Epistemologies of Ignorance in Education

Epistemologies of Ignorance in Education

edited by

Erik Malewski

and

Nathalia Jaramillo
Purdue University

INFORMATION AGE PUBLISHING, INC.
Charlotte, NC • www.infoagepub.com

Library of Congress Cataloging-in-Publication Data

Epistemologies of ignorance in education / edited by Erik Malewski and
Nathalia Jaramillo.
p. cm.
Includes bibliographical references.
ISBN 978-1-61735-345-1 (pbk.) – ISBN 978-1-61735-346-8 (hardcover) –
ISBN 978-1-61735-347-5 (e-book)
 1. Critical pedagogy. 2. Education–Philosophy. 3. Ignorance (Theory of
knowledge) I. Malewski, Erik. II. Jaramillo, Nathalia E.
LC196.E65 2011
370.1– dc22

2010052691

Cover art: Sisyphus by Mathew Felix Sun.
Matthew lives in the San Francisco Bay Area. In depicting life frankly and critically in both its visual surfaces and interior aspects, his work addresses history
and social commentary. He has exhibited in several national competitions and
his work is collected in the US, Canada and China. His work can be viewed at
http://www.matthewfelixsun.com

Printed in the United States of America

CONTENTS

PREFACE

Towards a Decolonizing Epistemology

Peter McLaren

One of the great axial problems of humanity is the relationship between the production of knowledge and the process of our quest for the Anthropos, that is, our quest for our own humanization. It is no secret that the question of epistemology and its relationship to pedagogical humanism has been sorely neglected by writers within the critical educational tradition, which is why this volume of essays edited by Erik Malewski and Nathalia Jaramillo is to be welcomed by critical educators everywhere. That this book has arrived at a very precipitous time in world history cannot be understated, as the planet is under siege by a complex of forces and relations that are the direct result of epistemologies of ignorance and which demand immediate attention not only by educators in urban areas with high-need student populations, but by humanity as a whole. For educators, however, this historical moment is of heightened concern, given the egregiously inadequate funding systems for education that cruelly exacerbate inequality and promote what Jonathan Kozol (2005) calls educational apartheid. This is even more the case at a time of budget shortfalls and a test-and-punish status quo that is strongly endorsed by the Chamber of Commerce and the Business Roundtable (Karp, 2010). And all of this is especially worrisome in light of the recent pronouncement by President Obama's basketball partner, and Secretary of Education, Arnie Duncan:

"Let me be really honest. I think the best thing that happened to the education system in New Orleans was Hurricane Katrina. That education system was a disaster, and it took Hurricane Katrina to wake up the community to say that "We have to do better.""

The early days of critical pedagogy offered an example that would be articulated by subsequent generations less hampered by the impossibility of pursing the tension between conflicting terrains—such as reform and revolution—that ultimately neither confront nor obliterate each other, but rather the opposite. While Freire's work provided unprecedented force in *Pedagogy of the Oppressed* (Freire, 2000), it had become domesticated throughout the 1980s until it was taken up and augmented by Marxist and neo-Marxist educators in fin-de-siecle North America and elsewhere, who were eager to free Freire from the bony grasp of liberal and progressive educators. It was clear to us then that we needed a new language of educational critique and transformation, a new way of thinking about knowledge, a new means of framing the entire discussion about what constitutes meaning and whose interests such meaning-making serves. But today, regrettably, we are at a stalemate. The logic of capital has kept a new language from emerging as we still seek answers within the very logic that has helped to create the crisis from which we are attempting to free ourselves. When Noam Chomsky warns that the "colossal toll of the institutional crimes of state capitalism" (cited in Rothschild, 2010) could lead this country into fascism not unlike what happened to the Germany during the Weimar Republic, it would be prudent to take note.

We cannot underestimate the tenacity and resilience of capital. Indeed, the tendrils of its poisonous vine are spreading into all the spaces and virtual spaces of potential capital accumulation. Globalized finance capitalism is the most widespread authoritarian structure in the history of civilization, giving the rich even greater riches and forcing the dispossessed to set up markets on moonlit streets to augment their exiguous incomes. We might be living in what is now called the "age of greed" but we should not be fooled that the current crisis of capital is linked mainly to the greed of corporate capitalists, since we believe that it is endemic to the system of capitalism itself. Our shadow grows large beside the flames of capital's vast furnace, a grotesquerie out of *Dante's Inferno*. We appear specter-like, Nosferatu the vampire with fingers extended across the wall of our flickering cave that we call civilization, all the better to grasp profits wherever our blood lust for capital finds them, and to palpate the farthest rim of the earth if necessary, even to squeeze out from the vacant eyes of the poor their last tears of sorrow, if they could fetch a price in the market.

This behemoth we call capital is not some creature encountered in the medieval surrealism of Hieronymus Bosch, a *bestiarum vocabulum* of the middle ages, or in a carnival act in a country midway. The beast is here among us, among both the living and the dead. Its indelicate stride is not an evolutionary gallop as we are too worldly wise to label it progress. Quite the contrary, it's conquest of the globe has laid waste to the land and has made civilization into a mausoleum, a place of dry bones in what once was a thriving metropolis of living, pulsating flesh, a place of hollow sockets in what once held the vitreous and the electrical charges that fashioned for humanity the gift of sight and foresight. Even a premonitory lunge from its febrile hand can cause havoc to cascade from its fingers of fire, like the unfolding scenes of the *Antichrist* by Lars van Trier. And when capital goes on a rampage, as it has this past decade, nothing can stand in its path and survive. Least off all the impecunious bystanders who seek out whatever diversions they can to avoid staring directly into the chaos. Inside the darkness they can see the junkyard world of the future. Finding relief in the light, they become blind to any and all alternatives to capital's value form.

Even in the midst of a crisis of capital, the likes of which the world has not witnessed since the late 1920s, the free market economy is championed vociferously as the guardian of democracy. Its faithful stewards remain studiously unaware of—or refuse to see—capitalism as a means of the exploitation of the labor-power of the worker and, even less, as a process of accumulation by dispossession. David Harvey recounts that accumulation by dispossession "is about plundering, robbing other people of their rights ... capitalism is very much about taking away the right people have over their natural resources" (as cited in Buzby, 2010, p. 99).

The extreme cheerleaders of neoliberal capitalism (the right wing populists, the antinomians, the premillenialists, the postmillenialists, the teabaggers and the White supremacist militia) view all those who would oppose their religion of profit and nation state triumphalism—the socialists, the liberals, the anarchists, the atheists and the communists, and other iraggamuffins—as in league with the AntiChrist. These "warrior Christians" (as some like to see themselves) send their children to "Jesus camps," while others join the Christian militias, like Hutaree, and plot to kill government law enforcement agents and train themselves to wage war against the AntiChrist (a recent poll indicated that one quarter of Republicans believe that Barack Obama could be the AntiChrist, the Beast of the Apocalypse in the Book of Revelation).

We slouch towards the future like a puerile old prison inmate, crawling towards the lost paradise of familiarity. Here we are told to be satisfied with being a detached spectator of our own history, by turning our bodies into means of producing or displaying commodities or by becoming commodities ourselves. Everywhere the concept of the self is being revised according to what will be most advantageous for the transnational capitalist class who weave the dreams of the world by using our sinew and bone as raw materials for the generation of profit. And even in an economic crisis such as the one that is savaging many nations around the world, the ruling class remains morbidly silent. In the United States such silence is deafening. Has the federal government given states and local governments interest-free loans to make up for all school and university budget shortfalls? Has the state shifted incentives away from financial capital toward human capital? A tiny one half of one percent tax on all financial transactions would generate about $200 billion a year, according to the Economic Policy Institute, but have any of these taxes gone into effect, taxes that could fund early childhood education, smaller K–12 classes, and lower tuitions and fees for public higher education? No, because Wall Street will not sacrifice its bonuses for the betterment of society as a whole, not even at this singular moment in world history.

And what have we done about it, you and I? We have set our imagination in motion like wind-up dolls not by newness but constant repetition. We have become indefatigable agents for the conquest of sameness by nurturing our compulsion for repetition. Great danger, we are told, lurks behind sudden changes. Stark shifts in the way we do things would pose too great a threat to our personality structures—or what has been called in popular psychology, "comfort zones"—so securely fastened to political inertia, like a rhinestone garter belt to a Sunset Boulevard mannequin. We pedal away on fixed bicycles. We make our bed in our quiet stupefaction, in the very *ne plus ultra* of political quietude.

We have made our home inside a swindle of the ruling class, a fetishistic inversion in which desire for emancipation has become cathected onto commodities, where the commodity is programmed to absorb the desire for liberation. Our emancipatory impulses for revolutionary struggle have become deconcretized, and mainly decorous, overlaid with habitual psychological mechanisms so that any attempt to unveil commodity culture leads to a kind of ambiguity, a "barroquismo" that conceals as much as it reveals (McNally, 2001).

Those who do not want to talk critically about capitalism should also keep quiet about the barbarism we are witnessing all around us. The earth shudders in agony. Present attempts at resisting the hydra-headed beast of capital are frozen like dried blood on history's stale proscenium where we dream our dreams and are dreamt in an overcrowded theater of destruction. In this country of strangers, the scourge of capitalism is met not with a momentous uprising by the oppressed but by isolated individuals enshrouded in a cynical resignation and a calcified hope, resulting in a paralyzing quietism awaiting its own dispersion.

We will not be bequeathed another Che Guevara or Paulo Freire (at least, not anytime soon) who will lead the fated triumph of the hardscrabble workers over the succulent and savvy bourgeoisie, who will transubstantiate the graveyards of political defeat into a victory march of the left, and who will bring us into a world of unbearable beauty and harmony, a land of Cockaigne devoid of Breughel's slothful peasants.

In our world of hand sanitizers, facebook identities, high gloss reality shows, mass media commentaries on world events that have as much analytical depth as petal dust sprayed from a vintage-style perfume bottle, and stylized varieties of adolescent rebellion with fast food marketing tie-ins, we try in vain to find a way out. But that proves as difficult as asking your own eyeball to stare back at itself, or requesting that Benjamin's Angel of History turn her head and face the future. Yet even against logo-swathed backdrops and image-based commentaries of daunting corporate grandeur, we keep ransacking Marx's tomb, especially when an economic crisis hits that demands some kind of explanation not afforded by the pundits of the *Wall Street Journal*.

Today's capitalism is spawned in a petri dish of virtual Faustian space, like those unfillable gothic cathedrals of Sevilla, where arches are poised to expand infinitely. Capitalism dresses itself up in vocabularies of commonsense. It can adapt to and absorb any language, even the language of the left. It works its discourse in the service of its self-expansion, having no master to serve but itself. Its favorite language is the language of mystification, of progress, of democracy. By fashioning itself out of the contradictory logic of progressivism and traditionalism, it can confuse and obfuscate. The editors of this important volume call this process the epistemology of ignorance.

We are told by the custodians of our research institutions that education should not be political, that it should remain neutral when it comes to questions of how best to effect the social order. But we never start from some zero point of prenotional experience, breathing the opiate air of mount Olympus in a some neutral space devoid of ideology. We need to take positions on issues that will effect not only present but future generations of young people, and we need to do so deliberately and protagonistically. We need, in other words, to seek an alternative to neoliberal capital or perish.

The corbelled vault of our imagination from which memories cry out and dreams are born has been constructed out of the debris of dead cities, destroyed civilizations, nations brought to servitude by the iron fist of the world-eaters, those whose imperial eyes sweep over the clearings when the dust of destruction has settled in their homelands and seek to plunder the resources of other nations, caring nothing of the aftermath, nothing of the blood that soaks into the earth or pools in the sewers of the heart, nothing of the blight brought to humankind. As critical educators, we are obliged to ask: Is it too late to re-enchant the world, to remold the planet in mytho-poetic terms, to create a past dreamtime as a sacred time for the present, to give ourselves over to divinities of our imagination, to live in the eternal present, to build totems from the clay of the riverbed? And while we ponder this possibility, the armies of the night march on, sneering at the pious surrender of the oppressed. We must bring this condition to a halt.

The crisis of capitalism has ravaged state and local budgets, most of which are not allowed to run deficits. So there have been major cuts in public schools and universities, and a giant deficit in our country's future. Thousands of teachers are being laid off across the country. Class sizes are expanding. School years have been shortened. Some school districts are moving to 4-day school weeks. Hedge-fund millionaires are organizing to push promarket education reforms. Angry parents in Detroit are demanding jail time for teachers whose students are scoring among the worst in the nation in math. The arts in our schools have been decimated. After-school programs have been canceled and even history classes are at risk of termination. Pre-K programs have been shut down. Community colleges as well as state universities are reducing their course offerings and admitting fewer students. Public universities, such as UCLA, have raised tuitions and fees, and closed their libraries to students on Saturdays. Students who are qualified to attend won't make it through the entrance gates. If public education is not reconstituted, and soon, then years from now the economic situation will worsen. But it is not the market that needs to save education but those toilers of the world who have fought to make public education play an important role in helping to shape and deepen democracy.

The market does not produce wealth but distributes the already available wealth. While, for instance, the stock market may seem to produce wealth, it is really just redistributing the wealth produced by the labor of the workers. Profit does not come from market relations (buying low and selling high) but from human labor power. Those who have to sell their labor power to earn a living (those who produce the profit for the capitalist) are part of one class. Those who purchase human labor and take the profit away from labor are part of another class (Ebert & Zavarzadeh, 2008). Yes, we are good—even eloquent—when it comes to appealing to moral sentiments. But this strategy is destined to fail because it rests on an appeal to the individual's consciousness—a move that does little to parry the most devastating structural effects of capital and is ineffective in bringing about capital's inanition (Lebowitz, 2010). As Istvan Meszaros (2008, p. 341) notes, an appeal to individual consciousness ultimately remains insufficient because "it avoids the social causes of the denounced negative symptoms." He adds that "what is absolutely excluded is the possibility of changing the structural determinations of the established social order that produce and reproduce the destructive effects and consequences" (p. 341).

We need to search, as do the contributors to this volume, for a knowledge of the good. Knowledge of the good is a knowledge of a practice designed to change reality, it derives from action as much as from contemplation. We judge the truth of our actions in their effects on the lives of the oppressed. But an epistemology of everyday praxis needs a larger optic from which to work, something to give the emancipatory act a political compass, something to guide its local struggles as a means of diminishing exploitation and suffering and promoting justice on a wider scale, a transnational scale, to be exact. Here we need to be strategic outsiders, and tactical insiders.

This movement to challenge capitalism requires that we jettison our epistemologies of ignorance and question normative ways of thinking about the world that corporate advertising and consumer-based culture continuously push upon us—ways of thinking dominated by class interests that have led to the current test and punish and privatization syndrome, to the competitive grants that drive top-down reform priorities, to the linking of test scores to teacher evaluation and compensation ("pay-for-test-score schemes") and high stakes exit testing, to the expansion of de-regulated systems of semiprivatized charters and private management of schools, to data systems that facilitate a remote control of classrooms and schools, to school closures, the firing of staff, forms of state and private takeovers by education management organizations, and efforts to move decision-making over education policy and curriculum away from schools and local districts to distant state and federal bureaucracies (Karp, 2010).

In addition, we must look beyond Western, Euro/U.S.-centric ways of knowing the world that are based in capitalist wastefulness and a lack of regard for the planet, in order to consider alternative and oppositional ways of thinking about and acting toward/against the imperialism of free-market, neoliberal, global capitalism. We need to look to fields that have been labeled as "other" or nondominant, such as women's studies, feminist theory, ethnic studies, indigenous studies and Chicano studies, so that we will be sufficiently self-reflective about our pedagogies, so that we can see how they may unconsciously uphold mainstream ideologies at the expense of nondominant conceptualizations of the world, so that we may seek solidarity with nondominant groups in the bringing together of the creative imaginaries of all people.

Radical critical pedagogy must find creative purpose and protagonistic agency in embracing all epistemologies by acknowledging how all people engage in a reciprocal relationship with the world from their own sociohistorical contexts and geo-political ways of knowing. We must engage with the entirety of diverse human lifeways and through that process we can envision an alternative social universe to capital's law of value. Indeed, this new social order should not be limited to Western/European responses to liberalism and capitalism alone, but rather should include the views of those who continue to suffer under the expansion of Western civilization.

Engaging indigenous perspectives requires that we be cautious about the "how" and the "means" of our engagement. Linda Tuhiwai Smith (2005) reminds us how researchers, academics, and project workers have always found "ways of 'taking' indigenous knowledge...[in a] systematic gathering of scientific data" that have proven dangerous to indigenous peoples (p. 2). Taking up indigenous perspectives can be an exploitative enterprise. In fact, it has often been as exploitative as the act of imperialism and colonialism itself; just as "Imperialism was the system of control which secured the markets and capital investments" of European and U.S. powers, research on indigenous knowledge and perspectives has become the accumulation of "othered" information as a form of subjugation that defined indigenous as "backwards" and Western as "modern" (Smith, 2005, p. 21). Of course, colonization's reach into the Americas and the development of the U.S. has become part of the legacy of modernity. We must challenge our concepts of "modernity" and recognize the limitations of our European-based epistemologies in order to allow for complete reverence for all other local and global views.

As racially marked bodies in geo-historical space, we require another artisanship of pedagogical practices, what Walter Mignolo (2009, 2010) refers to as a geopolitics of knowledge and knowing. This entails a political and epistemic delinking from Western Eurocentric practices and from a zero-point epistemology in which a knowing subject maps the world for everyone else. Developing another artisanship of pedagogical practices also means interrogating Eurocentered epistemologies as well as the production of decolonizing and decolonial knowledges through understanding our subjectivities as historical and biographical loci of enunciation. In other words, we need to engage in a geo-politics of knowing that will produce a geo-politics of knowledge that follows from a process of political and epistemic delinking from the grand Western episteme and cosmology.

The struggle for socialism must not be one in which we recuperate a Eurocentric center. We clearly need an epistemology of decolonialism that is not monological, monotopic, or imperial and that does not dilute the particular into the same (see Cervantes-Rodriguez & Grosfoguel, 2002; Quijano & Ennis, 2000; Santos, 2009; and Grosfoguel, Maldonado-Torres, & Saldivar, 2005). We need, rather, a diversality, a pluriversal universal—that is, a concrete universal that respects multiple and local particularities in the struggles against patriarchy, capitalism, coloniality and eurocentered modernity from a diversity of decolonial epistemic/ethical historical projects. In resisting a European/capitalist/military/christian/patriarchal/White/heterosexual/male/epistemological complex and transforming it by means of a decolonial and decolonizing pedagogy of liberation, a familiar

Zapatista saying proves instructive: "luchar por un mundo donde otros mundos sean possibles" [struggle for a world in which many other worlds are possible, (translation by, Nathalia Jaramillo)].

What we grievously need is an epistemology of the concrete. Epistemologies of the concrete are those that create a corporeally meaningful objectivity that is constitutive of our subjective awareness, an awareness guided by a wider praxis of transformation, a praxis dedicated to transforming a world of suffering and alienation into a world of struggle for social justice and for socialism. What we have in schools today are epistemologies of empire that remain trapped in the "what is." That is, they offer no strategies and practices of historical and geopolitical contextualization of the here and now such that learners can recognize the historically contingent nature of knowledge and meaning with respect to social structures, languages of experience, systems of intelligibility and what is presented to them as commonsense.

An epistemology of the concrete means escaping from pedagogical approaches to knowledge that are essentially circular, comprised of a polar reciprocity, or a frozen paradoxical juxtaposition—in short, a pseudo-dialectics (see Reitz, 2000). Most epistemologies of empire do enable at least a limited exploration of the paradoxical dimension of life, its polar tensions and complexities. We learn, for instance, to struggle for the good, the virtuous, and the true (most often embodied in the term, The American Way of Life), and avoid the bad, the ugly, and the false (examples often used are those of socialism and communism). However, within the epistemologies of empire not only are these polar oppositions caricatures of reality motivated by class interests, they remain fixed and permanently at war. The oppositions captured by epistemologies of empire remain a form of extreme dualistic vacillation. We need a pedagogy that can help students break out of this epistemological straightjacket. Either you embrace the good and reject the bad—either/or thinking—or you are on the road to perdition. There is never any serious engagement with "both/and" thinking. Students are not presented with any dialectical ground for moving forward, for breaking free from the narrow antimonies defined by the epistemology of empire.

Walter Benjamin recognized how capitalism has created new modes of mass experience that made people desire the same commodity images—dream images. He worked under the premise that dreams are disguised fulfillment of suppressed wishes on a collective scale. So dialectical critique for Benjamin involves engaging the core of these dreams and experiences to awaken from them to recollect them and translate the wishes they contain into "practical goods of historical action" (McNally, 2001, p. 198). Benjamin seeks to construct forms of experience in which the repressed that is embodied in the collective dreams of our ailing culture might be challenged by critical reasoning—by rational critique, but critique that is also embodied, and that can dissolve myth into the space of history (Mc-Nally, 2001). How can we demystify capitalist mythologies? We need to move beyond the communicative reason of Habermas, to a corporeal reason of Benjamin, where reason remains rooted in the body and its desire for happiness becomes the basis for an emancipatory politics" (McNally, p. 224).

Of Benjamin, McNally (2001) writes:

> Like the surrealists, he believed little is gained by instructing workers that capitalism is an irrational system in which people are dominated by things. Instead, the problem is to organize forms of experience that generate a new kind of bodily knowledge ... he believed ... that critical experience has to foster a sort of corporeal reason, one that fuses the body and the intellect in a radically new configuration where reason attends to—indeed follows—the messages emanating from the body, since "only the body can generate presence of mind." (pp. 197–198)

Reason, Benjamin averred, must connect with images that originate in the unconscious—primal longings and commodified dream wishes, a dreamworld of fetishes and phantasms—in order to disrupt the unconscious connections that tie people to a commodified society. Revolutionary critical pedagogy tries to follow Benjamin's example by undertaking a total and profound assault on the realm of preestablished understandings of how knowledge is to function in society. But in undertaking this task, revolutionary critical pedagogy sorely lacks a disciplined epistemological critique that can be augmented by a transformative praxis. *Epistemologies of Ignorance* fills this lacunae and promises to take educational theory into new uncharted directions.

Malewski and Jaramillo have given us necessary armor in defending educational discourses and practices from their participation, often unconsciously, in epistemicide, the production of violent knowledges of the other that leads to the manipulation and silencing of their own organic and indigenous modes of reasoning. Teachers will welcome this inspirational foray into decolonizing educational knowledges. Critical scholars will find a wealth of material from which to advance their decolonizing projects. *Epistemologies of Ignorance* is a one-of-a-kind book that is indispensible not only to the specialist critical scholar, but also to teachers and activists who remain committed to the idea that while education may not be sufficient to transform the world, it has to play a necessary role.

REFERENCES

Cervantes-Rodriguez, M., & Grosfoguel, R. (2002) *The modern/colonial/capitalist world-system in the 20th century: Global processes, antisystemic movements, and geopolitics of knowledge.* New York, NY: Praeger.

Grosfoguel, R., Maldonado-Torres, N., & Saldivar, J. D. (2005). *Latino/as in the world-system: Decolonization struggles in the twenty-first century U.S. empire.* Boulder, CO: Paradigm.

Karp, S. (2010, Spring). *School reform we can't believe. Rethinking Schools, 24*(3). Retrieved from http://www.rethinkingschools.org/archive/24_03/24_03_NCLBstan.shtml

Kozol, J. (2005, September). Still separate, still unequal: America's educational apartheid. *Harper's Magazine, 311*(1864). Retrieved from http://www.mindfully.org/Reform/2005/American-Apartheid-Education1sep05.htm

Lebowitz, M. (2010, February 20). Socialism: The goal, the paths and the compass. The Bullet. Socialist Project. *E-Bulletin,* No. 315.

Meszaros, I. (2008). *The challenge and burden of historical time: Socialism in the twenty-first century.* New York, NY: Monthly Review Press.

Mignolo, W. D. (2009). Epistemic disobedience, independent thought and decolonial freedom. *Theory, Culture & Society, 26*(7–8), 159–181.

Mignolo, W. D. (2010). The communal and the decolonial. *Pavilion, 14,* 146–155.

Quijano, A., & Ennis, M. (2000). Coloniality of power, Eurocentrism, and Latin America. *Nepantla: Views From South, 1,* 533–580.

Reitz, C. (2000). *Art, alienation, and the humanities.* Albany, NY: State University of New York Press.

Rothschild, M. (2010). Chomsky warns of risk of facism in America. *The Progressive.* Retrieved from http://readersupportednews.org/off-site-opinion-section/72-politics/1489-chomsky-warns-of-risk-of-fascism-in-america

Santos, B. S. (2009). A non-Occidentalist West? Learned ignorance and ecology of knowledge. *Theory, Culture & Society, 26*(7–8), 103–125.

Smith, L. T. (2005). *Decolonizing methodologies: Research and indigenous peoples.* New York, NY: Zed Books.

CHAPTER 1

INTRODUCTION

Epistemologies
of Ignorance

Erik Malewski and Nathalia Jaramillo

In lieu of the traditional introduction to edited books, we have decided to engage in a dialogue about the central questions that brought us together in collaborating on this collection. Esteemed colleagues and friends, we write from different—some might say incommensurable—philosophical and theoretical traditions. A dialogue allows us to speak to one another, and to you, the reader, in ways that would have been impossible had we written a common text. Our intent, as authors in this collection, is to provide the field of education with a distinct epistemological view on questions of marginalization, oppression, relations of power and dominance, difference, philosophy, and even death among our youth. We think it is necessary for those of us working in education to challenge the ambivalence and indeed, ignorance, we witness in the construction of curriculum, teaching practices, research guidelines, and policy mandates in our schools. We also find it necessary to think through ignorance as a necessary by-product of knowledge production. In this sense, we explore not only issues of complicity but also issues of oppression in spite of

Epistemologies of Ignorance in Education, pp. 1–30
Copyright © 2011 by Information Age Publishing

liberatory intentions. While feminists and critical race theorists have employed the concept of "ignorance" in their scholarship, little has been done in the field of education. Accordingly, this is the first systematic attempt to bring together emerging scholars in education to question ignorance, as the active production of 'unknowing' in order to keep in motion "the way things are" instead of thinking about "the ways things could be." In the sections that follow, we respond to five questions that we consider central to introducing readers to various perspectives on epistemologies of ignorance in education.

HOW DO WE CONCEPTUALIZE IGNORANCE?

EM:

What I find promising in epistemologies of ignorance is an attempt to read against efforts to constitute identity or the identity of a text as node of knowledge separate from its web. A tactical maneuver, this collection is comprised of counter-readings that work against the idea that beyond knowledge is a vast nothingness. In this sense, epistemologies of ignorance offer an alternate perspective to the assumptions that underwrite disciplinary knowledge, that of building up a canon of central texts and ideas that make up a field. My thinking echoes the teachings of Paul de Man (1983): that we must find the blind spots of identities and texts that serve as the very organizers of the space of the vision contained in texts, and therefore of knowledge production. Key to this collection, the visions we offer, as academics, are not separate from the ignorance that makes such visions possible and therefore our insights concomitantly produce blindness. Working against linear, structural models that tidy up what is replete with ambivalences, breakdowns, and "unstable oppositions that shift and collapse both within and between categories" (Lather, 2006, p. 36), the idea within epistemologies of ignorance is to think proliferation and contamination over our attempts to fully represent. In this sense, our very efforts toward solidification of categories and disciplinary knowledge become dangerous business in terms of all that is lost and covered over in the pursuit of intelligibility. In education, it is my contention that along with efforts to read for understanding we must also read against our very efforts to know. As state and national efforts successively work to narrow and contain what is deemed credible knowledge, education scholars in general and curriculum theorists in particular working out of epistemologies of ignorance are ethically obligated to trouble conventional notions of validity.

In an era of great anxiety over what constitutes credible knowledge, I look for new storylines to explain our epistemological and ontological realities, ones that seek out the status under which claims to knowledge are made alongside efforts to resist closure and "one right way" strategies toward understanding the world in which we live. Hence, older storylines that spoke of thesis/antithesis/synthesis on the way toward purer knowledge give way to newer storylines that forgo assumptions of salvation and progress toward multiplicity and deferral. Instead of a linear sense of development, epistemologies of ignorance work in difference that intentionally holds together disjunctive lines of thought in the search to map the variety and divergence of contemporary knowledge production in education. Baker (1999), among others, illustrates how postdiscourses teach us about the incommensurability of systems of thought and the danger of metanarratives that smooth over disjunctures. Yet, it is the very idea that such contestations lead us to the next step in development that those epistemologies of ignorance contest. Here the notion of establishing the truths of education is eclipsed by efforts to capture dominant and subjugated discourses competing for recognition in order to open up new spaces for understanding how disciplines contain knowledge and how knowledge is in excess of and shaped by that containment. Here a certain epistemological stuttering in our efforts to make truth claims disarticulates the positivity necessary to our knowledge production.

Proponents of disciplinarity worry that within the contemporary rage for accountability proliferation as an analytic tool will lead to further difficulties in identifying the boundaries of educational fields and a certain vulnerability when it comes to justifying our existence in terms of advancing knowledge (see Malewski, 2009). Rather than see epistemic breakdowns and ambivalences over what we know as evidence of failure, we make the claim that epistemologies of ignorance are necessary forays into the diversity of regimes of thought that exist in education in excess of consensus models. The series of binaries that have historically structured our meaning making practices in education are being displaced by what Morrison (2004) describes as "vernacular theory: multi-dimensional, tentative, pragmatic, touched by humans, interactive, passionate, and encompassing the human spirit ... less a theory and more clusters of concepts and reflective practices about people" (p. 491).

The notion of epistemologies of ignorance is a fruitful site at which to probe issues of ignorance and knowledge in relation to the production of both, particularly how blindness becomes the necessary organizer for the insights we make and the interplay of dominant and subjugated discourses jockeying for recognition. Asserting the gravity of racism, sexism, classism, and heterosexism upon knowledge—revealing its limits—epistemologies of ignorance demands of educators that they attend to the production of unknowing as imbricate to the production of knowing and foreground exclusionary practices in understanding how dominant discourses are shaped. As alternate feasible readings, some authors in this collection question just how fruitful epistemologies of ignorance are toward social justice and accordingly offer their own counter-positions on being and knowing. Their agendas together represent efforts toward emancipation that originate out of not knowing as a way of knowing as a vehicle for rethinking epistemology within education.

The scholarship that makes up this collection, then, becomes a middle way, a sort of "one foot in one foot out" of the positivity of knowledge, reading with and against disciplinarity, emphasizing ambivalence alongside certainty, unknowing alongside knowledge, and breakdowns alongside continuities. This is a conceptual move toward Derrida's (2007) wish "in organizing a critical examination of all the mechanisms that hold out the appearance of *saying* the event when they are in fact *making* it, interpreting and producing it" (p. 229), one where the lesson is "to see truth as that which escapes knowledge and is graspable only through the detour of its performance" (Lather, 2000, p. 155). As something other to the exhausted binaries of Western knowledge production, the urgent issues epistemologies of ignorance brings to education involve what it means to address complicity in epistemological violence in spite of efforts toward emancipation. Similarly, it also forces us to think through what it means to read for failures as well as successes, to examine how knowledge gets advanced and by whom, and to study how a reading performs via the interpretation it produces.

NJ:

There are various thinkers and writers that have shaped my position on epistemologies of ignorance. But perhaps my greatest teacher has been experience itself, and the memories I carry with me about growing up in a world of absurdities, incongruities, and extremely strict codes of personal and social conduct. My upbringing and schooling in the Roman Orthodox Catholic church has partly motivated me to question the mythic quality we ascribe to "truths" and to critically interrogate how we come to know "what we know." In this vein, the arguments set forward by writers such as Nancy Tuana and Boaventura de Sousa Santos have been most influential in shaping my thinking about epistemologies of ignorance, especially given the attention that both writers place on the active production of unknowing (in both the negative and positive). For me, this focus on the active production of not-knowing is central.

Ignorance is often considered an absence or lack in the "positive" flow of knowledge production. In other words, ignorance functions to actively obstruct or limit the range of possibilities for the full participation of all social beings to produce meaningful, nonsexist, nonracist, and "decolonial" (see Santos) knowledge(s). In Tuana's (2004) words, "Ignorance is frequently constructed and actively preserved, and is linked to issues of cognitive authority, doubt, trust, silencing, and uncertainty" (p. 195). Extending this conception of ignorance to education is a long-overdue and necessary intervention. Given the preoccupation and concern that we all share about the production of knowledge among our youth and institutions of learning, epistemologies of ignorance speak to the directives that we follow in pursuit of "higher learning" and the capacities that we support for contesting systems of (as you say, Erik) "containment." And when we link such obstructions with the dominant logic of production and consumption in capitalist society, then for me, the possibilities are numerous. This then leads me to the "negative" quality of ignorance, or "absent knowledges" in Santos' terminology, a point that is extended in my coauthored chapter with Sandro Barros in this collection.

Epistemologies of ignorance allow us to name and direct our attention to the gaps, omissions, and exclusions that our students and communities confront within dominant institutional settings, such as schools. What is insightful, especially in this edited collection, is the multiple and varied interpretations of how ignorance operates at the level of curriculum, teaching, philosophy, and teacher-student relationships. I think this demonstrates the specificity of ignorance (given the social dynamics of a given context, its people, and the "subject" of ignorance at hand), while at the same time exposing its common themes and relations within the society we inhabit. And importantly, epistemologies of ignorance also center the "subject"—woman, man, child, teacher, student—not as objects of knowledge production, but as sensuous beings who affectively live out the contradictions embedded within ignorance. Teresa Rishel's chapter in this collection, "Student Suicide: The Relevance (and Luxury) of Ignorance" exposes many of these constraints and contradictions, as evidenced in the professional preoccupation so many of us have with the content of our subject matter, as compared to the inter-personal relationships that give knowledge (and living) its meaning.

Importantly, even with particular and subjective interpretations of how ignorance is produced and sustained, I do think that epistemologies of ignorance can speak to the global and systemic forms in which the selective process of what is deemed worthy of "knowing" is institutionalized. Migration patterns, the media, labor production and consumption trends, social and economic policies, and the politics of warfare, occupation, resistance and social movements, are contextually embedded and unique, but by no means are they so distinct that we cannot see the relationship between and among them. These social and economic relations bring us together and push us apart, revealing the contradictions and antagonisms that have come to characterize the human and ecological condition of the twenty-first century. Is it an unworthy task to talk about the totality of ignorance on a global scale? Do analyses of totality lead to uniformity and linearity? I don't think they should, and I hope that epistemologies of ignorance can contribute to moving beyond the static and seemingly impermeable constraints that are often associated with concepts such as totality.

For educators, understanding the role that knowledge has in such social dynamics (in both the production and negation of 'ignorance') is imperative, in spite of the de-professionalization and de-intellectualism that plagues the disciplinary "containment" of education. Without question our schools and social institutions actively produce ignorance. The challenge, specifically for those working in the United States, is in understanding how efforts currently underway (i.e., standardization, teacher education restructuring, etc.) are done in the name of equality, social justice and the like, when they ultimately serve other agendas and interests, exclude other ways of knowing, and ignore the social and economic needs of our youth and communities. It is in this way that ignorance is most speciously produced, as a set of practices and initiatives whose results are "unknown" but followed regardless because of their perceived *promise* or because people feel "There Is simply No other Alternative" (TINA, as Naomi Klein writes).

The promises or "truth claims" that often accompany ignorance are historically embedded, culturally contested, subconsciously reproduced and politically motivated. There is a certain correspondence between claims to truth and actual, concrete everyday life. But when we scratch a bit deeper, we see how such claims have little to no basis in the "real" and have much more to do with what has been "imagined." This is not to say that the research or "science" behind educational reform is not grounded in so-called empirical evidence; I am suggesting that the very logic underlying such reform is not anchored in the real and concrete conditions of everyday life. If we look to the history of education policy and other reform initiatives, we come across an abundance of attempts to seemingly rectify the unequal distribution of schooling. In 1839, Horace Mann proposed "one model for all" in hopes of erasing inequities based on students' class position and racial/ethnic backgrounds; in 1964, Lyndon B. Johnson promoted the elementary and secondary education act under the mantra "War on Poverty," and most recently, we have the most clear example of a failed educational initiative, the No Child Left Behind Act of 2001. These, we could say, are "positive" attempts in education reform: at the most basic level, there seems to be an honest concern for the well-being of the poor, racially/ethnically marginalized, and an attempt to lessen the economic and social divide between them and the "better-off" segments of society. But they all operate in and are designed by the predominant logic of production and profit in capitalist society. And they also form part of what Sandy Grande (2004) addresses in her work on American Indian education as "rhetorical imperialism." In other words, the very terms (such as equality and justice) that accompany such reform efforts have been set, not by the afflicted communities who are targets of such reforms, but by the upper echelons of government administrators who function as architects of the wider social order. The "needs" of these communities are ignored, while dominant interests are met. Common across these efforts is the belief, and indeed assertion, that equal opportunity, democracy, and the values of a Judeo-Christian nation can be secured through such reform. In other words, that is the *idea*.

Breaking the correspondence principle (between thought and truth) and advocating in its stead a more grounded and material analysis of how ignorance is sustained and even embraced compels us to name and identify actions, practices, and relations that constrain us. Yes, we could say that such practices enable because they compel us to look for other alternatives, and other knowledge(s) that fulfill what we identify as missing in our current practice and thinking. And yes, all of this is shaped by the historical conditions that have led to the present moment. This is the very foundation of understanding the complex web of internal relations that constitute our society. Epistemologies of ignorance can break the very correspondence principle between thought and truth. In those omissions, gaps, and inconsistencies that are revealed, we come across an opening or passage. The opportunity is not only to think about other ways of knowing, but to translate and put into practice such knowledge for the particular and universal (pluriversal in the words of Anibal Quijano, 2000) rights of living a decent and just life. There is an element of utopian vision in epistemologies of ignorance. And as some of the contributors demonstrate, there is also rage, humor, sadness, and passion in this work. The detached, distant social scientist or educational researcher does not exist in these pages. Ignorance incites emotion and can be a catalyst for change–or so we hope.

WHERE DO WE GO FROM HERE?

NJ:

In my previous response, I briefly discussed the impact of Tuana's conception of epistemologies of ignorance on my own thinking about educational teaching and learning. For me, the social causes of ignorance are masqueraded in the realm of ideas, as a set of "thought processes" that are disinvested from the concrete and material conditions that people confront on an everyday basis. I would go so far as to characterize this phenomenon as a type of duplicitous ignorance that attempts to legitimize ignorance as the pursuit of ideals. We can extend this to the realm of institutionalized religion, science, industry, and so forth. Devotion, fear, presumed objectivity, and the politics of rationality can in some way contribute to our willful and "good-intentioned" ignorance. Clearly, ignorance does not operate in monolithic ways, and my emphasis here on "duplicity" is intended to highlight the very politicized and interested ways in which ignorance functions. This, I think, is a key site of intervention and interrogation in epistemologies of ignorance; it also represents one of the various polarities of ignorance (as the contributors of this book indicate). What then is the inverse of ignorance? What is the intended goal or objective of epistemologies of ignorance? Is it to engage in a praxis of knowing and a politics of transparency?

On this point, I am reminded of the compelling insights of poet-carpenter-farmer-scholar-writer-anarchist Henry David Thoreau (1851). On the topic of "useful knowledge" Thoreau advocated for "useful ignorance." He wrote:

> We have heard of a Society for the Diffusion of Useful Knowledge. It is said that knowledge is power, and the like. Methinks there is equal need of a Society for the Diffusion of Useful Ignorance, what we will call Beautiful Knowledge, a knowledge useful in a higher sense: For what is most of our boasted so-called knowledge but a conceit that we know something, which robs us of the advantage of our actual ignorance? What we call knowledge is often our positive ignorance, ignorance our negative knowledge. (p. 1)

Perhaps Thoreau had in mind the ways in which the technological and industrial revolution (i.e., the advent of capitalism) left little untouched or to the imagination. He was a minimalist, transcendentalist and astute naturalist who gave priority to sustainable living. A man disenchanted with what he perceived as an egregious consumerism and social division of labor taking over the simple pleasures of life, he disavowed knowledge for knowledge's sake. Thoreau warned against the accumulation, rote memorization, and insignificant and meaningless treatment of knowledge. He further noted:

> A man's (sic) ignorance sometimes is not only useful but beautiful – while his knowledge, so called, is oftentimes worse than useless, beside being ugly. Which is the best man (sic) to deal with: He (sic) who knows nothing

about a subject, and, what is extremely rare, knows that he (sic) knows nothing, or he who really knows something about it but thinks that he knows all?
(p. 2)

In the spirit of Thoreau's insights, moving beyond ignorance does not
imply a pure theory of knowing. The role, I think, of critical educators/
researchers working in epistemologies of ignorance is not to reconcile the
"unknown" with the "known" and assume that true knowledge will prevail
(i.e., thesis-antithesis-synthesis). This would be nothing more than a mere
reproduction of the same.

Epistemologies of ignorance reveal and interrogate. They bring
attention to the systemic, individual and collective forms that ignorance
assumes. In so doing, they generate an opportunity for us to inquire about
the different ways that ignorance operates and about the possibilities
of "useful ignorance." But the point is not only to reflect on where
ignorance has transpired and the reasons and social causes that have
led to ignorance. The point is to change the damaging consequences of
ignorance and to accept that in the process, we will come to recognize the
limitations of our own thought and actions. When knowledge is rooted in
doing, and when the act of knowing is based on interactions with others
and with our natural world, then perhaps we can accept that knowing
always involves unknowing. To me, education is not a life-long endeavor
towards the actualization of full or pure enlightenment. Ideas will only get
us so far; it is in our everyday activity that we give ideas their meaning.

Useful ignorance and beautiful knowledge are borne out of the commitment and struggle of peoples, whether they are community organizers, activists, professors, or academics struggling to make the academy
more relevant to the community and vice versa, or the ordinary man or
woman sitting on a stool at a kitchen counter somewhere, professing how
ignorance needs to be contested and mobilized for overcoming youth's
apathy. They are neither gifts nor deposits. They emerge from the particular histories and contexts in which communities are located. Ignorance
and knowledge stem from communities' relations to "others," to the ma-
teriality of the social world, and to the social relations of work, family, and
custom that are both specific and universal to the human condition.

EM:

In thinking through where we go from here I turn to the controversy
surrounding Rigoberta Menchú and issues of truth and interpretation.
More specific, I enter into an alternate reading (a reading of a reading)
of Patti Lather's (2000) "Reading the Image of Rigoberta Menchú:
Undecidability and Language Lessons" to shed some light on what might

be the future of epistemologies of ignorance. At issue is the controversy surrounding alleged inaccuracies in Nobel Laureate, Rigoberta Menchú's (1984) testimonio, *I, Rigoberta Menchú*. The book recounts Menchú's experiences as a Guatemalan peasant growing up in the midst of a civil war and the oppression of her people at the hand of the Guatemalan army. Over a decade and a half later, David Stoll (1999/2007) published *Rigoberta Menchú and the Story of All Poor Guatemalans*, a detailed study of newspaper articles, human rights reports, and interviews with Guatemalan people that underwrite his claim that some gross inaccuracies are embedded within Menchú's testimonio. Key to his argument, Stoll claims to have engaged the study to find out if Menchú's account was either a truthful story told by an oppressed Guatemalan Indian or a propaganda text crafted to meet her own political agenda. Stoll contends that the text errs toward the latter and portrays Menchú as mixing fact and fiction to meet the needs of the revolutionary organization of which she is a part. Central to this controversy are questions not only of differing worldviews but also of what might be thought of as incommensurable measures of what constitutes truth, the very limits of representation, and the slippage that occurs between the complex realities of a people and their representative.

What can be said about the Menchú controversy in light of the future of epistemologies of ignorance? The first is that epistemologies of ignorance make room for the idea that knowledge and its production, far from sitting in a complimentary relationship, are fraught with conflict and disjuncture. Here there are fissures between what we profess to know and the complex and textured experiences of people who educational researchers purport to represent. Rather than smooth over such slippages, epistemologies of ignorance teaches educators that ambivalences and breakdowns in our efforts to learn are the very terms by which we might read with and against disciplinary knowledge, to complicate rather than solidify our truth claims. In this sense, I agree with Nathalia's comment above that the idea is not to "reconcile the 'unknown' with the 'known' and assume true knowledge will prevail." For me it is undecideability that is precisely the key, the lesson that epistemologies of ignorance teaches us. In terms of epistemology and breakdowns in our efforts to know, what we might be compelled to consider in terms of knowledge production has to do with the impossible possibilities of truth. Is Rigoberta Menchú a propagandist, credible storyteller, community representative, or fiction writer? The inability to close down on the one right reading is the lesson epistemologies of ignorance bring to education.

It is tempting in terms of knowledge production to think only in terms of either mimetic representations or renunciation of truths as we come to terms with the slipperiness of language, playfulness of discourse, and limits of representation in educational research. The work included in this collection problematizes either approach. These authors are aware that knowledge gets produced when events are written about. They continuously point to ignorance as that which is beyond the grasp of knowledge but can be gestured toward by examining the performative aspects of knowledge production. In my own chapter, I focus on what indigenous/racialized knowledge teaches us about the unknown and the interrelationship between the seemingly disparate realities of Western and non-Western thought. Rather than "lock in" on singular truths and right translations, epistemologies of ignorance illustrate that within the original truth there is continuous movement and transformation, an uncertainty that opens toward a myriad of disjunctive interpretations and incommensurable truths. Epistemologies of ignorance teach us there is no truth without ignorance, no essential romanticized purity of grassroots communities and no essential complicit, contamination of Western ones. Rather, what these chapters attest to is the importance of attending to the ways stories are told, to the ways knowledge presents its objects, in order to save the world from our efforts to know it. In short, epistemologies of ignorance teach us that there is invaluable study in how knowledge and ignorance are produced in everyday practices of speech and writing.

Lather (2000) offers a simple yet profound claim: "To present something as the real thing is not the same as to produce it" (p. 154). When we study how knowledge and ignorance get produced, we are committing to complicity and numerous unavoidable distortions: that of our own desires to protect, advance, and serve; the limitations of language; the privileging of particular cultural worldviews; the psychological stress and concordant coping strategies of the knower and the known; the press of the protocols of academic research; and the limits of our efforts to read and know the world. In this sense, Derrida was right; the field of educational research and scholarship is less an archive of truths about the world than the very production of them. Epistemologies of ignorance is not about outcomes, the assembling of facts and figures toward a more complete picture of how the world works—the pursuit of intellectual transcendence if you will—but about the study of the performative in the effort to know and the corresponding pitfalls and breakdowns in our efforts to do so.

In summary, the question "where do we go from here?" demands critical examinations of how truth performs by way of its representations in educational speech and writing. As Nathalia so clearly demonstrates in her response to this question, the idea is not merely "to reflect on where ignorance has transpired" but to "change the damaging consequences of ignorance" while also recognizing ignorance as the very product of our efforts to know. Here we must accept that "knowing always involves unknowing" and therefore truth is always just beyond grasp in what we can represent, at least in any pure or absolute sense. The challenge then is to examine how truth performs by way of interpretation and translation, a very discomforting prospect for those who have great faith in what knowledge might provide in terms of salvation and progress. Deborah and Gregory Keller speak to this issue in their chapter "Socrates, Dialogue, and Us: Ignorance as Learning Paradigm" focused on Socratic thought and the ignorance born of the unrelenting quest for intellectual certainties. They turn to the value of "epistemic poverty" as a concept that opens spaces for resistance. For them, of key importance is "to break the hegemony of polemic certainties, such as the ones surrounding the so-called No Child Left Behind legislation" so as to provide opportunities for dialogue on what is unexplored and hidden in conventional understandings of politics and education.

To return to the controversy surrounding Rigoberta Menchú, what we are faced with are the dangers associated with confrontations between cultural worldviews, ones that contain within them different measures for credibility and truth, as well as unequal capacities to make their claims known to the larger world. Epistemologies of ignorance, then, is an attempt to intervene within the world, to make a difference in how we think, and to attend to those thoughts thought too difficult to bear. These are not comfortable reading practices but ones that trouble and invoke questions of trauma, neglect, and oppression. Accordingly, it is not surprising that truth in these chapters is often portrayed as a betrayal of truth, as what must be studied as truth that gets in the way of truth and its circulation. In regards to education, epistemologies of ignorance shift the focus on questions of truth content to those of truth effects. The latter is concerned less with traditional issues of validity and more interested in the study of how assumed truths impact knowledge and assumptions about the world. In other words, the study of truth effects raises questions over what forces shape systems of thought, corresponding perceptions of social and educational possibilities, and outlooks on the world. A central focus of epistemologies of ignorance involves the study of truths that contain within them the possibility for errors, partial truths, and the ambiguities associated with truths that do not easily extend beyond context and place. It seems to me, incorporating lessons about undecidability within educational theories and practices are "where we go from here" with epistemologies of ignorance.

WHAT CONDITIONS MADE POSSIBLE THESE MANIFESTATIONS OF IGNORANCE?

EM:

Tuana remarks (2006) that in addition to Donna Haraway's (1991) focus on "knowledge," we also need the capacity in part "to translate practices of ignorance among very different—and power differentiated—communities" (p. 3). To think through ignorance in context so as to address the conditions that make possible such manifestations, I turn to a recent handbook chapter I coauthored with Suniti Sharma (2010) titled, "Reading the Nebraska Safe Haven Law Controversy: Neoliberalism, Biopower, and the Discourse of Expendability." Key to this essay is a focus on the ways ignorance of certain groups is systematically cultivated and also how current interests/knowledge block such knowledge. Neoliberalism—a blend of increased privatization, government cutbacks, deregulation of business and industry, and increased international trade—underwrites the conditions by which those who utilize entitlement programs, such as safe haven programs, are demonized without regard for the subject positions available to them or sense of personal agency. Biopower speaks to the myriad of mechanisms by which people are rendered expendable. As this handbook chapter to which I refer illustrates, the poor and, increasingly, the middle-class, along with many non-Whites, are not only forced to take care of themselves when faced with hardship, they must do so quietly or find themselves accused of being "communists" or "socialists" if they speak out on the failed social policies that led to their troubling conditions. Neoliberalism and biopower are two forces insinuated in the Nebraska safe haven law controversy. Furthermore, when it comes to questions over what conditions allowed for the manifestations of ignorance explored in this edited collection, I see it as a by-product of what Fraser (1997) terms "weak" public spheres, ones where the opinions, experience, and knowledge of disenfranchised people lack practical force (p. 93). Expendable knowledge (nonknowledge) is linked to the expendable people (nonpeople) of a newly reformed state, one in "gracious submission" to global capitalism.

Before I continue on in a discussion of conditions, let me offer a little background. The Nebraska safe haven bill was made into law in July 2008 and, unlike safe haven laws in other states, covered not just newborns but all children up to the age of 17. If utilization was the measure, the law was an unquestionable success. Families suffering from the ravages of unfettered capitalism and the hallowing out of public services surrendered their children to the state, some driving from over 1,000 miles away. There was Tysheema Brown, a working class African American female, who made numerous attempts to set her son on the "right path" after he started talking back to teachers and was caught stealing a camera at school. After a tour of a detention facility did little to change his outlook and her application to enroll her son in Boys Town High School, a rehabilitation facility, was denied, she found out from her mother about Nebraska's newly enacted safe haven law. Sensing she was out of options, Tysheema drove her son from Atlanta to Nebraska, hoping to get him the services he needed, even if it meant surrendering him to the state. Then there is the story of Gary Staton, a working class White male and resident of Nebraska. Ironically, 17 months after the loss of his wife to a brain aneurism after she birthed their ninth child, he found himself at the same hospital ready to turn his children over to the state. The intervening months had not been good ones. Without his wife's assistance raising the family, Gary soon fell into economic and mental turmoil. On the financial edge, unemployed, and facing eviction, Gary felt Nebraska's safe haven law provided an opportunity for his children to have a better future, even if it meant they lived without him. Finally, there is the story of Lavennia Cooper, a middle-class elementary school teacher and single mother of a son with bipolar disorder. After years of inadequate health care that would only cover 3 weeks of psychiatric treatment at a time and expensive drugs that did little to quell her son's violent outbursts, Lavennia discovered, just as Tysheema and Gary did, that the only way to gain access to adequate care was if her son became a ward of the state.

What do these three stories have to do with the conditions that manifest ignorance among power-differentiated communities? Murray and Gibson in their chapter "Unknown Knowers: Mediating Knowledge in the 'Global Village' "focus on the phenomenon of the ways modern media culture shape "unknowing knowers" at the level of subjectivity, asking important questions about the relationship between knowledge and information, as well as its affects upon self-understanding and awareness of the conditions under which we live. In regards to the Nebraska safe haven controversy and media coverage, television, radio, newspapers would not let the stories of parents surrendering their children rest for long. As soon as the story of desperate parents turn their children over to the state would fade, another parent would surrender a child and the controversy would again heighten as discussions and debates over the appropriateness of the law reentered media channels. While the controversy initially opened spaces for democratic possibilities by way of discussions over state responsibilities towards its citizens, corporate lobbying to reduce the tax base, and the widening gap between the rich and the poor, neoliberal discourse was successively reinstitutionalized as the norm: The law was crafted with a "loophole," (Riccardi, 2008, p. 1), "abused" by citizens (Kavanagh, 2008, p. 12), and had "unintended consequences" (Koch, 2008, p. 10) that included relinquishing parents from responsibility for their children. Parents who surrendered their children to the state were characterized as irresponsible, lazy, unmotivated, and lacking the morals and character to raise good-natured children with a strong work ethic.

Equally telling, government official, initially in support of the law, quickly did an about face once the tides changed direction. Governor Heineman spoke of how the state's family services were abused and deflected attention from the plight of needy families and their entitlement as citizens of democracy they helped create and maintain. Over the months following the passage of the bill into law, Heineman would tell the media, " '[the law] needs to be changed to reflect its original intent' to protect infants" (Jenkins, 2008). After a number of parents came from surrounding states and beyond to relinquish custody at Nebraska's state hospitals, he returned to the media to offer a message with a different tone. This time he pleaded with the public, "Please don't bring your teenager to Nebraska. Think of what you are saying. You are saying you no longer support them. You no longer love them" (Lavandera, 2008, p. 5). Senator Mike Flood, the speaker of the Nebraska state legislature, summed up the perspective of legislators who passed the bill this way: "Looking back, a number of us would have voted differently" (Slevin, 2008, A03). It did not matter that these parents did love their children and were trying to get them help and support. The public would largely remain ignorant to their plight. Government officials and media pundits would cover up the struggles of these families and misrepresent them to the broader public.

Ignorance, then, is interrelated with the ability of the subaltern to tell their stories and the possibility that educators and policymakers have "ears to hear" the other. This would require that government "talk back" toward individualizing discourses that narrow conversations to the pathologies of the poor and issues of laziness, poor planning, or haphazard tragedy and not systemic forces that cultivate ignorance or how certain knowledge producing forces inhibit other forms of knowledge. At the very least, government in a participatory democracy must act as a buffer between the ravages of capitalism and its effects on citizens. Yet, in this instance, Nebraska's officials were strangely silent on the numerous gateways that had to be passed to make possible the conditions for such ignorance, of parents surrendering their children because they love them and media and government accusing them of a lack of love and irresponsibility toward their children.

Currently organized around the most effective ways to silence or subjugate populations that might constrain or absorb resources, ones that might otherwise support free markets, unregulated trade, and rampant consumerism, ignorance was the product of discourse focused on how to cut off citizens' access to state resources. Framed not as citizen entitlements, but as individuals robbing the state government and taxpayers, the poor and, increasingly, the middle-class were framed as communists or socialists if, in the face of tragedy, they spoke out against the failed social policies that led to their condition or turned to the state for help. Temporarily opening spaces for alternate readings, the media and government soon turned back to blaming families rather than ask more difficult questions about who has access to quality health insurance, what constitutes a living wage, and what the state might provide to offer the highest quality of life to all its citizens. Tuana (2006) frames these acts of government and media failure to ask difficult questions willful ignorance: "they do not know and do not want to know" (p. 10). Without question, the popularity of the program unmasked a dark underworld of U.S. Americans who suffered under the loss of strong public spheres, ones where the voices of the subjugated have practical force. Nebraska was blamed for letting such suffering rise to the surface of national consciousness and shaming the nation. The state did not receive accolades for servicing what was clearly a need among its citizens. "An active production and preservation of ignorance" (p. 10), those who used the safe have law were framed as expendable people of a newly reformed state, one in "gracious submission" to global capitalism.

In lieu of ignorance that is "the result of the configurations of interest" (Tuana, 2006, p. 4), the irony of a state going against global neoliberal precepts was not lost on the media. Ari Shapiro, correspondent for National Public Radio, asked in an interview with Nebraska's Director of Children and Family Services, Todd Landry, "I imagine this law has been a real embarrassment for you guys, huh?" (Shapiro, 2008). Other media pundits ignored the stories of parents who told of the difficulties they faced accessing resources and how they ultimately surrendered their children out of love, which further fanned the flames of demonization. For example, Catherine Arnst (2008), senior writer for *Business Week*, dismissed the important role of government checks into adoption eligibility, complaining that in her 18 month journey to become eligible she had to "jump through hoops and put up with invasion of privacy" while some parents do not want their children. Promoting further ignorance of the conditions that led to the frequent use of the safe haven law, she asserted those who relinquish custody of their children are "in many cases truly lousy [parents]. The kind of parents who should never have kids in the first place" (p. 2). Key to this collection, the question regarding whose interests are being served reveals not only how values and outlooks shape what we know but also how they shape what we do not know—our ignorance—and the interests and agendas at play that lead to such ignorance.

The Nebraska safe haven law controversy sheds light on the conditions that made possible contemporary manifestations of ignorance. Most telling was the government's support of a law that "highlighted what child welfare experts say was the widespread shortage of public and private aid" (Eckholm, 2008, A10) and later about-face when it was recognized that the law revealed the unprecedented desperation and suffering brought on by neoliberalism. In some sense, antidemocratic politics opened a space where global capitalism with its free market ideologies linked subjugated populations with the logic of expendability. Even as those demonized for their use of the safe haven law organized, fought back, and demanded that their stories be heard in front of the Nebraska state legislature, innumerable rationales for cutting state services and reconfiguring the discourse and terms for citizenship and entitlement eclipsed their voices. On November 21, 2008, the Nebraska legislature voted to amend the law; effective immediately after the vote, "no child over 30 days old can be dropped off" (CNN, 2008, p. 2). Without question, the Nebraska safe haven law controversy teaches us about ignorance manifest under conditions where (a) the knowledge that might be revealed does not connect to contemporary dominant interests; (b) contemporary systems of thought constrain other alternative forms of knowledge; and (c) the thoughts and ideas of the subjugated are remade ("re-represented") in ways that were not their intention or are simply misleading.

NJ:

There are so many complexities to understanding the conditions that give rise to ignorance, but central to this thesis, as you have indicated above, are the role of capital and the dominant mode of producing ourselves, our identities, and our relations to the broader society (whether we are talking about social institutions or Mother Earth). Social relations of capitalist society are conditioned by the abject ignorance that maintains social, political and economic hierarchies. Now, I am not applying a mere functionalist perspective to questions of ignorance, but we cannot afford to "ignore" the role of capital in how we organize society and spaces of learning and socialization. The magnitude of this logic is at times daunting, but without a due consideration of how people, nations, and our relationship to nature has been impacted by the forced omissions and exclusions that accompany a social system predicated on the unequal distribution of power, resources—on the alienation of woman and man, then we automatically limit the extent to which we can challenge ignorance.

On this point, I am reminded of the contributions of Dolores Calderon and Richard Kahn in this edited collection. Dolores' chapter focused on *colonial blind discourses* and *flattened epistemologies* in the curriculum of U.S. textbooks is a powerful example of how ignorance is "interested" in "normalizing the status quo" and protecting "White supremacy" (Calderon, p. x). Such "functional" attributes to ignorance reveal the history of knowledge production in formalized educational settings and the ways in which knowledge has been confined to a certain way of knowing and understanding the social world. Here, the epistemic underside of capital—rationality, discovery, and whiteness—is revealed in the careful examination of how schooling reproduces these dominant tropes at the expense of generating a critical and relevant education system for the benefit of our communities. From a different angle, Richard's *Towards an Animal Standpoint*, emphasizes the various aspects of "speciesist" relations that construct our reality. Both Dolores and Richard advance our understanding of how predominantly Western and Eurocentric modes of associated living and knowledge production frame human relationships. They identify the purposes and qualities of interested ignorance, or the conditions that make ignorance possible.

For me, responding to the question about the conditions that engender ignorance requires a broad stroke approach that does not reduce ignorance to a "function" or "determinant;" rather, ignorance needs to be understood in relation to a plural and complex society. Clearly, there is a general configuration and "order" to this society, and I would argue that the logic of capital is most clearly evident in the overriding structure that unifies us globally and transnationally. Within this argument, it is also important to recognize that the logic of capital is not evident on a-symmetrical scales across societies; indeed, there is difference and variance within and across social systems, even if we can call them "capitalist" across the board. The point then in discussing the multiple and plural conditions that reveal ignorance is to acknowledge the variety of claims that constitute "knowledge." The conditions of ignorance refer both to a structure and a set of processes that have historically led to a series of social and political conflicts that have yet to achieve resolution. In fact, we continue in the struggle to name, identify and contest interested ignorance. We remain in the fight to produce other knowledge(s) and frameworks that can transcend dominant modes of ignorance.

WHAT ARE THE IMPLICATIONS OF EPISTEMOLOGIES OF IGNORANCE FOR RESEARCH METHODOLOGIES IN EDUCATION?

NJ:

Over the last several years I have been reflecting on "ignorance" and its impact on research methodologies. This is not an easy question to tackle, because in order to decipher "ignorance" in educational research, we need to examine all aspects of the research process and break away from the traditional paradigms that fragment and isolate both communities and researchers from their "subject matter." But I believe it is critical for educators to tackle the notion of ignorance in methodology. Sometimes, I am baffled by the type of research that receives the most praise and "print time" in our research journals. I'm especially aggravated by research in education that only identifies their participants by classifications such as "dyads," "male," and "female." When did we get to the point of isolating everything "human" about our students and communities and determining their capacities based on a simple rubric of "control group" versus "treatment group?" There is a systematic approach (read, science!) in everything that we do; my point here is not to advocate for no measures of rigor of thought, expression, or methodology. But when "science" allows us to erase the faces and essence of the people with whom we work, turning them into "subjects" whose complexity is explained away as an "outlier," I take issue with that. I am alarmed when educational researchers spend more time contemplating their "device" or "intervention," than trying to understand what constitutes the social space of human exchange, of teaching and learning, and of producing knowledge to contribute to our mutual understanding and benefit. To this, I hope my comments are apropos.

Perhaps most importantly, research methodologies shaped by epistemologies of ignorance need to move beyond paradigms that deny the existence of other knowledge(s) or worldviews. There needs to be a concerted effort to undo the legacy of imposing one's worldview on making sense of another's social existence. In education, there are endless examples of how ignorance has operated at the level of research methodology. For one, we can recount the history of deficit-theory making and the ways in which educators reproduced the "civilized-uncivilized" narrative in explaining the conditions faced by communities afflicted by poverty (Brandon, 2009). Research in this vein has yielded and focused on the development of 'technologies' that could intervene in the academic trajectory of students. Such efforts represent ignorance in the way that researchers deny the importance of people's meaningful participation in the research process. In so doing, research "findings" actively produce ignorance, given that the researcher as "outsider" determines the visionary horizon, the field of analysis, and will undoubtedly miss many opportunities to contribute to shared knowledge between her and the community.

These paradigms oftentimes represent an apprehension of a community whose reference points are taken within the community itself. In other words, efforts to foster learning and "academic success" have not been pursued *with* the community, but rather *for* the community. Here the semantic distinction between "with" and "for" is necessary, because it signals a relationship developed between researchers and the groups they intend to inform or impact. But even so, this is limiting to the extent that research *with* a community opens up the space for a host of other contradictions to emerge. Who can ultimately determine whether or not the research was conducted *with* a community? Perhaps, then, what we also need are epistemologies of ignorance and research methodologies *by* a community. I'm not talking about the watered-down step-by-step manuals on participatory research collecting dust in a publisher's office. I'm talking about a transformation and re-articulation of research design, methodology, and ethics as conceived *by* and *within* communities.

Efforts to temper the effects of traditional and positivist research have been advanced by various fields and disciplines, from feminist philosophy of science to the late Colombian Orlando Fals Borda's treatise on research for liberation (see Fals-Borda, 1998). Within these paradigms, research is not considered a subject-neutral or value-free enterprise; rather, the biases, intentions and situatedness of research are laid bare from the beginning. Further, questions of oppression, empowerment, liberation and subordination figure centrally in this work. Research is done with a purpose; and we can say that purpose is to combat willful and malicious ignorance, and advance revolutionary ignorance instead.

Let's take for example, the notion of "situatedness." Situated observation implies an understanding of how communities interact and produce knowledge within a specific social-economic-political-spiritual web of human relations. The term has been *strongly* engaged by the feminist theorist Donna Haraway, who along with her colleagues in the science of feminism or, feminist science, have advocated for new definitions of such well-versed concepts as "objectivity" in social research. While I will not go into great lengths about the history or the exacting principles of "situated knowledges," suffice it to mention that this philosophical intervention into science attempts to undo the ignorance of teleological rationality by advocating for a "usable but not an innocent doctrine of objectivity" (Haraway, 2004). Situated knowledge also refers to the necessity of circumscribing our interpretations, ways of seeing and *evaluating*, with the limitations that we bring, as insiders or outsiders, to settings not of our own making. The point is to avoid binary oppositions—researcher/researched, immigrant/non-immigrant, man/woman—and degrees of cultural awareness or affiliation that range from, in my case for example, "more Latina" to "less Latina" or "more *gringa*" to "less *gringa*" as the core determinants of how we represent social life (and reproduce ignorance!). When the ways we identify with or differ from communities (according to economic, social, or cultural denominations) governs, a priori, the conclusions we generate about "them" or "us" then we have failed to see beyond the obfuscating veil of our own reflections.

Situated observations, the learning in our bodies, encompass various levels of "seeing" and analysis that bring together multiple voices and meanings that emerge within social settings. In this sense it is useful to consider the remarks made by cultural theorist, Teresa Ebert (2009), who refers to "abstract structures" as the social relations in which concrete actions acquire their meaning. For Ebert, a focus on concrete conditions and a disregard for the abstract may display the complexity of everyday life but also makes it hollow by cutting it off from the social relations in which experience generates its meaning. Meaning, she says, is not the correspondence of language to reality as realism implies, nor is it the endless play of the sign as linguistic theory suggests. Instead, she argues that meaning is a social relation, and the uncertainty of meaning and the existence of difference are not caused by the slippage of signs away from any fixed referent but by social change and contradictions. This represents a very significant intervention in the rather complex debates over the relationship between language and meaning. How we come to know power, authority, and our own position within institutional settings is based on both real and imagined social relations. Meaning spawns from language, but ultimately it comes from interactions, from the active production and exchange of knowledge.

Epistemologies of ignorance can aid in our attempts to enact more participatory and concrete research methodologies in the identification of the various "blind spots" that we enact in our daily activity. On this point, several of the chapters in this collection speak specifically to the relationship between ignorance and research methodology. I will mention just two. Alex Fidyk's "Suffering With: Seven Moments of Ignorance," for example, provokes a dramatically different reading of ignorance in the realm of ontology and epistemology from the standpoint of Buddhist philosophy; Molly Quinn offers a first-person narrative account of how ignorance methodically shapes our notions of freedom and liberation in her chapter, "Committing (to) Ignorance: On Method, Myth and Pedagogy With Jacques Rancière." These are all important contributions, ones that are not necessarily commensurate with the ideas I included above, but which advance our understanding of ignorance in the minutiae of life.

EM:

In a 2007 article titled "A Reading on Four Registers: Educational Reforms, Democratic Cultures, Research Methodologies, and the Question of the Posts," I wrote about how I was "searching through my files on underway projects, hoping to find something in my compilation of educational research that might foster my thoughts" on research methodologies (p. 11). In my search, I ran across Harry F. Wolcott's (2002) *Sneaky Kid and Its Aftermath: Ethics and Intimacy in Fieldwork*. His writing on the repercussions of his study of an educational dropout provides insight into the implications of epistemologies of ignorance for research methodologies in education. More specific, the text is constructed as a response to the fallout surrounding an ethnography, one that caused a firestorm in research communities for what it refused to reveal. To compliment Nathalia's interest in scholarship where "the biases, interventions, and situatedness of research are laid bare from the beginning," my interest is in what to do when the very act of representing constrains representation or, more specific, when the continuity of truth claims emanating from our research methodologies are shown to have embedded within them processes of silencing. Here Benjamin's description of "the very discipline" that is "constituted by what it excludes (and fails to grasp)" (Felman, 1999, p. 213) is helpful for understanding how the very act of going about our research brings with it a dark side of concealments, half-truths, and omissions. For me, this is not so much about what is laid bare as it is ignorance as necessarily insinuated with our efforts to produce and learn.

In the original 1983 article titled "Adequate Schools and Inadequate Education: The Life History of a Sneaky Kid," Wolcott described the experiences of a young man who had dropped out of school, freed himself (partly) from the trappings of the "establishment," and built a cabin in the woods just outside the city in what was revealed as Wolcott's backyard. Portrayed in great detail, this is the lived history of a 20-year-old who had been shuffled between divorced parents living in Oregon and California, sent to reform school, and found and lost (abandoned?) a series of second-rate jobs and substandard apartments. In thinking through the implications of Brad for educational adequacy, the topic of the 1983 article, we learn that Brad's thoughts and practices are difficult to classify. In some sense, he put his education to work. Brad learned how to enroll in a food stamp program and ration his meager benefits so that they would last over the month, eating "powdered milk" and "dry foods in bulk" (p. 20); and he lived rent-free behind Wolcott's house. More "insider" than "outsider" to society, Brad is portrayed as someone who has learned the cultural meanings of his practices and yet even with those understandings has decided to live outside formal educational structures. He both assimilated and resisted educational norms.

In the 2002 text, Wolcott sheds light on how ignorance was the very organizer of the ideas he put forth in 1983. Not discussed in the original article, we learn that the state of Brad's mental health underwent significant decline before he fled the makeshift cabin on Wolcott's property. Brad "became increasingly distraught and disorganized" (p. 46) and talked of a " 'sledgehammer to the brain' that was disordering his thoughts" (p. 47) Wolcott reported as he tried to intervene and help Brad come up with other options besides leaving his property. We learn that across the arch of his research and prior to Brad's departure, Wolcott and Brad developed a physically and emotionally intimate relationship. After

Brad left, Wolcott notes that for the next 2¹/₂ years he would occasionally hear of Brad's activities from his mother, with whom he lived at the time.

Research that started in 1981, resulted in its first publication in 1983, would take an unexpected turn in 1984 that would teach us a lot about the interrelationship of epistemologies of ignorance and material realities, what the continuity of academic writing belies, and methodologies that produce rather than mirror reality. Brad returned to Wolcott's property, drained nearly 500 gallons of heating oil into the house, attacked both Wolcott and his partner when they returned home, and set the house on fire. Fortunately, no one was hurt but what was revealed has much to do with issues of ignorance and research methodologies in education. After a highly publicized trial, Brad would go to prison; Wolcott would be taken to task for becoming intimate with Brad, failing to detail the full texture of his interactions in his writing, and violating professional standards for human subjects (see Ockander & Östlund, 2001; Schreiber, Rodney, Brown, & Varcoe, 2001). Wolcott would retort that the focus of the research, funded by what was then the U.S. Office of Education, was "educational adequacy," not intimacy in educational research; any description of their physical and emotional relationship would have sensationalized the research and detracted from the topic at hand.

What I have covered here are only select highlights from the study of "sneaky kid" and its "aftermath." The point is not to dramatize an already dramatic research project, but to explore breakdowns, half-truths, and omissions as the very sites of impossibility from which we might learn how to produce different ways of thinking about research methodologies within education. Key to my purpose, as an openly gay researcher, Wolcott re-reads his sneaky kid research, drawing from his own analyses, transcripts, field notes, memories, and the work of others, not merely to provide a fuller picture, but to interrupt his own writing. Troubling his previous research—and educational researchers troubling of his troubling—brings suspicion to the very idea of transparent research methodologies divorced from the production of ignorance. That is, issues of clarity and transparency in educational research have as much to do with processes and styles that hold credibility as they do the possibility of a bare and patent reality. A field kept ignorant, Wolcott's silences show how the unknown becomes the very organizer of the spaces between original events and efforts to access them via academic research and writing.

In this sense, epistemologies of ignorance points to a mobility in the original event—an original truth that is always just beyond the grasp of knowledge—that opens events to a multitude of interpretations and per-spectives that are partial, invested, and limited. Writing back to write for-ward to what remained unknown, here is knowledge that when confronted with its own constitution offers not fuller knowledge but a stranger within its knowing. Who is Wolcott? An ethical scholar? A victim of homophobia? A cutting edge methodologist? An opportunist researcher? Here undecidability and the unknown is precisely the lesson. When pressured to take a stand on his research with Brad, Wolcott (2002) commented that what seemed to him "at the time the best of individual responsibility" had become for others "the worst form of abuse of power" (p. 166).

My point in rehearsing all this is there is much to be learned from folding back to fold forward within a long-term research project to highlight ruptures, breaks, and refusals—the ways in which ignorance is unavoidably insinuated with knowledge production. What Derrida (1992) termed the ordeal of the undecidable in regards to how to think about justice sheds light on epistemologies of ignorance, "the urgency that obstructs the horizon of knowledge" (pp. 26–28). This is no mere oscillation between two significations: knowledge and ignorance. Epistemologies of ignorance speak to an academic duty, a sort of obligation to give oneself up to the unknown while taking account of the perspectives and guidelines embedded in our research methodologies. Because a just decision, and therefore a "just" or "good" methodology, cannot provide itself with unlimited knowledge, what we are left with is a horizon that is opening and limit, a mark of progress but also deferral. The instance of decision, of how to proceed in our research is, following Derrida, a moment of madness, acts taking place in the night of nonknowledge and nonrule. At its best, the unknown as a way of knowing illuminates how knowledge production tends toward concealments and omissions in spite of our best efforts toward clarity and transparency.

HOW MIGHT EPISTEMOLOGIES OF IGNORANCE SHIFT EDUCATIONAL PRACTICES IN SCHOOLS?

EM:

If we are to employ epistemologies of ignorance to enrich our understandings of curriculum and pedagogy, then central to any educational endeavor must be the examination of tactics and mechanisms by which not knowing is constructed and sustained. This might be thought of as "discomforting practices" in regards to finding spaces in schools which, in the contemporary moment, are overrun by the "rage for accountability," a testing culture of rote memorization and simple truths that belies both the complexity and politics of knowledge production. Yet, just as epistemologies have moved away from the reductive dream of a cure, salvation, or redemption by way of knowledge production— ongoing synthesis toward an elusive "one-right" true belief—so too must epistemologies of ignorance inform school practices around not knowing as complex, multidimensional, and situated. In this sense, epistemologies of ignorance shift educational practices toward place-bound and historically contextualized knowledges and against forms of curriculum content and instructional practice that are unlocatable and therefore irresponsible. This is not knowing that is complex, multidimensional, and situated; it comes from somewhere in space and time and therefore links to an ethics of responsibility because it can be called into account. Taliaferro-Bazile speaks to such contextuality in her chapter on emotion, rage, race, and what is refused, repressed, and dysconsciously acted out/ projected upon others. Her point is that the emphasis on rationality has made it difficult (impossible?) to teach about race in ways that account for feelings as sites of knowing. Furthermore, she argues, we as educators must begin to contend with the ways in which the pathologies of White ignorance, and suppression of Black rage as a logical response to it, have harmed the Black psyche. Where does that rage go, she asks, and attempts to answer by expounding on "the ongoing struggle between my rational professor self and my angry Black woman within" (this volume p. 268).

Just as there has been an emphasis in educational theory and practice to see from the borders and peripheries and therefore the very real danger of romanticizing and then appropriating the outlooks of the subjugated, as a context for claiming to understand their positions, so too is there a danger in claims to know out of the blindness created in insight. Not knowing, which takes place from below and through the study of the contours of knowledge production, is not easily learned or unproblematic and neither is its corresponding practice. As we consider the implications of epistemologies of ignorance for curriculum and pedagogy, it is important to recognize that in teaching and learning the positions of the subjugated are not innocent or reactionary. Just as ignorance is not a void but rather the spaces between filled with content and character— the unthought that is necessary organizer of whatever insights might be made—in subjugation there is value and agency. There is always already the unknown, knowing blocked by other knowing, and knowledge that remains hidden given current interests and agendas.

Equally telling, not knowing becomes crucial in regards to transformative curriculum content and instructional practice, as knowledge of the unknown is most likely in principle to engender insights into critical and interpretive centers. That is the unknown as a way of knowing tends to offer particularly effective modes for teaching through and with acts of repression, forgetting, and covering up—knowledge and its transmission that claim to be comprehensive while having no ground in which to stake its claims ("groundless claims"). Epistemologies of ignorance, then, function at the borders where knowing and unknowing meet and inquire into why this is so. Curriculum and pedagogy insinuated with epistemologies of ignorance have the potential "to be onto the God-trick and all its dazzling—and, therefore, blinding illuminations" (Haraway, 1988, p. 584). Here teaching from ignorance, from what is not known as a way of knowing, promises more in terms of sustaining and transforming accounts of the world. Peter Appelbaum teaches us about what is not known as a way of knowing in his chapter "Carnival of the Uncanny," focused on the "returned gaze" associated with epistemologies of ignorance. In multiple ways, he questions how that gaze haunts our practices and shapes our anticipation of what is next in uncanny ways.

Teaching from ignorance, then, is a pedagogical problem, requiring a focus on alternate readings and troubling absences; it invokes a pedagogy of problem detection, of locating the problems with knowledge prior to their designation as a problem or limit, of inquiry into the unknown that frames the insights present in the curriculum. Robust in seeking out what is not yet known, and investigating into how contemporary systems of thought block other thought, these are techniques and skills in teaching in excess of the "highest" orders of thinking that inform "teacher proof" curricula and "techno-scientific" instruction.

The common critique of teaching and learning that works against metanarratives and simple truths is that it risks relativism and generates cynical or noncommittal dispositions among students. Epistemologies of ignorance, however, work to disarticulate various forms of relativism, just as it does the one-dimensional totalization of curriculum content and instructional practice. Contrary to conventional thinking in regards to educational practices, an alternative to relativistic and totalizing curricula demands the study of what frames and organizes knowledge. That is, epistemologies of ignorance seeks, through the study of frames of reference, an investigation into partiality, place-boundness, and positionality among differential power relations, offering processes of schooling that mark the borders of intelligibility and the status under which claims to knowledge are made. Insinuated with a praxis of negotiation, reciprocity, and empowerment, here the unknown as a way of knowing meets the call of a solidarity in politics. To study in schools would consist of asking how concepts were brought together to usher knowledge forth, where, through what processes, by what individuals, and under what circumstances. And, concomitantly, study in schools would focus on the question, through what systems of unthought were the objects of knowing, the classifications of epistemology by which we see, specified.

Epistemologies of ignorance in teaching and learning, then, challenge relativism, which claims to be everywhere and at the same time claims no location. It also challenges objectivity and authoritarian regimes of meaning that are in fact a negation of studies of limits and confrontations with ethical responsibility. In this sense, epistemologies of ignorance in teaching and learning eschew ideologies of relativism and authoritarianism, ones that deny location, embodiment, and perspective. It is precisely this politics of interrelationship, of the insinuation of nonknowledge, that makes possible the answer to the question, "what knowledge is of most worth?" and that holds the possibility for sustained and potentially transformative curricular and pedagogical practices within schools. Snowber speaks to this issue of embodiment and authority in her chapter on the body and the academy. She asks why it is we can so acutely analyze the body as a text, turn to textual references to garner authority for our thoughts, but subjugate and erase the body with all its messiness, feelings, and ways of knowing. For her, we must come to terms with the fact that we always already know carnally, through a body that sweats, smells, senses through the skin, and relates to other bodies.

NJ:

At the time of this writing, Erik, public schools at the primary, secondary and tertiary level are under assault. Our schools are being challenged by the overriding logic of neoliberalism which attempts to insert market-based principles (i.e., standardization for efficiency, competition for productivity) into public affairs. We are also facing what I call the neocolonial logic of a capitalist republic. Here, I'm thinking of the glaring example of the Texas State board of education that recently passed amendments to the social studies curricula essentially upholding the values of individualism, whiteness, and capitalism over the struggles of the indigenous and people of color in the United States, as well as the shameful example of Virginia governor, Bob McDonnell, who declared April 2010 Confederacy History Month without mention of the history of slavery. We also have the case of Arizona, which following the controversial law allowing state police officers to act as immigration patrol (a federal jurisdiction) signed into law SB 2281, which essentially targets ethnic studies classes in public schools as "anti-American." Diversity, plurality, and a sustained analytical critique and interrogation of U.S. politics in ethnic studies classes has become synonymous with promoting "resentment of a race or class of people" and the "overthrow of the United States government." Collapsing dissent and critique in our curricula into anti-Americanism sets the stage for extremely one-dimensional and narrow interpretations of history and social phenomena. These shifts produce consequences at the level of knowledge production and at the development of a proactive and democratic citizenry that have not even entered into the debate. At this point, we cannot even discuss such blatant a-historical readings of the diverse peoples of the United States as ignorance, because it is not ignorance operating at the level of these policy decisions. It is a sustained and directed effort to unravel the progress that critical and concerned educators and citizens have made to make learning and teaching relevant and meaningful to the lives of students. Such efforts are not anti-American; they are constitutive of the processes needed to challenge ignorance and nativism in the social sphere that ultimately hinder our already weak democratic formations and secure the continued disenfranchisement of politically and socially marginalized peoples across the country.

So when it comes to schools, how do I think epistemologies of ignorance operate? I hope they can aid educators who are committed to the communities in which they work and who are concerned with the multidimensional aspects that constitute meaningful learning. I hope that epistemologies of ignorance are able to combat fear and resistance to discuss, engage, and seek to transform the depletion of the earth's resources; the resurgence of militant and reactionary political parties; the changing economy that leaves less and less in the hands of working people; the interpellation of war and subjectivity in our schools that can be found in the new technologies of video games and where youth have the capacity to maim and torture "dissidents" and in certain deleterious examples, rape and urinate on women; and the orgy of standardized tests, rubrics, reading materials, worksheets, practice sheets, practice tests, and interventions that establish the limits of knowledge formation among our youth.

Against this backdrop it would seem as though any notion of epistemologies of ignorance in education would fall on deaf ears. Education seems to be caught up on a runaway train with a discriminating fragment of the population yanking recklessly (and madly) at the throttle. The sheer odium with which the conservative right responds to any tendency to engage in critique of our social foundations is reflective of a new kind of authoritarianism in response to the ideas and practices set forward by frameworks such as epistemologies of ignorance. So in response to Erik's very insightful interrogation of relativism and authoritarianism in education practices and the role of epistemologies of ignorance in disrupting such processes, I am a bit dismayed by the willful, political, and ideological "ignorance" of so many officials who are given the privilege to make decisions about the education of our youth.

Yes, epistemologies of ignorance can shift educational practices in our schools. With vision, commitment, innovation, persistence and an openness to discover other methodologies and other ways of knowing we can return to the basic premise that guides education: knowing and unknowing.

REFERENCES

Arnst, C. (2008, November 17). What makes a good family? *Business Week*, Working Parents Blog, Retrieved February 8, 2009, from http://www.businessweek. com/careers/workingparents/blog/archives/2008/11/what_makes_ a_go.html

Baker, B. (1999). The dangerous and the good? Developmentalism, progress, and public schooling. *American Educational Research Journal, 36*(4), 797–834.

Brandon, L. (2009). Remembering Carter Goodwin Woodson (1875–1950). In E. Malewski (Ed.), *Curriculum studies handbook: The next moment* (pp. 125–137). New York, NY: Routledge.

CNN. (2008, November 22). *Nebraska lawmakers vote to limit safe-haven law.* Retrieved April 10, 2010, from http://www.cnn.com/2008/US/11/21/nebraska. safe.haven/

de Man, P. (1983). *The blindness of insight: Essays in the rhetoric of contemporary criticism.* Minneapolis, MN: University of Minneapolis.

Derrida, J. (2007). *The late Derrida* (W. J. T. Mitchell & A. I. Davison, Eds.). Chicago, IL: University of Chicago.

Derrida, J. (1992). Force of law: The "mystical foundation of authority.? In D. G. Carlson, D. Cornell, & M. Rosenfeld (Eds.), *Deconstruction and the possibility of justice* (pp. 3–67). New York, NY: Routledge.

Ebert, T. (2009). *The task of cultural critique.* Urbana and Chicago: University of Illinois Press.

Eckholm, E. (2008, November 21). Nebraska revises child safe haven law. *New York Times*, p. A10.

Fals-Borda, O. (1998). *People's participation: Challenges ahead.* London: Intermediate Technology Publications.

Felman, S. (1999). Benjamin's silence. *Critical Inquiry, 25*(2), 201–234.

Fraser, N. (1997). *Justice interruptus: Critical reflections on the "postsocialist" condition.* New York, NY: Routledge.

Grande, S. (2004). *Red pedagogy.* Lanham, MD: Rowman & Littlefield.

Haraway, D. (1988). Situated knowledges: The science question in feminism and the privilege of partial perspective. *Feminist Studies, 14*(3), 575–599.

Haraway, D. (1991). Situated knowledges: The science question in feminism and the privilege of partial perspective. In *Simians, cyborgs, and women: The reinvention of nature.* New York, NY: Routledge.

Haraway, D., (2004). Situated knowledges. In S. Harding (Ed.), *The Feminist Standpoint Reader.* New York, NY: Routledge.

Jenkins, N. (2008, October 30). Neb. to reconsider "safe haven" law: 23 abandoned, some from other states. *The Boston Globe.* Retrieved February 10, 2009, from http://www.boston.com/news/nation/articles/2008/10/30/neb_to_reconsider_ safe_haven_law/

Kavanagh, K. (2008, October 8). With teens being left at hospitals, Nebraska legislature sets hearing. *CNN.* Retrieved February 8, 2009, from http://www.cnn. com/2008/US/10/08/nebraska.safe.haven/index.html

Koch, W. (2008, September 26). Nebraska "safe haven" law for kids has unintended results. *USA Today.* Retrieved February 10, 2009, from http://www.usatoday. com/news/health/2008-09-25-Left-kids_N.htm

Lather, P. (2006). Paradigm proliferation as a good thing to think with: Teaching research in education as wild profusion. *International Journal of Qualitative Studies in Education, 19*(1), 35–57.

Lather, P. (2000). Reading the image of Rigoberta Menchú: Undecidability and language lessons. *Qualitative Studies in Education, 13*(2), 153–162.

Lavandera, E. (2008, November 14). Nebraska fears rush to drop off kids before haven law change. *CNN*. Retrieved February 8, 2008, from http://www.cnn.com/2008/US/11/14/nebraska.safe.haven/index.html

Malewski, E. (2009). Introduction. In E. Malewski (Ed.), *Curriculum studies handbook: The next moment* (pp. 1–40). New York, NY: Routledge.

Malewski, E., & Sharma, S. (2010). Reading the Nebraska safe haven law controversy: Neoliberalism, biopower, and the discourse of expendability. In J. A. Sandlin, B. D. Schultz, & J. Burdick (Eds.), *Education and learning beyond schooling* (pp. 531–542). New York, NY: Routledge.

Mann, H. (1839). *The Common School Journal*, vol. 1-2. Boston, MA: Marsh, Capen, Lyon and Webb.

Menchú, R. (1984). I, *RigobertaMenchú: An Indian Woman in Guatemala* (Elisabeth Burgos-Debray, Ed., Ann Wright, Trans). London: Verso.

Morrison, K. (2004). The poverty of curriculum theory: A critique of Wraga and Hlebowitsh. *Journal of Curriculum Studies, 36*(4), 487–494.

Ockander, M., & Östlund, G. (2001). To the editor: Comments on the Brad trilogy. *Qualitative Health Research, 11*(6), 725–727.

Quijano, A. (2000). Coloniality of power, Eurocentrism, and Latin America. *Nepantla: Views From South, 1*, 533–580

Riccardi, N. (2008, November 22). Nebraska legislature amends safe-haven law. *Los Angeles Times*. Retrieved February 8, 2009, from http://articles.latimes.com/2008/nov/22/nation/na-nebraska22

Schreiber, R., Rodney, P., Brown, H., & Varcoe, C. (2001). Reflections on deconstructing Harry, or when is good art bad science? [Letter to the editor]. *Qualitative Health Research, 11*(6), 723–724.

Shapiro, A. (2008, November 14) Nebraska legislators evaluate safe-Haven law. National Public Radio, Morning Edition, 11:00 AM–12:00 PM, Record #200811141107.

Slevin, P. (2008, November 16). Nebraska to alter safe-haven law: State hopes to care for abandoned children without becoming a dumping ground. *Washington Post*, A03.

Stoll, D. (2007). *Rigoberta Menchu and the story of all poor Guatemalans*. New York, NY: Westview. (Original work published 1999)

Thoreau, H., (1851). Useful ignorance. Reproduced in *Lapham Quarterly, 1*(4), (fall 2008). Retrieved from http://www.laphamsquarterly.org/voices-in-time/useful-ignorance.php

Tuana, N. (2004). Coming to understand: Orgasm and the epistemology of ignorance. *Hypatia, 19*(1), 194–232.

Tuana, N. (2006). The speculum of ignorance: The women's health movement and epistemologies of ignorance. *Hypatia, 21*(3), 1–19.

Wolcott, H. (2002). *Sneaky kid and its aftermath: Ethics and intimacy in fieldwork*. Lanham, MD: AltaMira Press.

CHAPTER 2

COMMITTING (TO) IGNORANCE

On Method, Myth, and Pedagogy With Jacques Rancière

Molly Quinn

One fatal Tree there stands of Knowledge
    Call'd
Forbidden them to taste: Knowledge forbidd'n?
Suspicious, reasonless. Why should thir Lord
Envie them that? Can it be sin to know,
Can it be death? And do they onely stand
By Ignorance, is that thir happie state,
The proof of thir obedience and thir faith?

—Milton, *Paradise Lost,* IV, 514

Upright and praying, keeping a colossal vigil, with its branches raised like
elbows to the light—it [the giant sequoia tree] is praying to some god of
life which I will never know, if I still know what praying means. Perhaps
today I should forget my knowledge.

—Serres, (1989, p. 62)

Epistemologies of Ignorance in Education, pp. 31–52
Copyright © 2011 by Information Age Publishing
31

There is a certain strong and generous ignorance that concedes nothing to
knowledge in honor and courage, an ignorance that requires no less
knowledge to conceive it than does knowledge.
                              —Montaigne, Essays III, 11, Of Cripples

I am thankful that the good God created us all ignorant. I am glad that
when we change His plans in this regard we have to do it at our own risk.
                              —Mark Twain, Letter to the Alta California
                                    [San Francisco] (May 28, 1867)

Perhaps today we should not nor can forget that still there stands one—at
least—fatal Tree called Knowledge, away from which we have not far ven-
tured, about which we gather still, perhaps before which we even pray with
offerings of faith and obedience in kind—even if with pronounced doubt
or resigned desperation. In these posttimes, indeed, our garden paradise
has become more a forest of disenchantment in profound and abiding
ways, as we live and die by the realization that our hopes for knowledge
have fallen tragically short—rotten fruit under rotten branches or rotting
yet thereupon. At the least, we wonder and worry if the path of knowledge can anymore raise us higher, lift us to a lightened view, free us from
ignorance or incapacity, give us a truer understanding of ourselves and
our place in the world, gift us with insight into the human condition and
humanity's "raison d'etre" or "joie de vivre" in the cosmos. Certainly, we
brood over its fate in addressing human injustice and suffering, seeming
to have already greatly contributed to it.[1]

Contemporary epistemological critiques have also confirmed that
which we have experienced: working within this postmodern forest,
poststructuralist thinkers like Michel Serres, Jacques Derrida, and Michel Foucault, among others, seem to have gathered around this tree of
knowledge—the one with tenacious roots in Western soil and yet grasping branches expanding out of measure in all directions—in a kind of
condemnation of it: as the tree of the knowledge of evil, in effect, intent
on killing the tree called life. This very tree, to which we have been so
committed, and its fruit—the Western journey of knowing, the intellectual traditions upon which progressive dreams via education for a free
and full humanity have been nurtured—has actually been the source of
death. As Serres (1983/1989) himself concludes: "To know is to kill, to rely
on death" (p. 128). The story he tells of the sacred wood involves rules
of protection, and priests, and kings and soldiers of knowledge: territory
around the tree must be occupied, controlled, ever by the one who put the
former kingdom's ruler—supporting another theory—violently to death
and is surely subject to the same; "the space of knowledge lies in the
hands of soldiery" (p. 48). Inquiring into this space, tracing ontological
and axiological genealogies of its and our epistemological foundations,

these scholars have discovered its secret wisdom: war—martial in method, power its purpose.

Yet, such is not exactly the story I wish to recount today, nor the one to which I here commit and invite others to enter. Today, I wonder more about the story of, our knowledge of, an epistemology of, ignorance. Surely, there are many stories to be heard and told, and ones regarding ignorance cannot so easily be culled from those regarding knowledge. In fact, ignorance, it seems, is something of knowledge's virtual opposite, or shadow. As if coconstituted, there would be no knowledge at all were not ignorance present or possible as well, and yet our knowledge projects seem to issue from this quest to irrevocably eradicate ignorance, which too I suppose if accomplished would effectively bring our knowledge projects to an end. While contested (Bernstein, 1991; Nussbaum, 1997), this dark tale of knowledge's evil deeds and deathly demises, is one of which many of us are familiar, and with which many of us can identify; we may even acknowledge an inkling of and for ignorance as true bliss, and concede a certain longing to forget our knowledge. Yet, as educators, scholars, teachers of teachers and students, are we really willing to profess ignorance? Our ignore-ance of ignorance? In troubling knowledge, are we willing to be thankful for ignorance; to entertain it as some "happie" state, with faith and obedience; to endorse an ignorance that is strong and generous, requiring honor and courage? Or would doing so be at our own peril, risking that forbidden fruit of knowledge, addictive and oft sweet, upon which, for all its dissatisfactions, we cannot help but continue to feed (not to mention upon which our very livelihoods and labors, perhaps even human life and hope as progressively conceived, depend)?

Yes. Yes. Exactly. Alas. We may nod at poststructuralist indictments of knowledge, but our disdain for ignorance we certainly continue to hold near and dear. In this, ironically, we may embody both the "pluralistic ignorance" of which social psychologists speak (i.e., Katz & Allport, 1931)—secretly disregarding such questions to knowledge, even as we endorse in our research *Getting Lost* with Patti Lather (2007), suspecting that most scholars among us do as much; and the economists' "rational ignorance" because the cost of taking ignorance seriously outweighs the benefit of ignoring it. We are all children of Socrates, as much as the serpent, in this regard, certain that ultimately it is ignorance that is the evil—a darkness from which all need deliverance—that ought be expelled to make ours a garden paradise once again. *Really, thank God for the tree of knowledge, and the forbidden fruit! Knowledge, whatever troubles it visits upon us, is in the end productive of the "happie" state, strength, generosity, gratitude and more goods beside.* Whatever our failures respecting knowledge, surely it still holds more promise for realizing freedom, equity and human happiness—perhaps more and better and different "critical" knowledge, engaged with or brought to others more, in better ways, differently, even "postcritically," shall yield more satisfying fruit—than ignorance.

But what of the forgotten or forbidden fruit—the delicious light, depth, darkness, or absence thereof—of ignorance itself, and what it might afford or teach us? Or what of the teaching or knowledge it might assist in delivering us from? What if it is as Serres (1983/1989) suggests that "if you are standing inside, nailed to your ideas, you cannot move without tearing yourself to pieces. The tree of knowledge has become a bush of painfully fixed ideas" (p. 51)? What if "outside our knowledge there exists a learning sealed off by our very science, killed by our very language" (p. 59)? Perhaps ignorance might be found then to be a saving grace, or space, apart from compulsive feeding, serving and stuffing ourselves and others beyond or without satiation on plucked or fallen knowledge fruit. Maybe sustenance and satisfaction, even the genuine call of hunger and nourishment that answers it, is only experienced and embraced from or in the ground of not knowing. I submit, admittedly, that there are probably in truth knowledges and ignorances, subsisting in relation and necessary each to the other. I here press for ignorance as the marginalized, excluded other to knowledge, as it were, and beseech an experiment here: leaving knowledge, this revered and feared tree and its ripe fruit, for but a while, to entertain ignorance, what committing ignorance, committing to ignorance, might make possible with respect to our work as scholars and as teachers, particularly in our thinking about and posture toward knowledge and ignorance, power and emancipation, and/in the pedagogical relationship. And yes, taking up such a charge, involves a little faith—at least a momentary suspension of disbelief (Doll, 1993), and in this, too, a submission of will and authority akin to obedience. Courage too, then, indeed.

Why and how do I expect to advance such a mad proposal—especially among those who while not exactly kings or priests of knowledge, surely its masters or "doctors," guardians of the tree with some substantial degree of authority and power with respect to its root, ground and fruit? Ignorant as I am, or wish to become, I cannot exactly present here a knowledgeable answer to such a question, nor can I explicate an introduction or thesis or proposed direction to any definitive satisfaction; for, in this, I embrace the adventure of the fool. But I should wish to share a few stories in this wise, issuing principally from an inspiration to ignorance afforded me by another French postphilosopher, Jacques Rancière (1940-), in his historical account of Joseph Jacotot (1770–1840), *The Ignorant Schoolmaster* (1991), who in 1818 discovered the gift of his own ignorance[2]—as well as from my own experiences of and affinities for ignorance perhaps. In the very least, such accountings and recountings may assist us in making our way to ignorance, or rather in getting lost and losing ourselves in or to it, via: (1) a foolish invitation to commit (to) ignorance explored; (2) a pedagogical experiment of ignorance revisited; and (3) a heretical confession of unknown implications and want of conclusions offered to the reader. Of course, it is left to the reader whether or not she chooses to take up this adventure—is willing to play the fool for a spell, and what he finally makes of or takes from it.

A FOOLISH INVITATION TO COMMIT (TO) IGNORANCE EXPLORED

Many abuses are engendered in the world, or, to put it more boldly, all…, by our being taught to be afraid of professing our ignorance…

—Montaigne, *Essays III*, 11, Of Cripples

Not ignorance, but ignorance of ignorance, is the death of knowledge.

—Alfred North Whitehead

Ignorance gives one a large range of possibilities.

—George Eliot, *Daniel Deronda*, II, 13

I invite the foolish student of this text who would too consider committing, and committing to ignorance. I do so to compel us to entertain the importance of ignorance, even its active profession in some fruitful light, particularly in its relation to knowledge, to education as a project of knowledge, and to method, so pedagogically central to this project's enactment. I do so, as well, to foreshadow our inquiry into the work of Jacques Rancière (1991), who in his study of the "ignorant schoolmaster," Joseph Jacotot, challenges us with the possibilities of an emancipatory epistemology of ignorance for our own scholarly work in education, curriculum and pedagogy. I also engage this invitation in this way to present and play with certain normative notions of ignorance that abound, one of which is ignorance as that which is committed, an act issuing from want of knowledge that is, in fact, an act of offense or sin. In contrast to taking and tasting of the fruit of the tree of knowledge as prohibition, embracing ignorance is deemed transgressive—ignorance doles out its own forbidden fruit, or fruit of fruitlessness.

Even a cursory look into established definitions of ignorance, or something of ignorance's conceptual and linguistic lineage, via the

Oxford English Dictionary (OED, 1989), reveals how powerfully ignorance is associated with sin, and even as an offense against knowledge itself, albeit also in some ways articulated as at odds with faith, too. Herein, ignorance is likely not anything one wants to embrace, nor have ascribed to him or her. Related words of description include: dull, credulous, bestial, barbarian, ill-mannered, uncouth, feeble, and wanton. Ignorance, like knowledge, we might add, is in this way embodied, such that moral and ethical indictments and antagonistic identity markers are attached to it. Thus, the ignorant is subject to admonishment, susceptible to manipulation and enslavement, possessed of vulgar speech, destitute of knowledge. Negligence, violence, calamity, and evil issue from mere ignorance, which is affiliated with darkness, blindness, and hell.

While a literal rendering might postulate the term, from the Latin *ig-norare*, as simply "not to know," ignorance as generally defined is less frequently portrayed principally in terms of an empty state or an absence, albeit when taken up in this way tends to be circumscribed in a deficit conception, allusions also made to emptiness itself as somehow worthy of rebuke. The unlearned, uninformed, unskilled, unconscious one suffers from want of knowledge, and thus is destitute of and has no share in knowledge, as well—living without intention, only accidentally rather than with agency; this attribution of lack of agency, too, raises perhaps even questions about the very humanity of the one deemed ignorant. Thus, it seems that about the tree of officiated notions of ignorance, established understandings thereof, lurk the priests and authors of knowledge, the hands of soldiery—with their belief in inequality, a hierarchy of intelligence—rationing out that which is sanctioned as knowledge's fruit, regulating the very language and action by which it may be received and blessed, rendering what they will outside their purview as ignorance to be vanquished or from which to be delivered.

Herein, to commit ignorance, to commit to ignorance, is in one way to attend to it as a place for understanding the workings of power, a site of knowledge creation and annihilation, of cultural inclusion and exclusion —and dominance and resistance; for interrogating that which is epistemologically grounded and also driven underground in designations of what constitutes and counts as knowledge and ignorance. We could, of course here, speak of some such ignorance, so called, as epistemological alterity, taboo-ed epistemology, subjugated knowledge, or counterknowledge—the null curriculum of all that gets ignored, unattended, unacknowledged and left out of dominant conceptions of knowledge. Herein is a hidden curriculum as well that privileges certain paradigms of knowing as others are relegated to the realm of ignorance—not just inferior, insignificant, altogether unrecognized, unworthy of attention or false, but even dangerous or evil. It is a curriculum too, perhaps that privileges knowledge itself, as though there were nothing besides—totalizing it via mind, thought, language, reason, intelligence, and so forth; and as such, co-opting and seeking to wholly absorb and encompass all experience, all that it actually means to be human or to be fully human.

In this way, honoring ignorance entails challenging that which is given and established, and acknowledging and inquiring into that which lies outside of it. For ignorance can here also embrace this "outside," and as in response to the power of the officiated, which can also be a kind of agency and experience of emancipation: the gift of the stranger (Huebner, 1999; Wang, 2004), the wanderer or nomad (Deleuze, 1973; Serres, 1991/1997), embracing *intermezzo* living (Deleuze & Guattari, 1980/1987), with his or her epistemology of ignorance—border-land, foreign, alien, negative epistemological unknowns, kept from the grasp of knowledge's soldiery. Ignorance here is constituted, then also, through an affirmation of another way of being and seeing and engaging—or not—in the world; that which is not merely knowledge's binary opposite or its absence, something other. As Lather (2007) has put it: "There is a being in excess of our languages of knowing, whether we know it or not" (p. 3).

There is an "ignorance" (at least, so-called), for instance, among other things, as Southerner, as woman, and "raised on" religion, as Louisianan —"third world and proud of it" (as one of the state's mottos reads), that I have acknowledged, embraced, and endorsed—to which I have sought to hold fast, maintain, and even cultivate, and not merely as that which is counter to dominant constructions of knowledge and their exclusivity (i.e., male, WASP, 'Northeastern' cultural capital of New York City where I now live, "first" world) as academically framed, or in the way of the scholarly legitimate.[3] I suppose such a stance could be postulated as the reclamation of the ground from which has been and continues to be generated my own "funds of knowledge" (Moll, Neff, & Gonzalez, 1992) or the possession of a space for the constitution and possibility of my own "culturally relevant pedagogy" (Ladson-Billings, 1994), as it were, or even somewhat ironically as my own argument for the "transformative intellectual knowledge" to which Banks (2004) and Sleeter (2005), among others, are so vehemently committed, and also in the way of "un-standardizing" and pluralizing curriculum and teaching via education as a knowledge project through critical encounter with historically-marginalized and excluded epistemological artifacts and agencies.

Holding on to this kind of ignorance can also be viewed in terms of "playing dumb"—a way of being and acting perhaps of note among historically oppressed groups dispossessed of power like African Americans and women in the United States, as a form of disaffiliation from dominant knowledge forms and the subjectivities generated by them; that is, via normative discourses reinforcing, oft in unacknowledged ways, White, male, "middle-plus" class, heterosexual or other privilege. Elisabeth Johnson (2009), for example, in her study of the discourses and identities of high school youth in an urban English education classroom, describes an event of a young man of color "performing ignorance," particularly of the language use characteristic of White businessmen, to distinguish his masculinity as something different from, and other than, theirs. As a female of the deep South, actually learning ignorance and playing ignorant proved to be a tool of resistance and empowerment[4]—paradoxically, in seeming to reinforce the authority of men and the femininity constituted by male superiority, from this subjugated location women undertook to use it to their advantage, artfully undermining and covertly operating outside of it, manipulating men and the inequitable hierarchical structures to another purpose—their own; whether as fragile flower or "steel magnolia," they could move men to move to their whims. In this sense, ignorance reflects an expression of will and agency, and intelligence—a struggle for freedom that also affirms an equality of intelligence in the face of discourses and practices that work to negate such. Of course, I came to critique and undermine such wolf-lamb power-relation postures, complications and inversions (Serres, 1983/1989) as well within Southern male-female relations, but continued to understand ignorance, as such, some counterpoint to knowledge as generally defined, as something to affirm, in some manifestations, a something, too, beyond this mechanism within the hegemonic ordering of things.

Yet, while this affirmation, in my case, means embracing a certain rocking-on-the-front porch openness, bourbon-sniffing and—sipping breathing-room for nothing but the shared moment of intoxicating and irresistible taste, or tall-tale-telling-over-the-counter-conversation that reflects a Southern, feminine (perhaps classed and even raced, as well) penchant for the nonlinear, indirect, metaphorical, intuitive, earthy, bodily, sensual, inexplicable, irreverent (i.e., politically incorrect?), mysterious, mystical, and unknown; it means more beyond this as well. Primitive, perhaps—but thus also fundamental, this posture honors that which lies before knowledge and knowing, and that which lies beyond and even exceeds knowledge and knowing, somehow: a "moreness" (Huebner, 1999) that supercedes thought, language, conceptualization and conceptualizing. As Dwayne Huebner (1999) so wisely, or foolishly, alludes to something of this understanding:

> There is more than we know, can know, will ever know. It is a "moreness" that takes us by surprise when we are at the edge and end of our knowing. There is a comfort in that "moreness" that takes over in our weakness, our ignorance, at our limits or end. It is a comfort that cannot be anticipated, a "peace that passeth all understanding".... One knows of that presence, that "moreness," when known resources fail and somehow we go beyond what

we were and are and become something different, something new. There is also judgment in that "moreness," particularly when we smugly assume that we know what "it" is all about and we end up in the dark on our behinds. It is this very "moreness" that can be identified with the "spirit" and the "spiritual." In fact, Kovel describes the "spirit" as "what happens to us as the boundaries of the self give way." Spirit is that which transcends the known, the expected, even the ego and the self. It is the source of hope. It is manifested through love and the waiting expectation that accompanies love. It overcomes us.... One whose imagination acknowledges that "moreness" can be said to dwell faithfully in the world. (p. 403)

Via Huebner, drawing support from Joel Kovel (1991), we might consider this appeal to acertain sort of spirit as that to which our 'ignorance' points—reflective and/or inclusive of the "ignorance" of religion perhaps too, and in a way that our "knowledge" tends to minimize, marginalize, exclude or outright even deny (Wexler, 2000). Relatedly, perhaps, Jim Henderson and Kathleen Kesson (2004), in seeking to push against the boundaries of and expand upon our conceptions of our work, speak of curriculum wisdom as a kind of "cultivated ignorance" (p. 14). In Southern parlance, we might speak more of "soul" though, which revels in that which belies comprehension and even betrays knowledge. As such, perhaps, soul advocates a "generous ignorance," taking up the honor and courage of which Montaigne speaks and the unknown realms of possibility Elliot considers. To consider soul, and soulful living as a way of faithfully dwelling in the world, as well, and with respect to my Southern identity, is not as far a field concerning our consideration of ignorance as it might at first seem. To some, soul speaks to an embodiment of spirit—body and spirit alike having been somewhat pitted against and excluded from intellect, reason and mind in Western projects of knowledge; and I have been returning via my argument here to my own embodied existence as knower and unknown, knowing and unknowing, in the world, and shall shortly revisit such from another experimental view.

The ignorant in being given such designations as promiscuous, wanton, evil, dull, unskilled speaks as well to embodiment, one's embodied subjectivity, as the site of knowledge and/or ignorance in some primary way—the way in which the question of knowledge or ignorance comes down to the one (or group) who is knowledgeable or ignorant, and thus also the relationship between the ignorant and knowledgeable, which ends up usually becoming a relationship that is pedagogical. It is from this vantage point that we move, then, from a cursory reconceptualization of ignorance—at least inquiry into dominant denotations and connotations of it—to this return to ignorance experimentally respecting the pedagogical relationship, via various embodiments across and in time and history, making our way into the stories of Jacques Rancière and Joseph Jacotot.

A PEDAGOGICAL EXPERIMENT OF IGNORANCE REVISITED

It may be said with some plausibility that there is an abecedarian ignorance that comes before knowledge, and another, doctoral ignorance that comes after knowledge: an ignorance that knowledge creates and engenders, just as it undoes and destroys the first.

—Montaigne, Essays I, 54, Of Vain Subtleties

Genuine ignorance is... profitable because it is likely to be accompanied by humility, curiosity, and open mindedness; whereas ability to repeat catch-phrases, cant terms, familiar propositions, gives the conceit of learning and coats the mind with varnish waterproof to new ideas.

— John Dewey, 1910, p. 177

A great deal of intelligence can be invested in ignorance...

—Saul Bellow, 1976, p. 127

Today I only want to tell you a story about a story of the story of an "ignorant schoolmaster." I do so, perhaps as well, in the manner in which Patti Lather (2007) begins her work *Getting Lost*—borrowing from Walter Benjamin; she says: "This is a book about a book about getting lost at the limits of representation" (p. 1). Except, maybe here my tale about a tale of a pedagogical tale is more about getting lost—and maybe even finding ourselves too—at the limits of knowledge or knowing more broadly, something perhaps other than or beyond representation albeit inescapably tied up in it too. Or rather this recursive recounting of accounts may find us about getting lost before knowledge, in the place that precedes its limits, or exceeds them, after knowledge and knowing.

But, maybe I should move along to the telling, and simply begin with: Once upon a time, in a land far away and yet quite near, there lived an American professor in a disenchanted kingdom called the University, or sometimes also known as "the Republic of Knowledge" (Rancière, 1991). Albeit for a number of reasons, far too detailed to relate here, she did find enchantments from time to time of a certain sort, particularly in poststructuralist critiques of said knowledge, and drew comfort from such forests of disenchantment strangely—critiques opening here to the unknown, unknowable, unforeclosed, uncertain, to mystery. Ironically, in the telling of this tale, these clearings, too—or densities—affirmed in her, before and beyond her, all that is, in fact, present and yet inarticulable, "non-narrativisable" (Butler, 2005), unrepresentable—the bliss of ignorance, perhaps?

By chance one day, among the tangled and mangled branches of web-net communications that seemed ever only to proliferate-ly[5] come at her and darken, even block her way, she happened upon an enchanting address, issued by another kindred professor—John[6] was his name—also taken to wandering his way into "post" wildernesses. By renegade-rather-than-royal invitation, John was hosting a gala—or humble, whichever you prefer—presentation of the French philosopher Jacques Rancière. Now, some plot lines vividly, though simply, drawn in the announcement of Jacques' story drew her in, such that she found herself wanting much to be in audience for this occasion. One such charm was word of a text, if only as translated in English, writ nonetheless by this, to her, unexpected visitor yet to come: *The Ignorant Schoolmaster: Five Lessons in Intellectual Emancipation* (Rancière, 1991).

As naïve, idealistic, nonironic, and passé—"Old School," from a land-really far away, as it was, she had to admit to herself she was stirred still by "emancipation," and also in relation to the intellect. But, it was the declaration of ignorance, and amid all these juxtaposing signifiers, that really caught her attention and interest. She supposed some might fancy her a schoolmaster herself—as problematic as the concept was, as a whole, and in "school" and as "master," in many respects to her scholarly and teacherly sensibilities and aspirations. And she had experienced much and many times the virtues of "ignorance" too: suspecting the paths, purposes, perspectives, suspended and issuing from this unclear uncertainty, "cloud of unknowing" (anonymous, 1957), as ignorance is defined —want of knowledge, to mark those places, in fact, points of time and lostness and discovery, most interesting and influential, even transformative and free (although not without discomfort, difficulty and struggle, as well). And this, not only for herself, but also in relation to the students she taught. Though one such as she could hardly ever openly admit it—committing to ignorance, the worst act of treason, heresy against reason, in the kingdom of her dwelling. The schoolmaster, most of all, may be many things, but not ignorant, which is in her work, too, of the greatest shame.

In any case, there were other allures for her in Jacques' story to be sure, and we may well get to them in our tales of these adventures, yet, for now, suffice it to say that she set off to find this treasured text, and sought to give it a reading before his arrival. This, she accomplished and began her entry into the text with a delightful freshness and abandon, and anticipation. As for the Rancière gathering, as the day for it drew near, alas myriad obstacles arose and began presenting themselves. In the end, she was actually left by herself just to the text alone, then, called to some schoolmaster's responsibility and unable to attend the coveted event. Sad to have missed any insightful explications of the text offered by its author, she continued to take it up nonetheless, losing herself in the story it related, and wondered at hearing Rancière likened by some who had heard him to Elmer Fudd, an eccentric yet intent on his purposes cartoon character. But that is another story. Missing the authorial word, while unbeknownst to her at the time, foreshadowed experientially key elements of the stories she would enter through this particular text of Rancière.

Now Rancière's tale is yet in the telling, as truly are all tales, and we are perhaps most interested to get to the place where his story meets that of the ignorant schoolmaster, Joseph Jacotot, whose story he tells through the text, what his translators call "a fable ... enacting an extraordinary philosophical meditation on equality" (Ross, 1991, p. ix), and one we can soon see presents Jacotot's living out and telling of what he titles "the myth of pedagogy" as well. So many stories upon stories, nested in stories' branches, connected somehow across time, space, knowledge—or ignorance, language and more—or less. What Lather (2007) considers, in what she calls the aftermath of poststructuralism, is strangely—though some of these times of which I tell are prepost, something perhaps our stories share: a query about what knowledge is possible after our disappointments with knowledge (though she focuses on science), an impetus to articulate a philosophy of inquiry—"toward a fruitful sense of dislocation in our knowledge projects" (p. 1). Surely, our location around the tree of knowledge has not always or perhaps ultimately even been all too fruitful, or maybe actually overly fruitful—fruitlessness may afford better a welcoming of the new and new possibility. Wasn't knowledge and trouble indeed borne when Eve and Adam sought this root, its fruit? But that's another story. We shall be lost to our knowledge projects a while longer, leave these roots and lose ourselves in the routes of our two friends, committed as they are to—relocating themselves in?—ignorance.

The projects of our friend Rancière emerge in the aftermath of the student riots in France in 1968, a time identified with the end of politics and fall of the intellectual left, particularly in which enduring debates about education and class in France abound. A student of Louis Althusser, his disappointments with knowledge, also perhaps oriented themselves around the growing influence of thought in the social sciences—not particularly among social scientists but especially educational reformers (particularly from the 80s on, after translations in English)—especially of Bourdieu and Foucault, something likened to a media campaign. Critical particularly of the "Bourdieu effect" that explains cultural exclusion as a result of ignorance, and ignorance as a result of cultural exclusion, Rancière has been named an intellectual maverick of sorts, whose turn to nineteenth century workers' archives in his own scholarship did not find him among the fashionable philosophical celebrities of the times. But, the French attention to questions of education and equality, especially concerning class difference, he did share with them (issues of education, equity and difference contemporary in many contexts, including Molly's present one, as well), and no doubt the structuralist/poststructuralist interest in the "hegemony of binary oppositions"—that is, inquiring into the pedagogical relationship his mentor Louis Althusser and others described as fundamentally respecting the relationship between knowledge and ignorance (Ross, 1991).[7]

It is not surprising perhaps, then, that he invited into his own story another intellectual maverick of another era, the character Joseph Jacotot, a French professor and schoolmaster exiled (maybe Rancière is a bit exiled as well) from France in 1818 who committed to ignorance as a result of pedagogical experiments this chance afforded him. Rancière dubs Jacotot's tale an intellectual adventure whose context is in an aftermath as well, the postrevolutionary era in France. A distinguished professor of French literature, Jacotot had taught rhetoric, prepared for a career in law, served as artilleryman in the Republican armies, held post as secretary to the ministry of war and been made deputy—until the Bourbons forced him into exile at the Second Restoration. Given a position at the University of Louvain by the King of the Netherlands, however, he had students who wished to learn from him, and whom he wished to teach, but they did not share the same language. "An unassuming lecturer," Jacotot sought to address the dilemma in a text he found, a bilingual edition of *Télémaque*.[8] Through the limited use of an interpreter, he asked them to learn the French text with the help of its translation in their language. This included on the part of students repetition and recitation by heart as well.

What Jacotot found was most unexpected: deprived of explanation, in the difficult context of negotiating an unknown language, the students were able to write in French what they had learned of the text, performing as well as many French students would have done. Called by some the results of a "desperate empiricism," the experience compelled Jacotot to experiment further with what was initiated by chance on what students could do if left to themselves—perhaps, desire, will, that was all that learning required; perhaps, all could understand what any other has or could understand, he thought.

Jacotot successfully taught piano and painting, arts he knew not; Hebrew, a language he did not know, to a child brought to him deemed retarded; and students how to litigate in Flemish, a language also not known to him. Overturning the thought and method of his day, he came to the understanding that: knowledge is not necessary to teach, and that the dominant pedagogical method of explication is, in fact, one of stultification, based on a false premise of inequality: "the annihilation of one mind by another" (Rancière, 1991, p. 32). Rather, he posited that all people are equal in intelligence, and advocated universal teaching, or intellectual emancipation, which acknowledges this equality—the (non) method of chance, that by which "what all children learn best ... what no master can explain: the mother tongue" (p. 5); and this, methodically repeated as that which gives one the measure of his or her power (p. 16). Through this work, he also taught poor and illiterate parents to teach their children to read.

So as not to defy the spirit of Jacotot's adventure and discovery, without the deadening dominance of much direct explanation, let you who receive these tales of telling tales hear a few jewels from his story itself as told and retold in Rancière's translated work:

> The revelation that came to Joseph Jacotot amounts to this: the logic of the explicative system had to be overturned. Explication is not necessary to remedy an incapacity to understand. On the contrary, that very incapacity provides the structuring fiction of the explicative conception of the world.... Before being the act of the pedagogue, explication is the myth of pedagogy, the parable of a world divided into knowing minds and ignorant ones, ripe minds and immature ones, the capable and incapable, the intelligent and the stupid. (p. 6)

In this experiment with students, Jacotot "had only ordered them to pass through a forest whose openings and clearings he himself had not discovered" (Rancière, 1991 p. 9). Necessity compelled him to leave his intelligence out as mediator—an act suppressing the imaginary distance [between the knowledgeable teacher and ignorant student] upon which is built the principle of stultification. Rather:

> The master is he who encloses an intelligence in the arbitrary circle from which it can only break out by becoming necessary to itself ... supporting a notion of mutual teaching in mind: that each ignorant person could become for another ignorant person the master who would reveal to him his intellectual power.... Whoever teaches without emancipating stultifies. And whoever emancipates doesn't have to worry about what the emancipated person learns. He will learn what he wants, nothing maybe. (pp. 15, 17, 18)

Jacotot claimed, then, thus: "Beneath the pedagogical relation of ignorance to science (or knowledge), the more fundamental philosophical relation of stultification (explication) to emancipation must be recognized" (Rancière, 1991 p. 14). And indeed, something was, in fact, recognized, and:

> People were affected in Louvain, in Brussels, and in la Haye; they took the mail carriage from Paris and Lyon; they came from England and Prussia to hear the news; it was proclaimed in Saint Petersburg and New Orleans. The word reached as far as Rio de Janeiro. For several years polemic raged, and the Republic of knowledge was shaken at its very foundations.
>
> All of this because a learned man, a renowned man of science and a virtuous family man, had gone crazy for not knowing Flemish. (p. 18)

Of course, if the story were to be further told out, it might proceed to some conclusive resolution such as this: while Jacotot's method was indicted by many for corrupting youth, instigating such schools of darkness against virtue and unity ((Rancière, 1991 p. 75), soon order was and had to be restored in some less overtly agitated manner—the "method" of Jacotot could be explicated and was thus re-constituted and re-formulated (much like the pagan rituals of old were in the rise of Christendom) such as to be accommodated a more comfortable-than-not place within the very Republic of Knowledge itself. But, of course, legend reports, too, that Jacotot was left or lost to his madness, committed to ignorance ever after.

Are we crazy for not knowing? Is ignorance as it is defined—akin to wantonness, offense, sin and even violence (OED, 1989)? Yet, what of our knowledge? Is it akin somehow to the ignorance, mystery, perhaps, we deny, eschew, and try to recast and explicate as certain and clear? What if we embrace—perhaps with Jacotot and Rancière—what Lather (2007) with Benjamin describes as "the praxis of stuck places and naked methodologies" (p. 1), the "losing of ourselves in" that calls for quite a different schooling? What if we commit to ignorance as that "space surprised by difference into the performance of practices of not-knowing" (p. 7), an undecidability that loosens that which normalizes and regularizes in its explicitness, that "makes room" for something else to come about? Molly entertained herself with such questions, pausing before tenure papers, wondering how she might commit here, rather than explicate her pure pledges of allegiance to the Republic of Knowledge. But, this story, it will continue, no, it must not conclude, or end here, but rather make room for another story upon story upon story to come forth. So you are left now to the text, to take up your own ignorance, see where it takes you, your own intellectual adventures and unfolding tales thereof. And if a final decree of sorts must of necessity on such occasions be made, may it always be thus in this wise.

A HERETICAL CONFESSION OF UNKNOWN IMPLICATIONS
AND WANT OF CONCLUSIONS

They moved along in a manner one shouldn't move along—the way children move, blindly, figuring out riddles.... Wasn't that shameful method ... the true movement of human intelligence taking possession of its power?.... All their effort, all their exploration, is strained toward this: someone has addressed words to them that they want to recognize and respond to, not as students or as learned men, but as people; in the way you respond to someone speaking to you and not to someone examining you: under the sign of equality. (Rancière, 1991, pp. 10, 11)

Emancipation is becoming conscious of this equality.... This is what opens the way to all adventure in the land of knowledge. It is a matter of daring to be adventurous, and not whether one learns more or less well or more or less quickly. (Rancière, 1991, p. 27)

Whoever looks always finds. He doesn't necessarily find what he was looking for, and even less what he was supposed to find. But he finds something new to relate to the thing he already knows.... The [school] master is he who keeps the [student] researcher on his [own] route, the one that he alone is following and keeps following. (Rancière, 1991, p. 33)

The fool in me would leave off telling tales and penning proposals here, without a benediction, as it were, of any sort: she wants to leave the reader to the text alone, would draw this story as the experiment of an enclosed circle out of which the reader's intelligence, as equal to her own and unimpeded by explication, of necessity must itself break out, if it should so choose. There would be no forced altar-calls to commit to ignorance, or conclusions articulated in conflict with or contradiction to the schoolmaster's presentation, no explicit attempt at representation, no discussion of implications either, which of necessity, it seems, when directly engaged make for explications as well. Yet, I am compelled to continue in all this, it seems, and wonder if all is undone in this movement, if I in the end come to betray the very ignorance to which I have sought to commit.

Perhaps, it is true: the ignorant lie, ignorance can never be trusted. Or perhaps, I know too much already—like Eve and Adam, and would that I were ignorant but find myself insufficient and immobilized (or oversufficient and overmobilized) before ignorance's call. Possibly, though, we also know, if not too much, at least some things, and this one thing clearly: that in the Republic of Knowledge we shall surely be banished without such obeisance to the sacred tree and its soldiery, its roots and fruits and their established methods of pruning; we must ask ourselves again to what we are willing to commit and to what extent. Herein we return to questions, too, of courage and strength as well as devotion; those that speak not only to the limits of our knowledge but also of our ignorance, or generosity toward ignorance. Perhaps, in this, I am not ready for such radical wandering, taking unknown routes away from or without known roots—such as espoused by Jacotot or Rancière; to will my own exile, to exile myself as a subject of knowledge, or knowing subject, to so radically challenge my own cognitive agency or epistemological significance (Code, 1991). In fact, though, as I am humbled before failures in my own knowledge projects, I am also humbled in present and past attempts to be delivered from them—condemned, it seems, to knowledge and ignorance, knowing and its undoing.

In this, then, we must also ever commit to being ignorant in our ignorance, and inspiration to ignorance. Care must be taken: ours is not to totalize ignorance or our committing (to) it, but rather perhaps unlearn, become de-skilled in, find breathing room from, totalizing regulatory knowledge tree-fruit. There may indeed be some ignorance to which knowledge is also a saving grace—that is, the Southern rebel alas can also be the Southern racist. In addition, while "meaning is a work of the will" (Rancière, 1991, p. 56), the will—motivation and desire—is profoundly impacted by and even constituted in context, and all contexts are not equal; even as we with Rancière and Jacotot affirm human equality, and equality of intelligence, not first as goal but as existing ground from which we relate and work, we must also reckon with this reality and force of context. Embraced, for example, in the taken-for-granted context of neoliberalism (Apple, 2006, i.e., globalizing capitalism and individualism), the discovery of Jacotot could all too easily be taken to endorse a kind of "pull-yourself-up-by-the-bootstraps" approach to education that leaves to themselves, with respect to teaching and learning, those who already long since have been left out of, excluded from, nearly any adventure in the land of knowledge whatsoever, who have yet to be addressed under the sign of equality, whose own routes, and roots, have already and ever been regulated, thwarted, denied.

Yet, let us reckon too with this ignorance of his—that addresses us concerning myth and method with respect to knowledge and our relationship to it—and to those with whom we share a pedagogical relationship respecting knowledge. What do we make, for instance, of Rancière's recounting of the "apostles of inequality" (Rancière, 1991, p. 48) in the "world of the explicated explicators"—pronouncing the "slogan of the enlightened" (p. 8), one of duality in which are exalted "all the thrones of the hierarchy of intelligence" (p. 25)—and all their "perfecting of the ways of *making understand*, that great preoccupation of men of methods and progressives, ... progress toward stultification" (p. 8)? How do we, as scholars and teachers, especially those of us with "progressive" affiliations, avoid being or becoming such apostles ourselves? And further, if this myth of pedagogy—temporally structured as it is, through which students are sought to be brought up to speed with their masters and some are designated as behind, slow, or developmentally-delayed—has been taken up as the fiction of all of society in the ideology of progress, is democratization as it has been cast on a global scale "just the new name for inequality," as one (Ross, 1991) who has taken seriously Rancière's 'ignorant schoolmaster" suggests? At least what constitutes ignorance and ignorant, and its and his/her relationship to knowledge and to the knowledgeable, calls for serious address in our contemporary context wherein questions of citizenship and ethics, cultural right and recognition, difference and inclusivity abound regarding world migrations, immigrant rights, ecological and financial crises, as well as profound injustices and inequities in and out of education.

I could also here exhaustively cogitate upon and complain about the (im)possibility of my un-thesis (thesis/antithesis), nonproject/project of knowledge's (un)doing, the (im)possibility of my present (im)position in relation to ignorance, and effectively abandon the reader, us all, in and to the depths of the forest or its perimeters. Such does afford the possibility of getting lost, at least. Herein I could proclaim even as I disavow a "thus" or "therefore" or something "ever after," and also seek to avoid (dis)locating the relationship between me and my reader as one between ignorant and knowledgeable, or vice-versa, or between kindreds—whether characterized by ignorance or knowledge. And yet such placating, "im"-placating or "ex"-placating, belies a kind of disingenuousness, faithlessness before my way of and to ignorance to which I have exhorted some sort of commitment. In the end, it seems here, I can but testify only to this brief encounter with ignorance in time, bear witness to entertaining—and that in entertaining—a relationship that has inspired (somewhat literally in relation to an embodiment of spirit, fresh breath and breathing room, and roaming) and fired-up openings to different possibilities concerning our work as scholars and teachers, and in our under-standings about the relationships that constitute such work. Perhaps, too, Rancière via Jacotot suggests, as well, that such is all that really is ever possible: to testify, to bear witness, to the uncertain journeys we take and make and re-take and re-make again and again; to tell others of our ventures, to re-tell our tales, and compel others—whether student or no—to the same, abiding pedagogical myths and methods aside. Beyond any method for learning or teaching, the heart of the matter a la Rancière (1991) lies essentially in receiving and in making the announcement of the equality of intelligence, the liberation of all each to this power.

Herein a sense, too, of freedom is felt and experienced. In a contemporary rendering of such a posture, Lather (2007) affirms the way of testimony in the work of research, in our knowledge projects, grounding her articulations of such in John Caputo's sense that postcritical thought as committed to demystifications (for us here, of pedagogy's myth and its underlying conception of the ignorance-knowledge relationship) and meta-criticisms concerns itself, in fact, with emancipation, only differently, most resonant perhaps with—in Derrida's theological understanding with Benjamin—"a more Jewish … ethico-political grasp of difference…that shatters understanding, that underlines the saliency of the incomprehensible, something we confess we do not understand" (cited in Lather, 2007, p. 7). Confronting that to which we can only bear witness, we also must confess our ignorance before it.

Without seeking to explicate, as such, then, might we gather at last (perhaps in some manner of conclusion?), rather than around the tree of knowledge, around the well-lit and warming campfire (not the one upon which heretics are consumed), roasting and toasting to delicious fruit we know yet not of, in solidarity rather than soldiery, counting and recounting our tales together? Here, might we too simply ourselves commit (to) ignorance, at least every now and again, to addressing the fool—ignorant as she is, and ask what such makes possible, has made possible for her?

> What makes a fire burn
> is space between the logs …
> A fire
> Grows
> Simply because the space is there,
> With openings
> In which the flame
> That knows just how it wants to burn
> Can find its way. (Brown, as cited in Intrator & Scribner, 2003, p. 89)

Of course she is likely, with sparkling eyes, and while planting seeds for the life of new and varied trees, to reply, "You tell me," and invite the reader each to light his or her unknown way with and inspiration in/to ignorance.

NOTES

1. For further explorations of this critique of knowledge and its relation to violence and subjectivity, see, for example: Butler, 2005; Quinn, 2001; and Serres, 1983/1989, 1991/1997.
2. I must confess upfront that to counter a certain obsession with explication, and interpretation, in our knowledge projects—as well as to attempt a posture that takes up in some approximation the argument for ignorance as set forth in Rancière's text, I have directly presented, even via in come cases lengthy citations, a number of quoted passages from Rancière and others in this text.
3. Some provocative examples of related work, and in the way of scholarly legitimation, include Snowber, 2004 and Whitlock, 2007.
4. Michael Apple (2004) has articulated a similar gendered and class analysis of teacher resistance in an institutional and cultural context in the U.S. that has worked to increasingly control and intensify the labor of teachers, largely female, via "professionalization." He problematizes the ways in which teacher resistance and agency may be construed, in that their engagements may actually reinforce existing inequities and hierarchies.
5. The teller is playing here, with the play of language and of ignorance in relation to knowledge, and not in any way in relation to "Bushian" (as in former U.S. president, George Bush) trips of public (mis) articulation or as a kind of soldier or executive of Western knowledge once upon a time.
6. Professor John Baldacchino of Teachers College, Columbia University, who cohosted a lecture of Jacques Rancière at the College last year, is a colleague to whom I am most grateful for introducing me, inducing me, to the work of Rancière through his own work and teaching.
7. Professor John Baldacchino of Teachers College, Columbia University, who cohosted a lecture of Jacques Rancière at the College last year, is a colleague to whom I am most grateful for introducing me, inducing me, to the work of Rancière through his own work and teaching.

REFERENCES

Apple, M. (2004). Controlling the work of teachers. In D. J. Flinders & S. J. Thornton (Eds.), *The Curriculum Studies Reader* (pp. 199–213). New York, NY: Routledge.

Apple, M. (2006). *Educating the "right" way: Markets, standards, God, and inequality* (2nd ed.). NY: Routledge.

Anonymous. (1957) *Cloud of unknowing* (I. Progoff, Trans.). New York, NY: The Julian Press Inc. (Original work published ca. 14th century)

Banks, J. A. (2004). Race, knowledge construction, and education in the United States. In J. Banks & C. Banks (Eds.), *Handbook of Research on Multicultural Education* (2nd ed.). San Francisco, CA: Jossey-Bass.

Bellow, S. (1976). *To Jerusalem and back: A personal account.* New York, NY: Penguin Classics.

Bernstein, R. (1991). *The new constellation.* Cambridge, MA: MIT Press.

Butler, J. (2005). *Giving an account of oneself.* New York, NY: Fordham University Press.

Code, L. (1991). *What can she know?: Feminist theory and the construction of knowledge.* Ithaca, NY: Cornell University Press.

Deleuze, G. (1973). Nomad thought. In D. Allison (Ed.), *The new Nietzsche* (pp. 142–149). Cambridge, MA: MIT Press.

Deleuze, G., & Guattari, F. (1987). *A thousand plateaus: Capitalism and schizophrenia* (B. Massumi, Trans.). Minneapolis, MN: University of Minnesota Press. (Original work published 1980)

Dewey, J. (1910). *How we think.* Boston, MA: D.C. Heath & Co.

Doll, W., Jr. (1993). *A post-modern perspective on curriculum.* New York, NY: Teachers College Press.

Henderson, J., & Kesson, K. (2004). *Curriculum wisdom: Educational decisions in democratic societies.* Upper Saddle River, NJ: Merrill Prentice-Hall.

Huebner, D. (1999). *The lure of the transcendent: Collected essays.* Mahwah, NJ: Lawrence Erlbaum.

Intrator, S., & Scribner, M. (2003). *Teaching with fire: Poetry that sustains the courage to teach.* San Francisco, CA: Jossey-Bass.

Johnson, E. (2009). Pop culture, literacy and identity: Performative politics in a high school English classroom (Doctoral dissertation, Teachers College, Columbia University, 2009). *Dissertation Abstracts International, 70,* AAT 3368357.

Katz, D., & Allport, F. H. (1931). *Students' attitudes: A report of the Syracuse University reaction study.* Syracuse, NY: Craftsman

Kovel, J. (1991) *History and spirit.* Boston, MA: Beacon Press.

Ladson-Billings, G. (1994). *The dreamkeepers: Successful teachers of African American children.* San Francisco, CA: Jossey-Bass.

Lather, P. (2007). *Getting lost: Feminist efforts toward a double(d) science.* Albany, NY: State University of New York Press.

Milton, J., & Verity, A. W. (1892). *Paradise lost.* Cambridge, MA: University Press.

Moll, L., Amanti, C., Neff, D., & Gonzalez, N. (1992). Funds of knowledge: Using a qualitative approach to connect homes and classrooms. *Theory Into Practice, XXXI*(2), 132–141.

Montaigne, M. D. (1965). *Complete essays* (D. Frame, Trans.). Stanford, CA: Stanford University Press.

Nussbaum, M. (1997). *Cultivating humanity: A classical defense of reform in liberal education.* Cambridge, MA: Harvard University Press.

Oxford English dictionary (2nd ed.). (1989). (J. Simpson & E. Weiner, Eds.). Oxford, England: Clarendon Press.

Quinn, M. (2001). *Going out, not knowing whither: Education, the upward journey and the faith of reason*. New York, NY: Peter Lang.

Rancière, J. (1991). *The ignorant schoolmaster: Five lessons in intellectual emancipation* (K. Ross, Trans.). Stanford, CA: Stanford University Press.

Ross, K. (1991). Translator's introduction. In J. Ranciere (Ed.), *The ignorant schoolmaster: five lessons in intellectual emancipation* (pp. vii–xxiii). Stanford, CA: Stanford University Press.

Serres, M. (1989). *Detachment* (G. James & R. Federman, Trans.). Athens, OH: Ohio University Press. (Original work published 1983)

Serres, M. (1997). *The troubadour of knowledge* (S. F. Glaser & W. Paulson, Trans.). Ann Arbor, MI: The University of Michigan Press. (Original work published in 1991)

Sleeter, C. (2005). *Un-standardizing curriculum: Multicultural teaching in standards-based curriculum*. New York, NY: Teachers College Press.

Snowber, C. (2004). *Embodied prayer: Toward wholeness of body, mind, soul*. Kelowna, BC, Canada: Northstone.

Twain, M., Walker, F., Dane, G. E., & Rogers, B. (1940). *Mark Twain's travels with Mr. Brown: Being heretofore uncollected sketches written by Mark Twain for the San-Francisco Alta California in 1866 & 1867, describing the adventures of the author and his irrepressible companion in Nicaragua, Hannibal, New York, and other spots on their way to Europe*. New York, NY: Knopf.

Wang, H. (2004). *The call from the stranger on a journey home: Curriculum in a third space*. New York, NY: Peter Lang.

Wexler, P. (2000). *The mystical society: An emerging social vision*. Boulder, CO: Westview Press.

Whitlock, R. U. (2007). *This corner of Canaan: Curriculum studies of place & the reconstruction of the South*. New Yor, NY: Peter Lang.

CHAPTER 3

TOWARDS AN ANIMAL STANDPOINT

Vegan Education and the Epistemology of Ignorance

Richard Kahn

TOWARDS AN ANIMAL STANDPOINT: VEGAN EDUCATION AND THE EPISTEMOLOGY OF IGNORANCE

historia ... II. an account of one's inquiries, a narrative, history....
　　　—Liddell and Scott. *An Intermediate Greek-English Lexicon* (1889)

A Klee painting named "Angelus Novus" shows an angel looking as though he is about to move away from something he is fixedly contemplating. His eyes are staring, his mouth is open, his wings are spread. This is how one pictures the angel of history. His face is turned toward the past. Where we perceive a chain of events, he sees one single catastrophe which keeps piling wreckage and hurls it in front of his feet. The angel would like to stay, awaken the dead, and make whole what has been smashed.

Epistemologies of Ignorance in Education, pp. 53–70
Copyright © 2011 by Information Age Publishing

But a storm is blowing in from Paradise; it has got caught in his wings with such a violence that the angel can no longer close them. The storm irresistibly propels him into the future to which his back is turned, while the pile of debris before him grows skyward. This storm is what we call progress.

—Walter Benjamin (1970, pp. 259–260)

Looking at the immediacies of the colonial context, it is clear that what divides this world is first and foremost what species, what race one belongs to.

—Frantz Fanon (2004, p. 5)

I became a member of the vegan movement[1] in 1998, after quitting my job in New York and having adventurously moved cross-country to Los Angeles, the City of Angels, in the search for love and some newfound direction. Up to that point, my whole life had been a sort of haphazard series of fragments in which my ethical commitment to nonhuman animals repeatedly attempted to articulate and realize itself in a manner akin to the way one tunes in a radio or satellite feed of relatively poor signal strength, there were pieces of a message I kept receiving, but always through a veil of immense feedback that muddied my comprehension and ultimately made me change the channel. In the years prior, I had committed to vegetarianism and even served as an unwitting diplomat of sorts for the philosophy, having introduced it to the small rural town of Szabadszállás, Hungary, when I lived there for a year in the mid-90s ("Ah, vegetáriánus," people would say to me dolefully and half-perplexed when I tried to politely refuse the honor, as a visiting American, to strike the first blow in a ritual pig slaughter or to eat the sheep intestines stew that had been painstakingly crafted for me as a sometimes dinner guest). I also became more political about my lifestyle as I grew steadily more responsive to the fact that my deployment of vegetarianism as a personal dietary choice, one often locked in the private confines of my lonely kitchen or occasional restaurant outings, was at best a meager remedy to a social and ethical atrocity of such huge proportions that I feared to seriously contemplate it in any sort of systematic fashion.[2] In part, my increased sensitivity toward the need for a more radical form of vegetarianism was undoubtedly catalyzed by those friends and acquaintances in my everyday life who were invariably curious as to how I had arrived at the decision to stop eating meat and therefore commonly put questions to me such as "Is this for health reasons or your love of animals?" Now I can only chuckle at the supposed dichotomy of the query, but at the time these inquiries into my beliefs seriously troubled me as I lacked a convincingly coherent answer for them. I remained lodged, at least partially, within an epistemology of ignorance (Tuana, 2004; McHugh, 2004; Mills, 2007) that served to occlude the full extent of my membership within a speciesist society and so I was without the critical literacy necessary to voice my dawning conscientization into the need for animal liberation as part of my own emancipatory journey. Yet, my initial succession from the hegemony of the standard American diet had granted me certain epistemological privileges as well such that I began to read my interrogators on another level. Hence, I learned to interpret their questions about my vegetarian lifestyle as implicit attempts to elicit my re-enculturation into mainstream values and the dominant culture. But, even more importantly, I also perceived others' suspicion of my motives as a continual opportunity to better grasp exactly why and how I came to stand in the particular social, cultural and historical position I in fact occupied.

In this way, I was led to follow an educational path that I remain upon today, the development of an "animal standpoint" (Donovan, 2006), a mode of "oppositional consciousness" (Collins, 1989) that I define variously as: (1) the "cognitive praxis" (Eyerman & Jamison, 1991) of the animal and earth liberation movements, which works to rupture and transform academic discourse in order to establish relevant knowledge interests that are held by movement members (Kahn, 2006); (2) the recognition of the sociopolitical and cultural agency of nonhuman animals that coconstructs our shared reality (Haraway, 2003; Latour, 2004); and (3) the attempt to radically shift our gestalt away from a Western cosmological legacy informed by the history of speciesist relations that has functioned ideologically to inscribe reified notions of "humanity" and "animality" throughout society (Kahn, 2007, 2010a; Lewis & Kahn, 2009). The critical theorist Steven Best (2009) writes:

> Whereas nearly all histories, even so-called "radical" narratives, have been written from the human standpoint, a growing number of theorists have broken free of the speciesist straightjacket to examine history and society from the standpoint of animals. This approach ... considers the interaction between human and nonhuman animals—past, present, and future—and the need for profound changes in the way human beings define themselves and relate to other sentient species and to the natural world as a whole. (para. 14)

Accordingly, a primary concern of the animal standpoint is to provide counterhistories to what Ivan Illich called "modern certainties," or the "epoch-specific apriorisms which generate not only our mental conceptions but also our sensual perceptions and feelings in our hearts about what constitutes social reality" (Cayley, 1992, pp. 172–173). These counter-histories can help to illuminate profound silences on the animal standpoint in the sociohistorical record as being often nonaccidental, and institutionally perpetrated and organized, in order to legitimate hegemonic regimes of truth and ways of knowing that are foundational to our present moment's "dialectic of enlightenment" (Horkheimer & Adorno, 2002).

Of course, as we continue to live under the hegemony of speciesism in which animal liberation is not the norm, and in fact is considered an act of "ecoterrorism" (Federal Bureau of Investigation, 2008), it is impossible to produce a definitive and unified chronicle of the animal standpoint at this time. Instead, the animal standpoint is very much anticipatory of a future possibility that is only realizable now to a certain extent. As the epigram by Benjamin alludes, those who would speak from the animal standpoint occupy something of a morally eschatological space in which they are left to piece together clues out of the catastrophic rubble of the past in order to map the prospects of hope. In this way, the animal standpoint actually seeks to understand the world from multiple evolving locations, and so there are at present a multitude of heterogeneous and contradictory animal standpoint situations, not a singular universal standpoint that can be utilized like a cryptographic key for a theory of everything. But as Sandra Harding (2004, pp. 127–138) has argued, while this form of subjugated knowledge may be unable to escape being pluralist and partial in nature, it can thereby serve positively as a powerful resource to increase our objective understanding of society and provide for a more robustly democratic public sphere beyond majoritarian accounts.

Lately, I have become interested in the ways in which the act of counterstorytelling as a methodological element of critical race theory can provide a compelling model for historical research from the animal standpoint. As Tara Yosso (2006) writes, by interpretatively blending social science data and critical theory with personal reflections, autobiography, and the experiences of colleagues and other acquaintances, counterstorytelling strengthens marginalized traditions of resistance, draws attention to the victims of systemic oppression, and documents the workings of this oppression from the epistemological standpoint of the victimized (pp. 10–11). This essay therefore attempts to employ a form of counterstorytelling to provide some summative exploration of my formal and nonformal educational experiences as a vegan academic working on animal standpoint theory.

ON BECOMING A VEGAN

I remember the day I told my father I had made the decision to become a vegan. "Congratulations, Rich," he said dryly over the phone, "you've officially found a way to get even weirder. Why do you have to be such a pain the ass?" His reaction continued: "A vay-gun, huh?" he muttered, sarcastically emphasizing his mispronunciation of the term (which is pronounced "vee-gun"). "Well, give my regards to planet Vega." Over the years, my father's stance has softened somewhat and, upon recent visits to him, he has shown real concern about how to provide proper hospitality and has even gone out of his way to cook special vegan desserts for the occasions. Further, to a small degree, he allows some discussion about social matters from a vegan perspective such as my own.

On the other hand, he is also clear about drawing a firm line in the sand where he will not cross over into discussions that require self-critique or transformation around his own viewpoints on nonhuman animals or their status in society. For instance, I can eat a vegan meal in relative peace next to him, he seems to have decided, but in order to do so I must silently tolerate his meat and dairy-based food choices and listen obediently to his stories about how he relates to nonhuman animals and the natural world, regardless of how far they might transgress my own ethical commitments. An analogy for this might be that an abolitionist could be considered welcome at a slave auction as long as she did not openly question the reason for being there in the first place.

When in my father's company I am also consistently needled by his "jokes" that I send my vegan children to spend time under his care so that he can "teach them how to eat hamburgers, hotdogs, and all other sorts of yucky stuff." Invariably, this line of half-comedy ends with his dramatic guffaws and an attempt to form the hand salute used by the *Star Trek* character, Mr. Spock the Vulcan. Only a few times has my father actually done the gesture correctly, spreading his fingers apart into a "V" at the middle and ring finger, while intoning, "live long and prosper." In any event, his point is clearly not to offer salutary blessings, but rather to remind me of my alien and outsider status as an invader of his normal cultural routine. I relate this story not because I intend to paint my father as a uniquely unfeeling ogre who is deserving of public scrutiny, but rather because I have found that my relations with him on this matter are broadly representative of how vegans (who comprise approximately 1.4% of the general population[3]) are generally treated in their day-to-day lives by the great mass of other people. In fact, I think dealings with him are somewhat better even.

MICROAGGRESSIONS

The vegan in a speciesist society is ubiquitously on the receiving end of an unending volley of "microaggressions," the "subtle insults (verbal, nonverbal, and/or visual) directed toward people ... often automatically or unconsciously" (Solórzano, Ceja, & Yosso, 2000) in situations when those who are the microaggressions' target are members of a marginalized class. Part of what makes pedagogy against microaggressions so difficult is that these acts are often perpetrated by people who are unaware of the repressive nature of their behavior and who may not even consciously intend to communicate hostile messages through their actions. In other words, such microaggressions are part of the transactional fabric of the conflictual encounter between standpoint epistemologies and the larger epistemology of ignorance that is manufactured to support the conservation of the social status quo.

Many times these microaggressions arise indirectly against vegans through people's everyday use of speciesist language (Dunayer, 2001), in which nonhuman animals are spoken of as unthinking, unfeeling, and lesser objects instead of rational, sentient, and equal beings. As part of common parlance, which socially reproduces desensitization, vegans are required literally to stop conversation and challenge these assumptions if communication is to take place in good faith. However, to do so is often highly impractical as communication does not take place in a political vacuum and so vegans can easily be outnumbered or outranked by their interlocutors. Moreover, if they do in fact raise questions about the assumptions buried in people's language, they run the risk of being tagged as strident, irrational, or otherwise extreme.

In other instances, vegans can be more directly singled out for microaggressions against them. A case in point took place in 2002, in a truck stop outside of San Bernardino, CA, when my wife (then an ovo-lacto vegetarian) and I stopped to investigate whether the Burger King located there was offering the new "BK Veggie" sandwich. The context for our decision was a raucous debate that was taking place within the animal advocacy community at the time about the food item. Liberal vegan ideologues like Erik Marcus and major animal rights groups like PETA openly celebrated its arrival and encouraged everyone to buy as many as possible, believing it to be a strategic opportunity to get vegetarianism solidly established within popular culture. On the other hand, a significant number of vegans (including myself) were highly skeptical that fast-food corporations like Burger King held liberatory potentials for anything beyond perhaps a highly contradictory and strategically useless form of vegetarianism as personal lifestyle addendum. Indeed, as with McDonald's fries that were revealed to be quietly slathered in meat juices, so too it was eventually found that Burger King's veggie burger was not even vegetarian unless one asked to have its standard mayonnaise and bun removed, for these contained polysorbate-60, a fatty-acid emulsifier, derived from animals. Further, some vegans pointed out that, unless Burger King also microwaved the patty on a separate plate instead of flame-broiling it, the veggie burger would share grill fats and residue from the other meat products that are cooked there. With these points being actively discussed between us as we drove down the I–10, upon seeing the Burger King sign listed for an upcoming truck stop, my wife and I decided to stop in and see for ourselves whether or not to believe all the hype.

A sprawling and somewhat unsanitary place for drivers to fill up on a wide-range of commodities in a hurry, it was at first difficult to even locate the Burger King within the travel center. Having eventually found it tucked in the back of the building, near the bathrooms and a small array of video game consoles, we stepped up cautiously toward the lone order-taker as we scanned the menu to see if the BK Veggie was an available item there. I had bet it would not be. The place was deafeningly quiet and seemed almost to be staged for our experiment. "Can I help you?" the young woman behind the cash register asked. We did not see the item on the menu. "Do you have the BK Veggie?" we inquired. "Uhm ... the what?" she replied. Our order-taker was baffled and so we quickly provided a run-down as to the national announcement of the new sandwich. "I'm not sure if we have that or not," she muttered confusedly, "I'd better check with the manager." With that she was off and disappeared into a back area behind the equipment. A minute later she returned with a smile, "Yes, we do have it!" Since it was available, my wife was determined to taste one and placed an order, careful to spell out that it should not have either the bun or mayonnaise and that it should be microwaved, as she was a vegetarian. "I don't think we can do that" the cashier wondered out loud. In a friendly but direct manner, my wife insisted, "I thought the motto of this company is "Have it your way" The young woman behind the counter disappeared again, this time to return with the manager himself.

"What seems to be the trouble here?" he drawled, "So you want one of those BK Veggies, but how do you want it?" I noticed that he had raised one of his eyebrows, as if doubtfully examining the strange customers before him, wondering if we were troublemakers with our out of the ordinary request. My wife reiterated her desire, calmly providing the philosophical explanation for it along the way. "Oh. Hmmm. So you want just a micro-waved veggie patty nothing on it? Alright we can do that," the manager concluded, as he directed to the order-taker that he would take care of it and then headed off to find the frozen patty for microwaving. Two minutes later he returned with a grayish, wet-looking specimen on a small paper plate and handed it to my wife, "One BK Veggie for you." Thinking it looked pretty unappetizing we took it and were about to head back to the car to explore it further when the manager suddenly exclaimed excitedly, "Call me T-Rex!" "What?" we thought, and looked up to see him thumping his chest fiercely with one fist. "Call me T-Rex!" he said again, very pleased with himself and then began to stomp back and forth across the cashier aisle floor like the carnivorous dinosaur. Finally, returning from the Cretaceous period, he turned back toward us, pointed to our order and began to shake his head from side to side. "I don't eat anything unless it's bled. I'd never eat one of those things," the manager resolved.

It was a fascinating reaction on the man's part, one that we had in no obvious way enlisted. Apparently, even the single order of a quasi-vegetarian item that was his to offer for profit had struck at his identity as a happy member of a speciesist society in such a profound manner that he felt compelled to provide a performative rejection of what he took to be our critical countercultural position. Quite literally, through a microaggressive burst, the Burger King manager had to underline for us all that what he knew to be true prior to his customers' order of the veggie burger (with all of its possible background context) had not been put in jeopardy by the encounter. In this way, he sealed any fissures that may have erupted in his epistemology of ignorance and eradicated any possible contextual messaging that might eventually lead him to overturn his cosmological certainties about the order of the universe or his own place in it.

Microinequities

Vegans not only encounter microaggressions across society, but also "microinequities," which Sue et. al. (2004, p. 273) define as "the pattern of being overlooked, underrespected, and devalued." Whether it is at the supermarket or the average eatery, shoe store, clothier, or anywhere else that the living animal body is brutally reduced to an unliving article for trade, there is a widespread structural ignorance to vegan issues in most communities in the United States. While tiring and thankless work, an interesting form of vegan education can be to visit these establishments and to inquire of them what they have that is vegan, thereby making shopping a form of "public pedagogy" (Giroux, 2004). As in the Burger King example, this often sends frontline help scrambling for supervisors in a desperate attempt to figure out what a "vegan" is and whether or not one can then be serviced there (the answer typically being, "no"). While the tactic is unlikely to foment thoroughgoing social change from the animal standpoint, it can at least serve to generate critical dialogue with people and possibly raise some metacognitive reflection about multiculturalism, as well as put veganism on their cultural radar thereby.

Businesses are hardly the only purveyor of microinequities, though. Even friends and acquaintances routinely overlook the need to find some way to demonstrate the thought of inclusion to vegan guests at parties or other gatherings. This is frequently revealed when a vegan is offered and rejects the barbeque, cake, or any list of items that is then rapidly produced thereafter, as it becomes more and more apparent to host and guest alike that the vegan attendee had not been considered during the event's preparation. At other times, friends will thoughtlessly engage in talk about the delightful qualities of the nonvegan meal they may recently have had or will display nonvegan merchandise to vegans in the search for their cordial approval, something that of course cannot come without involving the vegan in a fundamental self-contradiction.

Activists for other radical and progressive causes are themselves not above overlooking and devaluing advocates for the animal standpoint. For instance, I have been a part of many meetings where strong critiques of classism, racism, sexism, or other forms of structural oppression are delivered by people who then go on to consume commercial varieties of factory-farmed meat and dairy, entirely blind to the problematical aspects of doing so.[4] Moreover, vegans have had a hard-time being heard in some activist communities, as they can be stereotypically characterized therein as White liberals who have adopted a political cause that works to divert them from the need to examine the other forms of prejudice suspected to be rooted within their lives. I myself have been the target of such criticism, and while I would be the first to admit both my own imperfections and that there are some vegans for whom this charge is undeniably apt, it is also overly broad and misleading. Thus, allies in other struggles are sometimes surprised to learn that important vegan figures in the fight for social justice include people like César Chávez, Coretta Scott King, Alice Walker, and Michael Franti. While not a reason to adopt vegan politics in itself, opening dialogue about why vocal leaders like these became vegan or why other activists assumed they were not can serve to sow the seeds for the kind of collective intersectional analyses that are ultimately necessary to understand the "matrix of domination" (Collins, 2000) that is used to divide and conquer counterhegemonic groups by those who would legislate our everyday lives.

VEGAN EDUCATION IN THE PUBLIC SCHOOLS

Vegans can just as easily encounter micoaggressions and microinequities in the school as they can in the larger society.[5] While some schools have moved to try to incorporate a consistent vegetarian (and sometimes vegan) offering on the menu, the overall reality is that vegans are still treated like second-class citizens in most school cafeterias. Even when there is food provided for them to eat, the school experience is structured so as to reduce veganism to a personal "special dietary requirement" and not a collective political standpoint from which to mount a transformative critique of society. When exhaustive ingredient lists are not made openly available, or there is not clear transparency as to the manner in which the available food has been cooked, and staff are not properly educated so as to be able to easily answer questions about the food or its preparation, this constitutes a form of microaggression by school administrations against vegans (and by extension, all who eat at the school). It is crucial to remember, however, that behind these dietary microaggressions are macroaggressive institutional logics, not just the careless or uninformed aptitudes of individual administrators.

Consider the recent story of Dave Warwak, a fifth through eighth grade tenured art teacher in the Chicago-area Fox River Grove Middle School, who had previously exhibited at Northern Illinois University but who was suspended and then fired by his public school for teaching art from the animal standpoint.[6] In 2006, Warwak became a vegan and decided to respond to evidence of animal cruelty by students at the school by developing (and gaining approval for) a collective art lesson in which a number of students and teachers created and cared for their own companion animal made out of commercially-available marshmallow "Peeps" chick-shaped candy. As with school exercises in which students care for "baby" eggs, people at the school personalized their Peeps, spoke to them, and treated them as if they were subjects of a life that were deserving of protection. At the end of the lesson, however, Warwak surprised everyone by collecting the marshmallow chicks for a diorama school art exhibit he then created in which the Peeps candies were represented as locked behind zoo cages, hung on the wall as trophy game heads, squashed as road kill, boiled and fried in pots and pans, and enclosed between slices of bread as sandwiches. According to a September 12, 2007 *Chicago Tribune* editorial, this resulted in a rebuke from the school's principal that Warwak was trying to "influence students against the school lunch program" and he was warned to stick to the curriculum. In response, Warwak replied that part of teaching art to students is to get them to think about life and to have them connect their creativity to the social issues that they care very deeply about. He then turned his sights on asking for the removal of the National Dairy Council's "Got Milk?" and other promotional posters which adorned the lunch room walls. When the school's cafeteria manager refused to take them down, Warwak and his students posted their own vegan posters satirizing the issue. He also began a more public campaign to raise consciousness about the quality of school lunches being offered at the school, which resulted in his dismissal.

While one might question Warwak's collegiality, it also seems clear upon studying his case that his firing was not due to his pedagogical style, but rather his unwillingness to relent from using the art curriculum to explore his own school as a location in which to house the animal standpoint. By doing so, he quickly found himself immersed in a hot bed of political issues related to the existence of what could be termed the "school cafeteria-industrial complex" that lay just below the epistemological surface of the school's day-to-day code of normalcy. For instance, we might ask (as he did): Why were the Dairy Council posters in the school? What was the school's food quality? What's wrong with influencing students against the school lunch program if there is a sound educational point to be made in doing so?

Not only at Fox River Grove Middle School but also in thousands of schools across the country, corporate agribusiness has run amok in the attempt to utilize public education as a place to establish the naturalization of commercial meat and dairy as lifelong eating habits, to generate increased sales, to subsidize the food industry against decreased producer prices, as well as to funnel below-health standards food not fit for public sale. Warwak was correct to demand the removal of the Dairy Council's posters as the Federal Trade Commission had in fact already targeted them for removal from approximately 105,000 public schools. In May 2007, the Commission ruled that the advertisements' message on behalf of the dairy industry's "Milk Your Diet" campaign, that claimed that the regular consumption of milk promotes healthy weight loss, was scientifically misleading and false.[7] A story on the matter in *Alternet* captures the corporate duplicity behind this overt operation to infuse milk propaganda in schools:

> The Milk Your Diet campaign (also called BodyByMilk; Think About Your Drink; Why Milk?; 24oz/24hours; 3-A-Day; and Got Milk? as in, one of these slogans has got to work!). .. shipped truck-size posters of 'stache-wearing David Beckham, Carrie Underwood and New York Yankee Alex Rodriguez to 45,000 public middle and high schools and 60,000 public elementary schools last fall and conducted an online auction where students could use milk UPC codes as currency. ("It is an amazing experience," say the web promos, which were still up in May. "Did we mention you have a chance to win an iPod? And a Fender guitar? And cool clothes from Adidas and Baby Phat? All you have to do is drink milk to get it. Any sizes. Any flavors.") The campaign offered $1,000 America's Healthiest Student Bodies Awards to schools with the "most active" students and saluted them with what? Got Milk recognitions. (Rosenberg, 2007)

Schools across the country have utilized dairy industry materials in this fashion because it is tacitly demanded by the USDA's National School Lunch Program, the primary governmental vehicle through which food that is in oversupply is promoted and national prices thereby subsidized. In this case, schools are only reimbursed for their food expenses by the program if they promote items like milk, which it has deemed a nutritional good.

It should be pointed out that this is the same National School Lunch Program that was slammed by a March, 2008 exposé from the *Wall Street Journal*, which uncovered that:

> In reports dating back to 2003, the USDA Office of Inspector General and the Government Accountability Office cited the USDA's lunch-program administrators and inspectors for weak food-safety standards, poor safeguards against bacterial contamination, and choosing lunch-program vendors with known food-safety violations. Auditors singled out problems with controls over E. coli and salmonella contamination. (Williamson, 2008)

Worse still, the above phrase "known food-safety violations" is something of a euphemism. For a prime beef vendor for the National School Lunch Program has been the meat packing company Westland/Hallmark which, via undercover footage shot by the Humane Society of the United States, was revealed to be regularly slaughtering "downer" cows (i.e., mortally sick animals that have also been linked to Mad Cow and other fatal diseases in humans) for popular consumption. Though having repeatedly denied any illegal wrongdoing for years, the ultimate revelation of Westland/Hallmark's practices in turn led to the nation's largest ever recall of beef (Associated Press, 2008). Unfortunately, it was suspected that the large majority of the meat from Westland/Hallmark had already been eaten, much of it by school children. Dave Warwak's art program therefore sought to provide a form of epistemological rupture of the educational status quo in order to call attention to the role being played by this sort of food in his own school. In so doing, however, he threatened to parade the fact that the dietary norms constructed on behalf of those attending public schools (as well as in the larger society) are generally set in place by an emperor without clothes.

"ECOTERRORISTS" IN THE ACADEMY?

In closing, I would like to offer some cursory critical remarks about higher education from the animal standpoint. While many colleges and universities exert greater control over their food purchases than public schools, and have moved to respond to increasing student demand for vegetarian and vegan menu options, there has been far more interest in providing locally-produced foods as part of a potential cost-cutting program legitimated through the language of sustainability (Powers, 2007) than in engaging in campus-wide discussion about the ethical dimensions of dining hall food services. Furthermore, the forms of symptomatic micro-aggression that take place against vegans in elementary and secondary schools, and in the broader society, routinely occur on college campuses against students and faculty alike as well.

To my mind, the most ominous of these microaggressive themes is the tendency amongst academics to uncritically reproduce the sentiments of corporations and the state about the animal rights movement as being composed of irrational and increasingly criminal elements.[8] This has resulted in a hostile campus climate for vegan scholars working from the animal standpoint, in which their colleagues maintain a psychological disposition that functions institutionally to delegitimate research normatively informed by the unprecedented plight faced by nonhuman animals. Crucially, this also feeds into an atmosphere of repressive tolerance within higher education that stifles meaningful protest and just debate of vivisection practices on campus.[9]

The philosopher Steven Best perhaps represents the bellwether case for what can happen professionally to animal standpoint theorists, as the repercussions for his written inquiries on this matter have involved Best's being branded an "ecoterrorist" in the halls of the United States Senate, his having a permanent ban placed upon his visitation rights by the United Kingdom, and his subsequently having his departmental Chair removed under spurious circumstances that also allegedly involved attempts to revoke his tenure status as a professor (for more on Best's story, see Kahn, 2010b). In my own experience, I have been actively discouraged by mentors, "for my own good," from doing animal standpoint work, and when I have chosen instead to continue with it, have been coached to remove relevant references from my curriculum vitae, and to otherwise de-emphasize the research interest publicly wherever possible. I should add that the advice was not without some strategic merit, as my professional references informed me after my being hired last year that prospective employers repeatedly asked for assurances that I was "just studying these things" and was without any correlative background of illegal behavior. In a connected instance, dating back to September 2003, a professor in my PhD program easily wondered out loud with me if I had anything to do with a then recent series of alleged Earth Liberation Front attacks on Humvee vehicles in the San Gabriel Valley. "I figured it must have been you and some of your buddies," he remarked. To this day, I am not sure whether or not he was kidding.

More than ever before, we need students actively engaged in critical animal studies, yet it can be argued that the current academic trend is toward the penalization of animal standpoint research and vegan education. The counterargument might be that we are now witnessing an almost faddish rise of scholarship on nonhuman animals through the development of interdisciplinary posthumanist discourse and the emergence of fields such as "Human-Animal Studies." To be sure, these developments should be pursued as potential opportunities to shatter the long tradition of speciesist scholarship across the disciplines and to end the role that higher education plays in producing an epistemology of ignorance about nonhuman animals at this time. But as Frank Margonis (2007) has written, "One of the key philosophical strategies for maintaining the epistemology of ignorance is ... a tendency to abstract away from social realities" (p. 176). In this sense, I am skeptical that posthumanism or other forms of academese that are detached from the concrete requirements for animal liberationist praxis provide much more than a means to undermine the animal standpoint by co-opting its language and tempering its aims on behalf of the quest for professional prestige and more conservative political visions.

My skepticism about the academy's present desire to seriously confront the issues of the animal standpoint should not be considered cynicism about the larger possibility for positive change, however. On the contrary, if the previous century was marked by an assault on the lines of color, class, and gender, the twenty-first century will be defined in large part by the attempt to resolve issues of justice in relation to species. The critical educator Paulo Freire (2000) wrote, "While the problem of humanization has always, from an axiological point of view, been humankind's central problem, it now takes on the character of an inescapable concern" (p. 43). As I have tried to relate, there are significant historical forces at work affecting a culture of silence throughout mainstream society on vegan issues. Yet, in all sectors and levels of education, both formal and nonformal, the struggle for a new paradigm of nonanthropocentric understanding is taking place today at the grassroots. It is true that the end of speciesism cannot be guaranteed but, then again, neither can the conditions that would allow for its unquestioned continuance.

NOTES

1. The vegan movement began in 1944 when Donald Watson and Elsie Shrigley founded the U.K. Vegan Society in response to frustrations that vegetarians were increasingly normalizing the practice of consuming dairy products linked to highly exploitative and oppressive animal husbandry practices (Rodger, 2004). The society defines veganism as "a philosophy and way of living which seeks to exclude, as far as is possible and practical, all forms of exploitation of, and cruelty to, animals for food, clothing or any other purpose; and by extension, promotes the development and use of animal-free alternatives for the benefit of humans, animals and the environment. In

dietary terms it denotes the practice of dispensing with all products derived wholly or partly from animals" (Vegan Society, 1979). News media tend to characterize vegans as "avoiding" animal products of any kind, but do not emphasize that they do this as a form of political boycott.

2. A summary of the many aspects and broad extent of the evolving catastrophe for animal-kind, both human and nonhuman, can be found in Kahn (2008, 2010a). For a powerful filmic treatment of this horror, see the movie *Earthlings* (2003). Like most people I only became gradually familiar with the realities behind the conditions in industrial factory farms, slaughterhouses, and other institutional practices responsible for the standard American diet such as the overfishing of the oceans and the destruction of the Amazonian rain forests in order to grow endless acres of monocropped soybeans for cheap beef production. Interestingly, people's first response to consciousness of these problems is often to respond by saying something like, "If I had to know where my food came from, I don't think I could eat it." This is a profound articulation of the need for vegan education and the epistemological role that ignorance plays in allowing for grossly unsustainable cultural practices to continue without challenge.

3. This number is according to a 2006 poll conducted by Harris Interactive for the Vegetarian Resource Group, see: http://www.vrg.org/journal/vj2006issue4/vj2006issue4poll.htm

4. One could easily (and ultimately should) advance critiques of members of the vegan community in this same way. For example, an entire line of vegan-friendly "green" consumer products, including gourmet ice creams, cookies, pizzas, "chicken" nuggets, and the like, have sprung up in the last decade as both vegan manufacturers and other companies have raced to fill the needs of what is demographically considered a niche market with significant buying power. However, exchanging relatively low consumer cost meat for high-priced vegan frozen and boxed food simply assists the capitalist system to effect transformation through a period of potential crisis. It is no surprise, then, that companies selling vegan wares such as Whole Foods, Inc. have been repeatedly tabbed as grossly exploitative of labor. In this way, veganism that is not also anti-capitalist fails to strike at the larger structural problem and so can itself be a source of continued epistemological ignorance. On Whole Foods, see for example, http://www.wholeworkersunite.org and http://www.ufcw.org/press_room/index.cfm?pressReleaseID=3 , as well as http://www.coopamerica.org/programs/responsibleshopper/company.cfm?id=309

5. Due to issue's of space, I will not cover the range of issues that might be covered under this idea, which besides issues of school food include in-class dissection, the use of pesticides and rodenticides by schools, in-class pets, as well as the manner in which the history of nonhuman animals (as with women, people of color, the disabled, etc.) has effectively been written out of the majority of the school curriculum.

6. The details of this story are formed out of personal correspondence I had with Warwak in September and October, 2007, as well as the composite evidence and article links archived on Dave Warwak's websites: http://www.

inslide.com and http://peepshowforchildrenonly.com. The latter is dedicated to a self-published manuscript in which Warwak chronicles, his pedagogical saga and archives transcripts from resultant legal proceedings that took place when Warwak sued the school district for being improperly fired and for not abiding by mandated state standards for character and humane education.

7. The Federal Trade Commission ruling, while a victory for democratic science, came on the heels of countless petitions filed against the Dairy Industry campaign by the animal rights organization, Physicians Committee for Responsible Medicine, dating back to 1999. The Commission denied a hearing for all of the previous petitions.

8. It should be noted that standpoint theory has been used historically to question the right of capitalist society to define criminality in ways that privilege social leaders and further marginalize the struggle-from-below. See Lukacs (1971).

9. I deal with this issue at length in Kahn (2010b).

REFERENCES

Associated Press. (2008). *Beef recall hits school lunch program.* Retrieved August 28, 2008 from http://www.edweek.org/ew/articles/2008/02/19/24beef_ap.h27.html

Benjamin, W. (1970). *Illuminations.* London: Jonathan Cape.

Best, S., (2009).The rise of critical animal studies: Putting theory into action and animal liberation into higher education. *State of Nature* [Electronic version]. Retrieved from http://www.stateofnature.org/theRiseOfCriticalAnimal.html

Cayley, D. (1992). *Ivan Illich in conversation.* Concord, Ontario: House of Anansi Press.

Collins, P. H. (1989). The social construction of black feminist thought. *Signs: Journal of Women in Culture and Society, 14*(4), 745–773.

Collins, P. H. (2000). *Black feminist thought: knowledge, consciousness, and the politics of empowerment.* New York, NY: Routledge.

Donovan, J. (2006). Feminism and the treatment of animals: from care to dialogue. *Signs: Journal of Women in Culture and Society, 31*(2), 305–330.

Dunayer, J. (2001). *Animal equality: language and liberation.* Derwood, MD: Ryce.

Eyerman, R., & Jamison, A. (1991). *Social movements: a cognitive approach.* Oxford, England: Polity Press.

Fanon, F. (2004). *The wretched of the earth.* New York, NY: Grove Press.

Federal Bureau of Investigation. (2008). *Putting intel to work: against ELF and ALF terrorists.* Retrieved March 16, 2009, from http://www.fbi.gov/page2/june08/ecoterror_063008.html

Freire, P. (2000). *Pedagogy of the oppressed.* New York, NY: Continuum.

Giroux, H. A. (2004). Cultural studies, public pedagogy, and the responsibility of intellectuals. *Communication and Critical/Cultural Studies, 1*(1), 59–79.

Haraway, D. (2003). *The companion species manifesto: Dogs, people, and significant otherness.* Chicago, IL: Prickly Paradigm Press.

Harding, S. (2004). *The feminist standpoint theory reader: Intellectual & political controversies.* New York, NY: Routledge.

Horkheimer, M., & Adorno, T. (2002). *Dialectic of enlightenment: philosophical fragments.* Palo Alto, CA: Stanford University Press.

Kahn, R. (2006). The educative potential of ecological militancy in an age of big oil: towards a Marcusean ecopedagogy. *Policy Futures in Education, 4*(1), 31–44.

Kahn, R. (2007). Toward a critique of paideia and humanitas: (mis)education and the global   ecological crisis. In I. Gur Ze'ev & K. Roth (Eds.), *Education in the era of globalization* (pp. 209–230). New York, NY: Springer.

Kahn, R. (2008). Towards ecopedagogy: weaving a broad-based pedagogy of liberation for animals, nature and the oppressed people of the earth. In A. Darder, M. Baltodano, & R. D. Torres (Eds.), *The critical pedagogy reader* (2nd ed., pp. 522–540). New York, NY: Routledge.

Kahn, R (2010a). *Critical pedagogy, ecoliteracy, and planetary crisis: The ecopedagogy movement.* New York, NY: Peter Lang.

Kahn, R. (2010b). Operation get fired: a chronicle of the academic repression of radical environmentalist and animal rights advocate-scholars. In A. J. Nocella, II, S. Best, & P. McLaren (Eds.), *Academic repression: Reflections from the academic industrial complex* (pp. 200–210). Oakland, CA: AK Press.

Latour, B. (2004). *Politics of nature: How to bring the sciences into democracy.* Cambridge, MA: Harvard University Press.

Lewis, T. & Kahn, R. (2009). Exopedagogies and the utopian imagination: a case study in Faery Subcultures. *Theory & Event, 12*(2). Retrieved January 2, 2010, from http://muse.jhu.edu/journals/theory_and_event/v012/12.2.lewis.html

Liddell, H. C., & Scott, R. (1889). *An intermediate Greek-English lexicon.* Oxford, England. Retrieved from http://www.perseus.tufts.edu/cgi-bin/ptext?doc=Perseus%3Atext%3A1999.04.0058%3Aentry%3D%2316098

Lukacs, G. (1971). *History and class consciousness: Studies in Marxist dialectic.* Cambridge, MA: MIT Press.

Margonis, F. (2007). John Dewey, W. E. B. Du Bois and Alain Locke: A case study in white ignorance and intellectual segregation. In S. Sullivan & N. Tuana (Eds.), *Race and epistemologies of ignorance* (pp. 173–196). New York, NY: SUNY Press.

McHugh, N. (2004). Telling her own truth: June Jordan, standard English and the epistemology of ignorance. In V. Kinloch&M. Grebowicz (Eds.), *Still seeking an attitude: Critical reflections on the work of June Jordan* (pp. 87–100). Lanham, MD: Lexington Books.

Mills, C. (2007). White ignorance. In S. Sullivan & N. Tuana (Eds.), *Race and epistemologies of ignorance* (pp. 11–38). New York, NY: SUNY Press.

Monson S. (Producer & Director). (2005). *Earthlings:* Making the connections [Film]. Burbank, CA: Nation Earth.

Powers, E. (2007, Nov. 1). Campus food from around the corner. *Inside Higher Ed.* Retrieved August 28, 2008 from http://www.insidehighered.com/news/2007/11/01/local

Rodger, G. D. (2004). *24 carrot award.* Retrieved August 28, 2008, from http://www. vegparadise.com/24carrot610.html

Rosenberg, M. (2007, June 5). Milk is not a diet food. *Alternet.* Retrieved August 28, 2008, from http://www.alternet.org/healthwellness/53102/milk_is_not_a_ diet_food/

Solórzano, D., Ceja, M., & Yosso, T. (2000). Critical race theory, racial microaggressions, and campus racial climate: the experiences of African American college students. *Journal of Negro Education, 69*(1/2), 60–73.

Sue, D., Capodilupo, C. M., Torino, G. C., Bucceri, J. M., Holder, A. M. B., Nadal, K. L., et al. (2004). Racial microaggressions in everyday life: implications for clinical practice. *American Psychologist, 62*(4), 271–286.

Tuana, N. (2004, Winter). Coming to understand: orgasm and the epistemology of ignorance. *Hypatia, 19*(1), 194–232.

Vegan Society. (1979). *Memorandum of association of the vegan society.* Retrieved August 28, 2008, from http://www.vegansociety.com/html/downloads/ ArticlesofAssociation.pdf.

Williamson, E. (2008 , March 3). School lunch at risk for years. *Wall Street Journal.* Retrieved August 28, 2009, from http://www.greenchange.org/article. php?id=2097

Yosso, T. J. (2006). *Critical race counterstories along the Chicana/Chicano educational pipeline.* New York, NY: Routledge.

CHAPTER 4

LABYRINTH OF IGNORANCE

Nathalia Jaramillo and Sandro Barros

Say to a blind man, you're free, open the door that was separating him from the world, Go, you are free, we tell him once more, and he does not go, he has remained motionless there in the middle of the road, he and the others, they are terrified they do not know where to go, the fact is that there is no comparison between living in a rational labyrinth, which is, by definition, a mental asylum and venturing forth, without a guiding hand or a dog-leash, into the demented labyrinth of the city, where memory will serve no purpose, for it will merely be able to recall the images of places but not the paths whereby we might get there.

—José Saramago, *Blindness* (1995, p. 217)

In José Saramago's *Blindness* the world comes to an apocalyptic halt when no one is spared from "white blindness." The story revolves around the effect that a mysterious illness is having on the entire population of the planet, a form of contagious "blindness" that leaves people seeing only the absence of color: white light. The first victims to lose their sight are quarantined in a mental ward, with military guards instructed to shoot and kill if and when the inmates attempt to leave the barracks. Tensions are quick to rise, as the blind leading the blind are left to their own devices to make sense of their fate and newfound limitations. The thugs among the quarantined do not take long to submit to their vices, and quickly turn to rape and murder as they intimidate and attempt to dominate a microcosm

Epistemologies of Ignorance in Education, pp. 71–85
Copyright © 2011 by Information Age Publishing

of strangers blinded by white light. *Blindness* is a story of despair, loss, misery, retribution, love, and forgiveness. It cannot be understood as mere fiction, for in typical Saramago fashion, he compels us to take a serious look into the often silenced and ignored aspects of human sociability. But perhaps most compellingly, Saramago reminds us that the story of blindness cannot be told without its counterpart: vision. It is through the eyes of one woman spared from white blindness that Saramago unveils society's discontents and heartache, as it is she who is driven to the brink of madness because of her ability to see. Blindness is to vision as ignorance is to knowing. The dialectical unity of the concepts that we use to characterize the human condition challenges the "rational labyrinth(s)" that we rely upon to conduct our everyday activity.

Questioning the foundations of "knowing" in education not only reveals the processes in place, which connect students to their developing understanding and awareness of subject matter, but it also reveals what is left unsaid and unclaimed in the very field of knowledge production. For those of us working in the critical education tradition, such silences or absences are not considered innocent omissions; rather, they point to the systemic ways in which ignorance is sustained at the level of epistemology, institutional organization, and indeed, politics. In the face of increasing social and economic disparities in our communities, we are compelled to question how such forces operate at both the discursive and material level to substantiate practices that promote the dissimulation of the social complexities brought about by conditions of adversity and contradictions within capitalist society. Questions that guide our analysis can be framed as follows: how is the pursuit of equality pared with the perceived resolution of cultural, ethnic, racial and or/gendered differences in the educational system? To what extent can we challenge the blinding ignorance that seems to revolve around a critique of capitalist society and the ways in which teaching and learning unfolds in our communities? Is our ability to identify ignorance constrained by a seeming blindness to the object of our critique? How do we navigate this labyrinth of ignorance and transcend its most perplexing conditions?

While we do not claim to have definitive answers to the questions that we propose, mapping out the intraconnections within the educational field can—albeit modestly—afford a different view from which we can begin to hollow out the "complex" ensemble of practices and discourses that constitute education. Following Saramago's aforementioned trope, we are referring to this as the rational labyrinth of ignorance in education. This labyrinth is etched into the cognitive schemas that we rely upon in both our definition and execution of "education." It is communicated through language, materialized in our practices, and it conditions the range of possibilities that we pursue in seeking out new epistemes and social activity.

For the purposes of charting out the complex branching of path and direction within this labyrinth of ignorance, we have confined our analysis to the political, ethical, epistemological, and cognitive dimensions of ignorance.

POLITICIZING IGNORANCE

With a decades-long emphasis on "sameness as fairness" (see Gutierrez & Jaramillo, 2006) we have witnessed a spate of educational technologies, literacies, assessments, and various other curricular apparatuses that are promoted as both new and necessary to undo the historical legacy of students' marginalization in U.S. schools. The election of President Barack Obama has helped consolidate such differences on various levels, given both the populist tenor with which the administration reaches out to ordinary citizens (i.e., we are all Americans) and the pragmatist approach the administration is undertaking in educational reform. The general public is quick to announce the beginnings of a "postracial" society with the election of an African American president, suggesting that the history of racial and ethnic exploitation in the United States is not only irrelevant to the present, but that it is relatively untraceable as well.

This is not to say that media pundits and segments of the reactionary political right do not prey on the opportunity to engage in polarizing debate or that they do not continue to "racialize" political discourse. Even segments of the Democratic leadership during the Obama administration have been unable to resist their subconscious attempts to "see" race. Senate Democratic leader Harry Reid's comments on Obama's "light skinned" appearance and speaking patterns "with no Negro dialect, unless he wanted to have one" (Halperin & Heilemann, 2010) as characteristics that would secure his election, have been among the most obvious blunders. And when the topic has been President Obama's educational initiatives, his address to schoolchildren in September 2009 and the subsequent speeches he delivered on the state of education during the same time period were received with a torrent of ideological backwash and redbaiting (perhaps even his perceived "Blackness" registered as a marker of social and political liberalism). Media pundits urged parents to keep their children home during the highly publicized address and a heightened sense of panic accompanied the criticism directed to an administration that wanted to give students a "pep-talk." The Right chastised the administration for disseminating "anti-capitalist" ideology (McKinley, 2009) and seemingly socialist and/or nationalist rhetoric.

In reality however, the content of president Obama's speeches skewed very much away from criticism towards the country's unrelenting assault on the public sphere vis-a-vis deregulated capital and its implications on national education. To put it simply, there was no indication or suggestion that the administration was preparing to either restructure or radicalize the educational system in the U.S. or to call into question the capital-schooling relationship. Rather, the president's message concentrated on pragmatic issues of schooling such as the expansion of charter institutions, merit-based pay scales, retention, and the closing of the achievement gap of United States' students in the sciences when compared to those of other industrialized nations. In fact, we have witnessed both an intensification of high-stakes accountability systems for teachers and students alike since 2008 election and their attendant "choice" schemes that operate under the reigning free-market ideology. These are issues and educational reform efforts that we have heard not once or twice, but hundreds of times over dating, back to the advent of the "space wars" in the chilling climate of Cold War theatrics.

By and large, the generalized tone of President Obama's speech conveyed a middle-of-the-road approach to pressing issues related to education. His "stay in school" and "study hard" message corresponded to an apparent universalist prerogative; however, intrinsically, Obama's encouragement of larger investments for education and his emphasis on the science curriculum underscored the hidden ideology of education in the service of a capital need rather than education as a means to resolve society's most imminent problems. Poverty, hunger, violence, militarism, and joblessness among youth and their families— the bare bones of how the most impoverished sectors of youth come to understand themselves and their communities—were by and large left out of the script. Students were given a terse but encouraging nod, and while the Obama administration acknowledged the difficulties that many youth face in their poor and violence-stricken neighborhoods, they were implored nonetheless to mind their parents, teachers and nation and "work hard." Such remarks are endemic to the discursive strategies the successive administrations have has pursued in their education reform initiatives. Thus, the educational practice itself, with its inherent authoritative quality, comes into view as a polarizing agent, since the various elements present in its structure favor rigidity as a synonym for meaning and order. Regardless of how relationally and intrinsically complex disagreements may be between fractions of the political elite, the social experiment of schooling reinforces extreme oppositions based on a structural unpreparedness and unwillingness to deal with the social contradictions that are generated by the very industrial and service oriented system that serves and is served by education. This unwillingness, or intentional ignorance, is not only built into the system that aligns education with broader political and economic motifs, but also operates on cognitive and moral dimensions intended to bring together a diverse populace around the central relations of capitalist society. The logic of capitalist production and its rationality coupled with free-market idealism begin to take root in the very processes of thought, furthering the commodification of all things intrinsically "human."

PSYCHOLOGY OF IGNORANCE

C. Wright Mills (2009) once wrote, "Attempts to explain social and historical events, economics and political, religious and military institutions, on the basis of psychological theories about the individual often rest upon the assumption that society is nothing but a great scatter of individuals and that, accordingly, if we know all about these 'atoms' we can in some way add up the information and thus know about society" (para. 15, number 4). Taking these considerations in mind, it would be an error to critique the seemingly ignorant (and ignoble) deeds of Obama's address and educational proposals as a personal character flaw, or perhaps even a political maneuver intended to assuage his skeptics. Professing ignorance cannot be attributed to personality or intelligence; it is not the result of a cumulative calculus of figureheads, education secretaries, or other esteemed members of government who simply do not know better. Professing ignorance is as systematic and institutionalized as educational standards themselves, reflecting the historical and material processes that yield to the current moment of "compromise," renewed "hope" and "perseverance" for *all*. In fact, we might very well argue that it is not the personal psychology of individuals that actively produces ignorance, but rather the speeches and policy mandates themselves serve as psychological mechanisms to legitimize ignorance. Consider the messages that are sent to our youth and communities: America has to be among the leaders and not the led in science and engineering, students must persevere and work harder to beat the odds, mediocrity will not be tolerated, success and innovation will be rewarded and failure will be punished. Hundreds if not thousands of educators, researchers, students, and community members anxiously await the opportunity to be recognized as stellar among the rest.

We are compelled to question the overemphasis given to personal sacrifice and strife in matters of the state, especially education. It brings to mind remarks made by Barbara Ehrenreich (2009) in *Bright Sided: How the Relentless Promotion of Positive thinking has Undermined America*. In her analysis of high paid motivational speakers, Ehrenreich questions the message, "As fresh people advance in their speaking careers, what will be their message, the content of their speeches?" She responds,

> they will give speeches … insisting that the only barriers to health and prosperity lie within oneself. If you want to improve your life—both materially and subjectively—you need to upgrade your attitude, revise your emotional responses, and focus your mind. One could think of other possible means of self-improvement—through education, for example, to acquire new "hard" skills, or by working for social changes that would benefit all. But in the world of positive thinking, the challenges are all interior and easily overcome through an effort of the will. (p. 51)

Listening to Heads of States quibble about educational reform is turning more and more into a motivational speech. Granted, there is discussion of the acquisition of hard skills required by industry and ensuring that every child has access to the spectral "highly qualified teacher." These we can say are the "tools" that will jumpstart positive thinking. The assumption is that a change in affect can result in positive outcomes in teaching, learning and the acquisition of knowledge. But the intentional ignorance that resides in such polemics remains outside the realm of practical activity. Neither students nor educators are implored to understand the consequences of advancing an increasingly individualized and affective response to the mandates of the nation-state; rather, our communities are thrust into a highly politicized fracas of ideological posturing. This brings us to the second pathway in the rational labyrinth of ignorance, morality and the ways in which education processes and reform attempt to align morality with authority mandates.

MORALIZING IGNORANCE

The moral and ethical imperative to sustain and enforce the social relations of capitalism within a wider context of global competition for resources and dominance advances both the discursive and legislative measures to meet such a demand. Here, the very notion of what it means to become a 'global citizen' is underscored by the capital need to generate new markets and social innovation. The driving impulse behind such mandates is often presented in terms of safety and security, procuring the Earth's natural environment for a nation's independence amidst global competition for basic resources, and abiding by the meritocratic notions of industriousness, duty, obligation and hard work in order to satisfy the will of capitalist nation-states. Within this moral and ethical optic, the collective needs of a people are subsumed under the overriding logic of their elected and appointed officials. In the realm of education, this juxtaposition translates into a system of rewards and punishments for educators, students, schools and institutions of teacher education that to varying degrees meet their proposed objectives. The discourse that accompanies such moral and ethical claims is largely framed around an individual desire to overcome the challenges presented within the structural injustices and hierarchies of our communities. The assumption is that desire drives subjectivity, and, therefore, it is a fundamental expression of an individual's identity (McLaren & Jaramillo, 2010). But what if we understand desire not as an expression of freedom, but as a way culture interpolates the individual as a subject (Ebert, 2009)? In this sense, the overriding cultural logic of society and its attendant discourses of morality cannot be isolated from the personal attributes of an individual. In other words, there is no singular "I" within moral discourses of desire; there is only the collective "we" whose life choices are undoubtedly shaped by the very culture of capitalist society.

In the Obama administration, the ethical imperative to serve or contribute to the overall wellbeing of the nation has been converted into competitive policy mandates, "Race to the Top" initiatives, and a stalwart approach to a perceived unwillingness to follow the moral compass of capitalist society. The bourgeois morality of law enters into the larger polemics of moralizing ignorance as the mechanism that can either motivate or ensure compliance. Moralizing ignorance becomes a nation-state function in order to control social behavior and, in many ways, to guide the direction that education will take. The structure-agency relationship becomes seemingly less dichotomous because of the ways that structure begins to define what counts for 'meaningful' agency via political passivity, the production of intransitive consciousness and by means of ideological hegemony (Jaramillo & McLaren, 2009). On this point, Henry Giroux (2010) writes:

> Agency is now defined by a market-driven concept of freedom, a notion that is largely organized according to narrow notions of individual self-interest and limited to the freedom from constraints. Central to this concept is the freedom to pursue one's self-interest independently of larger social concerns. For individuals in a consumer society, this often means the freedoms to shop, own guns, and define rights without regards to the consequences for others or the larger social order. (p. 8)

In consideration of the aforementioned, we find it increasingly difficult to interrupt the degree to which politicians and education policies sustain ignorance through a moral optic. When the fundamental premises of individual desire and choice are translated into 'human' rights, then how do we contest the ignorance that underlies such assumptions? To quote Giroux further,

Freedom exclusively tied to personal and political rights without also enabling access to economic resources becomes morally empty and politically dysfunctional. The much heralded notion of choice associated with personal and political freedom is hardly assured when individuals lack the economic resources, knowledge and social supports to make such choices and freedoms operative and meaningful. (p. 8)

Moralizing ignorance signals a deep system of governance that is predicated on a universal imperative to sustain the virtues of the pursuit of happiness and freedom in society. Ignorance in this respect does not refer to a naiveté of ideals or goals; rather, ignorance signals the unwillingness to question the basic foundation on which "happiness" and "freedom" rest. The incommensurability of such ideals and moral imperatives with the concrete conditions in which the growing numbers of impoverished people are forced to live, do not come under question (Jaramillo, 2010). On the contrary, there is a seeming blindness, and we might say repulsion, to the actual conditions of our communities. In the process, we forget our reciprocal accountabilities to each other because we too often confuse autonomous self-identity with critical agency (Jaramillo & McLaren, 2009). The codes of civic conduct are written as youth progress through the educational pipeline, a pathway that often obliges them to find an "escape route" so that they can become captains of their own destiny.

Throughout their life courses, youth acquire skills linked to a variety of situated forms of activity (Nunes, 2007). The process of learning in a majority of our schools, however, is more concerned with obtaining a righteously moral and definitive answer "of value" that stabilizes the social order rather than it is interested in exploring the intrinsic relationships, the modalities, and the preconditions of the process of inquisition itself, or the "classification" and the "framing" of pedagogical codes within intrinsic norms and aesthetics (Bernstein, 1996). However, the comprehension of meaning as a mutable exercise of making sense *in* and *of* the world occurs within a rigid parameter of appreciation of both concepts, which ultimately translates into the pernicious acceptance of morality as a master and governing organism independent from the way in which individuals choose to relate to one another. Habituated practices of forming and informing opinions within the traditional school environment do not stimulate the conceptualization of ideology as an internally related and reciprocal way of critically conceiving differences in nuanced ways. Rather, schooling reproduces certain conditions that tend to categorize ideological positions in rigid terms, mimicking society's mode of production, namely capitalism.

Discussions on the meaning of public education as an instrument that propagates ideas of production and efficiency, which are diametrically opposed to decolonial, materialist and humanistic principles, are often disregarded outside a polarized frame of inquiry. Thus, to question if the source of such a polarization comes from the educational institution's inaptitude in its role as a moral agent of socialization is to attempt to resolve conflicts outside contrasting modes of reaction that disregard ambiguity as an essential modality of being and functioning within society. If schooling shares, indeed, a level of responsibility to the often virulent and intimidating tone with which certain groups of society react when engaging in characteristically polarized moral debates, how does the public institution facilitate such a reactionary response from the very beings it attempts to integrate and harmoniously socialize into the productive apparatus of capitalist society? What do our youth and communities learn along the way? This leads us to a discussion of how ignorance operates at the level of knowledge production, the final passageway that we will discuss in the labyrinth of ignorance.

EPISTEMOLOGICAL IGNORANCE

For those scholars working within the paradigm of decoloniality, the notion of ignorance is central to understanding the geo and body politics of knowledge (Mignolo, 2009). Modern epistemology, what Colombian philosopher Santiago refers to as the hubris of the "zero-point" was able to conceal the ways in which knowers were marked—racially, ethnically, and spatially—through the process of scientific rationality. In other words, when *raison d'être* was primordially defined by the processes of scientific discovery, autonomous development, and progress associated with the age of the Enlightenment, then where people came from, and how they had come to identify themselves and be identified as human subjects was erased from the production of knowledge. The classification and categorization of peoples based on binary oppositions, that is, savage versus civilized, Black versus White, servant versus owner, emerged not only in the purposeful and violent division of labor that characterized the transition from feudal to capitalist society, but in the coconstitutive processes of defining what it meant to be *human*. Officiating science on the metric of developing rationality (read as individual autonomy and European, male progress) erased all other forms of experiential knowledge. This transition from organic "science" (experiential learning is a way of coming to know, understand, challenge and transform the world around you) and "hard" science, turned the experiences, histories, cosmologies, and natural environments of peoples into "things" that could be strictly documented, analyzed and utilized. The utilitarian logic underwriting science was brought together with the overriding logic of capitalist expansion that perceived development in strictly technocratic and instrumentalist terms. On this point, it is worth quoting Walter Mignolo (2007) in extenso:

> Scientific local-knowledge overruled experience based knowledge in the name of efficiency. In the forest and in the fields a new category appeared: weed. Weed (like Indians and Blacks) was a scientific classification that eclipsed and erased (or used when relevant) the experience-based classification of persons who did not learn from the books of science but in the daily and yearly dealing and living with and in the forest. Weed follows the same logic of the categories of Indians and Blacks: the imposition of a classification of what shall be discarded. However, discarding Indians and Blacks and weeds implies also discarding the knowledge that Indians and Blacks have and on the other discarding the knowledge that people in India who had lived in the country and in the forest for centuries have about the complexity of what the ignorance of the Western expert reduces to weed, hiding what is his or her own ignorance. At that junction, the principle of a prudent knowledge for a decent life is overruled by the greediness of timber companies and their lust for wood—nothing better than declare primitives or ignorant all those who know what the civilized expert ignores, (p. 382)

Built, then, within the paradigm of modernity is an intentional ignorance that does not question the parameters of "what we know" and does not see the value in knowledge that falls outside the motives of Western, scientific reason. Ignorance, in this respect, is unremorseful and defiant. When the production of knowledge translates into a gaming war of resources and ideological posturing, then history has taught us that the side with the greatest military muscle often prevails.

The "paradigm of modernity" is evident in education policy and reform in the way that we systematically (and some might say, militantly) define what counts for "knowledge." Evident in the processes of standardization, testing, accountability, and opening public education to private and corporate intervention is a concerted effort to homogenize what educators and students are able to accomplish in an educational setting. And ultimately, they are being forced to comply with the simple truth of capitalist schooling.

While efforts have been made to "diversify" the curriculum; to attend to "bias" in testing instruments; and to afford students tutorials and other interventions to successfully pass their learning mandates, none of these "truths" challenge the epistemological ignorance that underwrites knowledge production in U.S. capitalist society. To be clear, we are not suggesting that true knowledge is devoid of any ignorance; on the contrary, ignorance and, we will argue, ambiguity are both necessary and constitutive to knowledge production. And we are not suggesting that the scholastic institution reproduces with exactitude the capitalist mode of production without accounting for individuals' agency or "puncturing" capitalism's master narrative, as is the case of post-structuralism's de-centering of the traditional subject (Sandoval, 2000). As Au (2009) succinctly observes, individuals within the school environment do "posses agency and consciousness which allows them to mediate and resist the dominant social relations reproduced through institutions" (p. 8). This critique withstanding, it is also important to recognize the potentiality of schools as formative mechanisms of divisive politics and social relations, which tend to group and reinforce categorizations within established parameters.

In essence, testing, among other recourses developed towards and implemented within the school institution, has been gradually dissipating any opportunities for understanding the meaning and the nature of knowledge not as an acquisition but rather as a construction. The absence of a recognized and legitimized "in-betweeness" in dominating educational discourses has facilitated the elimination of ambiguity as that which necessarily complicates the act of schooling beyond simple rationalism. The principle of complexifying education with the intent of liberating individuals from organizing their thoughts outside extremities constitutes a threat to the very social order under which we currently operate. However, one's liberation from the slavery produced by ideological discourses can only take place if mirror-image extremities of thinking are corroded, and, therefore, leave subjects free to choose according to present sociotemporal conditions. In the case of high stakes testing, capitalism's benevolent hand would be at risk if its ritual practice were to be abolished, for gradually capitalism has encroached itself into the fabric of education, altering its natural practices of free association precisely by reducing choice. Suffice to note the multimillion-dollar industry of textbooks, ancillary materials, and so on, that cater to schools and shape curricula to the detriment of the common interests of the people.

The harmful ramifications of standardized testing industry contribute further to the absolutist effect of schooling by suggesting the act of "passing" or "failing" a particular task as a terminal reality. Indeed, the options available through testing reduce existence to a diametrical opposition of success or failure, as if to succeed or to fail were terminologies with which it would be easy to come to terms, and that did not correlate to issues of race, gender, class, or even sexual orientation (Au, 2009). If the construction of knowledge is a developmental *ad infinitum* human capacity, grading in standardized forms, to be differentiated here from authentic dialogical assessment, is a counterintuitive action and a rather imperfect form of characterizing one's ability and potential to know. Essentially, once answers are restricted to *yes* or *no* without observing power relationships where there is a struggle to confer meaning to things, ideological choice is reduced to a wholesome pro or against stance that, in due course, disregards and silences marginal agents which struggle for the ability to signify and articulate meaning.

WHERE DO WE GO FROM HERE?

All knowing is knowing of a certain ignorance, as
all ignorance is ignorance of a certain knowing.

—Boaventura de Sousa Santos, 2007

If like the characters of Saramago's (1995) novel we are blinded, not by white light, but by the persistent and enduring ignorance that we encounter in all aspects of the education in and out of schools, then where do we go when we pass through the rational labyrinth of ignorance and enter into the labyrinth of the city, where "memory will serve no purpose, for it will merely be able to recall the images of places but not the paths whereby we might get there"? Santos (2007) writes of the necessity for developing an epistemology of "absent knowledges," one that does not reduce reality to what exists, but to "an expanded conception of realist knowledge that includes suppressed, silenced or marginalized realities, as well as emergent and imagined realities" (p. 431). For us, this includes advancing a historical and materialist conception of knowledge that is not determined by the relations of capitalist society, but one nonetheless that sees the point of departure in a mode of critique and a transformative praxis that does not ignore how capital has configured human sociability. In advancing a historical-materialist approach, we do not deny the importance of ignorance and ambiguity as constants in the process of constructing social meanings, but we do argue that is necessary to begin to carve out this epistemological undertaking by looking beyond the determinations of capitalist society.

At the level of language, uncertainty and inexactness constitute the products of the sensuous experience of individuals in the world mediated by a system of representation. Indeed, due to its very nature as a representation, language cannot escape ambiguity, for its underlying principle is precisely an approximation to an idea and not the idea itself. To claim ignorance and knowledge does include an analysis of what these terms convey. To not recognize the organization of thought as a potentially unstable process mediated by language is to fall prey to a system that categorizes reality in diametrical oppositions, or in the negation of premises that complexify notions of righteousness and falseness. As Paula Allman (2007) correctly notes, because grasping relationships within our particular realities constitutes a difficult task—since our experiences vary according to time and space—we often think of ideological opposites as uncorrelated principles and not, in a Marxist sense, the result of a process of mutual interaction. The fixation and ritualizing of methods of polarizing ideas become easily accommodated and reproduced within the industrial context because, once opposing ideas are de-historicized and made into "things," they are removed from a flexible cognitive system that recognizes truth and knowledge as contingent upon structures of power. Contained by the natural requirements of the capitalist system, among which are found the reproduction of knowledge and the illusion of choice, knowledge itself is transformed into an immutable subject, "conceptualized as existing separately and distinctly from the real world" (Allman, 2007, p. 60). In this reproductive context, truth and knowledge are devoid of ambiguity, which in essence corresponds to the acknowledgement of conflict as a "moral state of difference" (Barthes, 1972). Hence, any appreciation of the term polarization when it comes to ideology and schooling tends to be received either as a hyperbolic generalization or as an antagonist and isolated social manifestation.

When we examine the ways in which ignorance and knowledge function to sustain dominant notions of self-hood, we recognize the structural and functional mechanisms of ignorance in social regulation and control. Whether or not paying attention to how epistemological formations emerge within the dominant capitalist system makes it easy for us to discover and dismantle systems of knowledge that maintain and regulate social actions as diametrically polarized events is a question and struggle that we need to maintain. Perhaps the theorization of an "epistemology of ignorance" could reveal uncertainty and ambiguity as the true location of dialogue, which is, after all, natural in any process of knowledge acquisition/construction. However, ambiguity and uncertainty within the capitalist frame of mind are constantly concealed and re-signified as "weaknesses," socially pernicious human characteristics, thus having no place in society. But if we reframe the meaning of ignorance outside opposition in order to expose that it does not correspond solely to an absence of knowledge but rather to a condition perpetuated by certain antidialogical epistemologies characteristic of our current system of production, this very recontextualization could lead us to become more aware of those elements, within the educational setting especially, that formulaically perpetuate situations of dominance and oppression. In other words, ignorance could be seen not as the absence of knowledge but rather as an epistemological product that sustains "unknowing."

Citing Nicholas of Cusa, a fifteenth century philosopher and theologian, de Sousa Santos (2009) writes of the need for "learned ignorance," a designation that refers to the learner's knowledge process. The point argued by de Sousa Santos is to reject an absolute truth or end-point in the learning process. Taking this into consideration, we can speak in terms of "learned ignorance" or we can discuss this manifestation as set forward in

Freirian dialogical thought. In either case, learning is seen as a process of mutual understanding and recognition. We may question our outlook on reality with our method of analysis (Stetsenko, 2008), but ultimately we seek out and pay attention to how knowledge changes temporally and spatially, to how knowledge is mediated by the interdependence between social systems and between teacher and student.

Ultimately, applying epistemologies of ignorance to the learning process exposes the limitations of thought that we have in this finite world. We can become aware of what types of "ignorance" we need to identify and reject in the learning process—those that lead to a historical mystification about the development of our sensuous beings; but we also need to become astutely aware of how "radical ignorance" (Cusa, as cited in Santos, 2009) or the role of the dialectic in generating liberation of thought, is constitutive of the learning process itself. It is in rejecting, rewriting, renarrating, reconfiguring, situating, and making relevant and meaningful our educational praxis to ourselves, our community, and to the global totality that we can expose our humility and strength as educators. And yet, none of this will be given to the educational sphere. Pedagogical struggles are conditioned by political, economic and social forces that at times appear unscalable. We may feel cautioned by the plight of securing our livelihood and we may be silenced by the educational institution itself. We can maintain a sense of hope, however, that in passing through the labyrinth of ignorance, we may carve a different path that can collectively lead us onto the street, empowered by what we have come to see, and what we have yet to know.

REFERENCES

Allman, P. (2007). *On Marx*. Rotterdam: Sense.

Au, W. (2009). *Unequal by design*. New York, NY: Routledge.

Barthes, R. (1972). *Mythologies*. Toronto, Canada: HarperCollins.

Bernstein, B. (1996). *Pedagogy, symbolic control, and identity*. Lanham, MD: Rowman & Littlefield.

de Sousa Santos, B. (2007). From an epistemology of blindness to an epistemology of seeing. In *Cognitive justice in a global world* (pp. 407–438). Lanham, MD: Lexington Books.

de Sousa Santos, B. (2009). A Non-occidentalist west? *Theory, Culture & Society*, 26(7-8), 103–125.

Ebert, T. (2009). *Cultural critique (with an attitude)*. Champaign, IL: University of Illinois Press.

Ehrenreich, B. (2009). *Bright-sided*. New York, NY: Metropolitan Books.

Giroux, H. (2010). Democracy and the threat of authoritarianism: Politics beyond Barack Obama. *Truthout*. Retrieved February 20 2010, from http://www.

truthout.org/democracy-and-threat-authoritarianism-politics-beyond-barck-obama

Gutierrez, K., & Jaramillo, N. (2006). Looking for educational equity: the consequences of relying on *Brown*. In A. Ball (Ed.) *With more deliberate speed: achieving equity and excellence in education—realizing the full potential of Brown v. Board of Education*. Malden, MA: Blackwell.

Halperin, M., & Heilemann, J. (2010). *Game change*. New York, NY: HarperCollins.

Jaramillo, N. (2010). Liberal progressivism at the crossroads: Towards a critical philosophy of teacher education. In V. Hill-Jackson & C. Lewis (Eds.), *Transforming teacher education: what went wrong in teacher training and how we can fix it* (pp. 37–60). Sterling, VA: Stylus.

Jaramillo, N., & McLaren, P. (2009). Borderlines: bell hooks and the pedagogy of revolutionary change. In L. Davidson & G. Yancy (Eds.), *Critical perspectives on bell hooks* (pp. 17–33). New York, NY: Routledge.

McKinley, J. C., & Dillon, S. (2009). Some parents oppose Obama school speech. *The New York Times*. Retrieved December 12, 2009, from http://www.nytimes.com/2009/09/04/us/04school.html

McLaren, P., & Jaramillo, N. (2010). Not neo-Marxist, not post-Marxist, not Marxian: Reflections on a revolutionary critical pedagogy. *Cultural Studies/Critical Methodologies, 10*(3), 251–262.

Mignolo, W. (2007). The splendors and miseries of "Science": coloniality, geopolitics of knowledge, and epistemic pluriversality. In B. de Sousa Santos (Ed.), *Cognitive justice in a global world* (pp. 375–398). Lanham, MD: Lexington Books.

Mignolo, W. (2009). Epistemic disobedience, independent thought and decolonial freedom. *Theory, Culture & Society, 26*(7-8), 159–181.

Mills, C. W. (2009). Psychology and social science. *Monthly Review*. Retrieved on January 15, 2009, from http://www.monthlyreview.org/091228mills.php

Nunes, J. A. (2007). Pathways to cosmopolitan knowledges: in the aftermath of the discourse on the sciences. In B. de Sousa Santos (Ed.) *Cognitive justice in a global world*. Lanham, MD: Lexington Books.

Sandoval, C. (2000). *The methodology of the oppressed*. Minneapolis, MN: The Regents of the University of Minnesota.

Saramago, J. (1995). *Blindness*. Orlando, FL: Harcourt.

Stetsenko, A. (2008). Collaboration and cogenerativity: On bridging the gaps separating theory-practice and cognition-emotion. *Cultural Studies of Science Education, 3*, 521–533.

CHAPTER 5

SOCRATES, DIALOGUE, AND US

Ignorance as Learning Paradigm

J. Gregory Keller and Deborah Biss Keller

What has been the forgotten, the left out, the abandoned on the Western quest for knowledge, power, and self? Has it been the priority of the question and the inescapability of the spirit—an infinite that never falls prey wholly to totalization and particulars that can never be wholly subsumed under a universal? We find in Socrates a paradigm first of all of the ignorance that gives the lie to unrepentant certainties and, at the same time though often falsely hidden by that first, a dangerous obscuring of a second space for the resistance that lies at the heart of critical social practice. We aim in this chapter to contest the Socratic notion of ignorance, to the extent that it underlies and upholds the closing of minds to workable knowledge in favor of absolute and thus unreachable knowledge; yet also to play the value of Socratic not-knowing against Aristotelian categories of the perfect society built upon the subjection of "natural" inferiors by masters, men, and the virtuous rich. In the end we suggest that epistemic poverty carries its own virtues that must not, however, obstruct the shared construction of resistance and hope out of the everyday particular knowing supplied

Epistemologies of Ignorance in Education, pp. 87–104
Copyright © 2011 by Information Age Publishing

both by common human experience and by the uncommon experience of the hidden others who lie invisible behind the curtain of social cohesion.

THE FORGOTTEN

We begin by asking ourselves what has been left out of our teaching and learning, our ways of knowing and acknowledging, our ways of recognizing or, for that matter, of not cognizing at all. There is, of course, no single answer to this question—even seeking a unique answer reveals our lack of liberty in thinking. What we most often forget might simply amount to the priority of the question, the beginning that turns us away from "truth" and the (alleged) perfection of our (alleged) knowledge and turns us toward the endless quest(ion).

Let us suppose, then, that the forgotten constitutes a significant category and that we can approach it as such—never forgetting that remembering that which is forgotten presents us with a dilemma. Whatever remains truly forgotten cannot, of course, just be brought to mind. Let us assume, nevertheless, that we can hope to attach some legitimate meaning to the forgotten and begin there. First of all, we could begin with the forgotten on a personal scale, asking "what have *I* forgotten that plays a role in shaping *my* life" (equally, what have *you* forgotten, and what is its role for you). We could, on the other hand, address a larger sense of the forgotten and ask about social or cultural forgetting, about the missed or abandoned, the overlooked or invisible in our cities, our nations, our vast, inscrutable histories. In either case, we will find a mass of details and specifics, as well as of generalities—consisting of that which it is inconvenient to remember. It can be uncovered in a search to recover that which has been deeply covered by a veil of more desired information, has been paved over in the search for faster access, has been sunk beneath the sea of forgetfulness.

Speed and priorities for immediate action, as well as a need to ascertain who is in and who is out, lend credence to the contemporary push for answers, certainties, and Truth within the global economy. But this emphasis on knowing depends on a high level of ignorance. So we turn in our meditation here to a paradigm of questioning, based on the ideas of one who claimed that his only wisdom—for which he was renowned—lay in knowing, alone it seemed among his fellow citizens, that he did not know what he did not know. We are speaking, of course, of Socrates. We offer him as paradigm but also as question—how much may we lay claim to ignorance and how far must we act on whatever truth we see—however dimly. We will later offer a contrasting approach to understanding, one we find in Aristotle's *Politics* (1998) in which certainties about human nature are used to set up inflexible relations of power with masters "naturally" over slaves and men over women and children.

THE WESTERN QUEST FOR
KNOWLEDGE, POWER, AND SELF

We turn to a trio of Foucauldian ideas for help in describing the situation of the forgotten and the way of the question that we address—ideas he most aptly speaks of in terms of games of truth, relations of power, and practices of the self (see, e.g., Foucault 2003a, 2003b). Although we use these Foucauldian concepts as tools for our specific purposes, we do not mean to make Foucault in any way responsible for our conclusions nor do we claim that he would authorize our use of these terms or our conclusions.

Beginning then with games of truth, we see that rules for producing "truth" either broadly (within an entire society or culture) or narrowly (within a field, discipline, or given interaction) imply an emphasis first on the result to be produced and secondarily on the "games" or methods meant to leave us in possession of it. Here we see an important distinction between product and process (the result and the activity leading to it). More dogmatic aspects of society or culture place more weight on getting the product right, that is, on producing "proper" conclusions, hence lending credence to a distinction between orthodoxy and heresy. Valued processes thus are those that give "right" answers—ones that work to maintain power and status in its current forms. No one can deny the movement of processes in society, but control of that movement can be attempted in such a way as to maintain rather than transform the "normal" state of things, a state that keeps talk of truth and relations of power as much in the same form over time as possible.

Power then resides in right answers and agreement, party affiliation, creedal tests, acts of "faith," and in those functionaries who authorize, guard the gates, and pronounce anathemas on unbelievers. But even when the emphasis lies instead on process, such as rules of inference, moves of logical deduction, or scientific methods, the point of the process often lies solely in its product or result. Rules of inference, logical moves, and scientific methods are frequently defined wholly in terms of their adequacy in producing truth. We have no intention of implying that such rules or methods are worthless—as Foucault points out, we cannot, or at least need not, do away with games of truth.[1]

Moving our focus from product to process can itself be valuable in loosening dogmatism and replacing mere authority with procedures that can be refined or questioned. Here we are reminded of Marilyn Frye's (1983) comment that "The loving eye knows the independence of the other" (p. 75). Authority that subdues and subjects the other to its gaze and "truth"; dogmatism that closes the door of questioning and uncertainty —these do not acknowledge the independence of the other. There is no "loving eye" in the product-oriented world of absolutism. Epistemologies of ignorance help us to recall both the "willful ignorance [that] involves a cultivation of ignorance" and the "loving ignorance" of that which lies beyond our capacity for knowledge (Tuana 2006, p. 15). Dogmatism and authority for its own sake play upon and encourage willful ignorance and, at the same time, disparage any form of loving ignorance concerning the unknown/unknowable.

We can look at the situation with games of truth as follows: Results (alleged truths) can be questioned by turning to the processes (methods/ games) that produce or produced them. Processes can be questioned by asking whether they in fact produce truths. This second step of questioning can proceed through showing that an alleged truth (one produced by the method in question) is not in fact a truth. The methods used to demonstrate this methodological failure are multiple. We can show, for example, that the alleged truth fails to meet some broad criterion concerning what counts as a truth, or we can develop or apply an alternative method for truth production, showing that the method being questioned fails to produce truths authorized by the alternative method or that it produces alleged truths the alternative method rejects.

There is also an approach that discards the production of truths, or at least certainties, as an appropriate aim. Here we see the Socrates of the *Apology* (Plato, 2000) as a paradigm (and a method) of questioning that rejects certainties due to their function in closing the mind of the believer to further inquiry. He seems to accept a number of methodological "truths"—for example, that courage is of great value, that one should not fear death, that one should guard one's integrity at all costs, that questioning itself lies at the heart of our common humanity, that society is most fully benefitted not by following whatever its leaders say but by calling everyone in it to account concerning what they truly value and how they choose to live. At the same time, he denies that he or anyone else has a complete grasp on final truths. We will have much more to say about Socratic wisdom and method as we proceed, but this must do for now. The aim we discover in Socrates (and many other philosophers/spiritual leaders throughout history) points to a focus not on certainties but on enhancing one's life. The problem with "truths" is that they become indiscriminate patterns of thought and action that resist the multiplicity of moment-to-moment aliveness and situational variation. Hearing Socrates and the small but persistent crowd of lovers of wisdom who offer similar insights, we might uncover in ourselves a species of willful ignorance as well as a failure to love our appropriate ignorance of the unknown and unknowable, and we might see that these aspects of epistemologies of ignorance have been cultivated both by social norms and by our own fears of the unknown.

In this case, then, we employ questioning not to produce right answers and set limits to thought or community but to loosen our grasp so as to perceive more clearly and respond more adequately to whatever happens around us in the present. We do not *use* questions but rather *open to them*, allowing a loosening of the soil, a planting of new seeds, a growth that adheres to its own rules, rules that we do not control, that are not to be managed but received in surprise and hope.

This matter of control turns us to the question of relations of power and the ways and means by which ignorance is fostered or stifled through subjectification. We follow Foucault in seeing relations of power as encompassing the vast range of ways we influence one another. My actions, intentionally or not, affect the actions of others; this is the essence of the inescapability of relations of power (and of community). Power then, according to Foucault, is not a substance or a structure or set of structures; it is not confined to domination and is not merely political or positional, in the sense of existing as or consisting of official structures of government or culture. Relations of power cover *all* human relations and interactions. The historical perspective of the West, on the other hand, tells us that power must be hoarded and fought against or for, and, again, a key aspect of that process lies in truth claims and in the control of the various levels of those games of truth used to authorize and maintain the methods, rules, and procedures needed to create and hold in place whatever certainties happen to work in conjunction with the structures of power. Ignorance is then either strengthened or shunned under a reign of power that encourages us to remain ignorant of means or resistance and plays up our fears of accepting our ignorance of that which cannot be known.[2]

The truth must be captured, defended, and of course put into practice (as though truth and practice were distinct species that cannot mate). Attaining and keeping truth depends upon right methods, but historically it depends even more on proper access to and wielding of power. Different approaches to games of truth (that they exist merely to produce certainties or that they exist as socially constrained possibilities for thinking that must be kept fluid in order to function properly) parallel different, we might even say competing, understandings of power. On the one hand, is a traditional Western view of power as domination, as absolute — what Bakhtin (1981) refers to as "authoritative discourse" (p. 342), which functions not by persuasion since persuasion works only with at least the minimal consent of the persuaded. Authority, in this sense, works only as untouchable certainty—for Bakhtin this means that the words of authority cannot even be put in other terms but must be maintained and thus revered only in their original form. A second notion of power, presented by Foucault by means of the idea of "relations of power," stands for the ongoing relationship of mutual influence in which we all always find ourselves.[3] Mutual influence, of course, also connects with particular games of truth, ones that do not absolutize either procedures or products of the knowledge quest. Acknowledgment of ignorance or at least possible ignorance undermines power as domination or absolute authority and consistently presents relations of power as flexible and fluid.

In this regard there are practices of the self that lean toward absolutizing claims to truth and structures of power as well as ones that balance truth claims with recognition of possible ignorance and perceive relations of power in more mutual and supple ways. Foucault's idea of practices of the self covers a wide field of subject positions and subjectivizing processes. Our use of it here is to suggest that the dialogical approach to questioning and the recognition of possible ignorance leads us to think of ourselves and present ourselves in relationship. That is so see ourselves in ways that are less mired in endless defense of certainties than engaged in ongoing processes of increasing awareness and openness to newness and to a certain liquidity, so to speak, of relationships. We do not mean here that relationships are not valued or maintained but rather that they are both valued and maintained in process and openness more than in a defense of claims that demand constant defense and subtle or overt war.

THE PRIORITY OF THE QUESTION

Given the paradigmatic figure of Socrates and the historical situation we have roughly outlined above, we turn to an approach championed by Socrates that cuts across the Foucauldian categories of games of truth, relations of power, and practices of self. In Plato's reconstruction of Socrates' defense at his trial, Socrates tells the jury of his mission from god—to question those with a reputation for wisdom (and, as a side effect, to sting the great horse of the Athenian state into virtuous action despite its lazy indifference to its own good). The possibility of wisdom, in Socrates' terms, cannot be reached by digging trenches around what we believe ourselves to know. It can only be reached by the frightening openness of free discussion with the "barbarians" (both within and without) who fail to see the truth we find so obvious. Once we recognize the vulnerability of our claims, once we see with Socrates that the unexamined life is not worthy of human endeavor and energy, we see the priority of the question.[4]

We can, as we think about our thinking about things, focus on the answers we have received or the ones we wish to promote. Often this approach guides our thinking as individuals, as members of particular communities, and as human beings.[5] We begin with an alleged truth or, even when we begin with a question, we seek as quickly as possible to move on to the answer that dissolves the question. Socrates, among others, would have us turn this process around. Perhaps we should not only begin with questions but also see them as the crucial aspect of the thinking process.[6] It is, after all, the question that opens the door to thinking, that thaws our frozen notions of the way the world is, that leads us to journeys of thought in which the travel functions as far more important than the arrival. Of course, the occasional "perching" (to borrow a term from William James 1890) of thought is very restful and, as we will note subsequently, might form a launching pad for action. But it is in flight that the adventure of thought comes into its own, it is in movement that thinking attains its fullest life.

The approach taken by Socrates can be characterized as beginning with the hidden dialectic of the answers we cherish. Every statement can be seen as implying at least two questions: First, we might ask what question a certain statement answers. If, for instance, I say, "The sun is setting," you cannot understand the meaning attached to those words unless you understand the question, whether explicit or implicit, they answer. The question I might be answering could be, "What time is it?" or "What shall we do now?" or even "What do you see?" In each case, the meaning of the words takes its orientation from the question being answered. Second, though, every statement raises at the very least aquestion of "Is it true?" but often much more than that. The cultivation of ignorance, whether imposed or chosen, stands opposed to both forms of exploration—"truths" that are being enforced by others or by oneself require that we not notice the flow of questions in the midst of which those claims lie. The hidden purposes of truth claims resist this kind of placement.

To see our conversations, with one another as well as with ourselves, as primarily the propounding of claims, is to view them essentially as monologues. I tell my tale and you respond with yours. My people have their stories and your people have theirs, and so on. To see conversation as substantially a flow of questions pursued produces a dialogue in the most literal sense, a movement of thinking between us rather than an attempt to hand off our truths and then turn away. A metaphor that might help here is one presented by Foucault. Spiritual practices in antiquity, he recounts, were likened to preparation for a wrestling match more than for a dance. In dancing, prescribed moves were learned that could be repeated until one attained a sense of mastery—as long as the dance is properly circumscribed according to the music and types of movement expected. But in a wrestling match one must be prepared to respond to the unexpected and thus one cannot simply follow preset moves. One must train for acuity of perception and flexibility of response (Foucault, 2005). So it is with the process of genuine conversation. It can never follow the preset moves of a catechism in which one merely memorizes the "correct" answers with which to answer the prescribed set of questions. Genuine conversation follows the flow of those questions that come up as one moves further and further from the known. Epistemologies of ignorance remind us of the value of comfort with the unknown and alongside that comfort a sharply defined sense of who benefits from ignorance that has potentially been imposed upon us by those who use our lack of knowledge to their advantage.

An education, for instance, that emphasizes memorized answers leaves one with a comfortable sense of knowledge, even of certainty. Life, however, throws us questions at an unprecedented rate and from unexpected angles. In that case, a recognition of ignorance that sets the frame for discovery and invention fits the best. As Socrates tells us, those who believe they know because they are satisfied with simplistic answers fail the test of wisdom. Only those, like Socrates himself, who accept their ignorance play well at life's game of uncertainty.

SOCRATES AS PARADIGM OF IGNORANCE

In the *Apology* Socrates details the charges that have been brought against him (Plato, 2000); his offense being that of attempting to point out fallacies in the thinking of those with whom he came into contact through a probing question-and-answer model that the Athenian political leaders deemed threatening. In his claim that artisans and poets alike also considered themselves wise in aspects other than their respective vocations, he concluded after questioning them that they lacked knowledge about such matters and it would be more advantageous to be as he saw himself—having neither their wisdom nor their ignorance. For Socrates, then, the wise individual is the one who knows he does not know. This *Socratic irony* serves as a paradigm of ignorance through which we might more carefully and thoughtfully consider our claims in the quest to come closer to truth—to break through those unrepentant certainties to which we so carefully cling. The advantages of having access to such a paradigm would seem endless. Allowing questions to arise based on our prior held beliefs and claims affords a thought process that, if pursued with diligence, forces us to reassess our thinking in light of alternative perspectives brought about through questioning the various parts of our claims and beliefs to highlight fallacies that we might not otherwise become aware of. This would seem, then, to lead us closer and closer to truth as we continue to question our claims as they continue to evolve by means of the question-and-answer process itself.

This paradigm of ignorance can be useful to individuals as they engage in questioning themselves, allowing those unrepentant certainties to break open to expose subsequent questions that in turn inform the formulation of conclusions that fuel further questions. This ongoing process alerts the individual to remain ever open to questioning that serves to further facilitate an articulation of thought and belief. This paradigm of ignorance can be very effective in classroom practice as the teacher actively engages her/his students in questions alternately posed with their answers. As students become more and more familiar with the Socratic Method, they will potentially become increasingly adept at the practice and engage their fellow students in the process. Such a practice then leads students to the twin ideas of (1) discovering where ignorance has been imposed or taken on that puts them at a disadvantage, and (2) becoming increasingly at ease with not having answers to every question.

So what could be disadvantageous about this paradigm of ignorance? What could be a more efficient way to actively pursue truth than to keep open the line of questioning? Let us take up for a moment the subject of questioning more closely. That which would ostensibly lead us to particular conclusions via a line of logical reasoning that the Socratic Method entails also has the capacity to discard anything that obstructs this line of reasoning. The danger here lies in the fact that the discarded can have the potential to offer up a space for resistance that informs critical social practice. In the standards driven world of education, specifically, such legislation as the No Child Left Behind Act (NCLB) and more recently, the Obama administration's educational initiative, Race to the Top, might be justified as necessary if taken up in a debate that attempts to secure a legitimation of a system of quantifiable rewards and punishments in an effort to improve student performance in selected subjects with selected criteria.

What gets left out, however, is the plight of those students whose lived situations and experiences do not lend themselves to improvement through this line of reasoning. Here the emphasis on standards and test scores is so great and so omnipresent that it can leave teachers, students, and parents feeling suffocated—and in the case of many students and parents, with a lack of awareness of the cause of such feelings—and powerless to actively resist in any productive way. Now, in his defense, so to speak, we can hardly claim that Socrates would somehow lead individuals today to believe that the NCLB is somehow justified in its current incarnation. The point here, however, is that when we become so involved in trying to pursue the 'truth' for our own ends, it is often possible to argue "logically" for those ends. In doing so, we forget, ignore, and/or delete those spaces that are lying below the logic and at the heart of critical social practice.

Returning to NCLB, who is going to allow those spaces to "rise to the top" so that marginalized groups of students can be served in ways that offer them optimal opportunities? How can spaces be opened up for teachers to engage in the questioning that affords teachers and students the opportunity to *be* and *feel* empowered to effect change in their own lives? If our admitted ignorance leads us to accept the status quo (as in the case of the standards-driven curriculum in U.S. public schools) we make a mockery of the Socratic approach to wisdom. Ignorance, in other words, can be cited as a reason for inaction, and we need to recognize the possibility that certain approaches to admitting ignorance might aid the oppressor if we are to maintain critical practice grounded in and alongside of our recognition of what we do not know. As noted earlier, we must distinguish between two ideas in applying an epistemology of ignorance to engaging in critical practice: first, ignorance might be forced upon one by certain relations of power that gain from our lack of knowledge or by ourselves, when we believe that we gain from not knowing something; second, in at least some areas of life knowledge lies beyond our abilities and our ignorance can fruitfully be embraced. In both areas, questioning can help develop our understanding, and in both areas, we need to be less quick than we might want to be in determining what we can and cannot know.

Socrates then provides a paradigm not only in terms of individual intellectual endeavor but, as we have just suggested, in terms of social action and policy. We cannot open spaces for the questioning that empowers without placing questioning in a central position within our human endeavors, whether in education, as just suggested, or in politics, communal resistance, or individual experience. The heart of critical social practice remains tied to the Socratic paradigm of the centrality of the question.

CONTESTING THE SOCRATIC NOTION OF IGNORANCE

We are ready now to contest what we have so far valorized—the Socratic ignorance that problematizes the value of unquestioned certainties. There is no question that acknowledged ignorance holds great value when opposed to rigid categories of knowledge; as discussed in the last section, knowing when and what we do not know plays a crucial role in critical practice and in resistance to oppression whether our ignorance is forced upon us so that we need to overcome it or unavoidable so that we need to accept it. As emphasized earlier, questions surround our every claim, and conversation that presents itself as monologue fails to meet its own standard of meaning. Dialogue stands as a primary function of human interaction whether with oneself, with others, or with life itself. What those who would engage in critical practice must contest, however, lies in the Platonic Socrates whose vision of truth might block levels of actionable critique as discussed in regard to NCLB, for example. For the sake of simplicity, we might divide understandings of Socrates along the following lines: First is the Socrates of the *Apology*, in its most obvious reading, who values questions over answers and unveils his view of human wisdom as worthless because most of it falls prey to its own image-making. (For example, the "wise" people of Athens questioned by Socrates seem much more concerned about maintaining the public belief in their wisdom than about learning anything and thus becoming wiser.) We find a second vision of Socrates as one who questions the wisdom of his peers primarily on the basis of a greater wisdom of his own. This outlook appears at least in part in the *Republic* (Plato, 1991) where the story of the cave represents Socratic wisdom as being based in a divine vision of the truth that the ignorant simply lack. The pretense of wisdom found in the Athenian "wise" people is likened to those who mistake shadows for reality.

Even if we deny that in the second view Plato reflects the historic Socrates, the Socrates of the *Apology* seems intent on seeking truth, in much the manner of those who invoke epistemologies of ignorance to chart a path through the muddied waters of societal "truths" that often simply serve the powerful. Although Socrates claims that human wisdom is worthless, he makes some claims that sound very much like claims to knowledge such as that (1) he speaks the truth in contrast to the lies of his accusers, (2) he knows the truth about his lack of wisdom, (3) there are certain truths about how one ought to live and die, and (4) Athens benefits from his questioning of its citizens. It also seems that he raises questions as though there are truths to be found that his "victims" simply have not yet found. This is particularly apparent in certain other Platonic dialogues such as the *Meno* where Socrates questions Meno about the correct definition of virtue (Plato, 1924).[7] There seems in these accounts to be no question as to whether there is a truth about the essence of virtue, the question lies in whether they have yet found that truth. Even the ending of the *Meno*, aporetic as it is, suggests continuing the quest the next day, presumably in the hope that tomorrow the truth about virtue might be found.

We would like then to offer the following question about Socratic wisdom/ ignorance, as suggested above: Does Socrates in the end value his famed ignorance or does he settle for ignorance while wishing always to replace questions with answers, ignorance with knowledge, "worthless" human wisdom with the genuine wisdom of the gods? Let's suppose that the latter is the case. Then Socratic ignorance and the perpetual questioning that it embraces stand not as paradigmatic but as a temporary expedient on the (admittedly long and troubling) road to Truth. The following alternatives stand out, at this important juncture on this path: On the one hand, questions have primary value and can never be set aside. They are not temporary, to be left behind as soon as possible, but offer us the highest intellectual and practical value. On the other hand, answers are always the point. We settle for questions only until we turn them into answers, only until we replace them and finally put them to rest by coming to the truth they push us to seek. Socrates, and the whole intellectual tradition of the West, can be called as witnesses on either side of this duality.

A worst case scenario in relation to what Socrates offers us lies in the suggestion that even in the case of thinking of him as the ancestor of a view that places questions first we find in him a privileging of the abstract and theoretical over the practical and workable ideas we need for social liberation and personal freedom. The problematic point here is that either of the alternatives above might end up placing practice outside the range of real interest. Whether, in other words, one sees questions as primary, but essentially theoretical, or one see purely conceptual answers as primary, one can be left without any practical grasp of ways to form, reform, or transform society. When Socrates calls the "wise" to account, he attacks their ability to answer definitional questions, to provide proper conceptualizations, to offer the essence, in words, of those ideas he has asked them to address. He further suggests, quite directly, that what aids Athens, his ultimate value to his society, lies in his holding them accountable for their ideas.

SOCRATIC NOT-KNOWING AND ARISTOTELIAN POLITICS

Now let us place Socratic ignorance up against a rival notion, that of Aristotelian understanding of human nature and society. To begin with we admit that we intend to be less than fair to Aristotle, whose thinking was wide-ranging and of immense importance in Western intellectual history. It is easy to pick on such a figure and to make points at his expense that no one could make were Aristotle here to respond. We use Aristotle in our own teaching, both explicitly and implicitly—to make use of Western thought at all places us in a debt to Aristotle, and despite its flaws we make use of the categories and logic of Western thought as part of any attempt to work with the intellectual, affective, and pedagogical resources of our society. Having made our confession, we can proceed to the attack.

Aristotle presents us with a "science" of society and self—recognizing as he does so that the level of precision possible in this arena is far below that in mathematics or some other sciences. Nevertheless he explains the nature of human happiness, the best life, and the best society—both in terms of logical and attainable possibility. The highest good for human beings, called happiness or a satisfying life (eudaimonia), is to be found most fully in completing the highest human capacity, the capacity to reason or think (to engage in dialogue [*logos*] inner and outer[8]), that is, it is found in *theoria*, usually translated "contemplation." A secondary approach to the highest good lies in political involvement for the sake of creating and maintaining a good society. The best life is a life of intellectual and practical virtues lived in a society with a successful constitution. The highest human life is only possible for certain kinds of individuals; slaves, women, barbarians, and children can engage in a limited kind of virtuous behavior but complete virtue and therefore a fully happy life requires a full measure of human capacities—the ability to reason and the ability to carry out one's reasoning—which individuals on the preceding list lack (though male children of free and wealthy citizens carry within them the possibility of a good life through having the potential to acquire these basic human capacities).

Aristotle soundly renounces Plato's perfect society (found in the *Republic*), yet describes his own possibilities of social perfection in the *Politics*. We must recognize that Aristotle sees human society as both perfectible, within certain limits, and as necessarily imperfect, due to various antagonisms and struggles that naturally reside in any actual community. There are, for example, the natural antipathies held by the rich for the poor (and the poor for the rich) as well as by both of these for the group in the middle. It is further the case that various social and vocational groups tend to participate in a form of internal warfare and that the vicious and virtuous form a natural dichotomy. Due to these factors and to aspects of history, geography, choice, and other contextual features of human community, any group, although made up of human beings who are naturally political, cannot complete a perfect *polis*. The best we can do is form a proper society, based on a balance of factors and antagonisms that has the greatest potential for a satisfying, lasting "union." Such a proper union can only be attained when those who live within it each take an appropriate place in the whole. That, further, requires that the naturally superior and the naturally inferior be correctly distinguished and fulfill suitable roles.

Out of Aristotle's view (which, Aristotle might be surprised to find us suggest, seems remarkably similar to that of Plato[9]) we then get the common view of the West, in which everyone has an assigned role that must be rightly lived in order to produce a good society. Whether or not this ideal would in fact work, and neither utopian social experiments nor any known *polis* has been able to demonstrate its validity, its danger lies in the unthinking acceptance of assigned roles—even ones we assign ourselves.[10] Bluntly and briefly put, assigned roles make the players of those roles conceptual objects rather than persons. We might agree with Kant, for instance, that playing an assigned role (being a *means* rather than an *end* on occasion) holds no danger given our free acceptance of the role and it being a role that causes no damage to oneself or others. Even so, however, the playing of roles endangers our individual multiplicity and requires the (at least temporary) relinquishment of questioning and resistance—either of which might be given up briefly but both of which must be kept available if we are not to lose what makes us human and what makes a living community possible.

What makes society work, in the end, in the common view of Plato, Aristotle, and the West seems to be the subjection of "natural" inferiors by masters, men, and the virtuous rich. Even granted that the West has in recent decades placed some of this subjection under scrutiny, it still forms a core value of the social arrangements that make possible the style of life looked at as a natural right and both exported and understood as a key human value by the most powerful nations (and corporations) of the Western tradition. As a simple but central example, without the poverty of the workforce (slaves, women, subsistence-level workers) not only the rich but whatever middle class remains as well as the relatively impoverished members of "developed" countries could not acquire the goods and have available the services that they have come to expect and require—as part of a good life.[11]

We turn to Socrates—admittedly poor and carrying a dangerous value to his society—for a response to the Aristotelian "good life" and parallel "good society." We would maintain that there is much agreement between Socrates and Aristotle (and between both of them and Plato) about the crucial significance of virtue in one's life, about the necessary connections between self and society, and about the intimate coincidence of personal goodness and a good life.[12] What Socrates offers in response to the controlled, indexed, tagged, and ordered life of a society that holds everyone in place lies primarily in his unwillingness to accept society's given order as its correct one. The priority of the question, we maintain, undermines the authorized and "proper" control of persons under any reign of benevolent subjection. It offers instead wonder, uncertainty, and movement that always overflow the banks of certainty, that never cease to bring enforced order and harmony, however wise its proponents proclaim themselves to be, under profound and incessant attack, not because the questioners know better but because no one does.

THE VIRTUES OF EPISTEMIC POVERTY

Our concluding point, then, relies on a value we have tried to question: Epistemic poverty,[13] a fundamental recognition of our individual and communal lack of knowledge "goods," both constitutes a virtue and requires a set of virtues without which we wallow in false convictions about our access to truth. The most significant virtue needed to live out this voluntary poverty lies in placing a priority on questions rather than answers, on recognizing the centrality of ignorance not principally as a lack but as the space required in order to begin to move. We take Socrates as our paradigm here, without apology but noting that one possible Socratic approach can obscure what we must instead bring into the foreground, the need for ignorance not to paralyze but to galvanize.[14] When ignorance becomes an excuse for immobility, we lose the impetus that the priority of the question supplies, that is, the drive for resistance.

The value of the virtues of epistemic poverty become especially important as we seek to break the hegemony of polemic certainties, such as the ones surrounding the so-called No Child Left Behind legislation. Can no child be left behind? Can we actualize education that optimizes every person's possibilities?[15] Can we, for example, as suggested by Marcuse (1991), so supply everyone within our larger society (perhaps even at the level of planetarity[16]) with sufficient goods that we then, each and all, turn our released energies toward artistic (or similar) endeavors that fulfill our humanity, rather than embracing a corporate vision of merely becoming better and better consumers.

This leads us then back to the door through which we entered this discussion. What is left out and forgotten in our everyday and our political understandings? Our everyday particular knowing of our ignorance—that we do not know all that we might (or even all that we believe we do) and that the hidden presence of the other in our conversations and our world calls *us* into question and points to the priority of the question not only as a heuristic device or as a clever means for keeping hidden our aggressive agendas but as a living process for proclaiming the uncertainty we ought to feel in the fluid movement of thought, dialogue, and life.[17]

NOTES

1. See, for example, Foucault (2003b), "Thus, one escaped from the domination of truth not by playing a game that was totally different from the game of truth but by playing the same game differently or playing another game, another hand, with other trump cards" (p. 37). This does not mean that we should accept any given game of truth uncritically, simply that games of truth are a legitimate aspect of our social interactions.

2. So we are provided with answers that either reduce our involvement in learning about the power and possibilities of our own lives or provide reassurance that we understand (and appropriately shun) the outsider or the different.

3. Paralleled in Bakhtin (1981) with the words "internally persuasive discourse" (p. 342).

4. Nancy Tuana (2006) sets out a helpful taxonomy of epistemologies of ignorance in her section headings: Knowing That We Do Not Know, But Not Caring to Know; We Do Not Even Know That We Do Not Know; They Do Not Want Us to Know; Willful Ignorance; Ignorance Produced by the Construction of Epistemically Disadvantaged Identities; and Loving Ignorance. We have previously referred to some of these distinctions. Of importance here is the fact that the priority of the question plays a role in both what we fail to know and what we cannot know. Questioning opens us to seeking to know that which has been systematically withheld from us and to becoming comfortable with the truth of our epistemological limitations.

5. We are tempted to refer here to our being human as a "cosmopolitan" aspect of community, but do not wish to embroil ourselves in the heated on-going debates concerning this notion.

6. We would point to Foucault (2003a), Gadamer (1989), Collingwood (2002), and Russell (1959) as representative recent thinkers who have promoted the value of questions as crucial to thinking itself.

7. We acknowledge that the *Meno* provides us with what is likely to be Plato's later view of Socrates that is not to be confused with the earlier view found in the *Apology*. Nevertheless the view found in Socrates' questioning of Meno corresponds in some ways with the questioning in the *Apology* of the alleged wisdom of the leaders, poets, and artisans of Athens.

8. Friendship appears to be of substantial importance for Aristotle, not only in general and as an important aspect of virtue, but also in relation to fulfilling the highest human function of contemplation.

9. Of course there are significant differences between their views, which we do not mean to ignore. We point here only to the way in which the ultimate society gets portrayed by both thinkers as involving placing each individual in her/his "proper" role that cannot be evaded or denied at pain of loss to the functional whole.

10. This of course plays directly into various historic and current epistemologies of ignorance.

11. We would like to note here recent television commercials by a big box chain store extolling its value for providing a good life at a reasonable price—the

actors in these fictions appearing as members of middle class families able to engage in enjoyable pastimes through saving money at the stores in question—stores that frequently have been criticized for their treatment of workers and their encouragement of sweatshop production conditions.

12. Further, the "big three" ancient thinkers (Socrates, Plato, and Aristotle) all denounce in various ways those forms of ignorance that restrict, taint, or destroy a good society. Socrates denounces the "wisdom" of those who lead society and pass off their ignorance as truth; Plato (in the *Republic*) holds that society must be ruled by philosophers (genuine "lovers of wisdom"), and Aristotle points out the need for proper enculturation so that one sees virtue for what it is and does not fall prey to the ignorant aims of those who value pleasure or political honors over virtue.

13. A term we employ for the Socratic questioning we have been describing. It relates both to questioning forms of assigned ignorance and to allowing a judicious love of ignorance in relation to the unknown/unknowable.

14. Ignorance, in other words, becomes the spark for becoming. It is the recognition that knowledge is always lacking and to know is a verb and sets in motion the terms for ignorance, what must always be understood as unintelligible but also a force in our knowing.

15. We think here, though not exclusively, of Dewey's (1937) suggestion that equality requires equal opportunity to develop and that any legitimate form of democracy requires that form of equality.

16. We draw this term and at least some of its conceptual framework from Spivak (2003), also Pinar (2007) and, interestingly, Teilhard (1978).

17. Our sincere thanks and deep appreciation for the extremely useful critical comments on an earlier draft by the editors of this volume and by Erik Malewski in particular.

REFERENCES

Aristotle. (1998). *Politics* (C. D. C. Reeve, Trans.). Indianapolis, IN: Hackett.

Bakhtin, M. M. (1981). Discourse in the novel. In *The dialogic imagination: Four essays* (pp. 259–422). (C. Emerson and M. Holquist, Trans.). Austin, TX: University of Texas Press.

Collingwood, R. G. (2002). *An essay on metaphysics* (Rev. ed.). New York, NY: Oxford University Press.

Dewey, J. (1937). Democracy and educational administration. *School and Society*, 45, 457–462.

Foucault, M. (2003a). *Polemics, politics, and problematizations: An interview with Michel Foucault*. In P. Rabinow & N. Rose (Eds.), (Lydia Davis, Trans.) *The Essential Foucault* (pp. 18–24). New York, NY: The New Press.

Foucault, M. (2003b). *The ethics of the concern of the self as a practice of freedom*. In P. Rabinow & N. Rose (Eds.), (P. Aranov & D. McGrawth, Trans.), *The essential Foucault* (pp. 25–42). New York, NY: The New Press.

Foucault, M. (2005). *The hermeneutics of the subject: Lectures at the Collège de France 1981–1982*. New York, NY: Picador.

Frye, M. (1983). *The politics of reality: Essays in feminist theory*. Berkeley, CA: Crossing Press.

Gadamer, H. -G. (1989). *Truth and method*. New York, NY: Continuum.

James, W. (1890). *The principles of psychology* (Vols. 1–2). New York, NY: Henry Holt.

Marcuse, H. (1991). *One-dimensional man*. Boston, MA: Beacon Press.

Pinar, W. F. (2007). *Intellectual advancement through disciplinarity: Verticality and horizontality in curriculum studies*. Rotterdam, The Netherlands: Sense.

Plato. (1924). *Meno*. In *Plato with an English translation: Laches, Protagoras, Meno, Euthydemus* (W. R. M. Lamb, Trans.), London: Harvard University Press.

Plato. (1991). *Republic of Plato: Second edition*. (A. Bloom, Trans.). New York, NY: Basic Books.

Plato. (2000). *Apology*. In J. M. Cooper (Rev. ed.), *The trial and death of Socrates* (pp. 20–42). (G. M. A. Grube, Trans.). Indianapolis, MD: Hackett.

Russell, B. (1959). *The problems of philosophy*. London: Oxford University Press.

Spivak, G. C. (2003). *Death of a discipline*. New York, NY: Columbia University Press.

Teilhard de Chardin, P. (1978). *The heart of matter*. San Diego, CA: Harcourt.

Tuana, N. (2006). The speculum of ignorance: The women's health movement and epistemologies of ignorance. *Hypatia, 21*(3), 1–19.

CHAPTER 6

LOCATING THE FOUNDATIONS OF EPISTEMOLOGIES OF IGNORANCE IN EDUCATION IDEOLOGY AND PRACTICE

Dolores Calderón

INTRODUCTION

In previous work I examined a series of ideologies and practices that shape education in the United States and argued that they promote myopic educational ways of thinking that hamper the full development of indigenous educational ideas and practices. Some of the ideological categories I identified, for example, include the concepts of "colonial blind discourses" (Calderón, 2009) and "flattened epistemologies" (Calderón, 2006b). I also identified a related series of educational practices based on these ideologies, including "normative multicultural education" (Calderón, 2008) and the "Colonial Model of Education" (Calderón, 2008). In this chapter, I focus on normative multicultural education. I assert that the repeating themes I located in both these educational ideologies and practices originate from their foundations in what Vine Deloria and others

Epistemologies of Ignorance in Education, pp. 105–127

defined as Western metaphysics (Deloria, 1979, 1992; Deloria & Wildcat, 2001; Smith, 2001). Together the ideologies of colonial blind discourses and flattened epistemologies and the practice of normative multicultural education (NMCE) operate to promote what I refer to as *colonial ontologies*[1] that leave little room for truly diverse educational discourses and practices to flourish.

In this chapter, I continue my examination of these ideologies and practices in education, drawing from the work of indigenous scholars who have developed the critique of Western metaphysics in education (Cajete, 1994; Champagne, 2005; Deloria & Wildcat, 2001), and an indigenous politics of action (Smith, 2002), while coupling these insights with recent research on epistemologies of ignorance (Mills, 1999; Sullivan & Tuana, 2004, 2006, 2007). I am examining epistemologies of ignorance because many of the claims and insights foundational to them parallel my own research. Furthermore, epistemologies of ignorance are constructive because the model helps explain how colonial blind discourses, flattened epistemologies, and NMCE function. I also seek to further a research platform that cultivates the decolonizing work promoted by critiques of Western metaphysics, particularly as it relates to what I define as NMCE. By doing so, I hope to continue to make the case that much of NMCE practice is poorly equipped to promote indigenous informed educational needs that originate from radically different epistemologies and metaphysics and that also retain the goal of encouraging Native Nation-building.

For this work, I rely on critical interstitial methodology (CIM) (Calderón, 2006a, 2006b, 2008). Critical interstitial methodology "is briefly defined as a methodology, or way of examining, two or more theories/methodologies that are generally viewed as mutually exclusive, or incompatible [citations omitted]" (Calderón, 2008, p. 140). For instance, CIM is a valuable tool with which to examine theories, methodologies, and research founded upon differing epistemological foundations, in this case indigenous informed critiques of Western metaphysics and largely Western informed critiques offered by epistemologies of ignorance in ways that are complementary.

I developed these concepts in response to what I saw as gaps in the education literature and in response to Daniel Wildcat's (2001) call for indigenous educators to explicitly identify the "features of the Western tradition or worldview that produce many of the problems we are immersed in today" (p. 10). Indeed, as Wildcat insists, "the hope for American Indian education lies" in this identification and the active reconstruction of indigenous knowledge systems (p. 10). Finally, while my work parallels epistemologies of ignorance, it also begins to uncover important originary Western assumptions that help show us why epistemologies of ignorance are commonplace, indeed normalized ways of knowing and not knowing.

METHODOLOGY/ THEORETICAL FRAMEWORK

CIM (Calderón, 2006a, 2006b, 2008) allows for an analysis of how Western metaphysics, ideologies, and practices, as identified by indigenous methods and perspectives, reveal how epistemologies of ignorance operate in curriculum, for instance. To understand my approach in this chapter, I want to first offer an outline that highlights the basic tenets of CIM:

- CIM utilizes the concept of interstice, or "space in between in order to rebuild useful and strategic uses of theories and methodologies, which originate from differing epistemological sources" (Calderón, 2008).
- CIM, drawing from feminist theory, critical race theory, and indigenous models (Deloria & Wildcat, 2001; Harding, 1997; Hill-Collins, 1997; Hurtado, 2003; Solórzano, 1998; Smith, 2002) explicitly "reconstructs the analytical relationship between theories and methodologies framed from differing epistemological frameworks in ways that promote and illuminate tangible and organic needs of non-Western communities" (Calderón, 2008, p. 141).
- CIM requires analysis, deconstruction, and reconstruction of different approaches in ways that promote indigenous practices (Smith, 2002).
- In this intellectual interstice, or "no person's territory," non-Western theories are centered, destabilizing Western-informed approaches (for example anthropocentric orientations are de-centered in the critical interstice).
- Moving into this intellectual interstice requires border crossing (Anzaldua, 1987), and as I describe in previous work "because this intellectual territory is outside the realm of Western spaces, theories that are more strongly derived in Western spaces are more prone to critique because in this territory, the West is confronted with the fact it is not a universal" (Calderón, 2008, p. 141).
- In the interstice, "non-Western epistemologies are not labeled as marginal or in relation to a Western framework" (Calderón, 2008, p. 141).

- Most importantly, CIM demands one to investigate and trace the origins of theories/methods/methodologies to their originary worldviews. Without doing this, theories/methods/methodologies remain blind to their colonial ontologies.

As Sandra Harding (1997) describes, methodology is "a theory and analysis of how research does or should proceed" (p. 161). In this case, CIM guides me to: first move my own work and epistemologies of ignorance (EOI) into the intellectual interstice; center a strategy of indigeneity; map the epistemological origins of difference; and finally promote a comprehensive dialogue. In addition, as Harding explains, "*epistemology is a theory of knowledge*" which determines who can know, "what kinds of things can be known" and, in her work, how feminism has pointed out that traditional Western epistemologies "systematically exclude the possibility that women could be 'knowers' or *agents of knowledge*" (p. 161). CIM demands that I trace how epistemological exclusion occurs and how the cosmos of what is known can be expanded. Accordingly, I am interested in locating how current epistemological frameworks informing educational discourses and practices actively produce gaps that have concrete consequences for many communities that are not allowed full participation in educational knowledge production. For this reason, I explore how the critical framework of Western metaphysics, in conjunction with EOI challenge fundamental knowledge claims that are made in educational research and practice. Yet, as a researcher of color, I am confronted with what Villalpando and Delgado-Bernal (2002) refer to as the "apartheid of knowledge" in academic knowledge production that excludes non-Eurocentric ways of knowing that provide alternative research agendas, methods, and frameworks (Delgado-Bernal & Villalpando, 2002; Villalpando & Bernal, 2002). However, Daniel Solórzano (1998) reminds us that as researchers:

> we must realize that most of the methods we use as social scientists are rooted in these 'racist epistemologies.' It is our responsibility to acknowledge these epistemologies and, where appropriate, use them for transformational purposes while continuing to move toward more antiracist and antisexist epistemologies and related methods. (p. 133)

CIM demands this type of accountability. Aída Hurtado (2003) argues a similar point: "Feminists of Color are motivated to produce knowledge from the position of the 'politics of urgency.' Theirs is a commitment to changing social conditions now by whatever means necessary" (p. 222). In this regard, the combined understanding offered by EOI and Western metaphysics is a powerful tool because it challenges the apartheid of knowledge (Delgado-Bernal & Villalpando, 2002) encountered not only in research but in educational practices as well.

In the next section, I examine the ideologies of colonial blind discourses and flattened epistemologies, in conjunction with epistemologies of ignorance, to examine why and how knowledge gaps persist. In section four, I examine the corresponding practices or forms of these ideologies, specifically NMCE, investigating how epistemologies of ignorance enhance these insights. In section five, I examine the foundational ideology of Western metaphysics, providing a brief review of its development and how I characterize it. Last, I examine Western metaphysics and epistemologies of ignorance together in order to clarify how the ideologies of color blind discourses and NMCE. However, I begin with a discussion of the ideologies I encountered in previous work.

IDEOLOGIES: COLONIAL BLIND DISCOURSES AND FLATTENED EPISTEMOLOGIES

Colonial Blind Discourses

Informed by Dolores Delgado-Bernal's (1998) notion of cultural intuition—the distinctive standpoint and insight of the world that, according to Delgado-Bernal, Chicana researchers bring to their work—I found that much of education research, literature and practice blindly incorporates colonial ontologies through what I refer to as colonial blind discourses. Delgado-Bernal (1998) explains that "cultural intuition" is informed by four sources that Chicanas use in their research. These include: personal experience (which consists of collective experience and community memory), existing literature on a topic, professional experience, and the analytical research process itself. In my analysis of colonial blind discourse, I drew from the combination of my own subjectivities, experiences, literatures explored, and research processes. Cultural intuition allowed me to see colonial blind discourses in action and name it as well.

My own subjectivities as an indigenous/Mexican/legal/education researcher inform and shape how I interact and interpret various literatures, research, and practices in education (Calderón, 2008). An additional element shaping my cultural intuition is the role of place, or geography (Deloria & Wildcat, 2001). Place leads me to understand what I describe as the "oscillating nature of the politics, policies and practices of Nation-State, the legal landscapes (Delaney, 1998) of nation-states," (Calderón, 2008, p. 9) a formative aspect of the community memory I draw from. Furthermore, "the experience of place leads me to understand very intimately how the changing nature of the settler-state, its laws, economics, politics, and cultural practices impact communities' lives" (Calderón, 2008, p. 11). In addition, this cultural intuition reminds me that the memory and collective experience of my community serves as a witness to the recent history of the settler-state; thus, cultural intuition signals the intimate knowledge and understanding of settler-state processes that comes from my community (Calderón, 2008). From the position of my personal experience (informed by collective experience and community memory), legal background or professional experience, interactions with several research areas, and my own research—as well as accompanying literatures such as multicultural education—I discovered a recurring blind spot, or gap in knowledge production. The propensity of discourses, like colorblind ideologies (Bonilla-Silva, 2001), to "normalize Western knowledge organization and assumptions, promote Western notions of being (metaphysics) and promote Westernization of knowledge and its institutionalization through means perceived as neutral" (Calderón, 2008, p. 167) in my experiences and resulting research is captured in colonial blind discourses.

Colonial-blind is a play on the concept colorblind, which is characterized by education researchers as the dominant racial ideology of the contemporary moment (Bonilla-Silva, 2001). For example, Bonilla-Silva argues that colorblind ideology or racism represents the new racial ideology of our era. While in the past, he explains, "the racial practices typical of the Jim Crow era were overt and clearly racial, today they tend to be covert, institutional, and apparently nonracial" (p. 138). Similarly, Laurence Parker and David Stovall (2004) posit that in K–12 education,

> the ideology of color-blindness and "racial progress" has also been reflective of an overarching trend ... to ignore race and racism in their schools, by assuming that if attention is not paid to racial implications of problems. .. then these issues will simply disappear. (pp. 170–171)

Undeniably, this formulation of colorblindness parallels Charles Mills' (1997) and Nancy Tuana's (2004, 2006) characterizations of epistemologies of ignorance as they relate to race and gender. For instance, Tuana (2004) argues that ignorance is actively produced and preserved and is many times linked to systems of oppression. In the same way colonial blind discourses are closely linked to systems of oppression.[2] While similar to contemporary colorblind ideologies, colonial blind discourses have a much longer history of institutionalization. This institutionalization can be traced back to the colonial origins of European expansion and the nation-building processes of the United States. In this regard, it is harder for many to "see" or acknowledge that they are engaging in these types of discourses as they have been normalized for so long, and are in fact a functional component of American identity and nation-building (Calderón, 2008). To be sure, this formulation of American identity is structured around Eurocentric foundations that necessitate an ignorance of the other. Charles Mills (2007), in articulating his theory of "White ignorance" points out quite simply that "the White delusion of racial superiority [or White ignorance, which is not only confined to White people] insulates itself against refutation" (p. 19). On the other side of White ignorance is Black knowledge, which Mills (2007) describes as consisting of "the self-conscious recognition of White ignorance" (p. 19). It is not a surprise that I was able to see color blind discourses, indeed intuit it as described earlier. In addition, Mills' (2007) point that White ignorance is not only confined to White people bears repeating because as indigenous scholars point out colonization occurs not only institutionally, but physically, emotionally, and spiritually as well (Deloria, 2006; Smith, 2002).

In education, colonial blind discourse, indeed White ignorance, manifest themselves in a multitude of ways. For example, civic education emphasizes the discussions of minority rights with regards to African Americans, American Indians, Asian Americans, and Latino/as (Calderón, 2008). This discourse imputes an instance of *colonial ontologies* that ignores the fact, as David Wilkins (2002) points out, "tribal peoples, unlike any other groups in the United States, are sovereign nations, not minority groups" (p. 47). This omission is not a surprise. Knowledge organization in the United States is preoccupied with upholding the racial hierarchy of White supremacy. Outlaw (2007) describes this hierarchy as a racial ontology. Historically this racial ontology resulted in particular types of knowledge concerning the other. Outlaw (2007) explains that for Whites, "there was no need to know living persons of supposedly inferior races in their own right and on their own terms, only that they be 'known' *by race* and 'known' as such by White folks" (p. 198). This racial ontology, he continues, "produced ignorance," but more importantly,

> the "knowing" and concomitant ignorance were ordered and valorized by the requirements of ordering political economies and social-cultural life-worlds in which the enslavement and exploitation of Africans and their descendents ... were enforced as the normal way of life. (p. 198)

The epistemologies of ignorance embedded in social studies curriculum follow the same logic. In the United States, Whiteness is transformed into nativeness, requiring a process of unlearning immigrant narratives (Calderón, 2008). The treatment of American Indians as minorities in textbooks affirms this ordering of "political economies and social cultural life-worlds" of Whites, thus promoting colonial blind discourse. Like colorblind ideologies, epistemologies of ignorance offer further insights into the production of colonial blind discourses in curricula. In this case the framing of American Indians as minorities has to do with what Tuana (2004) refers to as "the result of the configuration of interest" (p. 4), and "knowing that we do not know, but not caring to know" (p. 4). In this case the "configuration of interests" is the framing of Whites as the new natives. Tuana (2004) continues that it is important to account for the "practices that resulted in a group *unlearning* what was once a realm of knowledge" (p. 2). Whites treated tribes on a sovereign-to-sovereign basis, but over time, history has diminished this relationship. The decreased negotiating power of tribes over time translated into an ideological distancing on the part of the U.S. from this sovereign-to-sovereign relationship facilitating dubious land acquisitions (Williams, 1986). These configurations of interests more than promote miseducation, they promote a gap in knowledge, a blind-spot, and are more suitably identified as colonial blind discourses as they relate to American Indians. The configurations of interests in education are further explained by the reliance on flattened epistemologies and the practice of NMCE. Yet, a simple inspection of colonial history and contemporary legal narratives reveal otherwise, and specifically demonstrate how what once was a common realm of knowledge is now unlearned.

For instance, in previous work I examine how jurisprudence in the United States configures racialized groups and American Indians (Calderón, in press). I elaborate on Supreme Court jurisprudence, focusing on cases having to do with the classification of race and the status of American Indians. For example, in the case of *Morton v. Mancari* (1974) non-Indian plaintiffs sued the Bureau of Indian Affairs for what they claimed were discriminatory employment preferences in favor of Indians citing the 1972 Equal Employment Opportunities Act, EEOA (417 U.S. 535). However, the Court held that the employment preference did not violate the EEOA because the "preference, as applied, is granted to Indians not as a discrete racial group, but, rather, as members of quasi-sovereign tribal entities whose lives and activities are governed by the BIA in a unique fashion" (417 U.S. 554). The Court found that the employment preference in place was reasonable and "directly related to a legitimate, nonracially based goal" (417 U.S. 554).

Similarly, in *Regents of the University of California v. Bakke* (1978), the petitioner in *Bakke* attempted to use *Mancari* to argue that the State of California "may prefer members of traditionally disadvantaged groups" (438 U.S. 304). Here again, the Supreme Court differentiated the facts of *Mancari* from *Bakke*, finding that the *Mancari* preference was not racial but "an employment criterion reasonably designed to further the cause of Indian self-government and to make the BIA more responsive to ... groups ... whose lives and activities are governed by the BIA in a unique fashion"(438 U.S. 304). Both *Mancari* and *Bakke* differentiate tribes from racialized groups in the United States, emphasizing the sovereign status of Indians. While I am not arguing that education should look to Supreme Court jurisprudence to inform its content, as this would simply be replacing one colonial discourse with another, it is a useful example of the colonial blind patterns I have traced in social studies curriculum (Calderón, 2008). The question remains, however, if the U.S.'s own legal doctrines recognize American Indian tribes' differentiated status from minority groups why do civics and U.S. history textbooks adopted widely in classrooms across the country fail to incorporate this basic premise?[3]

The configuration of interests promoted in textbooks demands that history portrays Whites as the new native (Calderón, 2008). However, other issues also influence the presence of colonial blind discourses in curriculum. On the one hand, curriculum content changed over time in response to the demands of racial minorities and Indians for increased representation and culturally sensitive curriculum (Banks, 2004). However, this resulted in simply adding more multicultural content into existing content, rather than more critical representations (Calderón, 2008; Council on Interracial Books for Children, 1977; Sleeter & Grant, 1991), leaving the same racial ontologies unchallenged. Furthermore, this development is filtered through the same *colonial ontology* that favors whiteness and, as such, promotes colonial blind discourses.

In addition, colonial blind discourses are able to operate because of the type of epistemological models they rely on; they reproduce themselves because they rely on an epistemological model that is flat, reductive, and unidirectional in the way knowledge is created, produced, and disseminated. In particular, colonial blind discourses are enabled by what I refer to as a *flattened epistemology* (Calderón, 2006b). When paired with epistemologies of ignorance this concept reveals that the gap in knowledge I identify as colonial blind discourse is much more than a gap but an "active production" (Tuana, 2004, p. 195).

Flattened Epistemologies

Engaging the work of Herbert Marcuse (1991) has allowed me to flesh out the concept of a flat epistemology, particularly his work in *One-Dimensional Man*. Hence, using Marcuse's critique of one-dimensional society in conjunction with the insights of critical race theory and whiteness studies, I characterize the epistemological process of modernity as flat (Calderón, 2006b). Indeed, flattened epistemologies have a particular configuration. They tend to be hierarchical, totalitarian, and reductive (Calderón, 2006b). They also have a unique function—they normalize the status quo, which protects White supremacy. Epistemological production in the United States is closed and totalitarian and thus flattened epistemologies produce specific outcomes, including the suppression and de-legitimization of other forms of knowledge, especially if they are threatening to the status quo.

It is worth quoting Marcuse (1991) at length to demonstrate how flattened epistemologies are a product of the racialized nature of one-dimensional society many label Whiteness:

> The flat epistemic nature of whiteness is attributed to the unidirectional mode of capitalist relations, which always progress towards the reproduction of capital and disallow critical engagement of the system. Marcuse (1991) explains that modern society's technological rationalism operates as an apparatus that "imposes its economic and political requirements for defense and expansion on the labor time and free time, on the material and intellectual culture. By virtue of the way it has organized its technological base, contemporary industrial society tends to be totalitarian. (pp. 2–3)

These increasing economic and political requirements demand a flattened culture which flows singularly from the Establishment.

> In essence, the totalitarian or flattened rationalism is ideologically produced in the one-dimensional epistemology of whiteness. Individuals come to understand themselves, for the most part, only in relation to the universal or totalitarian notion of whiteness. Whiteness appears to be commonsensical, universal and value-neutral. George Lipsitz (1998) points out that "whiteness is everywhere in U.S. culture, but it is very hard to see" (p. 1). Whiteness represents the normative practices and discourses upon which everything is measured, but this measurement is not an explicit act. Rather, it remains an unseen, or invisible measure. "As the unmarked category against which difference is constructed, whiteness never has to speak its name, never has to acknowledge its role as an organizing principle in social and cultural relations" (Lipsitz, 1998, p. 1). As I have indicated elsewhere, "Whiteness silently pervades all sectors of life, both public and private." (Calderón, 2006b, p. 75)

This characterization of flattened epistemologies explain how colonial blind discourses function, rendering gaps in knowledge invisible. As illustrated earlier Tuana (2004) asserts: "An important aspect of an epistemology of ignorance is the realization that ignorance should not be theorized as a simple omission or gap but is, in many cases, an active production" (p. 195). Colonial blind discourses are more than an omission or gap; they are actively produced and enabled by flattened epistemologies. Tuana (2004) continues. "Ignorance is frequently constructed and actively preserved, and is linked to issues of cognitive authority, doubt, trust, silencing, and uncertainty" (p. 195). Specifically, flattened epistemologies shape how colonial blind discourses are produced through the epistemological reliance on issues of cognitive authority that actively silence other knowledge forms. For instance, regarding race, Tuana draws from Mills' (1997) insights:

> Charles Mills, for example, argues that matters related to race in Europe and the United States involve an active production and preservation of ignorance: "On matters related to race, the Racial Contract prescribes for its signatories an inverted epistemology, an epistemology of ignorance, a particular pattern of localized and global cognitive dysfunctions (which are psychologically and socially functional), producing the ironic outcome that Whites will in general be unable to understand the world they themselves have made" (1997, p. 18). (Tuana, 2004, p. 195)

Indeed, this inverted epistemology identified by Mills (1997) is akin to the flattened epistemologies model I developed aided by a variety of theoretical frameworks.

Additionally, Mills'(1997) insights as detailed by Tuana (1994) on the cognitive dysfunctions produced by racialized epistemologies of ignorance echo those of Marcuse's (1991), specifically the process of "mimesis"—the individual's immediate and uncritical identification with his/her society. Mimesis, I add,

> is the silent process with which whiteness extends its ideology into all facets of life in advanced industrial society in the United States. Through mimesis, individuals thus establish a non-critical relationship with whiteness. Simultaneously though, this mimesis of whiteness announces itself through a variety of institutional and narrative means. (Calderón, 2006, p. 75)

A configuration of interests, indeed. Therefore, the cognitive dysfunctions identified by both Mills and Tuana rely on flattened epistemologies that do not provide room for alternative perspectives. Enabled by the flattened epistemologies that rely on epistemologies of ignorance, colonial blind discourses lead to particular types of educational practices. One of these is normative multicultural education.

PRACTICES: NORMATIVE MULTICULTURAL EDUCATION

Normative multicultural education (NMCE) is characterized by the following features:

- NMCE folds Native Americans into minority discourses with African Americans, Asian Americans, and Latino/as;

- NMCE defines multiculturalism within *colonial ontologies* that operate from the foundations of whiteness;
- NMCE emphasizes multicultural goals in relation to equality and citizenship rights, including integration and individual rights;
- NMCE is informed by colonial blind discourses and flattened epistemologies;
- NMCE is framed by Western metaphysical frameworks.

I also want to add here that NMCE promotes epistemologies of ignorance.

In much of my work, I am driven by the concern that native educational issues are many times subsumed within NMCE, thus alienating indigenous educational desires.[4] While native nations are consistently shaping their own educational practices, this is problematized by the inconsistent nature of Indian education policy, exemplified by the current standardization movements of No Child Left Behind (Beaulieu, Sparks & Alonzo, 2005; Freeman & Fox, 2005; Lomawaima & McCarty, 2006; Reynolds, 2005). Additionally, because the majority of Indian students, about 90 percent, attend public schools (Freeman & Fox, 2005), there are fewer opportunities for implementation of Indian specific curriculum. Instead, public school curriculums favor normative types of multicultural education (Banks, 2004; Gay, 2004). And, as research demonstrates, both textbooks and content standards merge Indian narratives into larger multicultural discourses that are shaped by colonial blind discourses that rely on flattened, epistemologies of ignorance (Calderón, 2008).

Geneva Gay (2004) argues that multicultural education found in schools does not reflect the more critical scholarship and multicultural education models developed by critical educators. This, according to Banks (2004) is,

> widespread because curriculum reform was the main focus [of multiculturalism] when the movement first emerged in the 1960s and 1970s [citation omitted], and because the multiculturalism discourse in the popular media has focused on curriculum reform and largely ignored other dimensions and components of multicultural education [citation omitted]. (p. 4)

The reformist orientation of multicultural education reflects the configuration of interests illuminated by epistemologies of ignorance, further characterized by the dominant flattened epistemologies of whiteness. Regarding White supremacy, Outlaw (2007) points out that historically "Education became a principal means by which to effect the production, mediation, and legitimation of ignorance-sustaining knowledge, via schooling especially, that would achieve this defining and ordering" (p. 200). Education, I argue, particularly NMCE, maintains this tradition.

Geneva Gay (2004) clarifies, "Multicultural education is essentially an affective, humanistic, and transformative enterprise situated within the sociocultural, political, and historical contexts of the United States" (p.39). This point of contention is emblematic of the problems I see in attempting to incorporate and address indigenous peoples in NMCE based scholarship, theory, and policy—because authentic engagement with indigenous peoples challenges Whites' claims to native status. Gay reminds us, "because multiculturalism originates in the liberal pluralist paradigm it is limited in its ability to create long-lasting substantive social change" (p. 54); thus, it is unwilling to engage with paradigms that are radically different.

Like Outlaw (2007), McLaren and Farahmandpur (2005) challenge normative formations of education, paying close attention to multiculturalism, arguing that the dominant trope of multiculturalism seeks "to legitimize the social order through racial harmony, and a national identity based on the 'Americanization' of marginalized cultures" (p. 147). This type of multiculturalism promotes colonial blind discourses, particularly as it relates to American Indians, as both the cultural and political reality of tribes in the United States is antithetical to the types of "Americanization" sought (Calderón, 2008). Similarly these standardizing discourses of NMCE, facilitated by flattened epistemologies, do little to capture the complex identities and subjectivities of immigrant/transnational/diasporic communities (Bhabha, 2004; Lukose, 2007).

Building on this characterization with Western metaphysics, I add that NMCE fails to engage Western metaphysical assumptions. Specifically, many of the key themes tackled by NMCE including citizenship, equality, and diversity embody Western metaphysical assumptions that are not congruent with indigenous needs that emphasize sovereignty, self-determination, and tribal culture.

WESTERN METAPHYSICS: INDIGENOUS INFORMED PERSPECTIVES

Thus far, I have described colonial blind discourses and how they produce knowledge gaps in social studies curriculum through flattened epistemologies which help to sustain White supremacy. To enable this, the production of knowledge in curriculum relies on epistemologies of ignorance in order to maintain what Mills' describes as White ignorance, or a narrow definition of American identity (Calderón, 2008). Yet the flip side of colonial blind discourses and epistemologies of ignorance are that American Indians demand and articulate an entirely different set of educational needs[5] built upon on very different epistemo-ontological paradigms.[6] As the Supreme Court cases I describe earlier illustrate, American Indians' relations with the United States are political, yet tribal sovereignty is inherent, originating in the unique cultural and spiritual dimensions of tribal sovereignty (Champagne, 2007; Wilkins, 2002). Nevertheless, as I argue above, both the inherent nature of indigenous sovereignty and the unique political status of American Indians are missing from how educational practices are conceived, theorized, and put into place. Moreover, indigenous controlled education is challenged by the increasing rigidity of No Child Left Behind (Beaulieu et al., 2005; Reynolds, 2005; Senese, 1991). These cultural fissures remain because the foundational ideologies that inform colonial blind discourses and their operationalization in NMCE occur through the flattened epistemologies that rely on "ignorance."

Peeling back another layer of both the systemic and ideological narratives common in the U.S. reveals the origins of these fissures—Western metaphysics. Deloria (2001) define metaphysics as the "first set of principles we must possess in order to make sense of the world in which we live" (p. 2), which is congruent with much of Western philosophy's definition of metaphysics (Aristotle, 1966; Baumgarten, 1743; Grube, 1966; Plato, 1992). Deloria, however, takes a different trajectory than that of Western philosophy's definition of metaphysics by developing an understanding of metaphysics informed by indigenous perspectives (Deloria, 1979, 1994, 1992, 2002, 2006). I add that Western metaphysics is "the set of assumptions and systems of knowledge derived from European traditions, their historical origins, and colonialism that form the foundations of education in the United States" (Calderón, 2008, p. 1). For indigenous educational practices, this work is critical as it centers a politics and urgency of indigeneity. Deloria (2001) assert that metaphysics can be a powerful concept for assessing Western culture's basic and fundamental assumptions and normative frameworks.

Hence, I argue it is important to utilize the concept of metaphysics, despite its origins in Western philosophy, because as Deloria demonstrates, it is a useful concept with which to critically engage Western thought and practices that remain unrecognized in Western circles because they are completely normalized. More importantly, these perspectives pose serious challenges to indigenous peoples. Deloria's work has not found its way into broader educational discourses. While taken up by scholars interested in Indian education and predominantly Indian scholars, I argue that Deloria's work shines a light on education in ways that move the field towards a truer form of diversity.

But why metaphysics? Scott Pratt (2006), answers this question: " *'The fundamental factor that keeps Indians and non-Indians from communicating is that they are speaking about two entirely different perceptions of the world,' that is, he [Deloria] says later, two radically different metaphysics"* (p. 4) [emphasis added]. It is worth noting here, that while I draw on the breadth of Deloria's work, the impetus of his work changed over time. In *Metaphysics of Modern Existence*, Pratt (2006) explains, Deloria (1979) attempted to "develop a new philosophical ground between Native and Western worlds that is suited to responding to the crises faced by the world as it approached the twenty-first century" (p. 4). Deloria (1979) was searching for a possible "new metaphysics," or a metaphysics that took into account both indigenous and Western scientific approaches (Pratt, 2006), which Deloria (1994, 2001) later rejected, responding to Western peoples inabilities or lack of desire to search for this common ground with indigenous peoples (Pratt, 2006).

Instead, Deloria, with Wildcat, in *Power and Place: Indian Education in America* offer, as Pratt (2006) describes, an "attempt to provide Native people themselves with a philosophical framework that will at once preserve their traditions and provide resources for negotiating the schizophrenia of their interactions with European-descended culture" (p. 4). While Deloria's goals changed overtime, his extensive work on outlining Western metaphysics remains central. Acknowledging and illuminating that Western metaphysics is foundational and omnipresent in Western education has widespread implications. Indeed, as Daniel Wildcat (2001) maintains "we must begin a discussion of education in America with the metaphysical assumptions of Western civilization implicit in and underlying modern notions of curriculum and pedagogy, given that so little attention is paid to the topic today" (p. 9).

William Cobern (1988) also provides another important reason to forefront and critically engages Western metaphysics in education. Although he speaks in the context of science education, his perspective applies to education broadly:

> It has been demonstrated that students do not come into the science classroom with minds "tabula rasa." Students bring with them ideas and values about the natural world that they have formulated on their own or have acquired from previous educational experiences...Some students come into class already holding a high value of science. Others come with value systems

that will readily incorporate a high view of science given the proper circumstances. Others are prepared to resist. (p. 5)

Cobern (1988) continues, "it is assumed that students come into secondary and college science classes with relatively homogeneous, fundamental views of the natural world capable of assimilating and valuing modern scientific understanding" (pp. 5–6). Cobern wishes to challenge such assumptions and focus instead on how students' worldviews influence how they learn, and how they are taught.

Furthermore, Deloria, Wildcat, and Cobern's work provide useful points of comparison with multicultural education research that has been influential in shaping the multicultural content of curriculum. It is true that multicultural research in education identifies the need to bring student's particular worldviews and epistemologies into the classroom. It does not, however, identify how the metaphysical understandings behind worldviews influence student learning. Moreover, because multicultural education is firmly embedded within the cultural archive of Western metaphysics, much of the discourses, practices, and research maintains Western metaphysics, thereby excluding other worldview systems. In this regard, ethno-science education research is at the forefront of this metaphysical challenge because it is beginning to engage these basic metaphysical dynamics. Yet, in the United States, Western perceptions of the world continue to dominate orientations toward education. If Indians and non-Indians are potentially coming from such different perspectives of the world, what does this mean for indigenous students within Western education? How do we begin to confront this more foundational ignorance in the conceptualization and implementation of education in the United States?

Scholars such as Mills, Tuana, and Sullivan have laid out a framework for beginning to articulate ignorance in contemporary society. However, this work only begins to get at the tip of the iceberg. The issue is more foundational—it is one of worldviews. For indigenous peoples, the legacy of Western metaphysics is more than a mere set of ineffectual ideas and values; to the contrary, the legacy of Western metaphysics locates and reproduces itself in institutions, communities, families and individuals. As Maori scholar Linda Smith (2002) points out, ideas are made real by specific "systems of knowledge, the formation of culture, and the relations of power in which these concepts are located" (p. 48). Smith explains: "The individual, as the basic social unit from which other social organizations and social relations form, is another system of ideas which needs to be understood as part of the West's cultural archive" (p. 49).

In previous research, I mapped out the key components of Western metaphysics, focusing on concepts identified by Deloria in order to explore how these orientations shape ideology and structure in relation to education (Calderón, 2008). Here, however, I am interested in examining how Western metaphysics institutionalizes epistemologies of ignorance in ways that appear controversial. Deloria's work, for instance, is useful in illuminating the entanglement of Western metaphysics with Judeo-Christian ideas. This argument is not unique to Deloria as others have explored how, for instance, Western modern science and Judeo Christian ideas are intertwined (Rubenstein, 2003). Hence, if we are to begin to deconstruct the cultural archive of Western metaphysics it "depend[s] upon the manner," as Deloria (1979) suggests, "in which we examine the general conceptions of reality held by Western peoples rather than upon a precise knowledge of what the most advanced thinkers have intuited" (p. 19). In order to do this, Deloria (1979) turns to "the religious and philosophical beliefs traditionally held in Western civilization" (p. 19). I contend that this aspect also represents one of the most challenging features of Deloria's work because it touches upon deeply held and internalized belief systems; indeed, it touches upon the foundations of epistemologies of ignorance.

For example, the foundational components of metaphysics Deloria identifies—time, place, reality and being—are culturally and institutionally enacted and understood differently by Western and indigenous peoples. In the West, for instance, the metaphysics of time, place, reality, and being produce particular ideas such as linearism, separation between humanity and nature, and the object status of geographies. In turn these paradigms produced specific types of knowledge forms and approaches, such as the discipline of history. Returning to my previous research on social studies textbook I found that "history as chronology is the major form of historical master narrative developed in the west, and ... chronology, or linearism are central concepts of Western metaphysics" (Calderón, 2008, p. 288). History is a particular knowledge branch of the Western metaphysical approach to time that is based on linearism and progressivism. Both these concepts owe their conceptual development to Greek and Judeo-Christian thought, revealing a deeper ontology that extends extant examinations within epistemologies of ignorance:

> Shepard Krech (2006) explains that Western metaphysical temporality is linear, originating in Judeo-Christian ideas: "Equally well understood are the deep roots of linear time in the West and its importance in ancient Hebrew thought, and the unidirectional teleology of Christianity" (p. 576)..... This construction of temporality produces concepts such as linearism, chronologism, and progressivism. From its Christian and Greek origins, time is constructed as progressive. It is imbued with the belief that the future represents progress over a past that is culture that is heralded with representing and realizing perfection for humanity. Deloria (1992) explains that this particular

product of Western metaphysical views of time, "involves the assumption that time proceeds in a linear fashion; further it assumes that at a particular point in the unraveling of this sequence, the peoples of Western Europe became guardians of the world" (p. 63).

History, as a paradigm in the West is constructed from these particular conceptualizations of temporality. In the west, historical narratives are largely constructed through written texts and function mainly as chronicles of Western peoples exploits (Deloria, 1992), and within the United States, promote settler-state mythologies. In addition, Krech (2006) explains "..that the systems in which literacy is embedded privilege linearity, which either reinforces or undermines extant temporal systems" (p. 576), such as those of indigenous peoples. It is therefore important to expose how the historical narratives favored in social studies curriculum promote narratives that center Western peoples and ideas, thereby marginalizing other knowledge systems. (Calderon, 2008, pp. 101–104)

Applying epistemologies of ignorance to these metaphysical insights is useful. Tuana (2006) describes, for instance, "Another category of ignorance involves topics that *we do not even know that we do not know* because our current interests, beliefs, and theories obscure them" (p. 6). Deloria's work in Western metaphysics challenges this type of ignorance.

Mills (2007) importantly reveals the asymmetry between White ignorance and Black knowledge. Citing Weldon Johnson, Mills draws our attention to the notion that: "colored people of this country know and understand White people better than the White people know and understand them" (p. 17). Wildcat (2001) concurs, adding that indigenous educators use this to benefit Indian communities:

American Indian educators, in particular, unlike their non-Native counterparts, are better prepared and well suited by experience to critically look at the deep roots of Western-inspired institutions and practices. Because of their bi- and often multicultural experience we can and should explore creative ideas and ways of establishing healthier Indian communities and sovereign Indian nations. (Daniel Wildcat, as cited in Wildcat & Deloria, 2001, p. 19)

Mills' (2007) cautions, though, that White ignorance is not confined to White people alone. Similarly indigenous scholars (Deloria, 2006; Smith, 2002), and others (Fanon, 1967) recognize that the process of colonization leads to a type of ignorance, which Deloria identifies as colonization and thus advocates work towards decolonization. However, Tuana (2006) cautions that once the knowledge "we do not even know that we do not know" is identified it can "slip into the previous category of knowing that we do not know but having no interest in coming to know" (p. 6).

I find this condition of ignorance one of the most difficult challenges I face as an educator—people dismissing or not caring about the insights provided by indigenous scholars and communities. Other scholars attempt to address this lack of interest as well as it relates to schooling and democracy but there is still a lot of work to be done in this area (Lomawaima & McCarty, 2002).

CONCLUSION

Clearly, research on epistemologies of ignorance offers much to education as they play a prominent role in producing knowledge and learning. Yet, a critical examination of epistemologies of ignorance alone is not enough. Such a critique must be part of a comprehensive strategy that targets how current educational ideas and forms, including those promoting diversity of thought, perpetuate colonial blind discourses. Indeed, epistemologies of ignorance are reproduced because of the one-dimensional, flattened manner in which knowledge is produced in the West. However, many non-Western communities' lived experiences are situated in a context of relational knowledge as opposed to knowledge production that is one-dimensional and reductive. For example, the No Child Left Behind Act and its affiliated practices continue to promote flattened epistemologies. The challenge is to not simply replace one colonial discourse with another, as this leaves unchallenged the specter of Western metaphysics so many indigenous scholars make explicit in their critiques of Western culture. As Charles Mills (2007) reminds us, the flip side of White ignorance is Black knowledge of White ignorance, or what Du Bois refers to as "double consciousness." Deloria eloquently remarks about the impacts of a type of "double consciousness":

> No matter how well educated an Indian may become, he or she always suspects that Western culture is not an adequate representation of reality. Life therefore becomes a schizophrenic balancing act wherein one holds that the creation, migration and ceremonial stories of the tribe are true and that the Western European view of the world is also true. (p. viii)

The schizophrenia occurs because one perspective assumes a totalizing view of the world, insisting that its version of truth is singular. However, if the Western worldview were to shift, there is hope of a more complex understanding of truth (and its situatedness in particular contexts) and education must play a central role in such a project.

Epistemologies of ignorance offer educators a strong pedagogical opportunity to explore, for instance, historical narratives. We cannot continue to rely on the typical methods offered by NMCE as this simply adds content onto an educational paradigm that relies on ignorance, indeed colonial blind discourses. Social studies curriculum must take seriously the incorporation of comprehensive lessons on tribal sovereignty, including indigenous perspectives. Rather than maintaining disingenuous narratives around American identity, recovering these gaps in knowledge reinserts the complex nature of American identity that one would hope disrupt narrow lessons that maintain intolerance.

NOTES

1. In previous work, I define a colonial ontology as a project that "promotes a hierarchy of being in which settler nation-state citizenship is defined as the dominant form, and the racialized "minority" other is defined as the subordinate. This hierarchy of being is mediated by a number of corollary rights defining the parameters of access to this ontology (such as integration, diversity, and equity), and promoting settler dominance over indigenous groups (doctrine of discovery, federal supremacy, and limited sovereignty) (Calderón, 2009).
2. Colonial blind discourses are analogous to majoritarian narratives identified in critical race theory as "the bundle of presuppositions, perceived wisdoms, and shared cultural understandings persons in the dominant race bring to the discussion of race" (Delgado & Stefancic, 2001, p. 462) .
3. Tribal sovereignty is inherent, not derived from tribes' relationship with the United States. Unlike federal or state sovereign powers, "tribal sovereignty" has a unique cultural and spiritual dimension (Wilkins, 2002, p. 48).
4. Without a doubt, the transnational nature of many immigrant communities is also not served by NMCE.
5. There are exceptions to this, but for the sake of this chapter, I will focus on the majority trends in Indian Country.
6. I purposely use the concept epistemo-ontological, as opposed to traditional Western divisions between epistemology and ontology.

REFERENCES

Anzaldua, G. (1987). *Borderlands, la frontera: the new mestiza* (1st ed.). San Francisco, CA: Aunt Lute Books.

Aristotle. (1966). *Metaphysics*. Bloomington, IN: Indiana University Press.

Banks, J. A. (2004). Multicultural education: historical development, dimensions, and practice. In J. A. Banks & C. A. M. Banks (Eds.), *Handbook of research on multicultural education* (2nd ed.). San Francisco, CA: Jossey-Bass, Wiley.

Baumgarten, A. G. (1743). *Metaphysics* (2nd ed.). Halae, Magdeburgicae: Hemmerde.

Beaulieu, D., Sparks, L., & Alonzo, M. (2005). *Preliminary report on no child left behind in indian country*. Washington, DC: National Indian Education Association.

Bhabha, H. K. (2004). *The location of culture*. New York, NY: Routledge.

Bonilla-Silva (2001). *White supremacy and racism in the post-civil rights era*. Boulder, CO: Lynne Reinner.

Cajete, G. (1994). *Look to the mountain: an ecology of indigenous education*. Skyland, France: Kivaki Press.

Calderón, D. (2006a). Developing critical interstitial methodology: taking greater control over our resistance. In B. Kozuh, R. Kahn, A. Kozlowska & P . Krope (Eds.), *Description and explantation in educational and social research*. Czestochowa, Poland: Rodn "WOM" Publishers.

Calderón, D. (2006b). One-dimensionality and whiteness. *Policy Futures in Education, 4*(1), 73–82.

Calderón, D. (2008). *Indigenous metaphysics: challenging western knowledge organization in social studies curriculum*. Doctoral Disseration, University of California, Los Angeles.

Calderon, D., (2009). Multicultural education as colonial education?: Indigenous disruptions of "colonial-blind" discourses. In A. Kempf (Ed), *Breaching the colonial contract: Anti-colonialism in the U.S. and Canada* (pp. 53–78). New York, NY: Springer.

Champagne, D. (2005). Education, culture and nation building: development of the tribal learning community and educational exchange. In D. Champagne & I. Abu-Saad (Eds.), *Indigenous and minority education: international perspectives on empowerment*. Beer-Shiva, Israel: Negev Center for Regional Development.

Champagne, D. (2007, January 19). Self-governenment's roots: communities. *Indian Country Today* [Electronic version]. Retrieved from http://www .indiancountrytoday.com/archive/28208114.html

Cobern, W. W. (1988). *"World view" theory and misconception research*. Paper presented at the National Association for Research in Science Teaching, Lake of the Ozarks, MO.

Council on Interracial Books for Children. (1977). *Stereotypes distortions and omissions in U. S. history textbooks*. New York, NY: Racism and Sexism Resource Center for Educators.

Delgado, R., & Stefancic, J. (2001). *Critical race theory: An introduction*. New York, NY: New York University Press.

Delgado-Bernal, D., & Villalpando, O. (2002). An apartheid of knowledge in academia: the struggle over the "legitimate" knowledge of faculty of color. *Equity and Excellence in Education, 35*(2), 169–180.

Deloria, V. (1979). *Metaphysics of modern existence*. San Francisco, CA: Harper's.

Deloria, V. (1994). *Indian education in America: Eight essays by Vine Deloria, Jr.* (2nd ed.). Boulder, CO: American Indian Science & Engineering Society

Deloria, V. (1992). *God is red: a native view of religion*. Golden, CO: Fulcrum.

Deloria, V. (2002). *Evolution, creationism, and other modern myths*. Golden, CO: Fulcrum.

Deloria, V. (2006). *The world we used to live in: Remembering the powers of the medicine men*. Golden, CO: Fulcrum.

Deloria, V., & Wildcat, D. (2001). *Power and place: Indian education in America*. Golden, CO: Fulcrum Resources.

Du Bois, W. E. B. (1903). *The souls of Black folk*. Chicago. IL: A. C. McClurg.

Equal Employment Opportunity Act of 1972, 42 U.S.C. 2000e-16.

Fanon, F. (1967). *Black skin, white masks*. New York, NY: Grove Press.

Freeman, C.,&Fox, M. (2005). *Status and trends in the education of American indians and Alaska natives*. Washington, DC: U.S. Department of Education, National Center for Education Statisticso. Document Number.

Gay, G. (2004). Curriculum theory and multicultural education. In J. A. Banks & C. A. M. Banks (Eds.), *Handbook of research on multicultural education*. San Francisco, CA: Wiley.

Grube, G. M. A. (1966). *Plato's thought*. Boston, MA: Beacon Press.

Harding, S. (1997). Is there a feminist method? In S. Kemp & J. Squires (Eds.), *Feminisms*. Oxford, England: Oxford University Press.

Hill-Collins, P. H. (1997). Toward an Afrocentric Feminist Epistemology. In S. Kemp & J. Squires (Eds.), *Feminisms*. Oxford, England: Oxford University Press.

Hurtado, A. (2003). Theory in the flesh: toward an endarkened epistemology. *Qualitative Studdies in Education, 16*(2), 215–225.

Krech, S. (2006). Bringing linear time back in. *Ethnohistory, 53*(3), 567–593.

Lipsitz, G. (1998). *The possessive investment in whiteness: How white people profit from identity politics*. Philadelphia, PA: Temple University Press.

Lomawaima, K. T., & McCarty, T. L. (2002). When tribal sovereignty challenges democracy: American indian education and the democratic ideal. *American Educational Research Journal, 39*(2), 279–305.

Lomawaima, K. T., & McCarty, T. L. (2006). *To remain and indian: lessons in democracy from a century of native American education*. New York, NY: Teachers College Press.

Lukose, R. A. (2007). The difference that diaspora makes: thinking through the anthropology of immigrant education in the United States. *Anthropology & Education Quarterly, 38*(4), 405–418.

Marcuse, H. (1991). *One-dimensional man* (2nd ed.). Boston, MA: Beacon Press.

McLaren, P., & Farahmandpur, R. (2005). *Teaching against global capitalism and the new imperialism: a critical pedagogy*. New York, NY: Rowman & Littlefield.

Mill, C. (1997). *The racial contract*. Ithaca, NY: Cornell University.

Mills, C. W. (1999). *The racial contract*. Ithica, NY: Cornell University Press.

Mills, C. W. (2007). White ignorance. In S. Sullivan & N. Tuana (Eds.), *Race and epistemologies of ignorance*. Albany, NY: SUNY Press.

Morton v. Mancari, 417 U.S. 535 (1974).

Outlaw, L. (2007). Social ordering and the systemic production of igno-rance. In S. Sullivan & N. Tuana (Ed.), *Race and epistemologies of ignorance* (pp. 197–212). Albany, NY: University of New York Press.

Parker, L., & Stovall, D. O. (2004). Actions following words: Critical race theory connects to critical pedagogy. *Educational Philosophy and Theory, 36*(2), 167–182.

Plato. (1992). *Republic* (G. M. A. Grube, Trans.). Indianapolis, IN: Hackett.

Pratt, S., (2006). Persons in place: The agent ontology of Vine Deloria, Jr. *APA Newsletter on American Indians in Philosophy, 6*(1), 4–9.

Reynolds, J. (2005, April 8). Problems outweigh goals of no child left behind. *Indian Country Today*, p. 1.

Rubenstein, R. E. (2003). *Aristotle's children: How Christians, Muslims, and Jews rediscovered ancient wisdom and illuminated the middle ages*. San Diego, CA: A Harvest Book/Harcourt.

Senese, G. (1991). *Self-determination and the social education of native Americans*. New York, NY: Praeger.

Sleeter, C. E., & Grant, C. A. (1991). Race, class, gender, and disability in current textbooks. In M. A. Apple&L. K. Christian-Smith (Eds.), *The politics of the textbook*. New York, NY: Routledge.

Smith, L. T. (2002). *Decolonizing methodologies: Research and indigenous peoples*. New York, NY: Zed Books.

Solórzano, D. G. (1998). Critical race theory, race and gender microaggressions, and the experience of Chicana and Chicano scolars. *Qualitative Studies in Education, II*(1), 121–136.

Sullivan, S., & Tuana, N. (Eds.). (2007). *Race and epistemologies of ignorance*. Albany, NY: State University of New York Press.

Tuana, N. (2004). Coming to understand: Orgasm and the epistemology of ignorance. *Hypatia, 19*(1), 194–232.

Tuana, N. (2006). The speculum of ignorance: the women's health movement and epistemologies of ignorance. *Hypatia, 21*(3), 1–19.

Williams, R. A., (1986). The algebra of federal Indian law: the hard trail of decolonizing and Americanizing the White man's Indian jurisprudence. *Wisconsin Law Review, 1*, 210–299

Villalpando, O., & Bernal, D. D. (2002). A critical race theory analysis of barriers that impede the success of faculty of color. In W. A. Smith, P. G. Altbach & K. Lomotey (Eds.), *The racial crisis in American higher education: continuing challenges for the twenty-first century* (pp. 243–269). New York, NY: State University of New York Press.

Wilkins, D. E. (2002). *American Indian politics and the American political system*. Oxford, England: Rowman & Littlefield.

CHAPTER 7

SUFFERING WITH

Seven Moments of Ignorance

Alexandra Fidyk

Suffering With: Seven Moments of Ignorance
To relieve ourselves of suffering, we must learn the path of bringing
suffering to the forefront.

—Reverend Soun Hoshi

Psychoanalysis may indeed relieve suffering, but only in Zen-like fashion: not by
trying to suffer less, but by submitting to what life is about.

—Michael Guy Thompson

In Jung's words, a great deal of our suffering is neurotic, or unnecessary, suffering.
Both Buddhism and depth psychology recognize that to let go of one's obsessions, and
to break through them so that they no longer constitute the world, is a way to suffer
less and be freer.

—Polly Young-Eisendrath

Epistemologies of Ignorance in Education, pp. 129–165
Copyright © 2011 by Information Age Publishing
All rights of reproduction in any form reserved

"Knowledges and pleasures are complexly interrelated," Tuana (2004) argues in her study of the science of sexuality (p. 225). Here she and other feminist health activists named "epistemologies of ignorance" in a radical move to uncover the "ways women's bodies had been ignored," to examine knowledge that has been withheld from women and some men, to reclaim knowledges that had been suppressed or denied, and to develop new knowledge untethered to traditional frameworks (Tuana, 2006, p. 2). She extends her argument of the value of such epistemologies and their contribution to the women's health movement by making a case that epistemologies of ignorance are integral to resistance movements. In outlining a taxonomy of ignorance Tuana (2006) emphasizes that *we need the ability partially to translate practices of ignorance among very different—and power-differentiated—communities. Ignorance like knowledge is situated*" (p. 3). It is this situatedness that I would like to address.

Tuana (2004, 2006) Harding (2006), Ortega (2006), and Britzman (1995) in their attention to epistemologies of ignorance question knowledge claims, particularly what criteria is used to distinguish between knowledge and nonknowledge. They point rightly to the values and assumptions concerning goals from which knowledge and ignorance production arise. Their critique, while necessary for some kinds of knowledge production and for the empowerment of marginalized voices, fails to consider the ontological framework within which such knowledge lives. Indeed, these authors speak of epistemologies as if there is only one ontological perspective. Harding (2006), on the one hand, brings Freud and the role of the unconscious into the discussion, but she withdraws the importance of the unconscious and contends that Freudian accounts are still, for the most part, "grounded in suspect biological theories" and "tend to essentialize Western, bourgeois values and lifestyles" (p. 23). In making any knowledge claim, it is not only a matter of appeal to logical and universal rules, since all knowledge claims involve justification, but also a matter of social arena. Claims are justified within contexts of collectively held conceptions about the world, and how to relate to them and know them. These underlying conceptions are embodied in particular epistemologies. Still today the most powerful conceptions are those of empiricist epistemology although those of postmodernism (wherein the subject is decentred, enmeshed in the "text" of the word, constituted in intersubjectivity, discourse and language) run rival in many disciplines especially in the academe. One implication of the methods (tools for data collection) of any epistemology is as much a matter of politics—power—as it is of logic (Usher, 1996).

Ontology, then—what is the nature of the world—directly shapes the ways that we come to know and cannot know, and, indeed, connects to axiological considerations of what knowledge is worth knowing.

Epistemological and ontological questions are inherently related since claims about what exists in the world or universe imply claims about how what exists may be known. Epistemologies of ignorance, thus far, have been locked within a worldview that sees knowledge as producible, reproducible, and to a degree, controllable. Whether modern, or its antithesis, postmodern, these worldviews are complimentary but often in discourse, modernity values the singular and postmodernity the multiple, but neither values both, nor recognizes the other as part of each other's position. To situate oneself in a worldview that includes and values the unconscious, transpersonal, transgenerational, transspecies, feeling, imaginal, and emergent dimensions is to radically reconsider the ways that we come to know and thereby what we know. Such a worldview has been named integral (Gebser, 1984; Wilber, 1982) or post-post-modern (Shaker, forthcoming; Shaker & Heilman, 2008) in Western cultures. Further, if one includes ways of knowing such as contemplative practice, active imagination,[1] and knowing fields,[2] then the methods of collecting and representing such knowledge change as well. These ways of representation challenge the use of language, methods, and structures of both thinking and writing.

In other words, methods are embedded in commitments to particular versions of the world (an ontology) and ways of knowing that world (an epistemology). Method is, thus, inseparable from epistemology and ontology. And every ontology and epistemology is itself historically located, culturally specific, and value-laden. In writing from within Zen Buddhist and Jungian perspectives, it is the intention of this chapter to locate the reader in a different version of the world than what has been heretofore illustrated in discussions of epistemologies of ignorance and the studies of limits in education. The world, herein, is organic, paradoxical, minded, alive, and inclusive of its own values. Such relocation asks the reader not only to be open to the new but also to suspend the expectation of a text written in a single, linear, cumulative fashion with a definitive conclusion. Another reading of the world invites other forms of representation; using a method that challenges the dominant structure of organization and use of language, the text invites the reader to become engaged with a different way of knowing through circumambulation—a form of spiraling both inward and outward toward greater inclusion and complexity. Composed as moments, I highlight images, ideas, and processes of knowledge/ignorance inherent to these two perspectives; they offer another worldview that is at once individual and unique (relative, particular, phenomenal), as well as, simultaneously interconnected and interdependent (universal, collective, noumenal).

Ignorance here is understood as a conscious and unconscious agreement not to know as supported by "very different and power-differentiated" groups. These moments, part of the internal structures of Zen

Buddhism and Jungian psychotherapy, birth new knowledge, possess a memory, unfold creatively and place the fecund case of suffering into the dynamic relationship with "knowledges and pleasures." They redress the opening sentence: Knowledges and pleasures *and* suffering are complexly interrelated. In this view suffering engenders a deepening of life into our pains and our pleasures, our terrors and our delights.

Education stemming from a Western worldview located in modern and postmodern perspectives, in general, sees knowledge as a commodity, a tool to control or wield power. Its worth is assessed by its material or political use. From the overarching empirical position, education's core values are monotheism, dualism and progress. Rarely is knowledge related to one's being, by extension, one's action and nonaction (*wu-wei*). Suffering, a condition inherent to being human and experienced in multiple forms in our schools, is seen as a problem— something to avoid, annihilate, deny, repress—and is often treated with behavior modification or pharmaceuticals. Rather than looking at our "humanness" where disease, sadness, illness and death are "normal" natural conditions; they are seen as states that need correction. This perspective runs amok in the widely polarized view of "Be Happy"— the new mantra for summer camps where students are taught skills to pursue happiness and positive thinking. Many new therapies, most notably cognitive behavioral therapy (CBT), have had great success in obtaining crucial healthcare funding because they are in accord with the "techno-scientific mind-set" that dominates government, medical professions, and schools (Colman, 2009, p. 21). While CBT does "restore people's *functioning*," its quick and effective relief of symptoms does not seek wellness, balance or wisdom (p. 22). It aims to restore happiness—the assumed natural condition—to which we aspire. Analyst Colman (2009), however, suggests that the online CBT character, Noproblemo, of the Mood Gym program designed to prevent depression,

> will never grow or develop. And it is exactly his well-adjusted contentment that will limit the depth and meaning of his experience of life. He may be happy, he may be a decent and loving person, but he will never be wise. And this is because wisdom can only be achieved through *suffering*. "Wisdom grows up in strife".... This I think brings us close to the essential difference between analysis and other forms of therapy whose aim is the relief of pain. Our aim is not to relieve pain but to transform it, to show the patient a way to suffer their [*sic*] pain so that something creative and compassionate might be made of it. *Deo concedente*, as Jung says, the patient comes to a deeper and ultimately more satisfying, more fulfilling involvement in life. (p. 22)

Here, in a worldview that seeks to deny "negative thinking," "unpleasant" emotions and symptoms—the shadow side of humanity—both personal and collective, has no place.

Particular to this invitation to and praise for suffering is the current global situation. The extensive violence in the world, rationalized through political ideologies and/or religious belief systems (including secularism —all of which are supporting and supported by education), contributes to human and ecological (both flora and fauna) suffering and represents contemporary manifestations with extensive life and death implications. In what ways are these global and local conditions appearing in the bodies and minds of students, classrooms and communities? How might other images, ways of being and knowing offer ways to perceive and address suffering differently? Further, might our ability to move through and beyond different ontological positions affect the way we approach, in our daily lives, the other, as well as violence, in education, political, cultural, and economic events?

What are offered here to address epistemologies of ignorance are just two possibilities from a different ontological position. Each perspective, however, has been dismissed in education. And yet, I propose these perspectives are capable of contributing significantly to individual transformation and thus social change. They might be described using one of Tuana's (2006) categories of ignorance—"we do not even know that we do not know because our current interests, beliefs, and theories obscure them" (p. 6). However, each runs counter to the assumption that knowledge is produced by us separate from the rest of the world (Tuana, 2004, 2006). Knowledge arises, appears, unfolds, disappears, and dies in conjunction with all life. In this way, knowledge is not just a case of "turn[ing] inside out and upside down" as in the case of revealing and privileging women's genitalia (Irigaray, as cited in Tuana, 2004, p. 199) for such flesh is still visible, touchable and belongs to a tangible world. How does one come to privilege knowledge that emerges from a universe that has a mind and works in conjunction with other intangible forces?

With that said, there remains the inescapable importance of understanding social, cultural, and historical location in the terminology used to describe various Zen Buddhist and even Jungian concepts to Western readers. These moments, however, when known intimately, not as information to be retold, but understanding to be integrated into oneself, thereby altering one's consciousness and action, have the power to release one from suffering. This rendering of knowledge and ignorance values complexity, interconnectedness and inclusion toward greater wholeness and freedom (such wholeness is fleeting and degenerates to regenerate).

I ask the reader to suspend judgment and allow each moment to reshape the currently held view of the universe. Imagine: what does this way of knowing mean for what one knows, how one knows, and how one does or does not act? What is offered, then, are seven moments central to another ontological perspective (post-postmodern or integral). When positioned alongside current discourse on epistemologies of ignorance and the current limits of education, they have the potential to radically transform relationships and shift one's understanding and experience of suffering—*dukkha* (see Figure 7.1).

For I am knowledge and ignorance.
I am shame and boldness.
I am shameless; I am ashamed.
I am strength and I am fear (Robinson, 1990).

Figure 7.1.   Image of Jung's mandala. Retrieved from http://www.netreach. net/~nhojem/mandala.htm

A COMMENTARY

When I was a teenager, I came close to death on more than one occasion. In many ways I was an "at-risk kid," not because my teachers failed me (Haberman, 1995), and not because my parents were divorced or of minority status; rather, I suffered greatly. Even though I grew up in an extended family, was involved in school activities, and was a good student, I was both involved in and witness to pain, aggression, and violence. The way that I read and reacted to these events was expressed through "reckless behavior."

Twenty years ago when living in Japan, I discovered and began studying Zen Buddhism. More recently I completed Jungian psychotherapy
training, a journey which began in the study of Eastern philosophy and
the readings of T. S. Eliot, Marion Woodman, and Laurens van der Post
to name a few. Both Zen Buddhism and Jungian psychotherapy have allowed me to see how human suffering[3] rooted in ignorance can teach us
compassion, once we come to understand the meaning of our own suffering. This learning has revisioned my own suffering and reshaped my
orientation to life—enriching my practice as both a teacher and a therapist. We can be liberated from suffering, but it requires a "letting go" of
attachments, and/or a descent into one's psyche, accompanied by a shift
in consciousness. Both ways of knowing are not seriously entertained as
credible forms of knowledge within current systems of education.

Suffering, more accurately translated from Buddhism as discontent or
dis-ease, comes from the Sanskrit term *dukkha* and refers to a vast range
of phenomena, from the inevitable aspects of illness, decline and death
to the ordinary discontent of everyday life. It refers to conditions of life,
not merely a subjective situation; *dukkha* arises from natural processes and
crosses the self/subjective and other/objective realms of human reality. Etymologically, *dukkha* is composed of the prefix *jur* (bad) and the root *kha*
meaning "the hole in the nave of a wheel through which the axis runs"
(Mornier-Williams as cited in Spiegelman & Miyuki, 1994, p. 118). The
terms convey a metaphor that sheds insight on what it means to be a human being, literally, to be out of balance or in a state of being off-center,
like a wheel riding off its axle. This off-centeredness is most often experienced as irritability, "negativity," restlessness or being "out of the flow."
The teaching of *dukkha* stems from the Buddha's experience of life and
has become the basis of much Buddhist doctrine.

Essential to the Buddha's teaching are the Four Noble Truths, which
are concerned with the belief that no one can change life itself, but that
we have the ability to change our perspective and reorient ourselves to
the nature of *dukkha*. The First Noble Truth states all life is suffering.
The Second tells that *dukkha* arises because we are attached to particular
outcomes, such as an A-average. The Third Noble Truth describes an alternative perspective to concrete reality (First Noble Truth) that is called
emptiness (*sunyata*), arising when we loosen our attachments to desiring
that life unfold according to personal projections, values, and expectations. The methods to attain such emptiness and *nirvana*, the Fourth Noble Truth, are outlined as the Noble Eightfold Path, namely, right speech,
right action, right livelihood (these three comprise ethical conduct), right
effort, right awareness, right concentration (these comprise mindfulness),
right thought and right understanding (this stage of wisdom, *samadhi*, includes the previous two). Right (*samma*), in this context, means "in the

right way," "straight," not bent or crooked; right extends from love and compassion (*metta*), and the action is beneficial to both self and collective, while not in the promotion of the ego (Fidyk, 2008). For example, right livelihood signifies work, which like right action, does not result in intentional harm to others, including ecological systems and animals.

Contemporary psychological research on "flow experience" (Csikszentmihalyi, 1993), understood as "engaged, unselfconscious activity that eliminates the experience of a separate self," reflects the possibilities as described by the Third Noble Truth (Young-Eisendrath, 2002, p. 72). When we are no longer attached to things, we move with the flow of life. If much of our suffering originates from projecting our own desired outcomes into the flow of life, rather than surrendering to its unfolding (as in nonattachment), we create fear, a sense of separateness and a limited repertoire of possibilities. Once in this limiting position, the potential to move back into the flow can be attained through the knowledge inherent in the Third and Fourth Noble Truths. Knowledge that addresses our basic habits of mind is valuable and essential in education.

Currently, in Western education knowledge that is privileged belongs only to the perspective of the First Noble Truth. Furthermore, Jungian thought from Western analytic psychology, brings another perspective to the limits of education. In each given moment there may be multiple dynamics, conscious and unconscious, interplaying among members of the classroom that cannot be explained by causal relations. Our beingness, our human condition, is shaped by both our conscious and unconscious orientation to the world. For instance, our psychological complexes, unknown to the ego, frame our habitual mentations that develop early in our relationships and become the hook for our personal emotional patterns of reaction and defense. Complexes, a given emotional condition of being human, are "driving forces in generating and regenerating images of self and others, through distortions and delusions of fear and desire, dominance and submission, and power and weakness" (Young-Eisendrath, 2002, p. 73).

A complex, from a Jungian perspective, is the "image of a certain psychic situation which is strongly accentuated emotionally and is, moreover, incompatible with the habitual attitude of consciousness" (Jung, CW[4] 8, par. 201). It develops through archetypes or inborn patterns of thought and behavior that are common across culture and history. Archetypes are the natural tendencies to form coherent, emotionally charged images in states of arousal wherein regularities occur. There are "types of *situations* and types of *figures* that repeat themselves frequently and have a corresponding meaning" such as Mother, Father, Child, Teacher and Student (Jung, CW 9i, par. 309). They organize our perceptual and emotional patterns, at first adapting to the conditions into which we are born and later are projected onto others in our families, at school and in our daily encounters. Nowhere is this multilayered, multidirectional dynamic more apparent than in the classroom where a child's orientation to his or her teacher and classmates may reconstitute the home patterning. "Negative" experiences from childhood are particularly potent. For example, if a child was treated aggressively by a sibling or a parent, that child will have a strong tendency to recreate both the roles of victim and aggressor, at times identifying with one and projecting the other, and at other times, reversing the pattern. Complexes hijack thoughts and actions, dictating the perception and experience of an event.

Furthermore, both the complexes of the unconscious and the ego complex of conscious awareness can bring about a sense of off-centeredness through defensive emotional patterning. The ego complex forms around the core of an archetype of self, that universal human tendency to form a sense of "me"—a coherent image of being an individual, an embodied subject who exists over time. Forming around age two in normal development, the ego complex can be triggered by self-conscious emotions such as embarrassment, envy, greed, shame, pride, self-pity, and guilt in addition to fear and desire. From this age on, we experience ourselves as separated and isolated from others and the world; herein lies the root of subject-object duality. Believing that we are separate and unto one's own, masks both knowledge and ways of acting in the world that stem from a deep sense of interrelatedness. Rarely, however, are the insights of complexes offered by depth psychologies, understood as energies at work in students' behaviors in the classroom or on the playground. The reaction of the teacher or classmate may lack understanding of unseen and unconscious aspects at play in that child's actions or words. Such repetitive patterns—often part of bullying—can be understood through methods belonging to both Buddhism and psychotherapy, other ways of knowing, which to a great extent, have been ignored, even banned, from teacher training and education in general.

In what follows, seven moments of ignorance within Zen Buddhism and Jungian psychotherapy are highlighted. While representative of two systems of a different order—Buddhism belonging to the field of philosophical-spiritual meaning systems, and psychotherapy to the field of psychological-medical treatment—there is a significant conceptual overlap between the two fields. While one is old and the other relatively young, Buddhism and the wider purview of psychoanalysis belong to Wisdom Traditions (Miller, 2002). While neither grand narratives nor theories of everything, they both aim to understand suffering and how it may be ended. Both invite their followers to explore the depths of psyche, exhorting them to confront the challenging psychological experiences that arise during any in-depth exploration of mental process (Miller, 2002). The attention herein is not a comparison between the two discourses. While there are many similarities, there, too, remain many differences and certainly misunderstandings. What is critical is the way educators, researchers, administrators, and policy makers think about teaching/learning, and curriculum/pedagogy (includes methods); we must become informed by other epistemologies, but more importantly, by other ontologies and cosmologies.

SEVEN MOMENTS

Interconnectedness and Impermanence

The universe is an interconnected web where we are always participators in what is and what unfolds. At the subatomic level, quantum mechanics has provided evidence to support the experience and knowledge that time and space become a continuum; matter and energy interchange; observer and observed interact. Such knowledge is not limited to quantum mechanics but foundational to Wisdom Traditions, Zen Buddhism and Jungian thought (see Lindorff, 2004; Meier, 2001). The unity and interrelationship of all phenomena and the intrinsically dynamic nature of the universe can be experienced in the body through simple meditation, *bhavana*, which best translates as "mental development," for instance (Epstein, 1996, p. 195). As more sophisticated instruments have advanced the sciences, more sophisticated methods of consciousness exploration have evolved, finding parallels to understandings derived from the Eastern meditative traditions and their precise applications of methods for examining inner states of consciousness. This web of relations of matter, energy and information suggests that there is no separateness in consciousness and manifested form. This view directly contrasts Cartesian and Newtonian thought, which promotes dualistic thinking and dominates much of education. Its dynamic nature prevents permanence; all things are constantly changing. For both animate and inanimate entities, life is inescapably connected, so our full self (which includes multiple selves, seeing other as self, and an overarching Self), extends beyond the boundaries of our skin. Indeed, our skin breathes, lives and dies— transforms on an ongoing basis. We codependently arise with all entities in the universe; we are interbeings. Jung called this the *unus mundus* or interconnected dependency. Such interconnectedness does not exclude individuality. The "one" is not subsumed by the collective as formations are unique, and separate, yet fluid, continuously degenerating and regenerating, and not containing or restricting new relationships or formations (Fidyk, 2008, 2010).

We, as a species, are not defined by human fellowship but by the subtle and essential interdependency with animals, insects and landscape. The web is inclusive not only of our immediate surroundings, our geology and biology, but also of space and time. Seen in this way, consciousness becomes the epiphenomenon. South African Jungian analyst Ian McCallum (2005) reminds us of our molecular origins to our geology, to those first cellular membranes and to the eventual expression of a species capable of reflecting upon itself. He writes:

> The animals, then, are in us and with us; we share their genes and their juices. Made up of countless molecules, cells and complex organs, each one of us is the carrier not only of the pattern of embryonic gill slits and tails, but the entire history of life also. It would appear that the aboriginal "water of life" still circulates in the blood of every animal, including us. (p. 65)

This image of the web, then, applies to all elements and creatures that came before and continues to evolve along with us, giving life transspecies and transgenerational qualities. Further, all phenomena exist in a patterned universe, one with an underlying primal source to which "I" am connected. This relationship in Eastern and Wisdom Traditions is typically known intuitively and not something rationalized or intellectualized. Consider the words of Lao Tzu, in the *Tao te Ching*, the ancient roots of Buddhism: "The Tao that can be named is not the eternal Tao." While intangible and not readily expressed in language, poetry and metaphor permit proximity.

> The Tao is like a well:
> used but never used up.
> It is like the eternal void:
> filled with infinite possibilities. (Lao, 1963, #4)

This eternal *Tao*, a unifying principle in the universe to which everything relates, underlies the major Eastern religions—Hinduism, Buddhism, Confucianism, *Tao* philosophy and Zen, and is akin to Jung's notion of the Self.[5]

Self and Subjectivity

Connection and unity do not exclude the perception of subjectivity; subjectivity is not bound to separation-individuation as it is in the Western mind that underlies most curricula and even epistemologies of ignorance. In Buddhism, one cultivates a form of non-self-centered subjectivity, characterized by attention, mindfulness and tuning in to the other as well as to oneself. Often misunderstood is the statement, "You have no self," the intent is not to deny or reject the self but to recognize the self-representation as *representation*, as a concept without existence of its own. Returning to the earlier example of the child treated unfairly by his sibling, he most likely plays out both sides of the dynamic—victim and aggressor—in different situations, identifying with both positions as part of who he is. By learning that he is not his reactive self, he can come into relation with his own internal processes. In a state of not having to react he can begin to be. With practice he can distill this reacting self from the core experience where the nonself dwells. Through different techniques, including bare attention, he eventually touches a state of unconditioned openness where he may turn to the other with a similar attentiveness rather than a charged emotional state. In other words, his "I" is not his "ego" or his desires to compete, achieve or possess. These desires are only outward representations of a psychological state; they are not the core of his being. So this idea of dissolution of the self or ego means dissolution of self-centric-ness not of the ego itself. The ego by attending unconscious material becomes replenished and comes to selfhood (Spiegelman & Miyuki, 1994). Individuation, is a term used by Jung "to denote the process by which a person becomes a psychological 'in-dividual', that is, separate, indivisible unity or 'whole' " (172).

To state it another way, it is to become aware of one's multiples yet to hold them together in an un-divided fashion where there is an inner integrity and an outer cohesion; "the Self [has] a predisposition to unity and coherence within the context of multiplicity and diversity in inner and outer life" (Young-Eisendrath, 1997, p. 58). This notion of self is very different than typical notions of the Western ego whereby one "adds to" it as in cumulative growth, or one becomes as if by will, or self remains stable and eternal as in an essentialist position—in each of these beliefs, development ceases when the goal is reached. Indeed, it was reading Richard Wilhelm's translation of the Chinese text the *I Ching* that confirmed for Jung that psychological development is not linear but circular. Accordingly, there is no linear evolution; "there is only circumambulation of the self. Uniform development exists, at most, only at the beginning; later, everything points toward the center" (Wilhelm, 1967, pp. 196–197).

In the Jungian perspective, "self," in general, is understood as a central organizer in the psychological space of every human being, from which our subjectivity *and* its accompanying "otherness" emerge. Philosopher Charles Taylor (1989) says something similar. Individual subjectivity means dependence upon others: "One is a self only among other selves. A self can never be described without reference to those who surround it" (p. 35). Consistency, coherence and continuity in the experience of the self are vital. Lacking self-coherence or self-esteem is problematic for development (as is overzealous self-esteem). Self can be seen as the representation of a function of coherence, agency and relationship that allows us to perceive ourselves as a single, integrated, subjective embodiment that exists in a fluid and impermanent universe (van Waning, 2002).

The trick is not to create a fixed sense of self (a fixed identity) as is typically done with "things," but to hold a fluid, impermanent, relational sense of self and a sense of constancy with a core Self. Any sense of a separate self is really paradoxical: self and no-self. This shift in self-concept—conceptually, emotionally, experientially—is what makes Buddhist teachings and psychotherapeutic practices effective; it is the aim in attending *dukkha*. Recognition of this paradoxical meaning can be observed in relationship. For example, often when two people meet, each discovers in the context of their relationship how the self-centered, self-conscious subject mistakes the world and others to be separate, passive, external, and permanent. In place of this separateness, a deeper union may exist between two as in a therapeutic or mentor relationship, wherein the two come to see and experience their mutual, fluid self-other constructions that are rooted in the emotions and desires of the moment. Both can see how clearly the ego complex constructs others and the environment to be reflections of its own wishes and needs. In the safe bounds of such a mutual relationship, the two begin to awaken to greater compassion and insight through their knowledge of how suffering is created. The interdependence of such a dyad, as in a close teacher-student, master-disciple, therapist-patient relationship, respects the individuality of each and does not coerce one or the other for the ego's desires. To illustrate Zen Master Dogen explains:

> "The self attains the other" and "the other attains the self" while the self never abandons itself to the psyche of the other. Self and other are not one, and they are not two. If it is possible for the self to attain the other without dissolving its individuality, ... then the traditional concept of a separate self does not apply to our subjectivity.... [And further] self and other are ultimately interdependent; the self does not exist prior to, or outside of, the other; we only have the possibility of experiencing self or other through relationship. (Kopf, as cited in Young-Eisendrath, 2002, p. 75)

When Zen Buddhists and psychotherapists talk about overcoming the ego and, in the latter case, making room for the Self, they mean transforming the way of seeing subjectivity. In other words, Self has to be seen as a transformation of the everyday waking individual—the ego—from a "normal," narrow-minded awareness of itself and its autonomy in consciousness to the realization that there are reaches of the mind (conscious and unconscious, personal and collective) out of its control but essential to its development. And yet, one has to become responsible for one's own subjectivity: do not simply project one's complexes (often negative) onto others; do not blame the world or others for one's suffering; do not attempt to control in someone else that which has been excluded from the self and so on. The aim is not less ego but a reformed ego, less self-sufficient, less centered on controlling perception and experience, more open to the unknown and uncontrollable dimensions of mind and life's emergent properties. The idea of the Self serves to remind the individual that knowledge of life's mysteries begins in awareness of the presence of "greater" forces. It also serves to remind one never to presume that the unknown and uncontrollable workings of the mind can be reduced without remainder to categories of rational meaning, nor to allow the powers of the conscious ego to be swallowed up passively by the nonrational realm of the unconscious. It is significant to note that the "totality of the psyche is not unintelligible, but only *inexhaustibly* intelligible" (Heisig, 2002, p. 52). Epistemologies, here, embrace an unknowability, extending beyond those epistemologies of ignorance that remain certain of what is known and faithful to expansion and accumulation.

Within these complementary, mutually reflective functions of ego and Self, Jung (1961) realized the "cosmic meaning of consciousness" as creator of "objective" culture: once the self-enclosed ego has awakened to its own illusory nature through the wider world of the unconscious, it is able to step from the unconventional view of the world and give "objective" reality to the Self in the world of space and time to "complete creation" by "living out one's myth" (p. 256). In both the *I Ching* and psychotherapy, the goal of the work is directed toward greater consciousness and wholeness (however fleeting), or the realization of the Self as illustrated in Jung's commentary to *The Secret of the Golden Flower*. Here, Jung places "emphasis on *living* the *Tao* (the Self) in all of its paradoxicality rather than only interpreting it intellectually" (Stein, 2005, p. 218).

Synchronicity and Acausal Principle

Both Zen Buddhist and Jungian thought dwell within an image of the unity and interrelationship of all phenomena and the intrinsically dynamic nature of the universe. Herein lives the hermetic law, "As above so below." In other words, the macrocosm is expressed in the microcosm. Jung specifically addressed this relationship, describing synchronistic events as manifestations of the acausal connecting principle, which he also developed through Eastern thought. Indeed, development as circular and synchronicity are two essential ideas that Jung gleaned from the fundamental principles in Indian and Chinese perspectives.

Basic to all Buddhist teachings is the ontological reality of "Interdependent Origination"—no individual can exist in itself alone; it exists by support of everything other than itself or *pratityasamutpada*[6] (*engi* in Japanese) (Spiegelman & Miyuki, 1994). The episteme of such thought is very different from the conceptual mode of Aristotle that explains phenomena by the relationship of cause and effect. While this method has been effectively used predominantly in modern science, medicine, and some branches of psychology, consideration must be given to the limits of education and the problems that stem from the habit of viewing all phenomena in a cause-and-effect mode. Jung's concept of synchronicity, a noncausal principle, belongs to a dynamic world of pattern continuity, interaction, interdependent and spontaneous emergence (not dependent on that which precedes it only). Simplified, synchronicity is the coinciting of events, varying from the dramatic to the commonplace, whereby each event has felt significance. A synchronistic event, too, can be like a premonition or a sense that something is going to happen, something akin to an unexplainable knowing. Like dreams, such events are related to the concerns of the psyche and speak metaphorically about something psychologically important. We are often struck by such happenings and their occurrence points to an invisible, unknown connection; indeed, to a pattern of underlying relationality. In this way, attention is paid to all elements, all relationships of the constituting elements, both dominant and passive or powerful and powerless—the bully and the bullied.

Acknowledging synchronicity, like attending dreams, enriches our inner lives and adds another facet to our awareness, one that extends beyond those offered in modernist and postmodernist paradigms. To understand ourselves, others and events better, we need to receive and process information from metaphoric as well as logical sources. The same is true of imaginal expression or representation through drawing, painting, or dance. Education has become increasingly limited and limiting through its one-sided emphasis on a separate and independent self, linear thinking, and sensory perception. Even epistemologies of ignorance are limited by their situatedness, confined to ways of knowing that are reproducible and reducible. The symbolic, creative and intuitive functions have been forgotten or denied as a valuable way of knowing. An intuitive, feeling (as in value judgments) and affective component are required to appreciate music, art and symbolic experiences, which are vital to the fullness of life. While we need to be cautious not to become fascinated by or engrossed in the symbolic, a balanced approach aims against impoverishment or skewed development.

Synchronicity invites us to participate in the symbolic level where there is underlying meaning, where we share a collective unconscious with life (including our ancestors, homelands and extinct species), where time and space become relative and where, in the course of our everyday lives, we experience a nonordinary reality. Here the space between entities, animate and inanimate, rather than empty, is conjoined by an invisible web, a membrane or a transmission medium. Through synchronicity we experience the intersections of the timeless with time, "where the impossible union of spheres of existence is actual, and where what is inside of us and what is outside of us is unseparated" (Bolen, 2004, p. 48). Wherever synchronistic events occur (although it happens always and in multiples, we may only be consciously aware of it on occasion), the visible and tangible "ten thousand things" are experienced as being aspects of the one, while the invisible matrix, the inexpressible, ineffable, intangible connection, the *Tao* is ever present. Both worlds simultaneously exist; we live in the visible, unfolding and the invisible, enfolding realms simultaneously.

> The great Tao flows everywhere.
> All things are born from it,
> yet it doesn't create them.
> It pours itself into its work,
> yet it makes no claim.
> It nourishes infinite worlds,
> yet it doesn't hold on to them. (Lau, 1963, #34)

For Jung "acausal orderedness," which has many similarities to chaos and systems theories, occurs continuously in nature, but synchronistic events, which are deemed meaningful by the participant, are acts of creation that are noticed at specific moments in time (Jung, CW 8, par. 965). Such orderedness can also be explained by Einstein's theory of general relativity, where space and time are not separate, but are connected and part of a larger whole—a space-time continuum. Physicist David Bohm (1985) adds that *everything* in the universe is part of a continuum. Despite the apparent separateness of things, everything is an extension of everything else, where the implicate and explicate orders blend into each other.[7] In other words, the visible world blurs with the invisible world; at a subatomic level, no separation exists between the manifest and the unmanifest. Likewise, in depth psychology, the conscious blurs with the unconscious; there is no separation.

Collective Unconscious

Jung described the relationship between the collective unconscious and synchronistic events in a letter to Dr. J. B. Rhine, the noted extrasensory perception researcher:

> [the collective unconscious behaves] as if it were one and not as if it were split into many individuals [and manifests itself] not only in human beings but also at the same time in animals and even in physical conditions. (Bolen, 2004, p. 20)

While we each have a personal unconscious composed of forgotten or re-pressed feelings, images and memories, we also are threaded to and draw from deeper layers of the unconscious. This deeper layer, the collective unconscious, Jung considered universal.

Archetypes or innate patterns of behavior manifest as events such as birth and death or as themes of relationship and conflict as portrayed in Greek tragedies, myths or Shakespearian plays. Because they touch a common chord in us, we can say they have universal appeal. Similarly, archetypal figures become activated and clothed with personally derived affective colouration, when an emotional situation develops that corre-sponds to a particular archetype (Bolen, 2004). For example, someone may attend a class by an elderly woman, whose presence and words evoke an emotional response to the archetype of Wise Old Woman. She is, then, experienced as being wise and powerful where every word becomes charged with significance; she becomes numinous. Accepted as Wise Old Woman, what is said is not critically examined. The archetype has become personified—clothed as this particular woman, who is given all the attri-butes of the archetype. In schools we see other archetypal figures mani-fested in teachers, such as the mother, coach, or sage—all are symbolic, recurring figures in dreams, literature, and religion.

When the archetypal level of the collective unconscious is touched in a situation, there is emotional intensity as well as a tendency for symbolic expression. The usual everyday experience becomes altered, enhanced by greater meaning and infused with awe. When charged and active, dream images of great intensity and symbolic meaning may arise, and synchro-nistic events are more likely to be noticed, illustrating again a common connection to the collective unconscious. Through the study of uncon-scious material: dreams, visions and fantasies, Jung conceptualized the Self as an archetype that provides a sense of order and meaning to the personality. The Self is seen as a midpoint related to both the ego and unconscious, equivalent to neither, yet a source of energy that urges us to become who we are, not by linear progression, but by circling back and leaping forward. And yet, while understood as a midpoint, Jung later con-curred with Hisamatsu, a Zen Buddhist and Jungian analyst, that the core self or Self is "without form and substance and is therefore never bound by the ten thousand things"—a no-Self (Young-Eisendrath, 2002, p. 117). Thus, the goal in both psychotherapy and Buddhism is liberation where one is "no longer captivated by the ten thousand things" (p. 116), no lon-ger bound by *dukkha*.

It is important to note that Jung and others believed that modernity engendered a revolutionary self-consciousness in human development, a new awareness that allowed for self-reflection and accountability. Where we exist historically extends from the preceding periods, development and unexpected bursts of creativity—traditional, modern, and postmodern—as does the birth of post-postmodernism. In post-postmodernity, each previous period becomes nested or integrated within it becoming inclusive of the others rather than in opposition to them. On one hand, consciousness has evolved through time; it is a common experience. And, on the other, it has emerged, where consciousness has leapt forth from within gaps of discontinuity (Cambray & Carter, 2004; Johnson, 2002). An example of such emergent consciousness, I expect would accurately describe the experience and life of some youth in schools today. These students may well possess "borderland consciousness"[8] yet their behaviors and thinking most likely are mistaken for symptoms of underlying pathology and, thus, erroneously identified, coded, and treated in our schools. Those with "borderland personality" embody and reflect an evolving psyche that displays *"new psychic forms"* that are entering and affecting the collective Western psyche (Bernstein, 2005, p. 9).

Children's consciousness develops out of the collective unconscious. Emotional life, worries, joys, sufferings, hate, these are present before consciousness fully develops. This development can be read as a mixed blessing for excessive self-consciousness can result in the alienation of the ego from the rest of the Self. All of our complexes, including those that are typically unconscious have a degree of autonomy or intention of their own. For example, one only has to recall a highly charged emotional reaction to an event to realize how "taken over" we can become. Excessive self-consciousness of the ego can lead to the denial of other complexes and their motives, believing that our actions are only the result of conscious intentions (Young-Eisendrath, 2002). Believing thus reinstates causal relations. By being aware of and attending to the relationship between the ego and unconscious complexes, depth psychology offers an alternative to epistemologies of ignorance. Where epistemologies of ignorance shut down, take a position and formulate certainty, thus, limiting themselves, a Jungian perspective, on the other hand, willingly takes on such positions as vital to emergent consciousness.

The universal features of emotion and embodiment encouraged Jung to propose a shared common ground of unconscious experiences in which individuality is embedded. When someone projects an unconscious complex into another, it is likely that the other has had emotional and conceptual experiences for receiving and identifying with that projection. In other words, the projection sticks because there is something to which it clings. The projection of "alien states" onto others is an unintentional invitation to another to enact those concretized states. In hierarchical and intimate relationships, people often project and enact each other's repressed feelings and images, often creating pain and confusion in human relationships (Young-Eisendrath, 2002). Consider such projection unfolding and multiplying within large school populations or university settings where emotions are often not addressed, the body and its inherent knowing denied (later addressed), and the pressure to stay in timed, linear sequence, prevents the address of psychological material. Even the simple acknowledgement that more might be at play than the visibly seen or causally explained may alleviate some suffering of both students and teachers.

Transcendent Function

The Tao doesn't take sides;
it gives birth to both good and evil. (Lau, 1963)

Writings on the *Tao* and the doctrine of Interdependent Origination, while paradoxical in nature, speak of the tension between apparent opposites. Like the Chinese *Tao*, the Hindu *rta*, is a uniting symbol and signaled for Jung the existence of a uniting archetype in the collective unconscious (Coward, 1985). Psychologically speaking, third and fourth modes of being (see below) often symbolized in *mandalas* may be seen as an expression of the emergence of a renewed personality built on the ego-Self axis.[9] *Mandalas*, which figure prominently in Eastern traditions, are drawings that have a centre point, often a circle within a square and imply a circular movement (see images). The *mandala* is a mental image or a ritually enacted symbol which aims to engage all sides of one's personality —all the positive and negative opposites of one's nature, and, thus, represents the individuation process.[10]

In his commentary on *The Secret of the Golden Flower*, Jung points out that "the union of opposites on a higher [or deeper] level of consciousness is not a rational thing, nor is it a matter of will; it is a process of psychic development that expresses itself as symbols" (CW 13, par. 31). As part of the psychic process, the ego-Self individuates in terms of a ternary rhythm: it moves from the unconscious to conscious to transcendence and integration and circles back to the unconscious. Individuation (self-actualization) unfolds through developing and emergent moments which contribute to greater wholeness and integrity but not as a final stage of completion. In the case of renewed personality, the ego (first mode) recognizes the Self as nonego or its opposite (second mode). The tension created by this duality is released in the creation of a third mode of being in which the ego-Self interacts. Jung takes it one step further, suggesting that this psychological process continues to be resolved in a fourth condition: "the unspeakable conflict posited by duality resolves itself in a fourth principle. The rhythm is built up in three steps but the resultant symbol is a quaternity" (Jung, CW 11, par. 175).

Stated otherwise, a transcendent moment may occur in the classroom when the student(s) and teacher are so taken by the topic that all become animated or energized whereby the boundaries between self and other blur. Fleetingly, a third entity arises which is not the teacher or the student(s) or topic. A. N. Whitehead, educational philosopher, referred to this as the emergence of the superject where the subjective and objective polarities disappeared. He is included here to illustrate that these ideas are not new to education, only forgotten, ignored or denied. Remember, too, that Whitehead greatly influenced the work of John Dewey whereby a careful historical analysis of his writing indicates a shift in Dewey's educational thought toward art, aesthetic experience and a more organic view of the world. Whitehead's process ontology parallels Jungian and Zen Buddhist thinking for he conceives of bodily feelings as an ongoing flow of energy linking all entities together on a preconscious level, making possible within us the conscious experience of emotions, hopes, desires and mental activities (Fidyk, 1997). Whitehead refers to feelings as "vectors" that ebb and flow in streams of energy. The vectoral or webbed nature of bodily feelings enables all organisms to feel "what is *there,*" and transform those feelings into "what is *here*" creating the possibility of transcending and unifying the two poles of experience (Fidyk, 1997, p. 75; Whitehead, 1929/1941, p. 105).

Again, this occurrence of unification is the third mode of being. This process of merging occurs where the self grows by feeling (often unconscious), experienced as a certain fleeting unity achieved between itself and aspects of the world with which it is intimately related (Whitehead, 1929/1941). The rhythm of achieving unity, followed by the separation of the poles of experience, enables the entire process to be reiterated, varying in magnitude and duration. Whitehead, like Jung, believed that this rhythm of becoming includes creation, destruction and maintenance, carrying both self and other from an initial dim awareness of one another through a process in which their bodily feelings have the potentiality to merge in a sense of contentment in which they become fully integrated with each other. This fleeting unity provides an organic link not only between human beings but also with the "ten thousand things"—including ocean, air, landfill, frog and cow—a relationship that makes new and creative configurations possible (Fidyk, 1997).

The fourth mode, then, is this division of the two conjoined polarities into two new forms of the subject and object, self and other, or ego and Self. In terms of education, Whitehead believed that bodily feelings were the basis not only of our direct experience of the world, but also the source of our understanding and knowing the world. Thus, the teaching of any abstract idea must always be related to the bodily feelings at the core of one's own and her/his students' experience. For Whitehead, this meant grounding learning in art and aesthetic experience for bodily feelings give rise to the appreciation of beauty and creativity which are inherent in nature and so an intrinsic part of the process of becoming. The inclusion of bodily feeling and knowing is another element missing from the conventions of epistemology.

To restate, out of the two-ness of apparent opposites, or arising and ceasing, comes the three-ness of their conjoining—the Buddhist principle of Interdependent Origination, Jung's transcendent function; and White-head's superject. This simultaneous affirmation or synthesis of the opposites is, psychologically, the transcendence or dissolution of the boundary between "I" and the "other" or "world." In Jung's terms, the transcendent function is a creative expression of mind, psyche or soul. It is called "transcendent" because it "facilitates the transition from one psychic condition to another by means of the mutual confrontation of the opposites," namely, conscious and unconscious (Jung, CW 11, par. 489). It is not a disembodied state. This state of consciousness or fourth mode of being which arises through the transcendence of opposites is experienced without losing awareness of the transcendence that occurs.

In a doctoral class this winter, we experienced several occasions where we slipped into this third and fourth mode of consciousness; indeed, several students wrote after class asking "what happened?" or "how did that happen?" My best explanation beyond the readiness of one's ego, the group's cohesion, and the safety created in our weekly classes was the ability of the group to hold tension, conflict, and opposites without prematurely moving to judgment of "good" or "bad" or to closure. Such holding, a capacity for dialogical space, allowed us to unconsciously move more deeply into the experience. Here not-knowing took precedence over knowing, and holding a question open took precedence over quick closure on meaning. Further, when called to confront the concept of teacher-as-knower, I admit uncertainty, confusion and not-knowing. Certainly this acknowledgment of "limitation" allows a freedom to invite and explore other possibilities, while hosting a kind of curiosity that keeps the topic alive, fluid and meaningful. Trust in my pedagogical approach, permitted the students to shift the way they related to each other so that they were more relaxed, yet willing to risk and keep an open mind when momentary impulses, feelings and pressures arose. Rather than reacting to others' points of views or charging forward to prove "expert authority," they developed skills to wait and respect what emerged. Through our interdependence we discovered, uncovered, made and lost meaning about the topics, texts, processes and our own individual consciousness. The students, too, developed compassion for others in their ability to entertain confusion, contradiction and adversity. At the same time, they had a sincere desire and ability to attend the other when challenged. This response also required shedding pretenses, releasing the grip of personas, relaxing the ego's desire to be seen or heard and an ability to be honest about one's strengths and weaknesses – "no shame nor boldness." Resisting judgment, categorization and closure, as well as permitting things to arise, fall through time, to happen—under lays an alternative to conventional assumptions surrounding epistemology.

This unity between opposites is described in Buddhism as dependently coarising: "Each opposite is a foundation for the other[;] they seed each other" (van Zyl, 2009, p. 110). Applied to the classroom, the aggressive child or sibling "seeds" the nonaggressive child just as the inverse is true —in our classrooms, a wide spectrum of diversity is necessary for the development of all members. For Jung, the pairs of opposites are "not," because each balances the other. For Lao Tzu, it was the conjoining of the polarities of *yin* and *yang*, "feminine" and "masculine" that lead to the creation of the new:

> The way begets one; one begets two; two begets
> three; three begets the myriad creatures.
> The myriad creatures carry on their backs the *yin*
> and embrace in their arms the *yang* and are the blending
> of the generative forces of the two. (Lau, 1963 #42)

Here the path of *Tao* reinforces the generative energy of holding and movement, not unlike my pedagogic practice; carry on one's back theyielding *yin* and embrace the aggressing, *yang*. Both are necessary for balance, development, and continual renewal.

Intuition, Feeling, and Love

To appreciate cause and effect, one needs the ability to observe outer events and to think rationally. To appreciate a synchronistic event, one needs the ability to note an inner subjective state, a thought, feeling, vision, dream, or premonition and to intuitively connect it with a related outer event. Central to Buddhist, Jungian, and Whiteheadian thought is the psychic reality wherein all opposites unite in a paradoxical whole, not once but continuously. Odajnyk (1993) writes: "In the West, only a few individuals have glimpsed this truth. And usually these individuals have had to remain silent, for there is almost nothing in our civilization to enable anyone to appreciate this insight" (p. 109). He adds, "the entire Judeo-Christian tradition is inimical to such a radical, nondualistic conception

of reality [and yet it is a] 'break-through of total experience' in the West"
(p. 109). Thus, the most basic paradox is the paradoxical inseparability of
relative and absolute reality.

> Relative truth—the protocol of logic, distinctions, cause and effect—guides
> our everyday, conventional experience of ourselves and the world. Relative
> truth is the life of the individual and dynamics of the individual mind. Abso-
> lute truth is the vision of unity—of the emptiness—that binds the collection
> of relative truths [image of web]. It is the universal mind that transcends
> cause and effect, conditions, and categories. However, even though the ab-
> solute transcends and contains the relative, the relative and absolute are
> identical; hence the paradox that arises when a class of things is equated
> with a thing that is a member of the class (Jichaku, Fujita, & Shapiro, 1984).
> The life of the individual is the life of the universal, as illustrated by Jung
> in his concept of the collective unconscious, or in the idea that ontological
> development recapitulates phylogenic development. The individual mind is
> the universal mind, the particular is the general. If not, how could psycho-
> analysis derive any "laws" of intrapsychic dynamics, or physics derive any
> laws of nature? (Suler, 1998, p. 333)

Looking to right and left cerebral hemisphere brain functioning may
assist in elaborating this underlying pattern of coherence that speaks
analogously to causal and acausal principles and holds veracity for non-
Western thought. While there is communication and functioning between
the hemispheres, there is a directionality to each side; both sides are imperative to whole brain functioning (which is more than the sum of the
two). The left hemisphere contains our speech centres, controls the right
side of our bodies, and uses the logic and reasoning of linear thinking to
arrive at assessments and conclusions. It focuses on what is tangible and
measurable; left brain thinking is the basis for scientific experimentation
and observation. It follows that the left hemisphere sees in fragments or
bits and the cause-effect relationships between them, rather than the interconnected and dynamic whole. Its relationship to the world (and its
forms) is seen as separate from itself, something to use, predict and control; it is active and "masculine" —*yang*.

The right cerebral hemisphere is quite different: images, art, poetry
and myth belong here rather than the literal use of words. Through intuition it knows the whole picture and experiences a sense of historical
belonging with a future orientation—what it may become. The right side
can hold tension, ambiguity and contradiction. It holds "all" of an event
rather than focusing on parts and can simultaneously perceive and feel
what it takes in. It compares through metaphor rather than measurement.

Its style is receptive and reflective, a more "feminine" mode than that of the left hemisphere—*yin*.

In a broad stroke, the "masculine," *yang* culture of the Western world, with its privileging of rationality, Newtonian science and economic gain, has devalued right hemisphere functioning and our experience individually and collectively is poorer for that devaluation. This devaluing exists as a limit of and to our education; anything that cannot be perceived through the five senses and quantified (to some degree qualified) according to preset agreed upon determinants is considered of little value, and gradually many individuals cease to experience what it is like to be moved emotionally, bodily, or soulfully by music or image, for example, by the intuition about an underlying reality. The repeated message rings clear: artists, musicians, poets and, in general, the "feminine" function through the "inferior" way or the right hemisphere. Teaching methods, too, tend to follow blindly with an emphasis on the testing of repeatable verbal, literal and "scientific" skills and information. Coupled with the elimination of art, image, metaphor, dance and poetry from curricula and the repression of intuitive perceptions, this imbalance leads to a skewed education. By extension, it suggests a limited understanding of epistemology—how it is that we know. Because intuition perceives via the unconscious and is not dependent on concrete reality or the scientific method, it has been forbidden, dismissed, and in many cases, annihilated as a valid and valuable form of perceiving and responding to the world.

Intuition, like sensation, according to Jung, is an irrational function because its apprehension of the world is based on the perception of given facts. The perception of concrete facts is highly valued in education and Western culture. Indeed, this is the basis of most evaluation and knowing. Conversely, with intuition, content "presents itself whole and complete, without our being able to explain or discover how this content came into existence" (Jung, CW 6, par. 770). A kind of instinctive knowing, it presents with an inner certainty and conviction; recall those students who could not explain "how they knew"—they just knew.

Similarly, the feeling function as a subjective process may be quite independent of external events. However, feeling as a psychological function is not influenced by perception (as is intuition) but by reflection. Feeling in this context is not to be confused with emotion. Emotion and bodily feeling are vital to its differentiation but "when [feeling] is differentiated, it is not emotional at all" (von Franz, 2008, p. 16). The feeling function determines the value of something or someone and can be distinguished from affect in that it "produces no perceptible physical innervations, [for example,] neither more nor less than an ordinary thinking process" (Jung, CW 6, par. 725). Like eros, it is a dynamic energy that plays between emotional extremes, yet is not emotion itself (Fidyk,

2009). For Jung, differentiated feeling is a "new form of love" (von Franz, 2008, p. 16). Jung wrote in a 1933 letter to Albert Oppenheimer that we have become too "lopsidedly intellectual and rational" (von Franz, 2008, p. 14). Too intellectual may not be accurate today but certainly there is too much emphasis on left-brain qualities. He added:

> [we] need to be more than just reasonable and level-headed ... offer a cre-
> ative spiritual, non-materialistic view of reality as a whole—namely a real
> connection with the *unconscious* as a supramaterial, extrasensory reality to
> which we must relate, not only with our minds but also with feeling and emo-
> tion. (von Franz, 2008, p. 14)

In today's language, a "supramaterial extrasensory reality" may be read as an interconnected fluid web where synchronicity and intuition are valued means of perception. Taken further, Jung calls for the development of a differentiated relatedness or a "rehabilitation of Eros" (von Franz, 2008, p. 18). He emphasizes: "We must return to [love], to a general human empathy, but on a much more differentiated level" (von Franz, 2008, p. 16). This form of love, Jung called, "a whole-making effect of a certain kind of Eros [relatedness], which is an emanation of the individuated personality" (CW 10, par. 389–390, as cited in von Franz, 2008, p. 16). Love, here, is understood as "a dynamism which needs form and direction" (von Franz, 2008, p. 17; also see Fidyk, 2009);

> A differentiated feeling relationship would include a deep empathy and
> closeness to the other *and* a certain distance based on differentiation: an un-
> derstanding and a not-understanding, the latter consisting of a silent respect
> of the mystery of the other's individuality. (Jung, as cited in von Franz, 2008,
> p. 17, italic in original)

Again, we see a call for a balanced approach to our ways of knowing. *Eros* needs not only closeness and distance but also union with *Logos*, as *yin* with *yang*. Conversely, logos-driven approaches to teaching and learning need be coupled with love, stemming from a differentiated feeling that respects others (including animate and inanimate entities) and their different systems of values. Taken one step further, in a letter to Gerda Hipert in 1937, Jung wrote: "Ethics cannot exist without differentiated feeling, for without feeling it becomes a schematic rigid code of rules of behavior, a mere collective apparatus" (as cited in von Franz, 2008, p.13). To make a distinction here, Jung, I believe, is not only calling for individuals to develop differentiated feeling but also for a population and infrastructure that supports such feeling as a collective value and way of knowing. To make such a shift would press upon the current limits of education, requiring a reconceptualization of our curriculum and teaching practices so to value, support and include creativity, imagination, art and aesthetic experience.

Compassion

To develop and value the feeling function or to rehabilitate *eros* alongside *logos* would be to simultaneously develop compassion. Compassion is considered a virtue in numerous philosophies and is one of the greatest virtues in all the major spiritual traditions. Compassion is at the transcendental and experiential heart of the Buddha's teachings. Buddhists believe that knowing we are interconnected leads to the state of *metta* or loving-kindness that characterizes the *bodhisattva*.[11] With loving-kindness we become the ally of all beings everywhere. Like an effective therapist or teacher, the *bodhisattva* is there to assist those in hell see themselves—the lowest realm on the Wheel of Life in Buddhism where human beings are driven by fear, aggression, rage, and pain; they are restless and unable to do anything to tend themselves (Young-Eisendrath, 1997). When they recognize themselves as creating the conditions from which they suffer, they can gain awareness and techniques to release themselves.

In this way, without exception, our own liberation from suffering is intertwined with the liberation of others. It means rather than seeing other beings as adversaries, we must see them as fellow participants in this endeavor to freedom. This endeavor is central to transformative education (Fidyk, 2008). Such freedom is not a final, attainable state but the process of working toward fewer restrictions and for the incremental gains made along the way. Rather than viewing others with fear or contempt, which arises from a belief in separation, we see them as part of who we ourselves are. Seeing such fundamental interconnectedness is what is known in The Eightfold Path as right view (Fidyk, 2008). While most are unlikely to follow this path, attributed to that of the *bodhisattva*, developing a greater capacity for empathy and compassion is central to what we know and how we know, again an alternative to current epistemologies of ignorance.

Dukkha can arrest us in our ability to become conscious and make transformative use of suffering. Jung, similarly, talked about neurosis as a kind of unnecessary suffering, childish, or perhaps "immature" response to an experience of stress, difficulty, challenge, or frustration. This perspective on relationships and "problems" is imposed when we assume that life should unfold according to personal wants and desires as in the First and Second Noble Truths. Indeed, current epistemologies of ignorance, situated in a paradigm that values individualism, separateness and accumulation of knowledge is limiting in its self-promotion. For example, drugs to treat depression—one form of suffering—are a multibillion dollar industry. To educate people that depression is a transitory state wherein one way or another, all depression arises from and is "continued by shame, resentment, disappointment or despair at the limitations of one's own life or life in general" (Young-Eisendrath, 1998, p. 349), would not serve the current values of our culture. Indeed, if this view put forth by Zen Buddhist and Jungian perspectives could be entertained and attended through appropriate methods, the effects on the health profession would be drastic.

Unnecessary suffering, according to Jung, implies that adults (also children) do not take responsibility for themselves and, thus, believe that others are in control or that circumstances have doomed their life. While focusing on the limits and constraints of human life adds to suffering, it also offers a door for redress. As Buddhist and Jungian analyst Young-Eisendrath (1998) contends: "These limits teach us" (p. 348). She continues:

> From the facts of our discontent, dependence, vulnerability, and lack of omnipotence and omniscience, we learn what it means to be truly human. These 'negative' experiences open our hearts and allow us to connect to others through gratitude and compassion. (p. 348)

The only real freedom from suffering and death is to accept them (Third Noble Truth) and to recognize how they connect us to ourselves through meaning and value and to others through compassion. We cannot transform our discontent without recognizing how we create it.

Here, from within a different ontology, I echo Tuana (2004): "the question of how ignorance is sustained, cultivated, or allowed is one that must be asked explicitly and without assuming that the epistemic tools cultivated for understanding knowledge will be sufficient to understand ignorance" (p. 196). In the U.S. alone a recent advertisement for *Abilify* reported that two out of three people took medication for depression (September 18, 2009). From this perspective, depression is seen as abnormal, useless, and undesirable—the unwanted intruder. This viewpoint, I believe, confirms epistemologies of ignorance whereby depression is not viewed from within a larger ontological context as in Zen Buddhist and Jungian perspectives. Depression is not valued as an informing event; hence, its capacity to foster transformation remains ignored. By embracing the tenets of the seven moments, a new epistemology emerges wherein depression is located and understood as informing the continuum of life arising.

"True compassion," writes Young-Eisendrath (1996), "is a powerful antidote to our own suffering because it counteracts alienation" (p. 59). To engage in compassion—empathy and care for the other—relieves suffering and makes pain tolerable. Here, I equate suffering with a psychological state and pain with a physical one. In learning the freedom and wisdom of suffering-with, literally the essence of "com-passion," the resilient discover a wider context in which life has meaning. Many believe that here is where deep and authentic creativity is born, outside the boundaries of self-consciousness and within a perspective of love, compassion, and inter-relatedness.

For Jung, the Buddha's message was essentially about self-healing. First, in the way that it is concerned with the healing *of* the self, explained as that "which aims at the transformation of the ego in order to help an individual to overcome the dis-ease of life brought about by impermanence" (Spiegelman & Miyuki, 1994, p. 172); and second, in the way that it is concerned with the healing *by* the self, that is, "not through the medium of an external agency, but through the agency of the autonomous individual" (Clarke, 1994, p. 120).

Jung's interest in Buddhism was from the perspective of a doctor and therapist whose central concern was to attend psychic suffering. Toward the end of his life, he writes: "I acknowledge the immense help and stimulation I have received from the Buddhist teachings" (CW 18, par. 1580). He claims that the study of Buddhist literature enabled him to "observe suffering objectively and to take a universal view of its causes," and to confirm his belief in the possibility of extricating human consciousness from what he called "the entanglements of emotion and illusion" (CW 18, par. 1575).

Relevant to this attendance of suffering, Jung said "if the illness is caused by things that are unconscious, then there is the possibility of healing by making these causes conscious" (Jung-Hisamatsu, 2002, p. 114). Not all causes of suffering and illness lie in the unconscious; however, some cases point to symptoms with psychic causes, albeit, most fall into the other type. Therapeutic work has four elements: confession, elucidation, education and transformation. The fourth is most characteristic of Jung's focus and approach (Kawai, 1996, p. 115). Here, Jung says, "the therapist is no longer the agent of treatment but a fellow participant in a process of individual development" (CW 16, par. 8). Such practice likewise characterizes "good teaching" whereby the teacher or in Jung's case, the therapist, is no longer the "superior wise man, judge, or counselor; he is a fellow participant who finds himself involved in the dialectical process just as deeply as the so-called patient" (CW 16, par. 8).

The interdependence and mutuality of the teacher-student, master-disciple and therapist-patient relationship opens to the discovery of meaning and the emergence of the transcendent function, as the student (or patient) over time becomes more conscious of anguish—to suffer-with self and others. Buddhist methods focus attention on the behaviors of craving, aversion, and ignorance as experienced particularly through sustaining and defending the illusion of a separate, stable, independent self. Here, a teacher's task is to guide the process of awakening to the reality of interdependence and compassion (love), through methods that have already been well practiced and integrated by the teacher. These might include art, myth, fairy tales, symbols, dance, and even breathing techniques. Similarly, Jungian therapists and analysts are required to undergo their own work (requirements vary) and are encouraged to continue with supervision after certification. In both Zen Buddhism and Jungian psychology, the teacher or therapist is one who undergoes the transformation process first. It stands as a necessary requirement for teachers to partake in their own inner practice and healing. Not that students' "maturation" is fully dependent upon the teachers' self-awareness and self-knowledge, but it certainly resonates and may be guided (or lack thereof) from such knowledge and ignorance, being and action.

COMMENTARY CONTINUED

I began by speaking of the suffering that I experienced as a teen. In North America today there is a tendency toward wanting to protect children, students and ourselves against hardship, anguish and "negativity." It is believed that if we focus on "be happy," "be positive," buy more or better material things, or take the latest pharmaceutical treatment, we can avoid suffering. This dread of suffering, I believe, is based on ignorance about what suffering teaches and how it can be transformed.

In attending seven moments of ignorance: interconnectedness and impermanence; self and subjectivity; synchronicity and the acausal principle; collective unconscious; transcendent function; intuition, feeling and love; and, compassion, I point to the necessity of curriculum and pedagogy to include other worldviews. The perspectives belonging to different ontological orientations, such as Zen Buddhism and Jungian psychotherapy, confront the narrow focus of much current education that predetermines "what is worth knowing," thus, maintaining limited epistemologies of knowledge/ignorance. Such education suppresses, annihilates and remains blind to knowledge that will have a radical effect on students and teachers alike. If education is to inform and integrate different epistemologies of knowing, then the inclusion of specific and systemic methods of analyzing subjective distress is vital to the well-being of all those involved.

Buddhism teaches that our suffering arises from the illusion that the individual self is enduring, separate and needs protection. The schools of depth psychology warn of our tendencies to repeat experiences of fear and gratification through our psychological complexes and repetition compulsions. In particular, Jung believes that Eastern philosophical and wisdom traditions could aid the "suffering peoples of the [W]est to recover their own selfhood" (Clarke, 1994, p. 73) through yogic practices (used here as the general term for any physical or mental relaxation and as a spiritual path such as meditation and breathing techniques) for those who could align with Eastern thought and for others through methods such as active imagination. Both perspectives rest upon the belief that all living things, through the interaction of opposing elements within themselves, have a natural tendency towards a state of harmonious balance (homeostasis or equilibrium). With human beings, however, this bringing together of the disparate parts of the self, a state of more complete individualization, becomes a deliberate process through which a conscious sense of meaning and purpose can be achieved. This unity, Jung insists, is not that of undifferentiated oneness but a harmony achieved through the interplay of opposing but complementary opposites. In Buddhist, as well as Taoist and Hindu practice, the development of the personality, inclusive of both *yin* and *yang*, is the goal of all yoga. What binds Jung and these traditions together is the pursuit of liberation through transcendence of opposites (third and fourth mode consciousness). This pursuit, for the various reasons outlined, contrasts these two perspectives as a way of knowing to that which has been heretofore offered by epistemologies of ignorance.

A limit of current curricular work in teacher education programs is the lack of interest in or recognition of other epistemologies and ontologies. As illustrated in the case of human suffering and knowledge about its roots, in particular, knowledge of psychological and emotional reality from different paradigms, ways of knowing that are confined to only one worldview, unknowingly promotes suffering. Indeed, most programs have removed any relationship to pedagogy or philosophy and train teachers to become neutral and predictable technicians. Teachers would rather categorize students as "at risk," refer them for medication, and restrict their choices both in and out of school than challenge their own and others ways of thinking about behavior and entertain something new.

Defending ourselves against events and feelings judged as "negative" makes us desire only those things we believe, often through limited knowledge and experience, to be favorable, and, thus, to abhor what we believe is not. Seeing only one side of any event is limiting, destructive and does not reflect an image of the universe that we know through new science, new medicine and experience (phenomenology) to be simultaneously unfolding and enfolding. These conditions only lead to overwhelming experiences of despair, anxiety and envy, as well as, compulsions and addictions when old habits and approaches to treatment are continued, rather than question and redress our own knowledge/ignorance. It is precisely at the border of support and challenge, order and chaos that maximum development of any organism occurs. Simply, we need both—pleasure and suffering.

Our suffering has a purpose: when it is transformed, it gives rise to insight, compassion and renewal. Herein lies the root of our calling or service to the world. The fear, anguish and anger of my early years unconsciously directed my desire to become a high school teacher. I took the path that would enable me to attend people of the same age and in the same place where I experienced suffering. Later through attention to underlying complexes, trauma, injury and a one-sided perspective, I gravitated toward deeper philosophical, spiritual, and psychological (analytical) studies and practices. The shape of my service has broadened and currently stems from a deeper place of knowing rather than driven from old injuries, unattended complexes, and unconscious desires. While I have not mentioned the effects of trauma, abuse or loss, often the results of ignorance, oppression, and the uneven distribution of material and educational resources, I do not underestimate their mark on human life. Suffering as a gift may seem an affront to those who believe that suffering and pain, especially among the poor, ill and oppressed are simply unredeemable. I hope, however, that those in disagreement pursue these fields further because with time they may see that adversarial events such as trauma can be integrated beyond epistemologies of ignorance which view trauma from a victimized nonevolutionary position. To become compassionate entails our own individual confrontation with suffering and pain, the penetration of their meaning and the awakening to our interdependence and interconnection with all beings.

Limits in education for both curriculum and pedagogy are herein framed around the current literature on epistemologies of ignorance, their privileging of only one ontology and their inability to be open to new and other ways to know. Welcoming other epistemologies and ontologies, particularly one that is organic, inclusive and emergent, challenges what it is to know and what is of value. This shift has been highlighted in the case of suffering. A radical reorientation to suffering would permit a wide range of transformation as realized by students, teachers and communities that would allow for greater compassion, healing, and renewed perspectives on life. As we shift our subjective perceptions, the perceived (other) also changes and so, too, the one perceiving, and with that shift comes freedom from the constraints of the old. In so doing, we have changed both individually and collectively; we have changed the world.

Figure 7.2.   Three images of Jung's mandaldas. Retrieved from http://www.
netreach.net/~nhojem/mandala.htm

NOTES

1. Active imagination is a method of assimilating unconscious contents such as dreams, fantasies and images through some form of self-expression. The aim is to give a voice to sides of the personality (particularly the shadow and anima/animus) that are typically not heard, thereby creating a line of communication between consciousness and the unconscious. Even when the drawing, painting, writing, sculpture, dance and so on (the creation) is not interpreted, something happens between creator and creation that contributes to a transformation of consciousness.

2. The term "knowing field" was coined by Dr. Albrecht Mahr in 1997 at the first international conference on Family Constellations in Germany. Family Constellation is an event-oriented healing modality used to address transgenerational systemic entanglements. In Family Constellation work, representatives do not act out roles according to personality descriptions given by the client as in psychodrama or role play. With a set-up of a constellation, the representatives move into and become part of the knowing field of the family and notably "take on the actual feelings and impulses of the real family members" (Payne, 2006, p. 20).

3. T. H. Stcherbatsky, a Russian scholar of Buddhism, maintains that yogic practices, which appear in all Eastern schools of thought—be they Hindu or Buddhist—train the mind to release from suffering (Coward, 1985).

4. CW refers to the collected works volume number and paragraph of this reference.

5. The Self for Jung is the archetype of wholeness and the regulating center of the psyche; a transpersonal power that transcends the ego. By way of definition Jung wrote:

> As an empirical concept, the self designates the whole range of psychic phenomena in man [sic]. It expresses the unity of the personality as a whole. But in so far as the total personality, on account of its unconscious component, can be only in part conscious, the concept of the self is, in part, only *potentially* empirical and is to that extent a *postulate*. In other words, it encompasses both the experienceable and the inexperienceable (or the not yet experienced).... It is a *transcendental* concept, for it presupposes the existence of unconscious factors on empirical grounds and thus characterizes an entity that can be described only in part. (CW 6, par. 789)

In addition, he added:

> The self is not only the centre, but also the whole circumference which embraces both conscious and unconscious; it is the centre of this totality, just as the ego is the center of consciousness. (CW 12, par. 44)

And in relation to its manifestations, he directed that the Self appears in dreams, myths, and fairytales or....

in the form of a totality symbol, such as the circle, square, *quadratura circuli*, cross, etc. When it represents a *complexion oppositorum*, a union of opposites, it can also appear as a united duality, in the form, for instance of Tao as the interplay of *yang* and *yin*, or of the hostile brothers, or of the hero and his adversary (arch-enemy, dragon), Faust and Mephistopheles, etc. (CW 6, par. 790)

6. The Sanskrit word *pratitya-samutpada* is variously translated in English as follows: "Dependent Origination, "The Law of Dependent-Together Origination," "Dependent Production," "Conditioned Genesis," "The Law of Dependent Origination," and so forth. Etymologically speaking, the term *pratitya-samutpada* consists of two words. *Pratitya* is a gerund derived from *prati-i* which means "to go towards or against," and thus denotes "dependent on, based on." *Samutpada* is a noun derived from the verb *sam-ut-pad* which denotes "to spring up together, be brought forth or born of...." The hyphenated term suggests "origination by dependence of one thing on another," and indicates the "phenomenon" of the "dynamic mutual interdependence of each and every *dharma*" (Spiegelman & Miyuki, 1994, p. 133).

7. Bohm (1985) calls the deeper level of reality the implicate, which means the "enfolded" or unseen order, and he refers to our own level of existence as the explicate, unfolded or seen order. He uses these terms because he sees the manifestation of all forms in the universe as the result of countless enfoldings and unfoldings between these two orders.

8. Bernstein (2005) describes Borderland people as those who:

    personally experience, and must live out, the split from nature on which the Western ego, as we know it, has been built. They feel (not feel *about*) the extinction of species; they feel (not feel about) the plight of animals that are no longer permitted to live by their own instincts, and which survive only in domesticated states to be used as pets or food. Such people are highly intuitive. Many, if not most, are psychic to some degree, whether they know it or not. They are deeply feeling, sometimes to such a degree that they find themselves in profound feeling states that seem irrational to them. Virtually all of them are highly sensitive on a bodily level. (p. 9)

9. The ego-Self axis represents the vital connection between ego and Self that must be relatively intact if the ego is to survive stress and grow. This axis is the gateway or path of communication between the conscious personality and the archetypal psyche. Damage to the ego-Self axis impairs or destroys the connection between conscious and unconscious, leading to alienation of the ego from its origin and foundation. Erich Neumann who initially coined this phrase said it thus: "The ego stands to the Self as the moved to the mover.... The Self ... is an a priori existent out of which the ego evolves. It is, so to speak, an unconscious prefiguration of the ego" (as cited in Edinger, 1972, p. 38).

10. A *mandala* is a symmetrical structure consisting of ternary or quaternary combinations symbolizing the dynamic process of development or growth,

whereas the quaternary configurations represent a static structural wholeness or completion (Edinger, 1972). Jung observed that in the numinous experience or confrontation with the self, *mandala* symbolism often emerged in the manifested unconscious materials.

In Buddhism, a mandala, known as the Wheel of Life or Bhavacakra, contains depictions of six realms of existence that show what is possible in forms of life. Each realm is regarded as both a psychological state and a "place" or situation. It is believed that an individual is born into one of these realms because of the way in which one previously lived: deva (bliss or gods' realm), asura (actions were based on jealousy, struggle or rationalization), human being (passion, desire, doubt and pride), animal (strong mental states of stupidity and prejudice), preta or hungry ghost (hungry cannot be satisfied because of possessiveness and desire), and a being in naraka a woeful state —hell (hatred).

11.   In Buddhist traditions, *bodhisattvas* are those who, aspiring to enlightenment, resolve to attain full enlightenment for the sake of all sentient beings. The *Bodhisattva* vow acknowledges the suffering of both self and other.

REFERENCES

Bernstein, J. (2005). *Living in the borderland: The evolution of consciousness and the challenge of healing trauma*. Hove, England: Routledge.

Bohm, D. (1985). *Unfolding meaning: A weekend of dialogue*. London: Routledge.

Bolen, J. S. (2004). *The Tao of psychology: Sychronicity and the self.* San Francisco, CA: Harper San Francisco.

Britzman, D. (1995). Is there a queer pedagogy? Or, stop reading straight. *Educational Theory 45*(2), 151–165.

Cambray, J., & Carter, L. (Eds.). (2004). *Analytical psychology: Contemporary perspectives in Jungian analysis*. Hove, England: Brunner-Routledge.

Clarke, J. J. (1994). *Jung and Eastern thought: A dialogue with the Orient*. London: Routledge.

Colman, W. (2009). Response to Umberto Galimberti. *Journal of Analytical Psychology, 54*, 19-23.

Coward, H. (1985). *Jung and Eastern thought*. New York, NY: State University of New York Press.

Csikszentmihalyi, M. (1993). *The evolving self: A psychology for the third millennium*. New York, NY: HarperCollins.

Edinger, E. (1972). *Ego and archetype*. Boston, MA: Shambhala.

Epstein, M. (1996). *Thoughts without a thinker: Psychotherapy from a Buddhist perspective*. New York, NY: Basic Books.

Fidyk, A. (2008). Democracy and difference in education: Interconnectedness, identity, and social justice pedagogy. In D. E. Lund & P. R. Carr (Eds.), *Doing democracy: Striving for political literacy and social justice* (pp. 139–158). New York, NY: Peter Lang.

Fidyk, A. (2009). A "rehabilitation of eros": Cultivating a conscious relation with love. *Jung Journal: Culture & Psyche*, *3*(4), 59–68.

Fidyk, A. (2010). "Invisible loyalty": Approaching suicide from a web of relations—A chapter response. In E. Malewski (Ed.), *Curriculum studies— the next moment: Exploring post-reconceptualization*, (pp. 439–444). New York, NY: Routledge.

Fidyk, S. (1997). *Experience and learning in the educational thought of Alfred North Whitehead: A teacher's perspective.* Unpublished master's thesis, University of Saskatchewan, Saskatoon, SK, Canada.

Gebser, J. (1984). *The ever-present origin* (N. Barstad & A. Mickuas, Trans.). Athens, OH: Ohio University Press.

Haberman, M. (1995). *Star teachers of children in poverty.* Bloomington, IN: Kappa Delta Pi.

Harding, S. (2006). Two influential theories of ignorance and philosophy's interests in ignoring them. *Hypatia*, *21*(3), 20–36.

Heisig, J. W. (2002). Jung, Christianity, and Buddhism. In P. Young-Eisendrath & S. Muramoto (Eds.), *Awakening and insight: Zen Buddhism and psychotherapy* (pp. 45–66). Hove, England: Brunner-Routledge.

Johnson, S. (2002). *Emergence: The connected lives of ants, brains, cities, and software.* New York: Touchstone.

Jung, C. G. (1961). *Memories, dreams, and reflections.* New York, NY: Pantheon.

Jung, C. G. (1953-1971). Collected works of C. G. Jung (R. F. C. Hull, Trans.). In H. Read, M. Fordham, G. Adler, & W. McGuire (Eds.), *Bollingen Series 17.* Princeton, NY: Princeton University Press.

Kawai, H. (1996). *Buddhism and the art of psychotherapy.* College Station, TX: Texas A & M University.

Lao Tzu. (1963). *Tao te ching.* (D. C. Lau, Trans.). London, England: Penguin.

Lindorff, D. (2004). *Pauli and Jung: The meeting of two great minds.* Wheaton, IL: Quest Books.

McCallum, I. (2005). *Ecological intelligence: Rediscovering ourselves in nature.* Cape Town, ZA: Africa Geographic.

Meier, C. A. (Ed.). (2001). *Atom and archetype.* Princeton, NJ: Princeton University Press.

Miller, M. E. (2002). Zen and psychotherapy: From neutrality, through relationship, to the emptying place. In P. Young-Eisendrath, & S. Muramoto (Eds.), *Awakening and insight: Zen Buddhism and psychotherapy* (pp. 81–92). Hove, England: Brunner-Routledge.

Odajnyk, V. W. (1993). *Gathering the light: A psychology of meditation.* Boston, MA: Shambhala.

Ortega, M. (2006). Being lovingly, knowingly ignorant: White feminism and women of color. *Hypatia*, *21*(3), 56–74.

Payne, J. (2006). *The language of the soul: Healing with words of truth.* Findhorn, Scotland: Findhorn Press.

Robinson, J. M. (Ed.). (1990). The thunder: Perfect mind. In *The Nag Hammadi Library in English*(3rd ed.). Retrieved September 17, 2008 from, http://www.chsbs.cmich.edu/David_Smith/313/thunder.html

Shaker, P. (forthcoming). Jung and post-postmodernism: Symbols in education. In A. Fidyk & D. Dobson (Eds.), *Jung in the classroom: Education for meaning and diversity*.

Shaker, P., & Heilman, E. E. (2008). *Reclaiming education for democracy: Thinking beyond No Child Left Behind*. New York, NY: Routledge.

Spiegelman, J. M., & Miyuki, M. (1994). *Buddhism and Jungian psychology*. Temple, AZ: New Falcon.

Stein, M. (2005). Some reflections on the influence of Chinese thought on Jung and his psychological theory. *The Society of Analytical Psychology, 50,* 209–222.

Suler, J. R. (1998). Paradox. In A. Molino (Ed.), *The couch and the tree: Dialogues in psychoanalysis and Buddhism*. New York, NY: North Point Press.

Taylor, C. (1989). *Sources of the self: The making of the modern identity*. Cambridge, MA: Harvard University Press.

Tuana, N. (2004). Coming to understand: Orgasm and the epistemology of ignorance. *Hypatia, 19*(1), 194–232.

Tuana, N. (2006). The speculum of ignorance: The women's health movement and epistemologies of ignorance. *Hypatia, 21*(3), 1–19.

Usher, R. (1996). A critique of the neglected epistemological assumptions of educational research. In D. Scott, & R. Usher (Eds.), *Understanding educational research* (pp. 9–32). London: Routledge.

van Waning, A. (2002). A mindful self and beyond: Sharing in the ongoing dialogue of Buddhism and psychoanalysis. In P. Young-Eisendrath, & S. Muramoto (Eds.), *Awakening and insight: Zen Buddhism and psychotherapy* (pp. 93–106). Hove, England: Brunner-Routledge.

van Zyl, D. (2009). Polarity processing: Self/no-Self, the transcendent function. In D. Mathers, M. E. Miller & O. Ando (Eds.), *Self and no-Self: Continuing the dialogue between Buddhism and psychotherapy* (pp. 109–120). London: Routledge.

von Franz, M. -L. (2008). C. G. Jung's rehabilitation of the feeling function in our civilization. *Jung Journal: Culture & Psyche, 2*(2), 9–20.

Wilber, K. (1982). *The holographic paradigm and other paradoxes*. Boston, MA: New Science Library.

Wilhelm, H. (1967). *The I Ching*. (R. Wilhelm, Trans.). Princeton, NJ: Princeton University Press.

Whitehead, A. N. (1929/1941). *Process and reality*. New York, MA: The Free Press.

Young-Eisendrath, P. (1996). *The gifts of suffering: Finding insight, compassion and renewal*. Reading, MA: Addison-Wesley.

Young-Eisendrath, P. (1997). *Gender and desire: Uncursing Pandora*. College Station, TX: Texas A&M University Press.

Young-Eisendrath, P. (1998). What suffering teaches. In A. Molino (Ed.), *The couch and the tree: Dialogues in psychoanalysis and Buddhism* (pp. 344–353). New York, NY: North Point Press.

Young-Eisendrath, P. (2002). The transformation of human suffering: A perspective from psychotherapy and Buddhism. In P. Young-Eisendrath, & S. Muramoto (Eds.), *Awakening and Insight: Zen Buddhism and Psychotherapy* (pp. 67–80). Hove, England: Brunner-Routledge.

CHAPTER 8

STUDENT SUICIDE

The Relevance (and Luxury) of Ignorance

Teresa Rishel

In an era of an apparent hyper-focus on standardized testing and curriculum, students are further separated swiftly and decisively into groups by academic prowess, with a diminishing regard for the once popular focus on the "education of the whole child." While teachers continue to care—or attempt to care—about students and the social contexts that impact students' education, they are stretched to find enough emotional energy, let alone time, to attend to the deeper and more decisive elements that guide any particular student's abilities to navigate schooling. Teachers and students are increasingly corralled into a scripted version of teaching and learning, where reaching and maintaining a specific standard at a designated moment in time has become the status quo. It is not the intent here to debate the usefulness, effectiveness, or necessity of the standards movement within education, but more to point how this focus has overridden a crucial and threatening undercurrent of students' unhappiness, disappointment and fear, and the propensity towards self-harm through participating in at-risk behaviors and suicide.

In working with my undergraduate and graduate pre- and in-service teachers, the main thrust of their worries and concerns, and their

Epistemologies of Ignorance in Education, pp. 167–186

continued monologues, are about "the standards." These undergraduates adopt their mentor teachers' refined focus on "what" to teach instead of how to teach; the graduates commiserate over whether their students have retained enough knowledge to pass "the test" and to what degree this learning will reflect on their abilities as a teacher. Taking this into consideration, my teacher education students become overwhelmed and overtly resistant when course topics veer towards students' emotional health and well being and the impact they will have on future students' ability to succeed in school.

I have found increasing resistance by colleagues and administration to my teaching about adolescent and young adult suicide because they are deemed irrelevant to the focus on "academic standards." Because the preservice teachers witness the effects of their students' poor emotional health while teaching in the field schools (i.e., poor attendance, lack of participation, apathy, lack of concentration, etc.), they quickly grasp the importance of knowing how to recognize and respond to students' problems. And although I continue to teach about this important topic (along with child abuse and neglect), my preservice teachers often struggle with the importance of learning about what they internally know to be valuable, such as student emotional health, and the demands of teaching towards meeting state academic expectations. While students' academic success is often considered the "bread and butter" of an educator's job and the way to measure one's own worth as a teacher, it is also the perceived culmination of the journey of learning and knowing for its own sake that fulfills teachers within, regardless of administrative rewards.

As educators, we share a common understanding of the importance of homework, class work, school attendance, and student involvement at school. We "get" that we need to encourage and support students in their quest for higher grades, honor role placements, and ultimately, making the school's report card a symbol of exemplary achievement. What we often fail to understand, though, is that we frequently exacerbate problems for emotionally at-risk students by seeing them as merely objects to be tested, measured, and graded. Without taking into consideration the circumstances of a particular student's life and the causes behind their lack of success or engagement in schooling, we summarize their existence simply by applying a numerical value to them. As long as we attempt to "standardize" students in this manner—by judging them on academic merit—we are overlooking the fact that these students cannot succeed until their lives are in order, they feel valued by school personnel in spite of their lack of academic focus, and their life experiences are part of the curriculum of schooling. Unfortunately, attention toward at-risk students is lacking or nonexistence in many schools, there is a peculiar type of educational ignorance at work that threatens the lives of students.

Charles Mills' (1997), for example, argues that ignorance of race is not necessarily an absence of knowledge or unawareness, but instead a conscious or unconscious agreement not to know. As such, when there is an unconscious agreement not to know about any particular topic, subject, or issue, racial or otherwise, this indicates unawareness that one should know, which does not result in the possibility to learn or understand. If one consciously chooses *not* to know, then they are aware, but have decided not to further pursue the topic. This *choice* in what one wants to know or is deemed worthy of knowing, could indicate indifference, resistance, or apathy, or a combination thereof, the by-product of the choice not to know.

Similarly, Howard (2006) describes how the "luxury of ignorance" (p. 61) plays a key role when White educators purposefully avoid what they do not know, thus alleviating them of responsibility towards social justice, empathy, and action. In *We Can't Teach What We Don't Know: White Teachers, Multiracial Schools,*" Howard describes how historically the dominant social group has been able to "determine the structure and content of schooling," and "have institutionalized our ignorance in the name of education" (p. 63). As a result, the dominant social group has defined the "other" by not having to *know* much about them, their cultural backgrounds, or how to interact with them. Howard makes it clear that the luxury of ignorance is a choice, but can also be a lack of awareness or understanding that one *needs to know*. Further, he states that because of the "truths" that the dominant group upholds, they have "projected only a narrow wavelength of light, usually tinted to favor our own countenance" (p. 63). The concept of the luxury of ignorance can also be applied to how we view those who fall outside of the dominant group of "normal" and well-functioning students.

My research in adolescent and young adult suicide, based on the suicide of a former student, Dalton, exposes a "choice of ignorance" among those who have had the opportunities and means to impact the reduction of student suicide. I met Dalton, a fifth grade student, at the school where I was the principal. Dalton led a difficult life, which as the reader will learn, contributed to his inability to acclimate to the school culture and to be accepted by many of those within this culture. The dynamic friction between Dalton's personal troubles out of school and those heaped upon him by others at school set the stage for a difficult and long-lasting situation. In the end, his suicide in junior high put an end to the challenges he faced; however, for those he left behind, it was the beginning of the search for answers and understanding.

A highly taboo and unpleasant topic, suicide resides in the dark and forbidden recesses of society, where the status quo is a formidable opponent. Often associated only with people who are considered highly dysfunctional, emotionally imbalanced, and deemed at a substandard level of humanity, suicide has no place in a "normal" and highly functioning and achievement-oriented society, or so it appears. Moreover, in the various camps of religiosity and morality, the idea of suicide exists as a glaring form of possible sin and serves as the quintessential expression of the culmination of a life gone awry.

If this is so, then one would expect that all measures of possible prevention, education, and knowledge about suicide would appear in the facets of society where "knowing" is important. For example, it would appear frequently in regards to public education. If society judges suicide as the ultimate act of moral failing and religious desecration, then it would seem that we would ensure its avoidance to the best of our abilities. It would seem, as well, that our youth would know the facts, have the myths related to suicide dispelled (i.e., only teens who are insane or mentally ill commit suicide) and have an deeper understanding of the realities of such life and death decisions (i.e., dispel the romanticism of suicide). They would be armed with factual knowledge, resources and information on where to seek help and from whom, and the fullest extent, what measures could be taken to provide them an emotionally balanced life.

Unfortunately, suicide research is difficult since the subject carries with it a stigma of silence, which limits research on student suicide and its impact on schools. In addressing sensitive issues such as suicide in research, Sieber and Stanley (1988) assert that researchers circumvent taking responsibility when they avoid controversial topics just because they are in fact, controversial. Yes, research on student suicide has many controversial aspects, but the dearth of research may actually be due to ignorance on the part of educational researchers and erroneous attempts to avoid stigmatizing students, and less with the controversial nature of suicide itself. While ignorance among educational researchers perpetuates a lack of knowledge and awareness about suicide, this void unfortunately informs the ways that school personnel address the issue on the ground, so to speak. The controversial underpinnings of student suicide research and practice emerge mainly due to the myths surrounding suicide. For example, it is believed that by talking about suicide, it will *cause* youth to be more inclined to commit suicide. For school administrators, this fear is compounded by the idea that suicide pacts will be made among peers. It is also feared that attention given to suicide will make it a glamorous or romantic way to die, thereby giving the deceased a type of attention they desire. In other words, they feel that the attention they receive upon death will be greater, and somewhat earned, than the attention they received in life. Coinciding with the idea of "attention-getting," it is commonly believed that young people use the threat of suicide as a method of getting attention when in reality they have no intention of doing it.

The fact that a student might go to the extreme to threaten suicide as a method to garner attention, then they are certainly to a point where they need it. To deny them attention is in effect giving them the unfortunate message that they are not worthy of it and are free to commit suicide. In fact, according to the American Association of Suicidology (AAS, 2008), 75% of those who commit suicide tell someone about it in advance. As previously stated, one of the most common myths or beliefs is that only the insane or mentally ill are capable of suicide. When young lives are at stake, and suicide continues to remain concern, especially now when suicide is dipping into lower age categories such as 10–14 year olds, it seems more contentious to take a passive stance and do nothing.

Even within the suicide research community itself, a form of hegemony exists that surprise and dismay me, furthering my frustration that ignorance, the choice not to know, could be the culprit. I formerly attended the annual conference of a highly respected suicide research organization, but eventually abandoned it due to the lack of attention to the educational (school and student) side of suicide. What appeared most important were the medical and psychological aspects of a suicidal person, treatments, medications and testing. While these are certainly important and necessary in addressing this global dilemma, in my opinion, the philosophical orientations underwriting the conference limited what were considered acceptable approaches to suicide prevention and delegitimized research on adolescent and young adult suicide. This is particularly disheartening considering that suicide is the third leading cause of death for those aged 10–24, preceded by accidents (often suicide attempts) and homicides (violent death) (AAS, 2008). Increases in suicide during the past 15 years are among those aged 10-14, where hanging by belts, ropes, or plastic bags are the most common methods.

In the United States alone, every 2 hours a suicide occurs by those aged 15–24 (AAS, 2008), which demands that educators become involved in addressing suicide prevention. Globally, youth suicides total around 100,000 adolescent deaths every year (AFSP, 2008). Although my conference presentations were accepted, my interest in educating about our youth and the impact of suicide on schools, students, and teachers was not valued. I abandoned the conference, resigning myself to the fact that the rather costly meeting was merely an avenue to garner funds for medical research and interests. Because of this, my research continues with people in schools, ones who confront the social realities of students' problems.

The point here is not woeful self-indulgence, but an example of how not knowing, or not caring to know, is an unacceptable form of ignorance with far ranging effects.

Epistemologies of ignorance provide an exemplary forum for discussions on how teen suicide research sits in relation within various types of knowing, not knowing and not wanting to know, particularly in relationship to the three types of ignorance outlined by Tuana (2006). That is, (1) how ignorance is manifested, ranging from not knowing that we do not know about a topic, subject, phenomenon, or issue, (2) caring whether we know, and ultimately, and (3) who wants to keep us from knowing. In terms of suicide, we must first understand that most educators do not even know that they do not know. As discussed above, teaching my preservice teachers about suicide is met with resistance at first due to their hyperfocus on educational standards and assessment. After sessions on student affect, school culture and climate, and Dalton's suicide, they understand how much they did not know and are much less reluctant towards addressing the topic of suicide in the event should surface while student teaching or as they enter the teaching profession. This is not the end of the story, however. Once they learn about suicide, they are positioned to act and react accordingly when a situation regarding suicide arises, or make the conscious decision whether to care or not. Consequently, because of the nature of schooling and the prioritization of academic matters, as well as the desire to avoid talking about suicide, it is common that "others" (administrators, school boards, and community) prefer that they not know or act upon this knowledge. In this example, administrators, school board members, and community members typically act among many forces that keep us from knowing.

In the next section, I discuss adolescent suicide following Tuana's (2006) second type of ignorance , one where the focus is upon what "we do not even know that we do not know" (p. 6). Ultimately, this form of "unknowing" establishes the foundation for providing the education and developing school personnel. Based on my narrative inquiry research and the resultant case study of Dalton's suicide, along with the lived experience of my own son's suicide, the reader can expect to have their ignorance challenged, their knowledge increased, and their awareness altered. Using this knowledge and taking action remains each individual's choice.

SUICIDE—WE DO NOT EVEN KNOW
THAT WE DO NOT KNOW

Not knowing that we did not know might be the the most troubling dimension of epistemologies of ignorance, often coming into our awareness only after the fact. At the time, we have little awareness of what we do not know—a juxtaposition or coincidence—of life. Hindsight, a good indicator of what we did not know and how much we did not know it, nips at our heels as we maneuver through the years. "Had I known…" we say to ourselves, torturing and testing the knowledge, actions or reactions replaying moments, which we felt we had little control, or now wonder if we chose not to control. Hindsight offers the opportunity to not only feel the weight of regret and the shame of avoidance, but also the pain of ignorance.

Part of my own ignorance and regret, among many, was that I never expected suicide to be a part of my job as an elementary principal. The topic was not discussed in my teaching or administrative preparation, or considered as an area of meeting students' needs. Within the first year as an elementary principal, however, several students sent to my office for disciplinary action discussed suicide. I was fortunate, though, because my actions and reactions to these students grew out of my experiences with suicide. This is not to say that I am less critical about many of my actions back then, but in the least, I feel my awareness and knowledge lent itself to helping most of the students over the long-term. That is, except for one, Dalton.

Dalton, one of the students with whom I worked most closely in part because he had threatened to take his life, ended up committing suicide a few years into junior high, an occurrence that still haunts me. My research (Rishel, 2003), an in-depth case study on Dalton's suicide, presented both my lived experience as his principal and also the memories and recollections of school personnel (teachers, administrators, counselors, and health care personnel) who knew him well. The study focused on the ways in which Dalton's suicide impacted or affected his former teachers, their perspectives, and instructional practices. It also addressed administrative perceptions and roles in dealing with his suicide. The findings from the study illuminated school personnel's lack of awareness and knowledge about suicide, the effects of the stigmatization of suicide on decision making, and how the nature and structure of schooling exacerbates problems for adolescents, particularly those who are prone to self-destructive behavior.

As studies go, most research findings provide avenues for scholars to explain and describe circumstances, construct and deconstruct events, as well as ways to formulate suggestions, plans, procedures, and so forth to advance the field. Themes emerge, categories are created, and ways of viewing "the" research are all a part of meaning making and disseminating the findings. However, an important and unexpected aspect of my research was the extent to which I, along with my participants, experienced the full throttle of regret, the realization of avoidance, and the shattering reality of ignorance. As educators, I believe we know where we fall short, where we are most effective, and where we need to improve. Constantly in a cyclical state of evaluation and assessment of our abilities—by our superiors and ourselves—we feel that we have a good understanding of ourselves as educators and usually, I would suggest, find ourselves to be above average in the least. Sometimes, though, our images are crushed by truths, hidden or not, that speak to areas where we lacked experience, knowledge, or intuition, among others. My (Rishel, 2003) study of Dalton's suicide certainly netted many of these aspects in hindsight, the indicator of what is known and not known, and is unfortunately, irreparable. The feelings and realities associated with this study and our memories of "how it was," are best understood as the title of this section suggests: we did not even know what we did not know.

In the remainder of this chapter, I weave an account of how participants in this study account for what they did not know. I also account for how this lack of knowing, as obvious as it is now, was hidden amongst the hegemonic practices of schooling, the lack of pedagogical and administrative knowledge, and acquiescence to the status quo in overall actions, reactions, and interactions with and about Dalton. Understanding what they learned in the aftermath (what they know now) might advance suicide research, which is, at least one positive effect remaining from Dalton's life. Therefore, this discussion will focus on the exacerbating effects of alienation. As such, this will allow the reader to understand the ways that ignorance impacted Dalton's life and eventually, his death.

THE ALIENATION OF DALTON

Dalton's story is centered on alienation—at home, school, and in society. While there is much to be said about the various forms of his alienation, a question that continued to nag at me throughout the research process was the following: How much of his alienation was *self-imposed and purposeful* in order to avoid and reject others (possibly before they could reject him) *or* how much *was imposed on him by and through others*? Attempting to ferret out from where the alienation originated can be elusive, and at times may leave the reader with more questions than answers; at other moments in the research, the source of the alienation is obvious. Study participants (represented by pseudonyms) as well, were left to think about the degree to which they aided in Dalton's alienation in the school environment.

Social Alienation

Throughout the study, participants described how the relationship between Dalton and his mother affected his life and schooling. Dalton grew up in poverty and constantly had to weather the struggles associated with symbolic and material deprivation. His mother, a high school drop-out who had Dalton at age 16, worked night jobs at local bars, returning home in the early hours of the morning. Reportedly angry, frustrated, and tired (personal communication), she dealt with life the best she could, which did not include copious amounts of free time to spend with her three children, particularly Dalton. Further more, Dalton was the product of a rape by his mother's stepfather, which left a severe emotional distance between him and his mother. As a result, Dalton was often left to fend for himself and his two younger brothers, with only a grandmother nearby to oversee at least part of his needs. However, in the end, it became obvious that even the staff at his school did little to help alleviate the problem by making adjustments in what they expected from Dalton (i.e., signed permission slips, homework, parent participation, etc.). Inasmuch as they "cared," their actions towards Dalton indicated that they added more to his burden, highlighting that although they "knew" about Dalton's home life they did not find ways to act upon this knowing.

When school staff who participated in the study shared stories about Dalton, they initially centered on his appearance, particularly his black, unkempt, and oversized clothes. Dalton never wore new clothes. One participant stated that Dalton's big and baggy clothes were not the problem; rather, he had an appearance of someone who lacked "someone caring a lot for him," or who had taken time to care. Other participants added that Dalton liked to draw attention to himself by having shoulder length hair, wearing a long, dark coat, and letting his pants purposefully sag below his waist (this was prior to sagging pants being a fashion statement for this age group). A few of the participants commented on how they were always telling him to get a belt. The reason, evidently one they failed to find out, was that he only wore a belt on days that he was the first child up because there was only one belt in the house.

Dalton's life at home affected his school life, which is not uncommon, but it is important to understanding how social contexts impact students' success at school academically and socially. We see more serious concerns expressed about Dalton's life in the following excerpts from study participants.

> He bragged about drugs. And you know, he enjoyed getting high...we had conversations about growing "it" on his property. (Jack, September 9, 2002).

> I'm sure he was surrounded by drugs and alcohol and you know, and poverty and a lot of different things. I'm sure he was left alone a lot. (Reggie, July 30, 2002)

Well sure, he's brought up with "that." When he was in my class he talked about their family reunions and how they'd have keggers. And there were times that he would come to school and say, "Well, I didn't get any sleep last night" and he'd be talking about all the things that were going on at the party. (Jane, July 24, 2002)

These data clips illuminate the degree to which Dalton's social life stood in stark contrast to his junior high school peer group. His knowledge and experiences surrounding drugs, alcohol and his family's partying lifestyle further alienated him from his peers who engaged in more age-appropriate social outlets, such as school dances, sports, and community events. While there was no evidence that school personnel distanced themselves from Dalton due to his exposure to drugs and alcohol, they felt that it caused him to remain an outcast at school.

The social alienation of Dalton, much of which was beyond his control, became more complicated when one took into account his school behavior. The principal described Dalton as one who would curse at other students in the hallways, causing them to fear him. Dalton found these interactions amusing, which did little to help his acceptance in any group other than by those whose experiences were similar to his. The participants felt that most students liked him because he added humor to the class, but had little regard for him in other ways and had no desire to include him as a friend. The principal's description clearly shows Dalton's role in the school:

And some of the other kids kind of liked him because of that [humor]. He would always do those things that you wanted to do in school but you'd never do. He'd be the kid that would come forward and pass gas right in the middle of class and whatever he needs to do that everybody's thought about but that you just don't do. And so they were amused by him. (Jack, September 9, 2002)

To Dalton, school was simply a social outlet and since he disdained schooling, he resisted by acting out as often as he could. Dalton's behavior in class caused great distress for his teachers: he was rude and insolent, and over time, his behavior grew worse and more unusual. Dalton was "accepted" when his sense of humor diverted the teacher's attention or lightened the classroom atmosphere, however.

Dalton also used intimidation to act out against students who were valued in the school culture, such as honor roll students and athletes. More often than not, his aggressive acts would be towards students who were respected within the school, which lends itself to a deeper understanding of both his alienation and who he blamed. Dalton was highly intelligent, and with the right support and guidance, could have been a member of an "in" (Howard, 2006) group. However, due to the school's lack of regard for his intelligence, and focus on it as a key to his success and thus his acceptance, they used homework as a method of assessing his academic abilities. At the same time, he used homework as his method of resistance. He should have been placed in advanced classes and had the opportunity to interact with a group more closely aligned to his abilities and the opportunity to associate with a more positive peer group.

Although his infamous humor was often the cause of classroom and school disruptions, netting him trip to the office, and resulting in disciplinary action (which usually began with a stern voice and strict demeanor), it rarely remained so. As reported by partcipants, his humor was appreciated by those who had to discipline him, causing both the disciplinarian and Dalton to laugh. The principal sometimes noted that it was difficult to *want* to discipline Dalton:

> In the course of our conversations when I'm giving him hell, okay, I'm in there, and he's just not letting anything bother him, kind of letting it go and I'm ranting and raving a little bit. And I stop. He's laughing and I start laughing, okay, in the middle of the conversation! I said to him, "You're missing your calling; you need to be a comedian." (Jack, September 9, 2002)

Dalton was often not adept at recognizing social boundaries, and even when he knew the correct response or behavior, disregarding such behavior was his method of coping. On one occasion, he was facing disciplinary action for calling one of his teachers a "bitch" (Jack, September 9, 2002). Dalton admitted to saying it and then added, "Well, she is." Jack said that both he and Dalton began to laugh because he agreed with Dalton's description of the teacher. Dalton knew how to confound traditional student-leader relationships and certainly set a tone of passive acceptance from school authorities.

Known only for the unusual, the outlandish and the unacceptable, the negative attention Dalton received was at least attention, and sadly, the type of attention he also received at home. During the time I was Dalton's principal, I witnessed his mother's lack of involvement with Dalton and his schooling. Having sat through many conversations with Dalton concerning his home life, his common complaint was that his mother was never home and had little to do with him and his stepbrothers when she was. Dalton's mother did not attend parent events at the school, volunteer for classroom activities and outings, and did not ensure that his homework was complete. Dalton's mother berated him when she felt that he was not being "good enough," yet failed to recognize him when his actions were indeed good. She placed a huge amount of responsibility on him in having to care for his younger siblings while she worked until the early morning hours, yet did not provide him with positive reinforcement or encouragement; only disdain for whatever negative behaviors he displayed.

At school, while he engaged his peers in amusement, he was still not accepted. Dalton shared that he knew he would never be anything more than the outcast and so he grabbed at whatever he could to get attention. His ability to make others laugh did not, in the end, result in anything other than further alienation. He often made comments about how he would never fit in with his peer group and usually added that this was "fine" with him. It was easy to see behind his false bravado and feel the pain of his alienation, yet it was not so easy to break through his shell and help him find a way to connect with his peers. Lending some insight into his alienation, on the day of his sixth grade graduation, after 2 years of working with him, he stated:

> "Mrs. R, you just *don't* understand, do you?
> I am not like the other students; I am different." (date unknown)

Academic Alienation

For many students, attending school is stressful, particularly as they attempt to acclimate to the culture of schooling. Negative attitudes develop as students learn where they fit in and where they do not, and realize that as one of a crowd, their problems seem insignificant (Butler & Novy, 1994; Elkind, 1989). Part of this problem lies in the fact that school practices "do not support every child's autonomy, nor provide a sense of meaning, or consistent social support, which results in poor academic achievement and negative feelings" (Schlosser, 1992, p. 128). The atmosphere and events that occur at school cause students to begin to skip school, participate less, allow their grades to decline, or act out while at school. One effect is that they have difficulty adjusting socially, bringing about their desire to withdraw, which results in further alienation (Elkind, 1989; Liston, 2000; Schlosser, 1992). Consequently, these factors contribute to suicide and suicidal tendencies in students (Portner, 1964).

A strong negative correlation was found to exist between suicidal activity and a decline in school performance, where the third most significant cause of suicidal behavior is academic pressure, regardless of the intelligence level of the student (Beane & Lipka, 1986; Butler & Novy, 1994). One method of applying academic pressure is through tracking and grouping, a system of competition and reward that further separates students, not only physically, but also emotionally and socially as well (Beane & Lipka, 2000). Tracking, the separation of students into specific academic classes (i.e., accelerated, advanced placement, college prep, etc.) disallows certain students from access to high quality schooling, often in spite of indications that may warrant the student's enrollment in such advanced programs. In Dalton's case, his standardized test scores regularly fell at the 99 percentile, yet his homework and class work grades lingered at the failing level. Had Dalton's true academic ability been recognized instead of his daily performance, which again was his form of resistance, he may have found a way to be accepted and valued in the school community. Because Dalton looked and acted differently than his peers, he was treated as less intelligent than he actually was, although his tests scores were high and study participants felt that he was "very smart." An apparent result of Dalton's behavior, and not his ability level, he was placed in an academic "out group" (Howard, 2006), a classification that reflected a shallow representation of him. Students such as Dalton learn not to care about school due to the focus on academic achievement and a system that elevates the "jumping through the hoops" instead of caring for the whole child.

Thus, academic achievement becomes a limited vision for some students due to the *preset boundaries of their track*, which draws them into passivity and lack of involvement. Less is expected or demanded of them and their complacency is accepted. Beane and Lipka (2000) warn that educators must "stare long and hard" (p. 35) at what they do concerning grouping and other forms of institutional alienation, which are proven methods of lowering self-esteem, "strip[ping] learners of their personal dignity" (p. 21).

Unfortunately, what surfaces from this study as highly important to Dalton's reputation and alienation is schoolwork. Teachers and administrators who reflected on Dalton's academic trajectory focused on his failure to complete in-class assignments and homework. Concerns began in grade two, which is as far back as we have Dalton's story, when his teacher worried about him not completing assignments. In an interview, Martha shared that while her "heart went out to him," she had "no skills in dealing with helping him with the problems that he had" (personal communication, July 26, 2002). She continued by adding that in spite of her awareness that he was highly intelligent, she made him do all of the "easy" (personal communication, July 26, 2002) worksheets so that he could earn free time and did nothing to tailor his schoolwork to fit his needs. She avoided Dalton's problems instead of working through them to help him succeed and in this manner; schoolwork became a punishment for having family and life problems. Over the years, Dalton learned that his only recourse, his only method of defense, was to resist through refusing to do schoolwork and behaving poorly at school. Dalton used this resistance when he encountered a new grade level, a new teacher, and the familiar demands placed on him to do his schoolwork. In junior high,

Dalton's continued to refuse to do his assignments; teachers continued to prod, beg, and reprimand him. This highly intelligent, yet not academically motivated student was retained in seventh grade, not once, but twice.

Emotional Alienation

When students enter junior high or middle school, they are often given less responsibility and fewer opportunities for decision making (Eccles & Roeser, 1999). They learn that teachers do not value participation and prefer adolescents not think for themselves or question the world around them. When the tendency is "to do and believe what they are told to do and believe" (Wassef & Ingham, 1995, p. 35), teenagers feel they are losing their individuality while being encouraged to conform. The irony is that students worry about not fitting in and being different than their peers, yet, educators warn against following the crowd and encourage them to think on their own, causing students to become caught between two conflicting perspectives. Students who underachieve, exhibit behavior problems, or are depressed, find middle schools to be very frustrating, especially when attempting to retain their autonomy (Eccles & Roeser, 1999; Elkind, 1988; Elkind, 1989; Oser, 1991; Schlosser, 1992). Thus, the atmosphere and situations that occur *at* school cause students to develop negative attitudes *about* school.

Ironically, Beane and Lipka (2000) referred to school as a "place of last resort" (p. 5) for many teens, where school, "may be the last institution where these young people may work with a group of adults who are willing to give them help and guidance, not just criticism" (p. 6). Students are caught in a dichotomous relationship between hating school because it is alienating, yet needing it for survival against the pressures of the outside world. The guidance counselor shared how he attempted to convince Dalton's peers (after his death) that although Dalton was caught in this cycle, school personnel still tried to help him:

> They were hurting ... there were comments like, "No one tried to help Dalton." And they knew that wasn't true. I said, "You know, the very teachers that Dalton had the most problems with were teachers who really cared about him." And they knew those things, but they were frustrated that no one was able to help him and there's a difference between able to help and trying to help. (Trent, July 29, 2002)

Many researchers explain the relationship between students' perceptions of caring and their actions against those who show concern (Eccles & Roeser, 1999; Elkind, 1988; and Schlosser, 1992). Regardless of how detached and uncaring students are about school and schooling, they regularly think about what goes on in the classroom, what their teachers do and say, and about school life. Although student perceptions are not always based on reality, the result of their detachment and teachers who are not prepared to cope is their inability to learn (Jackson, Boostrom, & Hansen, 1993). Dalton was certainly a detached and uncaring student, and probably held many misperceptions about school, yet many of the participants reported he really did not hate school, rather, that he hated himself, while school provided a forum for the attention he sought.

Further conversations with the principal focused on what it was like for an administrator to deal with Dalton. The principal explained that he felt since Dalton did not learn respect at home, he had no framework for respect at school, and was a "kid who hated everything about himself and his life" (September 9, 2002). He shared that Dalton had to grow up on his own, learn right and wrong on his own, and be his own boss. The principal felt that Dalton found schooling difficult because "he was not able to work within how we organize and structure schools" (July 2, 2002).

I wondered about that statement, "how we organize and structure schools" and Dalton's inability to fit within the culture I studied. Jack was referring to the notion that because there is a certain way of doing things at schools (i.e., homework, good behavior, respect, etc.), and that students such as Dalton who did not accept these ways, they were unable to fit in. Although Dalton had a small circle of close friends who mostly fit within the same social class and home situations, he was witty, a great conversationalist, and enjoyed the company of adults over students. He created detailed, yet violent, art, which depicted images such as those found in the game Dungeons and Dragons. He was not an athlete, did not belong to student clubs and did not participate in any part of schooling such as activities, sports events, dances, and so forth, mostly because he had no afterschool transportation or family support. Even his attendance at school declined as he entered junior high. Yes, most said he was troubled, very troubled. Jack stated, "I don't think there's anyone that didn't know that Dalton was a troubled kid of some sort. Trouble from home, trouble with his place in society and his home life" (personal communication, September 9, 2002). Yet, in spite of Dalton's ability to converse with and relate to adults, his artistic ability, and his high level of intelligence, school personnel could not find, or did not find, a way to connect Dalton to school life.

School Culture and Alienation

When I look at students like Dalton, highly intelligent and creative, I have to realize that his intelligence had nothing to do with success for him. School represented all that he could not have; it was a place he did not fit in and another form of oppression. His lack of interest in pursuing traditional notions of success and his resistance toward the official curriculum were ways that he could act out, resist, and refuse to subscribe to the authoritative framework of schools. By resisting, he had control over some aspect of his life, albeit it a negative one. Jack's view that there was a lot of rejection *of* him because of the nature and structure of schooling prompts me to also believe that there was a lot of rejection *by* him because he refused to buy into the normative nature of schooling. My research suggests Dalton was trying to tell school personnel something that they were not able to see:

> Dalton was ... he was just unusual. He had so much intelligence that you just couldn't tell it from his grades at all. But to sit down and talk to him ... he had knowledge about all kinds of things. (Allen, July 30, 2002)

> He didn't care that he was at the 99th percentile. He thought that was nice, but that was no big deal. He would've rather mom come on a field trip with him, or show up for parent-teacher conference, or not partied all the time. Or showed him some affection. Made him supper. (Brin, July 22, 2002)

Brin highlights a key point: Dalton wanted and needed more than the school or curriculum offered him. He existed in a situation that he did not create, yet had to accept. From all observations, he was alone to fend for himself when his needs were immense. He did not value his intelligence because others did not value it; it brought no attention, accolades, or acceptance from those who were closest to him. His efforts to fit in or succeed at school did not prevail over his need to be loved, cared for, or accepted. He wanted attention, a stable family, clean clothes, and a normal life, none of which were available to him. Understandably, he became apathetic and nobody was able to alter his destructive course. Although some tried while others' did nothing. His resistance to schooling was his resistance to the life he had to endure. A stalemate had been established: the structure of schooling was not going to change and neither was Dalton. In the end, was it a situation of not knowing what they did not know or knowing that Dalton needed more attention, help, and support but caring not to know? Either way, it resulted in his further demise, buried beneath a pile of hegemonic practices, pedagogical unawareness, and ignorance.

From where does this ignorance emerge? How can one consider educators to be "ignorant" about a topic such as suicide since their very profession is based on dealing with students on a regular basis? Unfortunately, suicide researchers (Davidson & Range, 1999; King, Price, Telljohann, & Wahl, 1999) found that teachers who "feel less competent, are in fact less competent, and are uncomfortable handling situations involving suicide"

(Rishel, 2007). Many educators recognize the emotional and mental instability of students yet feel unqualified to handle the depth of emotional trauma that students suffer. According to a study to determine teacher knowledge about suicide, it was found that less than 50% of schools educate their teachers on suicide's warning signs and that less than 66% of *school counselors* were aware of suicide's warning signs (King et al., 1999). While most teachers of adolescents are aware of the problem of suicide, they lack knowing appropriate ways to deal with it. The fact that they could make grievous mistakes due to their lack of knowledge is a serious issue.

Further indications of the overall state of suicide amongst students is found in an American Association of Suicidology (AAS, 2008) report that at least one person under the age of 25 commits suicide every 2 hours in the United States alone. Given this, the fact that "we" do not even know that we do not know does little to thwart off the hidden despair with in our student population. We cannot afford not to know, yet the fact is that we do not. It is imperative that in the least, educators have an awareness of the basics of suicide; not only recognizing the behaviors and characteristics common to many suicidal students, but in knowing what to do.

According to the Youth Suicide Prevention Program (YSPP, 2007) "about 80% of the time people who kill themselves have given definite signals or talked about suicide" (p. 2) further illustrating that knowing the warning signs and what to do are the keys to prevention. Often precursors to suicide, closely related "risky" adolescent behaviors include self-cutting, depression, and eating disorders, such as the development of anorexia and bulimia, the latter of which have been linked to self-punishing or suicidal teenagers (Beane & Lipka, 2000). Other indications that students' emotional health is at risk are the increased number who engage in life-threatening behaviors on a regular basis, such as drinking alcohol, smoking, taking illegal drugs, and practicing unprotected sex (Centers for Disease Control, 2008).

Combined, the above should give us a clear indication of when our young people are stressed, distressed, and unhappy. With the current focus on academic achievement and standardization, it would serve us well to understand that self-worth and self-care should preempt students' desire or capability to perform well academically. Educators may be the only safety net between life and death situations, which requires that they be well equipped to handle the initial intervention and provide the listening ear that may guide the student to safety. As I learned from my case study of Dalton's suicide, what school personnel readily know about their students, their patterns of behavior, their everyday interactions and

Elkind, D. (1989). *All grown up & no place to go: Teenagers in crisis.* New York, NY: Addison-Wesley.

Howard, G. (2006). *We can't teach what we don't know: White teachers, multiracial schools* (2nd ed.). New York, NY: Teachers College Press.

Jackson, P. W., Boostrom, R. E., & Hansen, D. T. (1993). *The moral life of schools.* San Francisco, CA: Jossey-Bass.

King, K. A., Price, J. H., Telljohann, S. K., & Wahl, J. (1999). High school health teachers perceived self-efficacy in identifying students at risk for suicide. *Journal of School Health, 69*(5), 202–207.

Liston, D. P. (2000). Love and despair in teaching. *Educational Theory, 50*(1), 81–102.

Mills C. W. (1997). *The racial contract.* Ithaca, New York, NY: Cornell University Press.

Oser, F. K. (1991). Professional morality: A discourse approach (The case of the teaching profession). In W. M. Kurtines & J. L. Gewirtz (Eds.), *Handbook of moral development* (Vol. 2, pp. 191–226). Boston, MA: Allyn & Bacon.

Portner, J. (1964). *One in thirteen: The silent epidemic of teen suicide.* Beltsville, MD: Robins Lane Press.

Rishel, T. (2007). Schoolyard to the graveyard: A curricular study of Dalton's suicide. Unpublished dissertation, Purdue University, West Lafayette, IN.

Rishel, T. (2007). Suicide, schools, and the young adolescent. In S. Mertens, M. Caskey, & V. Anfara (Eds.), *The young adolescent and the middle school: Handbook of research in middle level education Series* (Vol. 6, pp. 297–322). Charlotte, NC: Information Age Publishing.

Schlosser, L.K. (1992). Teacher distance and student disengagement: School lives on the margin. *Journal of Teacher Education, 43*(2), 128–140.

Sieber, J., & Stanley, B. (1988). Ethical and professional dimensions of socially sensitive research, *American Psychologist, 42,* 49–55.

Tuana, N. (2006). The speculum of ignorance: The women's health movement and epistemologies of ignorance. *Hypatia, 21*(3), 1–19.

Wassef, A., & Ingham, D. (1995). In search of effective programs to address students' emotional distress and behavioral problems part l: Defining the problem. *Adolescence, 30,* 523–539.

Youth Suicide Prevention Program.(2007). *About suicide and self-harm. Know the warning signs.* Retrieved January 15, 2008, from http://www.yspp.org/aboutSuicide/warningSigns.htm

CHAPTER 9

LET THE BODY OUT

A Love Letter to
the Academy From the *BODY*

Celeste Snowber

My Dearest Academy,

I need to commend you, for you have been very astute at giving me attention through all your cognitive capacities. You have thoroughly analyzed me and successfully grasped the ramifications of the body politics and the connections between the body, knowledge, and power. You have looked at the cultural understanding of how the body has been absent, present, misused and I have now managed to find myself in a wide variety of discourses, not to say at least infiltrate fields across disciplines. I am now actually a hot subject and object, and you researchers are taken seriously for scholarly discourse that connects issues with me. I mean, I am now even being discussed at the tables of some of the finest institutions around the world.

This is a big feat, given my absence over all these years. I have become more visible in theorizing and this is not to be minimized. Yet, in this presence, there are absences, ones that have implications for the health of developing the scope of full body intellectuals, scholars, and educators

Epistemologies of Ignorance in Education, pp. 187–198

who not only speak about the body, but also live from the body. So now it is time for me to speak, speak to you with a tender heart, with all the juice and even mess of what the body is. After all there is huge mystery and paradox when it comes to the body, and of course there is the aspect of living ecstatically. I am after all, not a text and cannot be distanced eternally, as letters on a page, which do not sweat or weep, moan or bleed. As much as I am analyzed, philosophized or dissected so as to be moved into the conversation, I can also become marginalized from the conversation. I have come to nudge you to remember a few ways to bring me back to center. I am actually more interested in being a centerfold than just a fold.

I am a gift for you, far more than you know. Think of me as a personal navigation system that guides you toward what can unfold within you, including the depths of pain and beauty. I am the map you have been yearning for, a free GPS system, the veins and capillaries of your innermost longing. I am not found in one neat package, but I am filled with all the limitations and wonder that a human being be invited into. It was I who led you to feel the delicious wind on your limbs, the delight of moisture on flesh, or the crispness of late fall air in your pores. I live through a sensuous knowledge. I am all about those many kinds of intelligences you speak of, that have been well theorized. I am the lifeblood of inspiration; it is I who puts breath into these intelligences. I am found not only in kinesthetic or visual intelligence, but how you viscerally feel the waves of movement within your flesh, the flutter in your chest, the sigh in your voice, the release in your shoulders, the way you walk into your class or how you glance at a loved one.

It is I who you can trust when you need to listen to your inner voice. I reside in the subtle sensations constantly flowing through you. I am the feast for your eyes, the tactile knowing for your skin, and the smell of your sweat. I speak in a language that defies the categories that even the plethora of bodily discourses articulate about me. It is the language of the flesh, ripe with carnal ways, which are often absent from the halls of the academy, not to mention the corporate world and realms of multiple forms of leadership and administration.

The body has a spontaneous path, circular, and circulating in ways, which cry to be spoken, but often silenced. Tears are familiar to the body's voice, passion, and com/passion form the parts, blood knowledge is the torso. Outbursts are normal. Sleeping is needed. Spilling is central. In a predictable fashion, I am known to be unpredictable. My sentences are formed with the grammar of the gut—a grammar that is left at the doors when policy is made or enacted. Administration and the thousands of meetings you are involved with are not always where I hang out, but this is where I am needed, and I want to go. I would even like an invitation, unannounced! What would it mean to lead by the pulse of the body? Could the body come in to the boardroom or the administration of the academy? Could attention to the body affect decision-making or policy?

You see, now it has become even in vogue to speak of intuition and imagination in many fields, including leadership, management, research, and teaching. The diverse fields within education after all have had major thinkers and scholars that have cultivated other ways of knowing, although I am always a bit of a side dish. The truth is sometimes the side dish, is the main dish, the ones you adore, like French fries!

AN ENFLESHED THEORY DANCES

There is a secret the body holds. How one accesses imagination, intuition and fresh ways of perceiving lies within the body. And this is the practice of activating what lies dormant within your own pulsing body, waiting to be awakened. It is like one can know all the steps, as any good dancer would know—the structure and form of a plie, a turn, a flamenco rhythm, or the hand gestures of Bharat Natyam Indian Classical dance. But the steps are the theorizing, to truly make the steps dance, one needs to breathe life into them, activate the soul—the bodysoul. I am calling you beyond the steps to a place where you re-familiarize yourself with me and you can dance again as a child both literally and metaphorically. This may not be a graceful dance, for even being clumsy is a bodily act, but it is a physical engagement. Or another example is that a team really figured out a more efficient way to play football or hockey, but never engaged their full bodies in the sport. It would certainly be good theory, but not enfleshed. I'm after a theory with flesh on it.

The body has become brittle; look how many of you let the rhythm of what delights you take second place or completely relinquish. If you attended to the body as you do to the computer, we could really have a party, if not tea! I love to be moved, walked, spun, stretched, and expanded. I need breath for living. I am often prohibited from yawning deeply, and how much I just long to do this in your endless meetings. Why don't you let me out in the middle of one of your committee or departmental meetings? What if I could stretch, sigh, or even sit on the ground? I am scrunched for hours in front of those boxes you call laptops, only the fingers are getting a work out. You have left a huge part of me behind. My goodness, you would think none of you had hips or pelvises for that matter. What about entertaining a pelvic inquiry? You have relegated the pelvis to the "third world" as if it is the forgotten sister. Bring her back!! From the pelvis you were born and it is the pelvis you must return to.

What knowing lies in the center of your belly that you have forgotten? I long to speak so you may hear—yet I am a hidden, a forbidden voice. Activate those hips dear and you may feel the sway of your own heart!

Perhaps it is time to make space for me as you did when you were a child. Then you abandoned yourself to skipping, jumping, and leaping when excited, and expressing with your whole torso when disappointed. You made all kinds of noises, relished in making sounds and made up stories like brushing your teeth. You, of course, like everyone else learned to "pay attention" by being still, but this was never a true attention or contemplative stillness, but more like a frozen immobility, which of course results in stiffness. The complete stillness knows the rhythm of the breath and is in close contact with the heart—a bodily attention where one recovers awe at each day.

Some of you had begun your early career as teachers, for you loved the child within yourself and the child without. I am asking you to attend again as a child, the child who knows the body does not lie, but is the place where truth lives, however you may define that. Let me arise from the sitting postures I am in all day. Let me come out and play! Take your students through the physicality of the earth, and transgress the boundaries of your confined spaces. The real act of transgression is to bring me to your class, let me out, find the body pedagogy of teaching. Here, all teaching is a bodily act as well as mentoring students or colleagues for that matter. Let your body be brought to the listening process, where one listens with all of his or her being. You cannot afford not to bring me.

And most of all remember this: It is time to *play* again. Yes, instead of just hashing issues out with colleagues, go back together in the woods, open up your sternum to the sky, smell the fragrance of the earth and be silent together. It is in the silences, the body has insight waiting to impart. One can research, collect data, analyze, reflect, but if we could only let the body with all of its senses into all these acts, there may be a different world, an enduring academy with flesh. You are not just called to survive, but to thrive—no one can work constantly without paying a cost. There are too many paying a price for not dwelling with the nourishing fruit of engaging with all of his or her physicality, with self, other, and the world.

After all this is about connection and I seek to connect you once again to the magic of the life force, the magic of the lifebody. You may all call it different things, but it is about living with joissance, living with vitality—being deeply alive. Sip of the body's glory and may the invitation deepen your endurance in the hard places. Even the broken body has its teaching place in our lives. There are times one is called to pause and pace. Slow down. Soothe oneself into the beauty of writing by hand, walking in shadow, eating mangoes and using more garlic. We are researchers and it is all too easy to forget our own search—the search to *befriend the body*.

The body is not perfect, either is your nose, back or hormones. Every human being lives with limits and some of them more than others. But here is the rootedness to humanness, human beingness. Those who live in the academy are often better human doings than human beings. The body lives in the spaces of being, the ontological space of being present— a bodily presence.

So ask yourself, and right now! What does your body know? What does your body remember? What is your body longing for and therein lies the landscape for rejuvenation. I am no longer satisfied to be in the pockets of the academy. I want to be part of the full clothing—animating your life from within. I was your first love, your first expression as the turning of your torso in your mother's womb. Come back to what I have given you in the beginning.

Speak tenderly to me and let the wild/erness return or perhaps emerge for the first time. Let your own tissues and cells surprise you into its great mystery.

WHAT HAPPENED TO BODY KNOWLEDGE?

Do you ever ponder how the intimate connection to the body has been lost in the first place, or more importantly how the connection to knowledge that is really stored in our bodies has been so dormant? How could it be that knowledge you might have had in the beginning of your life has actually become almost invisible? Knowledge is a strange creature, there is so much of it, epistemologies of all kinds, and yet there are continual splits between theorizing and practicing, knowing and acting, or listening and responding. There has even been attention in scholarly discourse to "the absent body," places where I have not been heard, seen, or felt. The deeper truth is that you were all born with the knowledge that you *are* bodies, not that you *have* bodies. This is the birthright of being human, but it is knowledge that is visceral, tactile, visual, audible, and deeply kinesthetic. As your first love, you moved in the beginnings of your mother's womb and took delight in greeting the world outside with all your senses. Yet, you soon found as you were schooled both within the culture, and institutions that this bodily knowledge was not high on the list of what was valued. You might not get many kudos if you said you excelled in feeling the joy of swinging on the swings, or playing in the mud, or the release of pounding your fist in your pillow. But you certainly would be praised for bringing the body to certain skill sets, particularly some version of sports, or sitting attentively in the chair at school. This is the first big mistake of schooling—equating mindfulness, alertness, with not only stillness, but also frozenness. The mind and body are so connected that, in fact, the mind turns off after feeling so cramped. No room to breathe can become an unexpansive mind! Of course, everyone is getting this brain/body connection, now there is scientific proof after all.

But what happens at an early age is even without being conscious of it, boys and girls and eventually men and women make contracts with themselves, about everything in life really, but especially concerning their bodies. You find at an early age, that what is important is the external body, not the internal body, and it does not take one long to make even a subconscious contract to NOT pay attention to the sensing, pulsing, and breathing body. For example, it is easy to become very attentive to what one looks like, if you are having a bad hair day, or your jeans are too tight —basically how one looks. But it is not so easy to be attentive to what is going on from the inside out, how shallow you breathe, where one feels tight or released, or listens to intuition. The mind takes over and the multiple splits set in where body is disconnected from many aspects of life, but most importantly, how we experience knowledge.

A loved one can tell you that h/she loves you over and over again, but unless you truly feel this with your heart, they are only words. Or the reverse can happen, and one cannot mention the word love, and you feel this affection deeply. As humans, you were designed to comprehend knowledge with your whole beings—mind, hearts, soul, imagination, flesh. Yet, not all knowledge is the same, content being vastly different. But knowledge that is only predominantly received in the mind can be dismissed, but once you get knowledge in the gut it is difficult to forget its impact. The nuances of knowing live in the places between your shoulders and loins, fingers and chest. There is a fragrance of knowing that seeks and longs for a fuller way. It has known all along. The smell of a crabapple tree may unlayer your whole childhood, or the scent of rhubarb pie baking has multiple stories to tell. Remembrance and, therefore, knowing lies in your senses.

So, when this book focuses on "epistemologies of ignorance" the body comes to mind as a place in culture that has been only relegated to the mind. What happens to the body is that all the knowledge is great head knowledge, but has not reached down deep in the bone. In fact it can be really accurate, even profound, but until it actually drops into the cells, one never gets it. Take, for example, if I gave you instructions how to walk for the first time or ride a bike for that matter. I could tell you how your arms and legs work together but in opposite patterns, how your breathing is connected to your stride, how your heel touches the earth and the pure mechanics of movement. It would all be precise and correct, but unless you actually engage in the practice and find the muscle and cellular memory, you will not be able to engage in the activity or remember it. It is not that different with any kind of knowledge. Knowledge likes to get under the skin to have long lasting effects. A tactile knowledge, one where the grammar of the gut has its way.

REMEMBERING YOUR FIRST LOVE

This may all sound simplistic, but deep truths often are. This is all knowledge you once knew and still do deep down. It just needs to be re/membered, re/bodied back to being. That is why I am writing you a love letter. I am your first love, and I am beckoning for you to return to me. Come with me and I will again teach you to listen to the churning in your stomach, the flutter in your chest, the loosening of your hips, the hidden scents in your life waiting to be discovered and uncovered. I am patient and long-suffering and sometimes I need to get your attention unfortunately by breaking down. Some of you just do not give me enough attention; you think your deadlines are more important. Well your deadlines are not life-lines. I am your lifeline, your lifeblood, and I wait for you to come home and find release in just the sheer joy of being alive. I am a built in spiritual director, able to guide you through most of the terrain in your life. Let me just show up in your life and bring me to all the miniscule places in your life. It is all about noticing, a day-by-day listening. Make some time for me—walk me in the fresh air, even if it is raining. Stretch in the middle of a meeting. Have your tears and your laughter, too. Luxuriate in the way I can comfort you, a thousand ways that your deep body wisdom knows. This letter is not going to tell you all the hows. There are lots of books, bodily practices already available on this. Choose one that suits you, that is helpful—yoga, swimming, walking, great lovemaking, skiing. But, it is the dailyness of listening to the body I am after. This letter is a beginning, an initial gesture to bring you home to yourself, and an initiation into embodied knowledge.

Ask yourself if you have made a contract to not listen to your own body. And what kind of contract is it? For example, it could be that you are so overly responsible, you answer all your e-mails on time, while your body is exhausted from not having any play time outside! Oh, and these are not one time questions, by the way. They are questions that you can have as a daily spiritual practice, a bodily practice, for the span of your life. You have lots of years to work it out, so just relax and move into it. Do not see it as one more thing to accomplish. Remember your body is calling you back as a lover. Sometimes lovers forget about time and just relish in the beauty of the moment.

Find a contract for yourself that honors your deepest bodily knowing and surprise yourself with your own mystery. Begin small—tiny, incremental steps are best. Even as you read this piece, or after you finish it, drop the text, take a deep breath, shake out your body and interrupt yourself for five minutes by attending to me. And return. In fact, maybe you should do that with all your reading and writing. Get distracted and take walks in between. The words will have more life than you know. And return over and over again to the living pulse, the skin under the skin, so you may once again be at home in your own skin. And you may find home where your longings have resided for many years. Begin to accept and honor your limits. Let them be teachers to you, as well as the paradoxes, and inconsistencies of your own body. And most of all, celebrate your quirks, for only you have them. That is the beauty. And thus, celebrate that you are always called once again to your first love, the body you have and are.

AND THEN, MOST IMPORTANTLY...

Your voice, your dear deep voice which you are constantly concerned about within the academy or any other profession for that matter, that it gets uttered, articulated, told, retold, spoken, written and reflected back through others. The academy has built this into your contract, your employment contract if not your personal contract of what it means to be an academic and researcher. We spend half our lives finding our "voice," and then we are asked to put it into an articulation of knowledge that is privileged over many other kinds of knowledge. And one wonders sometimes where is your *body* in your voice, both orally and in your literacy?

The body does not really like formulas. Yes, it likes forms where there can be containers for freedom to reside. But formulas or formulaic writing diminish what the body knew in the beginning: that all language comes out of the breath and tongue, the rhythms of language are visceral. And this has caught on, in a few circles, but there is a long way to go to recognize and remember the body back to language. This would be a good travel plan: bring the body home to language. An all-inclusive excursion where the body infiltrates the way we write, speak, and even think.

We have all been trained how to write and you would not be reading this text if you had not been exposed to sophisticated writing at some level. But I am calling you back to have your writing become a place where blood turns to ink, where flesh seeps into your words so they sing, pulse, play, writhe, leap off the page and dance into your hearts, and minds with a kind of knowing that is truly re/membered. A kind of knowing that breathes vitality.

Now I have to tell you that if anything has been privileged, and there seems to be a lot of talk about this in academic circles: race, cultural, class, and gender undoubtedly form our perceptions and ways of being in the world. But one of the ways I have been left out of the conversation is to have knowledge articulated in very similar ways (even when there are different languages). Knowledge becomes expressed in mediums where rational, cognitive thought is privileged over the poetic, artistic, intuitive, and visceral. Now this is really changing, and I say YIPEE to this, but what I am concerned about more than anything is how your voice could possibly disappear through all these discourses. For some of you, it might work, but I would suggest that many of you are longing or beginning to desire a more organic articulation of your voice. And when your voice truly comes out, you basically just show up for your own life.

And how fantastic is that?! The best aspect you can bring to both words and worlds is yourself, because no one can be like you. And we need all of us, in our hundreds of thousand different ways we live, perceive, think, in our different fields. And we need embodied voices, ones that not only have astute things to say or write, but to express in ways where knowledge is not distant. The world is craving a knowledge that is intimate, one, which throbs with humanity. Only when the body returns to our language can there be the kind of fullness that is possible. This is an act of transgression similar to of bell hooks' (1994) "teaching to transgress," but it is also an act of emancipation. Body wises people.

So I want you to return to your voice in all its beauty and depth. A kind of authentic hearing can occur to yourself and others when the mind, heart, soul, and body are given free reign in voice. Now, this invitation may sound a bit abstract, and you might ask, well, how do I do this? Or, you may already feel you are integrating your bodily voice in your writing and speech. But I would tell you this is just a small, day-by-day practice of honoring the body. As you do this, as you make room for me, you will be surprised how I pop up in your sighs and words.

What I yearn for you is to find the origin of words, which have breath in them. Words are dropping from within and without, which dance on your skin. There is, after all, the many kinds of knowledge that you know, then most beautifully is the knowledge that you do not know. The knowledge that is hidden, obscured, and waiting to be grown in your hearts and in your minds. Here is a knowledge that is absent, but in its absence is strength. In its absence is the unfolding of beauty on the edge of a new dandelion, on the cusp of a mountaintop. The absence is waiting. The wisdom is waiting. In our attention to letting the body have its way, letting the body be part of all we say, do, and write, a new kind of knowledge is born. This is what artists know. This is what athletes know in the flow of their movement. This is what scientists know on the edge of discovery.

This is the heart of the creativeness. And I long to have my academics be outrageously creative. Return to the play of language, which surprises you. Drink deep of your own flesh, which calls forth a listening to all the rumblings of your life. And here I am in your midst, in the small acts of dailiness within and without you.

You have got the "footnoting" styles down. And you may notice that this piece has no footnotes, as an intentional act of listening to rhythm! I am now asking for you to get your feet in your notes. Take notes with your feet. Teach on your feet. Let your soles become where your soul breathes. Take off those shoes, boots, high-heels and place your worn feet on the earth and let your feet tell you where to go, what to research, where to write the next sentences. You know when you really love someone, the word beneath the words tell all, the glances and actions are at the he(art). For too long you have left the body out of even discourses that have done amazing good in the world, and even opened up transformative possibilities. There just is never enough ways the body can be integrated within all the diverse ways of writing. The body does not want to be bracketed, or just be utilized as a semi-colon. The body wants to be a comma, constantly breaking up every little intention and action, and even sometimes gushing. I live in multiplicity and thrive in multiples. Oh, yes, somewhat like multiple orgasms, but this is a love letter you know. I am after ecstatic living, even within institutions, be they be the academic or corporate world.

To let me out is to truly let me be. It is the difference between letting the river flow through your life or pushing the river. By now you probably have already managed to get through several institutions, have several degrees and have had a variety of jobs and relationships. You are highly skilled, attuned to the nuances of your field and have a wealth of knowledge and experience. You might have too many books by your bed, too many e-mails to answer, and have way too many commitments for the next few months, if not the entire year. You really cannot afford to live without the wisdom of the body. I will be the one who will bring you balance, rhythm, health and delight. I also may be the place where much of your pain is either physical or emotional. So, I really need to be let out to play. It is like cultivating your immune system. I mean when was the last time you just dangled your feet? Or skipped on the beach, or lied on the grass and watched the clouds? This too is research. Perhaps lying on the grass is horizontal inquiry, but it connects your body to the earth, and the earth loves to hold you. Here your bodyspirit can imagine possibilities, if only how one form shifts into another, even if just clouds. They are sparkles of beauty dust.

You might be wondering why all this talk of the body when everywhere you look there is attention to practices of keeping the body fit, a gym in every neighborhood and a variety of classes to be taken at the local community center that focus on health, fitness, sport or dance. And you, in fact, may be in a very good shape and attend to being physically fit. But I am not only concerned with your physical sustainability, but I am concerned that you can come alive to yourself, others and the world through all your senses. I want you to return to a sensual knowing where you are rejuvenated in the *eros* of the everyday. What do all your senses have to tell you about wisdom, knowledge and experience? How do you honor them? How are you going to delight in them this afternoon or evening? How do sound, color, light, texture, touch, and smell inform your moments? What do the senses have to teach? And most importantly, how can you trust your senses as a place of wisdom?

Of course, in any relationship there is "trust." It almost sounds trite to speak of this, but the body is trustworthy. Perhaps it breaks down, shifts and changes and is unpredictable. You can trust this all will happen. But you can also trust there is a well of wisdom residing in your cells, an inner guide, and an inner pedagogue waiting for you to consult with. Thomas Merton (1961), the great contemplative said in the title to his work, "hurry ruins saints and artists" to which I would add academics, leaders, managers or teachers. Perhaps it is useful as a fireman though! Speak tenderly to your body, speak to your body as a lover, luxuriate in the seasons of who you are becoming. Even your limits are a source of grace.

And one must mention that the body is a huge place of paradox. It is the place I have often called, "paradoxology"—in praise of paradox. For, there is none of us who have been left untouched by pain, suffering, or loss in our bodies in one form or another. We are invited into deep vulnerability and it is in this place that worlds can open up to us. Now it is not as if we have to suffer to have meaning, but our fragility as humanness is something we share. It has its specific color in our lives, but too can be a place of beauty and transformation.

Take, for example, a dancer who has a severe injury and must learn to utilize the other places in her or his body to find the movement to express the inner resonances. This is not ideal, but dancers as musicians can both rely on the same forms, and sometimes not find new inspiration. An injury or limit can invite one into moving in ways and combining other forms as voice, poetry, or site-specific work that may not otherwise occurred. The limits in the body can be a place for grace, an opening to the unexpected. No matter what, the body does age, you can count on this reality, and needs to continually reinvent ways of moving and living within the body that create vitality. So you may not be able to run anymore because of your knees, but what about kayaking? Or you may not be able to play hockey, well perhaps yoga? Or you may be in constant pain, well get yourself to a massage therapist and indulge your body in comfort. In our limits, we are challenged to leave our predictable ways of moving and change our repertoire. The comfort zones can be left behind and discovery is a never ending source of delight. And this delight could really be to change the speed in which we undertake our days. Slowing down could be an act of transgression. When the body slows, it gives a chance to really feel our feet rooted on the earth, to experience a sense of being grounded. To once again feel our roots, we once again can fly. Or as the poet, Juan Ramon Jimenez (1973) says,

> Roots and wings.
> But let the wing grow roots
> and the roots fly. (p. 6)

The body roots us inward and connects us to the interior life and what most matters to us. And we may not even know what that is, but our deepest longings are waiting to be uncovered. We need all the strength – physical, emotional, intellectual and spiritual for the journey. Two lovers' strength and health resides in both their solitude and companionship. The body needs time alone and together with others. And as lovers need to rediscover the beauty in shared presences, delighting in small things and often simple, so the body needs to find these small delights. The smell of the sea or pine, an expanse of the chest, releasing to wet tears, or a spontaneous burst of joy.

Rediscover the scent of your own life, let it bloom daffodils on the inside of you and let your own dear body guide you, foot by foot, hip by hip, heart by heart. I have been longing for you to come home for quite some time now, and it really is about living more effortlessly. More ease. More delight. Bodily knowing and understanding are your spiritual guides always with you for your search and your research. Now go let your body out and once again find the infectious joy of coming home to yourself.

REFERENCES

hooks, b. (1994). *Teaching to transgress: Education as the practice of freedom.* New York, NY: Routledge.

Jiménez, J. R. (1973). Under the water. In F. G. Lorca & J. R. Jiménez (Eds.), *Lorca and Jiménez; Selected poems* (pp. 1–6). Boston, MA: Beacon Press.

Merton, T. (1961). *New seeds of contemplation.* New York, NY: Directions.

CHAPTER 10

UNKNOWN KNOWERS

Mediating Knowledge in the "Global Village"

Stuart J. Murray and Twyla Gibson

We are unknown to ourselves, we knowers, we ourselves, to ourselves, and there is a good reason for this. We have never looked for ourselves, so how are we ever supposed to find ourselves?

—Friedrich Nietzsche, *On the Genealogy of Morality* (1887/1994, p. 3)

Village people aren't that much in love with each other. The global village is a place of very arduous interfaces and very abrasive situations.... Terrorists, hijackers, these are people minus identity."

—Marshall McLuhan, *Understanding Me* (1977/2003, pp. 265–266)

Epistemologies of Ignorance in Education, pp. 199–219
Copyright © 2011 by Information Age Publishing

INTRODUCTION: WE WHO REMAIN UNKNOWN

This chapter takes a philosophical approach to the question of how the modern mass media contribute to an epistemology of ignorance by constituting the modern subject as a passive recipient of information, an "unknowing knower." While burgeoning electronic media provide easy access to information, scholars continue to debate the relationship between "information" and "knowledge." For example, recent articles focus on Google to ask whether online search engines are "making us stupid" (Carr, 2008). These sorts of questions are perennial; indeed, long ago Plato asked in the *Phaedrus* whether the technology of writing would lead inevitably to a decline in human intelligence, suggesting that the mere appearance of knowledge would supplant wisdom and truth (Plato, 2004). This chapter is not concerned with specific media technologies. To be sure, these can be powerful tools to help us fill in gaps in our knowledge. Instead, we take a step back to examine modern media culture and how it fosters an epistemology of ignorance at the subjective level. For, as Sullivan and Tuana (2007) write, "Sometimes what we do not know is not a mere gap in knowledge, the accidental result of an epistemological oversight" (p. 1). Instead, we suggest that to know ourselves at this juncture in history will require an account of the effects of media and the ways that these enable, as well as foreclose upon, epistemic self-certitude.

Friedrich Nietzsche wrote the epigraph above well over a century ago. Although Nietzsche could not have anticipated the shift to global communication networks, his criticism continues to resonate. These words represent his philosophical attack on Cartesian subjectivity and epistemology. For René Descartes, what is most certain is that humans are subjects who know and are known, what we might call "knowing knowers." His famous maxim *cogito ergo sum* is foundational, a "first philosophy," which declares that every time I reflect upon myself, I can be certain that I am, I exist. The subjective relation for Descartes is immediate, which is to say, *unmediated*. This is both an ontological claim about what is, and an epistemological claim about what can be known, and known with certainty. The kernel of human identity, the "I", is characterized as *res cogitans*, essentially a "thinking thing" or "thinking stuff": "A thing that doubts, understands, affirms, denies, wills, refuses, and that also imagines and senses" (Descartes, 1641/1993, p. 20). We know ourselves as subjects, according to Descartes, when we take ourselves at once, reflexively, as the immediate objects of our epistemological inquiry.

Nietzsche responds in terms that frustrate Cartesian epistemology. He states that we cannot be objects of our own knowledge because we cannot even "find" ourselves. Indeed, we have never even looked. But what would such a looking entail? Nietzsche (1873/2001) asks, "What does man actually know about himself? Is he, indeed, ever able to perceive himself completely, as if laid out in a lighted display case?" (p. 1172). The whole business of looking turns out to be fraught. If seeing is believing, then it is certainly not knowledge in any rigorous sense. Vision turns out to be mediated by expectations and conventions that are always already epistemic: a lighted display case, received taxonomies for ordering visual information as meaningful patterns, colors, and motion. The visual field is coded, multiplex, and saturated, informed by race, class, and gender. Where, or better yet, how, shall we look if we hope to find ourselves? And is this question not more daunting in the global village, in a world that is mediated through global telecommunications networks and their live-feed, their sleepless spectacles? If there is no return to Descartes, or even to the time of Nietzsche, how, in what ways, by what terms, and where, shall we find the truth of who we are?

More than ever, our media technologies constitute us as Cartesian subjects, "knowing knowers" whose epistemological self-confidence seems to increase with the advent of each new technology and with greater access to information. When we "look for ourselves," we stumble onto a phantasmagoria of mediatized representations, "media tropes" (Murray, 2009), and we have grown accustomed to experience these uncritically, as accurate reflections. But such self-knowledge is problematic. Along with Nietzsche, we argue that such epistemological self-certitude is illusionary, a dangerous epistemology of ignorance. We claim in this chapter that existing paradigms of identity, subjectivity, and knowledge are proving incommensurate with the demands of our networked society, and yet we hold to them all the more obstinately. Are networked subjects self-knowing or is identity fragmented and uncertain? Can we foster new forms of identity that will help us to negotiate the conflicts that arise from our rapidly changing technoculture? This chapter takes up the problem of ignorance and changing epistemologies in the age of information, media convergence, and technoscience. Extending the seminal work of Marshall McLuhan, we tentatively propose avenues for responding to some of the urgent educational challenges of our age, and argue for the importance of critical media studies.

THE GLOBAL VILLAGE

Marshall McLuhan predicted that a potentially catastrophic identity crisis would affect the inhabitants of the global village. Most people, however, misunderstand what McLuhan meant by the "global village," seeing instead a place of interconnected utility, prosperity, and progress rather than abrasion and conflict (see Gibson & Murray, forthcoming). This is the Cartesian ruse, by which technoscientific progress is believed to lead to the gradual enlightenment of humankind, the eradication of poverty and disease, the end of racism and ethnic violence, in short, a New Jerusalem, a utopia of affluence and happiness as the fruits of human reason. Clearly, this future has not yet arrived. While technoscientific knowledge has allowed us to communicate and work and live together in ways that were previously unimaginable, the digital age raises new and serious challenges to us as a people. In the most obvious sense, new technologies offer more than simply new ways to communicate, to work, and to live; they also offer us new ways to exploit, to enslave, and to annihilate the other, crimes that are all too often sanctioned in the pursuit of knowledge, progress, and happiness.

There is thus a danger inherent in "naturalizing" technoscientific progress, to imagine it as an evolution, in the Darwinian sense. With natural evolution, species undergo a process of natural selection and change over time. Those species that flourish are the ones that best adapt to their environments. Often, we mistakenly think of this adaptation as "progress." But as Darwin himself imagines it, a biofeedback loop is at work between the organism and its environment. The process resembles a self-improvement program, except there is no "self," the process is not self-conscious, it is blind. Indeed, it is brutal. Nature is "red in tooth and claw," as the nineteenth-century British poet Alfred Lord Tennyson wrote in 1850. In contradistinction, technoscience is not natural; it is the product of Cartesian subjectivity and epistemology, which are also founded in sociohistorical conventions, not "natural" in quite the same way. We are and must remain responsible for our technoscience and its effects. We are not responsible for nature in quite the same way that we are responsible for human creations. Natural selection has a built-in inevitability; evolution is driven by brute necessity. If organisms do not adapt, they will become extinct. Nature is vicious but survival is at stake. For technoscience, however, there is neither inevitability nor necessity. We have a choice with our technologies. Where nature is blind and without moral values, humans (when at our best) are thinking creatures who have moral values.

Thus, human "progress" in the social and moral sense might best be understood as a *revolution*, rather than an *evolution*. We are creatures who revolt. We are creatures who clash with each other because our values are not natural and necessary but always open to question and interpretation. We clash over what counts as real progress. For instance, does the technoscientific superiority of one nation mean that its citizens are more "evolved" human beings? Does their technoscientific superiority give them the moral right to rule others? To invade other lands? To exploit the inhabitants? To steal their resources? To colonize or enslave them?

Here we begin to see the danger in taking technoscientific progress as natural and inevitable, as justification for a set of actions. History provides countless examples of colonization and exploitation promoted as "civilizing missions," self-righteously justified because those who are colonized and exploited are deemed "under-developed," "less evolved," or "less civilized." The underlying premise of colonization in the name of "development" is that rationalistic technoscientific superiority is synonymous with greater human ethical, social, and political progress.

These are some of the abiding questions that our technoscience raises, but leaves unanswered and unanswerable according to its terms alone. In the global village, thanks to communication technologies, we are brought face-to-face with the desires, the needs, and sometimes the desolate misery of others in distant parts of the world. They appeal to us through our televisions, computers, and other communications media, those lighted "display cases" of the modern world. But what does it mean to look into the faces of these others? Shall we look or look away? And how shall we, each of us, find ourselves in this world picture? How, and by what terms, shall we understand our responsibility to grapple with images and information as they are shaped into proximate knowledge, raw human suffering? The metaphor of the village is important: in a village we know our neighbors, we recognize the faces of those we pass on the street, and we purchase our products in the local marketplace. In the global village, our neighbors are present electronically but often remote geographically. The faces that we see are the faces that are linked through our facebook accounts and through television and the Internet. They stare back at us, even if we have never met them in the flesh. And the products that we purchase and consume come increasingly from a global marketplace: plums grown in Peru, moccasins from Macau, computer chips from China. Seizing on the manifold possibilities of global networks of all kinds, techno-optimists declare a new age of love and global intimacy, a chance to reach out and to embrace the great beyond. Speaking in pentecostal tones, technoscience is heralded as the way to salvation. Consider the unbridled optimism demonstrated in the pages of NASA's website, where technoscience promises "to pioneer the future ... to push the envelope ... to do what has never been done before" (O'Keefe, 2006). These clichés are reassuring gospel for a secular world, suggesting that salvation is nigh, and not to worry because it is in the hands of scientists, those known knowers. To call this a secular religiosity is not farfetched when one distills the truth of NASA's "vision for the future": "Our mandate is: To improve life here; To extend life to there; To find life beyond" (O'Keefe, 2006).

THE DARK, ATAVISTIC SIDE OF TECHNOSCIENCE

Rather than uncritically accepting the rhetoric of Life and Salvation, an epistemology of ignorance, McLuhan (1995) bids us to confront the "dark atavistic side" of technoscience (p. 247). Equating technoscience with unmitigated "progress" and epistemic certitude is a mistake. When McLuhan (2003) spoke of the "global village," he was not always full of hope and optimism. There is often dread and foreboding: "Village people aren't that much in love with each other." He continues, "The global village is a place of very arduous interfaces and very abrasive situations.... When people get close together, they get more and more savage, impatient with each other" (p. 265). For McLuhan, this abrasive hostility is a direct result of the new technoscience that brings us together in unprecedented ways, forcing us to reevaluate what it means to live together, to share our planet and its precious resources. As our communities and their values shift, often imperceptibly, in response to our inventions, we must learn new ways to make sense of our social and political bonds. McLuhan argues that every time radically new communication technologies are introduced, a crisis occurs in the human lifeworld.

We can get a better sense of our current technoscientific revolution by analogy with earlier revolutionary crises in human history. Such historical understanding will help us to respond appropriately to current and future challenges. According to McLuhan (1994) and Walter J. Ong (2002), the first major breakthrough in communication technology was the phonetic alphabet, which allowed humans to represent the spoken word of their oral cultures in visual form, laying it out in space, and preserving it through time. Before the alphabet, prehistoric or tribal humans were thought to have lived in direct communion with the world and with others, synaesthetically, through sound, sight, smell, and touch. With the introduction of the alphabet, humans stopped listening in quite the same way; we became more visual, detached, linear, quantitative, analytic, and logical. The alphabet changed our relationship to time and to place, thereby changing the way we interact with the world and with others. To take one simple example, in some respects we no longer enjoy a direct and embodied connection with the tree. Instead, we have different ways to symbolize trees, such as through the letters T-R-E-E, which can be written down and preserved, referenced, cross-referenced, and passed along in communication. The word "tree" does not look, feel, smell, or taste like a tree in any way, even if the paper it is written on comes from trees; you cannot climb it, build shelter from it, or burn it to keep warm at night. Consequently, McLuhan and Ong claim that the alphabet slowly eroded our collective identity and our sense of belonging in a tribal community; eventually, this collective consciousness was replaced by the individuated consciousnesses of literate culture, the idea and experience of a distinct rational self. Descartes is an exemplar of this subjectivity, a mind distinct from its body, while much of Nietzsche's writing seeks to return us to the truth of our body, to "re-tribalize" us, as McLuhan would say.

The story of the shift from oral to literate culture helps us to understand the shift that is currently underway, one from which we have less critical distance because we are in the midst of it. The literate culture that gradually replaced oral or tribal culture is now itself being supplanted by digital culture. We are confronted with new ways of living and relating to one another. McLuhan (1995) writes:

> I believe that our survival, and at the very least our comfort and happiness, is predicated on understanding the nature of our new environment because unlike previous environmental changes, the electric media constitutes a total and near-instantaneous transformation of culture, values and attitudes. This upheaval generates great pain and identity loss, which can be ameliorated only through a conscious awareness of its dynamics. (pp. 238–239)

Those of us born into this culture have begun to move away from the rational self that the phonetic alphabet ushered in. Networked and connected in the global village, the identity of each individual is no longer the most immediate experience. When we are emailing or gaming with friends online, when we are "tweeting" on Twitter or sharing music and videos, we are node or relay in a vast interconnected network. McLuhan (2003) claims that instantaneous electronic networks return us to oral modes of existence, transporting us "back into the bicameral mind, which is tribal, collective, without any individual consciousness" (p. 265). Ong (2002) describes digital cultures as inaugurating what he calls a "secondary orality," which is not a true return to origins, but "a more deliberate and self-conscious orality, based permanently on the use of writing and print" (p. 136). We must develop a conscious awareness of these dynamics.

SHIFTING SUBJECTIVE AND
EPISTEMOLOGICAL PARADIGMS

To see how subjectivity is changing thanks to digital technoscience, we might look at how the concept of authorship, and by extension, proprietary selfhood and Cartesian epistemology, have begun to change in the global village. We used to think of a book's author as the unequivocal *source* of the book, and the content of that book as something that the author had individually produced. The author's identity is important in this model. Why should I trust what I read? Perhaps the author is a professor or has some other recognizable credentials on the subject. In the digital world, however, there is not the same author–authority connection, nor is there the same centralized system for verifying the author's identity (see, for instance, "Authors Analogue and Digital" in Poster, 2001). If we consider a Wikipedia article, it is impossible to point to one single author. Wikipedia entries are collaborations from many contributors across the planet, and there is no easy way to verify the identity or the authority of the person who contributes. McLuhan used to say that books would become obsolete for just this reason. Similarly, with rap music we can point to an artist but not to an author in the traditional sense. Rap artfully blends together a mix from various other artists. There is no one single source of the creation: the music is collaborative over time and space, a mix of various people who speak and perform, here and there. Their words and music are remixed and repackaged (see Blair, 2009). There is less emphasis on the "true" identity behind an artistic creation; there is greater emphasis on the artistic "brand" or "label" that is marketed.

Unsurprisingly, copyright law is ill equipped to deal with digital authorship. The law is Cartesian, based on the old-fashioned idea of a single author, a rational, known and knowable knower, who produces a single product, and who owns the rights to that "product." Copyright lawyers like to tell us that it is illegal to share music through Napster or BitTorrent technologies, but to those who have grown up online it feels like the most "natural" thing in the world to do, sharing is what you do as a node in a network and "ownership" of something on the Internet strikes young people, especially, as silly (see Murray & Poster, 2003). The digital world encourages the circulation and recirculation of these texts, whether it is a Wikipedia entry, a piece of music, an episode of *South Park*, a blog entry, or an amateur Youtube video. But given capital investments in the culture industry, it is not difficult to understand the legal crisis that arises when old and new values clash. Today a different paradigm is emerging, and the old legal paradigms do not fit. McLuhan (1995) writes:

> the instant nature of electric-information movement is decentralizing, rather than enlarging, the family of man into a new state of multitudinous tribal existences. Particularly in countries where literate values are deeply institutionalized, this is a highly traumatic process, since the clash of the old segmented visual culture and the new integral electronic culture creates a crisis of identity, a vacuum of the self, which generates tremendous violence, that is simply an identity quest, private or corporate, social or commercial. (p. 249)

This "vacuum of the self" is a widespread cultural phenomenon that begs the question of authorship, authority, and identity. McLuhan (2003) describes "Terrorists [and] hijackers..." as "people minus identity. They are determined to make it somehow, to get coverage, to get noticed" (p. 266).

Global terrorism is paradigmatic in many ways because it is a product of the mass media: today, to be somebody is to be on TV. The spectacle must be built into the terrorist act if it is going to be noticed (see, for instance, Nacos, 2002; Niedzviecki, 2005). McLuhan, who died in 1980, predicted that media networks and satellites "will distribute terrorist paranoia around the world in living color to match each accelerating disruptive event" (McLuhan & Powers, 1989, p. 115). We might think of the second plane smashing into the World Trade Center and how this short and shaky amateur video clip has been burned into our collective consciousness. McLuhan (1995) also predicted the end of political democracy (p. 260) and the rise of political leaders who are not "literate" men but who appeal to collective fear, who mobilize "the collective tribal image and the iconic image of the tribal chieftain" (p. 261). It is difficult not to read our own age here, when a barely literate man spent 8 years as U.S. Commander-in-Chief: and the literate one to follow cannot seem to escape his shadow. The value of literacy has become supplanted by marketing, propaganda, images, icons, and brands; the tribal chieftain can be a fool and a tyrant, as long as he is resonant with the global consciousness. Rather than leaders, we have an emergent collective identity, emotional connectedness, the end of privacy and the end of the Cartesian, "true self" as we know it.

In a recent newspaper editorial, the Canadian philosopher Mark Kingwell dramatizes the clash between literate and post-literate modes of knowing and relating. He gestures to the obsolete notion of authorship and individual responsibility in relation to plagiarism at the university. We teach our students that when they write an essay, if they use someone else's ideas or words, then they must take care to document their sources according to standard conventions. Just like the music industry, here too juridical principles are meant to shore up a sense of personal responsibility. But the conscientious student panics: Are we meant to document every last detail? From where did the ideas come? There is no way for us to remember. Much like the Wikipedia article, our own essays are collaborations over time from many sources. We should stop pretending, Kingwell (2007) writes, that there is any such thing as original work. We should give up the idea of "the single-author, my-brain-on-paper essay," and opt "instead for collaboration and group evaluation" (p. F8). Of course, it is difficult to imagine this being implemented in the classroom. But we must at least begin to acknowledge that the old-fashioned concept of the single-author as the source of his or her essay is a bit of a myth. Essay writing and examinations have been around for a long time, and we have only begun to imagine the kind of evaluation systems that would replace them. Something *will* need to replace them and the literate truth that they represent, but until then, there will be a struggle between the old and the new.

In the health sciences, too, we find the knowing, individuated subject in crisis, thanks to advances in technoscience. Just as the author is in question in the university essay, in the health sciences we find that the concept of the autonomous rational subject is eroding. To take just one example, in recent years digital imaging technologies have become so good at capturing images of the brain that the Cartesian foundations of our legal system are being challenged. Remarkably, in some legal cases in the United States (Rosen, 2007), evidence from technologically advanced neuroimaging has been used as a defense against murder charges. In a nutshell, neurologists are able to show in a statistically significant way that there is an increased likelihood of homicidal behavior if certain portions of the brain are physically enlarged. While we cannot conclude definitively that brain shape *causes* murder, it nevertheless looks like brain shape is an influential factor. If the link can be proven, is Mr. Smith still responsible for murdering his wife? Or is Mr. Smith's *abnormal brain physiology* responsible for murdering his wife? What would this mean? Does it even make sense to speak in this way? The old-fashioned view would be that Mr. Smith is a *person*, that he is the sole rational agent or *author* of his actions, and that we must hold him responsible for what he does. But technoscience demonstrates that the complex relation between Mr. Smith, his brain, and his actions is fuzzy indeed.

In a tradition that privileges Cartesian subjectivity and epistemology, the law must discount the physiological dimension of Mr. Smith, inventing instead Mr. Smith the autonomous person, the singular actor, the moral agent, the law's fiction of "the reasonable man." If, for a moment, we speak only of written texts, the post-literate or digital view would be that there is *no* single author, and this is difficult enough to grasp. But what crisis is unleashed when we start to think of brains and bodies and persons in this way? In legal and ethical terms, who is responsible? Is Mr. Smith a node in a complex neural, corporeal, and social network? Could we put Mr. Smith's brain on the stand? Could we *punish* Mr. Smith's brain for the murder of Mrs. Smith, without punishing *him*? Technoscience raises seemingly unanswerable questions concerning the "truth" of subjects who are presumed to know. While the law holds to the principle of rational autonomy, of subjects who are "presumed to know," our technoscience forces us to ask whether this is not an epistemology of ignorance, a belief system that is fast becoming obsolete. It turns out, somewhat ironically, that the very technoscience that was founded in and presumably meant to uphold the traditional sovereignty of the Cartesian subject is the same technoscience that has led the subject into an *aporia*, a dead end or impasse. In other words, technoscience is beginning to reveal subjects who are incommensurable with the theories of subjectivity that have been in force for centuries; meanwhile, no coherent theory of the subject yet exists to replace this anachronism.

CRISIS

We are at an epistemological *aporia*. Our legal system presumes that Mr. Smith is a person, an autonomous moral agent who is the sole rational author of his actions, and so on. Similarly, the education system presumes that each of us is the sole author of the essays that we write. And if we look a bit further afield, we can begin to see that the whole system of democratic capitalism equally relies on the presumption that we are acting rationally and making free and informed choices when we purchase a product in the marketplace we call "society." Certainly, savvy advertisers and political parties seem to know that this is untrue; they know that we are motivated by factors such as emotion, a sense of collective belonging, prestige, sexual desire, and myriad factors that have little to do with the consumer being the single-author source of his or her actions. The problem is, once we admit that there is no such person behind our actions, no "doer" behind the "deed" (Nietzsche, 1994), then what? We will need to overhaul the entire legal system, the education system, the political system, and so on. The truths of technoscience have surpassed and outstripped our rational–literate capacity to find ourselves in their web, in the virtual display cases of modernity.

We began above with the commonsense claim that technoscience does not "evolve" in a Darwinian sense, and that if we "naturalize" technoscientific advances, then we are entering dangerous territory, socially and politically, because we risk sanctioning crimes in the name of historical progress, knowledge, and necessity. Perhaps these assertions were no more than Cartesian conceits or an undetected humanism at work. Perhaps technoscience has a life of its own, after all. Perhaps these advances have run away from us and we cannot make sense of the sometimes monstrous implications they carry in their wake. Judging from the questions above, technoscience is marked, arguably, by its own necessity, its own inner logic, even a kind of inevitability. This is a familiar theme in science fiction. If we concede that technoscience is both evolutionary *and* revolutionary, then perhaps we will be forced to abandon our Cartesian conceits and to contemplate posthuman, which is to say, post-humanistic, conceptions of subjectivity (see, for instance, Hayles, 1999).

We are not subjects who unequivocally know and control the effects of technoscience any more than we can control the weather; on the contrary, the few anecdotal examples above suggest that survival in the global village will depend on a revolution in subjectivity and epistemology. And yet we remain wedded to old models, solemnly exalt them as "epistemology," and refuse to acknowledge the ignorance that sustains them. Again, Nietzsche's (2001) critique of Cartesian subjectivity and epistemology is resonant, delivered with characteristic rancor and wit:

> this intellect has no additional mission which would lead it beyond human life. Rather, it is human, and only its possessor and begetter take it so solemnly, as though the world's axis turned within it. But if we could communicate with the gnat, we would learn that he likewise flies through the air with the same solemnity, that he feels the flying center of the universe within himself. (pp. 1171–1172)

This is not to exalt the world according to the gnat, but it is an exhortation to contemplate the world from a radically different perspective. In the information age, we already find ourselves distributed in the network, in the midst of connections moving at the speed of light, without fixed identity, "like an exposed spider squatting in a thrumming web" (McLuhan & Powers, 1989, p. 95). This is dizzying and disorienting; we seem to lack the resources to re-orient ourselves. We have only just begun to think through the subjective and epistemic crises that have been precipitated by technoscience.

The question, of course, is how to foster a revolution in human thinking. The challenges are monumental. In citing from the NASA website above, we suggested that technoscientific progress is often cloaked in religious rhetoric, filling us with the promise of a time to come, ostensibly leading us toward prosperity, happiness, and human enlightenment. But pious faith supports epistemologies of ignorance, orienting us in a world by making sense of the nonsensical, a structural abdication of responsibility, fundamentalism. If we ask how we might begin to *find* ourselves, we may find that we are incapable because self-identity is mediated through images and in terms that our not our own. In what ways can we foster a critical resistance to the technoscientific fundamentalism that seems to have evolved beyond our capacity to control or comprehend it, and that has been co-opted at times by corporate ideologies and interests?

We would like to point to two popular forms of resistance to technoscience, broadly construed. While both perhaps rightly see some of the inherent dangers of technoscience, we suggest that they are deeply problematic because neither of them seeks to understand what it means to live in the global village. A true revolution would involve a revolution in thinking that does not simply reject technoscience outright, in a reactionary vein, but that builds toward a critical posthumanism. First, then, are those who resist technoscientific fundamentalism by various forms of old-fashioned religious fundamentalism. This is a retrogressive response and it is ultimately hopeless because there is no dialogue: fundamentalism prohibits us from asking questions, and worse, it condemns us morally and spiritually for asking questions. Religious fundamentalism demands obedience to a word that is taken on faith as fundamentally and universally true. The global village will always be a place of arduous interfaces so long as there is fundamentalism, so we must work to find other ways to satisfy the human needs that fundamentalism seems equipped to satisfy.

Second, there is the Luddite or conservative resistance to technoscientific fundamentalism, a resistance that is also reactionary. The conservative approach would abandon technoscience or seeks ways to understand it in terms of the old, literate value system. In other words, according to this approach we ought to return to the idea of the single-author, the rational agent, the individual self who is responsible and supposedly free. One obvious problem with this position is that we would be forced to abandon some of the insights that science and technology have given us, while ignoring the very real questions that they raise. If once again we consider Mr. Smith's brain, and we learn that neurophysiology influences murderous behavior, then we are ethically and intellectually remiss if we jettison this piece of knowledge because it does not fit our desired models of the human person or legal system. Instead, we argue, it means we are now responsible for finding new ways to accommodate this knowledge, and this will mean a paradigm shift in what we accept as true.

A CALL FOR MEDIA LITERACY IN EDUCATION

Perhaps there is a third way to critically resist technoscientific fundamentalism while accepting that we are, for better or worse, global villagers who live in the midst of a new subjective and epistemological paradigm. It does not mean retreating into another form of fundamentalism, nor does it mean clinging or regressing to the nostalgic values of an earlier time. In response to rising fundamentalisms everywhere, the task will be to offer other ways to satisfy the needs that fundamentalism seems able to satisfy. And in response to the conservatives who call for a return to the old values, the task will be to offer new values that will honor, rather than undermine, the gifts of science and technology. We must make the most of our distributed intelligence, to try to imagine together new ways of living with others. It means that we must learn to tap into the tribal consciousness of the digital age, to make use of our emerging collective identity, our emotional connectedness, and our creativity. The revolution in thinking and being calls for thinkers and poets and artists who will work together in our networked communities to struggle to invent new ways of thinking, new modes of living together, a new politics, and a new education system. If we are to survive the intimate press of the global village, we must find the ways in which thought, poetry, and art will foster an openness that resists fundamentalism and that works creatively toward a new set of values. In McLuhan's words, "the function of art is to provide some livable distance" (McLuhan & Powers, 1989, p. 87). "Without the artist's invention," McLuhan writes, "man merely *adapts* to his technologies and becomes their servo-mechanism" (McLuhan & McLuhan, 1988, p. 98).

As technologies converge and the pace of change builds momentum, media will increasingly saturate every facet of our lives. McLuhan saw that constant exposure to the mediated world has a numbing effect, inducing a kind of stupor, a "Narcissus narcosis," that leads to feelings of "alienation," "disembodiment," and "de-personalization" (Danesi, 2008, p. 114). He saw that those possessing the most efficient communication technologies tend to use them to anesthetize, dominate, colonize, and control others in order to further their own interests and ends (Murray, 2008; Tschofen, 2008). He diagnosed hostility as a symptom of the "quest for identity" (McLuhan, 1977/2003, p. 266), and warned of increasing violence along the borders and frontiers between different media systems and cultures. He proposed education in media and their effects as the only remedy for the somnambulism induced by constant exposure to media, and for the violence that results from the forms of control that media exercise (Gibson, 2008a, 2008b). Education awakens us from the narcosis slumber and helps us to "momentarily step out of the system" to see the larger picture, to resist exploitation and abuse, avoid violence, and to nurture new subjective and epistemological paradigms in the age of the global village.

Retreating from society, moving off the grid, cutting ourselves off, these are not viable solutions. For doing so entails yielding to our ignorance and our status as unknown knowers. We must instead learn techniques that will allow us to enjoy the advantages and pleasures provided by technoscience, and to simultaneously resist the poisonous effects that either paralyze and make us docile, or make us desperate and enraged. Becoming knowing knowers requires new forms of education; it entails learning how to be "in" the media environment and fully involved with it, but not "of" it or "for" it.

McLuhan (1995) argued that many core assumptions, goals, and practices underlying education programs in place today have been rendered obsolete by the shift to new technologies and the transition to global media. We need to re-evaluate the programs that we have, rethink our educational strategies at all levels, and foster inclusive interdisciplinary and multidisciplinary approaches to media and information (Gibson, 2008a). As we build new collaborative models for work, play, and politics, it is imperative that we acknowledge alternative points of view and recognize different modes of information literacy, so that everyone has an opportunity to acquire the knowledge and skills requisite to fluency in the processes of information organization, storage, and retrieval across many disciplines, to play a role in producing new products or perspectives, and to contribute to the task of finding and implementing solutions that go beyond established boundaries and current know-how (Ontario Ministry of Education, 2002, p. 4). For only then will there be peace in the global village.

McLuhan (1962) recognized the problems and tensions created by shifts in communication technology and invented educational techniques and strategies that help to remedy the systemic ignorance of negative media effects. He explained that media create "technological environments [that] are not merely passive containers of people but are active processes that reshape people and other technologies alike" (p. i). He viewed all media as extensions of our bodies and minds, intermediaries that connect two things, such as a sender and receiver, and through which some "system of 'signs' (pictographs, alphabet characters, etc.) for recording ideas can be actualized" (Danesi, 2008, p. 115). But the medium does not just sit between sender and receiver: it includes the sender, the receiver, and the message in a total system, habitat, or environment (Strate, 2008).

The problem with media environments is that they "work us over completely." It is difficult to see beyond the system in which we are immersed. Environments are total, "invisible." "Their ground rules, pervasive structure, and overall patterns elude easy perception" (McLuhan & Fiore, 1967, pp. 84–85). Humans have an inherent gap in our sensory perception that blocks us from grasping the total picture, and a perceptual bias that makes us tend to foreground certain contents and to ignore the background or environment upon which those contents figure forth. We can only perceive our environment when it is juxtaposed with an anti-environment.

Artists and their works create these sorts of antienvironments that generate heightened awareness, critical distance, and new modes of perception. Similarly, technologies can simulate the creation of anti-environments. Images broadcast from satellites make it possible for us to glimpse outside our system and to achieve the critical distance that allows us to see our planet as a kind of "exhibit" or work of art. "Anything becomes a work of art as soon as it is surrounded by a new environment," that is to say, it becomes visible, "it creates attention; it creates perception." Indeed, the function of art is to "teach human perception" (McLuhan, 2003, p. 93).

More than ever before, we need artists and poets and visionaries to counteract our myopia, to open our eyes to new modes of perception, to teach us to see and to think and to know. McLuhan (1962) was just this sort of visionary. He created a "field approach" (p. i) that concentrates on antienvironments, bringing to an examination of issues, questions or problems, repertoires of methodologies from multiple disciplines under the framework of media and mediation. His writings are exemplars of this interdisciplinary approach to media research (Ontario Ministry of Education, 2002, p. 31).

McLuhan (1964/1994) frequently warned that we are "blind to the character of the medium" and provided examples to bring perceptual lacunae to our attention. He incorporated an understanding of human perceptual limits into a technique for media analysis and created intellectual devices to compensate for our sensory shortcomings (p. 9). The first example was the figure/ground relation from Gestalt psychology; the second, the example of the jet airplane breaking the sound barrier. The diagram of the figure/ground relation reveals how a dividing line mediates between two related fields: one field is foregrounded as the content, while the other is suppressed into the background. A shift in attention reverses the fields. This redirection of attention transforms the perception of the image as we suddenly become aware of the total environment that encompasses both. Similarly, the example of the airplane accelerating past the speed of sound makes apparent a shift in perception that turns the audible noise of the jet engines into a vision of waves on the wings. Due to the structure of our perception, we are able to perceive figure or ground, sound or vision, but not both at once. At the same time, there is on some level an awareness of the unity of the total configuration and environment. Discriminating one image from the other, or sound from vision, implies the whole relationship because perception maintains and locates the thing to be foregrounded out of the background and then suppresses and hides the background. The shift is a dissociation, one of two phases of a total act of attention in which each stage is complementary to the other and implies it.

The line that mediates between the two images in the Gestalt figure, the barrier that is surpassed when the jet accelerates beyond the speed of sound, these are models of mediation that help us to see and understand our perceptual patterns and processes. Observing how the line is a "medium" in the figure/ground relation makes it possible to envision the symmetry that binds the alternate fields together in a unity. Attending to the moment when the airplane breaks the sound-barrier makes it possible to grasp intellectually the total environment that contains both sound and vision. By shifting the focus of attention back and forth between ground and figure, form and content, sound and vision, we can mentally grasp the "Gestalt" and understand the "total configuration." The key to resisting media effects is to avoid attending exclusively to the sensory data that are foregrounded, for these are mere appearances and "false resting places," as Plato cautioned long ago.

McLuhan was a careful reader of Plato. He synthesized ancient discussions of mediation with contemporary research findings, applying the insights from the figure/ground relation and the break-boundary to the analysis of media, the interfaces between media systems and cultures, and to pivotal points in history involving shifts in dominant media systems, such as the current migration from print to digital technologies. His aphorism, "the medium is the message," encapsulates the basic premise of this approach. Mapping the figure/ground relation onto the example of the televised newscast, we could say that the message is in the total configuration of the picture and sounds that appear through our sense perceptions as the 6 o'clock news. The medium includes the satellite and broadcast technologies, ownership of the channel and network, the television set, the cable box, the person sitting at the news desk, cameras, lighting, production techniques, employees, advertisers, all those elements in the background that allow the content of the news to be foreground. The content of the news refers to the way that the words and images on the program are organized symbolically. Thus, the "messages" are not communicated only or even primarily by the news content; messages inhere in the medium itself as the environment that grounds the content. So the message of the news is the total configuration of information that occurs through the interplay of form and content, figure and ground, sound and vision, operating simultaneously through the character of the medium. The real news message involves much more than what appears on TV.

We can use these techniques to analyze the interaction among the various shaping forces along the borders between two different media systems. Resistance involves refusing to hold our attention on one field while ignoring the other. To employ an historical example involving cultures dominated by different systems colliding on a frontier, we would decline to concentrate solely on the rhetoric of the Europeans who "discovered" and conquered the native peoples of the Americas. Instead, we would shift attention to evidence of the oral and tribal cultures that inhabited those worlds, their history, their traditions, their versions of events. We would alternate attention between the European and Aboriginal sides of the story, using as a point of reference the sites of the encounter as zones of mediation, examining hands, teeth, tongues, and eyeballs, and the extensions of these human body parts as words and weapons (Tschofen, 2008). The human body, and media as extensions of the body, are locations wherein the social and cultural processes associated with two different forms of power are made manifest, thereby exposing them to observation and analysis, to critique. It is this active process of directed attention and the concentration along zones of contact and sites of shifts that allows us to step out of the field or system of which we are part, and for a moment to mentally put together the two fields, to imagine the integral unity of the events that configured history during that time period, and to resist the bias that clouds our vision.

Similarly, the field approach can be applied to today's media environment, at the turning point in the shift from print to digital technologies. We should not attend solely to the content of the news and accept this information at face value. Instead, we would pursue a dialectic of attention, constantly questioning the information that is presented. How does ownership of the network influence the selection of the events that comprise the news for that day? And how are those news items presented? What commercial advertisements are shown during the news hour? How are these commercials edited and interspersed with the news? What products or ideas are being sold? What techniques do advertisers use to try to influence our perceptions and behaviors? What issues are foregrounded while others are buried in silence? How does the medium utilize rhetorical tropes, seduction, stereotypes, and other components of media images, dialogue, and texts that establish conventions and formulas for themes, motifs, and manipulations? How is scientific research concerning human mental functioning enlisted so that vested interests gain access to our inner life in order to "work us over" at psychic levels below the threshold of conscious functioning and awareness? (Curtis, 2002).

When the news reports on the acts of terrorists or hijackers, we would shift attention to those acts, to those people, and ask: Why have they sought coverage? Why are they trying to be noticed? What identity are they seeking? Further, we might ask how our technological environments and processes shaped these people and these acts: How did these particular people come to embody the collision between different media systems and cultures, and to serve as effects of media? And how are we ourselves, we unknown knowers, implicated and responsible?

To come to know ourselves, as ourselves, to ourselves and *for others*, we must engage in a search for ourselves. Nietzsche is correct. We can only *find* ourselves if we look. We must learn to face our ignorance squarely, to step back from the display case, to see beyond the spectacle, the images, appearances, and false selves that have been imposed upon us, to clear away these obstacles to our vision and begin to reconstruct authentic subjectivities and identities that reflect the truth of who we really are, shifting, multiple, collective, and tribal. This looking involves a conscious awareness of the dynamics of media, it involves a ceaseless questioning of images, information, events, and values. In the era of the remix, of digital manipulation of images, of disinformation and propaganda, this process of questioning is diametrically opposed to the unquestioning acceptance of fundamentalisms, of pre-fabricated ideas, values, and subjectivities fed to us by the relentless consumer machinery designed to support our epistemologies of ignorance. Coming to know and "see through" and beyond the techniques and manipulations of media that present the appearance without the reality involves cultivating a critical awareness as the only way we can come to know, understand, and dwell within the new subjective and epistemological paradigms taking shape in the networked world. We must all become artists, create anti-environments, new forms of education, new politics, new values, and new ways of seeing. Only then will we be able to "produce some liveable distance."

REFERENCES

Blair, C. H. (2009). Panic and plagiarism: Authorship and academic dishonesty in a remix culture. *MediaTropes*, 2(1), 159–192. Retrieved from www.mediatropes.com.

Carr, N. (2008, July/August). Is Google making us stupid? *The Atlantic*. Retrieved May 30, 2009, from http://www.theatlantic.com/doc/200807/google

Curtis, A. (Director). (2002). *The century of the self* [Motion picture]. London: British Broadcasting Corporation.

Danesi, M. (2008). The medium is the sign: Was McLuhan a semiotician? In T. Gibson (Ed.), *Marshall McLuhan's "medium is the message": Information literacy in a multimedia age* (Special issue). *MediaTropes*, 1, 113–126. Retrieved from www.mediatropes.com

Descartes, R. (1993). *Meditations on first philosophy in which the existence of God and the distinction of the soul from the body are demonstrated* (D. A. Cress, Trans.) (3rd ed.). Indianapolis: Hackett. (Original work published 1641).

Gibson, T. (2008a). "Double vision: McLuhan's contributions to media as an interdisciplinary approach to communication, culture, and technology." In T. Gibson (Ed.), *Marshall McLuhan's "medium is the message": Information literacy in a multimedia age* (Special issue). *MediaTropes*, 1, 143–166. Retrieved from at www.mediatropes.com

Gibson, T. (2008b). "Introduction." In T. Gibson (Ed.), *Marshall McLuhan's "medium is the message": Information literacy in a multimedia age* (Special issue). *MediaTropes*, 1, i–xiv. Retrieved from www.mediatropes.com

Gibson, T., & Murray, S. J. (forthcoming). Global village. In M. Danesi (Ed.), *Dictionary of media and communications*. New York, NY: M. E. Sharpe.

Hayles, N. K. (1999). *How we became posthuman: Virtual bodies in cybernetics, literature, and informatics*. Chicago, IL: University of Chicago Press.

Kingwell, M. (2008). The end of the single-author, student-brain-on-paper essay. *The Globe and Mail* (Toronto Edition), 13 October 2007, p. F8.

McLuhan, M. (1962). *The Gutenberg galaxy: The making of typographic man*. Toronto: University of Toronto Press.

McLuhan, M. (1994). *Understanding media: The extensions of man*. Cambridge, MA: MIT Press. (Original work published 1964)

McLuhan, M. (1995). Playboy interview. In E. McLuhan & F. Zingrone (Eds.), *Essential McLuhan* (pp. 233–269). Don Mills, Ontario, Canada: House of Anansi.

McLuhan, M. (2003). Violence as a quest for identity. In D. Staines & S. McLuhan (Eds.), *Understanding me: Lectures and interviews*. Toronto, Canada: McClelland & Stewart. (Original work published 1977)

McLuhan, M., & Fiore, Q. (1967). *The medium is the massage: An inventory of effects*. Toronto, Canada: Random House.

McLuhan, M., & McLuhan, E. (1988). *Laws of media: The new science*. Toronto, Canada: University of Toronto Press.

McLuhan, M., & Powers, B. R. (1989). *The global village: Transformations in world life and media in the 21st century*. New York, NY: Oxford University Press.

Murray, S. J. (2008). Psychoanalysis, symbolization, and McLuhan: Reading Conrad's *Heart of Darkness*. In T. Gibson (Ed.), *Marshall McLuhan's "medium is the message": Information literacy in a multimedia age* (Special issue). *MediaTropes*, *1*, 57–70. Retrieved from www.mediatropes.com

Murray, S. J. (2009). Editorial introduction: "Media tropes." *MediaTropes*, *2*(1), i–x. Retrieved from www.mediatropes.com

Murray, S. J., & M. Poster (2003). Network digital information humachines: A conversation with Mark Poster. *Qui Parle*, *14*(1), 1–19.

Nacos, B. L. (2002). *Mass-mediated terrorism: The central role of the media in terrorism and counterterrorism*. Lanham, MD: Rowman & Littlefield.

Niedzviecki, H. (2005). Packaging the suicide bomber. *Tikkun*, *20*(3), 67–69.

Nietzsche, F. (1994). *On the genealogy of morality* [Zur Genealogie der Moral]. (K. A. Pearson, Ed., C. Diethe, Trans.). Cambridge, MA: Cambridge University Press.

Nietzsche, F. (2001). On truth and lies in a nonmoral sense. In P. Bizzell & B. Herzberg (Eds.), *The rhetorical tradition: Readings from classical times to the present*, (2nd ed., pp. 1168–1179). Boston, MA: Bedford/St. Martin's. (Original work published 1873)

O'Keefe, S. (2006, April 12). *Pioneering the future: Address by the Honorable Sean O'Keefe, NASA Administrator*. Retrieved December 7, 2006, from http://www.hq.nasa.gov/office/codez/plans/Pioneer.pdf

Ong, W. J. (2002). *Orality and literacy: The technologizing of the word*. London: Routledge.

Ontario Ministry of Education. (2002). *Interdisciplinary studies: The Ontario curriculum, grades 11 and 12*. Toronto, Canada: Ministry of Education. Retrieved from http://www.edu.gov.on.ca/eng/curriculum/secondary/interdisciplinary1112curr.pdf

Plato (2004). *Phaedrus and Letters VII and VIII*. (W. Hamilton, Trans.). New York, NY: Penguin.

Poster, M. (2001). *What's the matter with the Internet?*. Minneapolis, MN: University of Minnesota Press.

Rosen, J. (2007, March 11). The brain on the stand: How neuroscience is transforming the legal system. *The New York Times Magazine*, pp. 49+.

Strate, L. (2008). Studying media *as* media: McLuhan and the media ecology approach. In T. Gibson (Ed.), *Marshall McLuhan's "medium is the message": In-*

formation literacy in a multimedia age (Special issue). *MediaTropes, 1*, 127–142. Retrieved from www.mediatropes.com

Sullivan, S., & Tuana, N. (Eds.). (2007). *Race and epistemologies of ignorance*. Albany, NY: SUNY Press.

Tschofen, M. (2008). "Agents of aggressive order": Letters, hands, and the grasping power of teeth in the early Canadian torture narrative. In T. Gibson (Ed.), *Marshall McLuhan's "medium is the message": Information literacy in a multimedia age* (Special issue). *MediaTropes, 1*, 19–41. Retrieved from www.mediatropes.com

CHAPTER 11

CARNIVAL OF THE UNCANNY

Peter Applebaum

Not only did he disbelieve in ghosts; he was not even frightened of them.

—Freud (1905)

Even the uncanny itself is uncanny. The very definition of the term, as Freud pointed out in 1905, is uncanny. We might wish to avoid it. But that is the point of the uncanny, isn't it? Our initial experience is one of avoidance, which is what I want to explore in this essay. There is a concept of the 'uncanny valley' that seeks to capture this limbo feeling of paralytic avoidance. Yet there is also the notion, prompted by the extended valley concept that one might climb out of the valley, or fly over it. With such an opportunity come pleasures of both the uncanny and the canny. I begin in my prologue with three of the many descriptions of the uncanny—a haunting, a returned gaze, and an anticipation. The uncanny is a nexus of these varying feelings and experiences, each of which shares a great deal with the others. While epistemologies of ignorance are primarily concerned with the returned gaze, they act as well to haunt our practice, and to cause us to dwell in uncanny anticipation. This is the focus of the section following the prologue. Educational theory is always both "about educational experiences" and the description "of the educational experiences," focusing on some things while necessarily, according to epistemologies of ignorance, ignoring others that we should or do not yet know about, at the

Epistemologies of Ignorance in Education, pp. 221–242
Copyright © 2011 by Information Age Publishing

same time. So it is always a space (or valley) between two things, an uncanny interplay to say the least. How we navigate this terrain is the question at hand. I discuss the notion of the uncanny valley, and apply it to theorizing about educational theory as an uncanny artifice, that is, design science. I offer Border Pedagogies as a theoretical field that I claim has the potential to traverse the valley. Curiously, this is accomplished by seeking to dwell in the valley itself, exploring the microgradients of its slopes and crannies.

For some people, educational practice is *real*. It is simply a methodological and discursive challenge to *illuminate it,* as with much curriculum theorizing that attempts to deductively reveal essential features or manifest the essence of curriculum. Curriculum is brought in from the dark, disclosed in the light of deductive clarification as an entity unto itself. But for others the ambiguity is not so easily resolved by the disclosure of curriculum through an act of clarification. "Who or what clarifies?" (Bruce et al., 2003). Rendering of curriculum is as much an act of exclusion as of inclusion. And with that awareness comes a sensitivity to the indeterminables of any rendering. I claim Border Pedagogies constitute a carnival of the uncanny because curriculum as lived interpretation is an uncanny gesture that we can embrace: they push the limits of what we know and do so by making us *want* to be haunted, to be gazed at, or to ambiguously anticipate. They make the uncanny the method and the experience at one and the same time in their insistence on the creolization of culture and the annihilation of fake universalism

Educational theory is a haunted house. And this house provides an especially favored locus for uncanny disturbances, "its apparent domesticity, its residue of family history and nostalgia, its role as the last and most intimate shelter of private comfort[,] sharpen[ing] by contrast the terror of invasion by alien spirits" (Vidler, 1987, p. 7). No/Yes, it is a mirror, which when held up to our gaze shows us an image of ourselves, but not exactly ourselves, instead an uncanny likeness, "Seeing, not as one sees oneself, but from an objective positioning, from outside of oneself—as in looking at photographs of the self " (Middleton, 1997).

> But imagine that one could see one's mirror image close its eyes: that would make the object as gaze appear in the mirror. This is what happens with the double, and the anxiety that the double produces is the surest sign of the appearance of the object.... Here the Lacanian account of anxiety differs sharply from other theories: it is not the anxiety of losing something (the firm support, one's bearings, etc.). On the contrary, it is the anxiety of gaining something too much, of a too-close presence of the object. (Dolar, 1991, p. 13)

Maybe/and educational theory is an anticipation. Inhabitants of Hiroshima used the Japanese *bukimi* (weird, ghastly, unearthly) to describe the experience of impending catastrophe combined with uneasy, continued good fortune in the months before the nuclear bombing (Lifton, 1967; Saint-Amour, 2000). We are not here to equate schooling with nuclear holocaust. That would inadvertently minimize the unspeakable horrors of the atomic tragedies; yet we can "anticipate" the consequences of *theorizing as anticipation* through this juxtaposition. Theorizing as *bukimi* enables us, too, to name this game of alarm, fear, and celebratory delay.

THE UNCANNY

Modern recognition of the uncanny is usually attributed to a 1919 essay by Sigmund Freud, *Das Unheimliche*, now easily available in numerous translations. *Unheimlich* is the name Freud used for those things that ought to have remained secret and hidden but have come to light. It is a rather enlightenment notion, and scholarship on the essay has pointed out that the uncanny seems to be a specific cultural and historical outgrowth of the enlightenment project (Dolar, 1991; Park, 2003). The boundaries between the enlightened and the uncanny—and by extension, the unenlightened— are far more equivocal than we might otherwise believe: not just resulting from Enlightenment standards of reason and lucidity, the uncanny constitutes these standards in much the same way as the canny itself implicitly carries the seed of the uncanny in its own meaning. As Park (2003) notes, this critique of the uncanny also carries traits of a tendency for people to regard the historic moment of the Enlightenment as "our contemporary." We describe the present, for example, as latent in the thinking of the eighteenth century.

> Such a proleptic tendency, in addition to suggesting a problematic ownership, approaches the Enlightenment as a "mirror to ourselves," thus "sacrificing its specificity" to "the need to find projections of ourselves in the past." (Outram, 1999, pp. 39–40)

Simply stated, enlightenment pedagogy is as follows: if only the learner could see what the teacher sees, she or he would then know what the teacher knows, instead of being ignorant. Sadly, as Plato so eloquently illustrated centuries prior to the enlightenment era in his parable of the cave, the learner is living in a dark and dingy cave, and only sees shadows on the wall of what is really there in the world. The teacher has turned from that wall and "seen the light"; well, actually, the teacher has seen the world in a new light, and is trying to show the learner how to see. But the learner is blinded by the brilliant light, and can see nothing when she or he first looks, turning back to the cave wall and continuing to watch the shadows. The learner has already developed an elaborate and meaningful theory of these shadows, and they work, since learners have no clue about what the teacher has seen. This blinding light of truth is one metaphor for the resistance to learning that Freud found at the heart of psychoanalysis, and which is such a pivotal critique of the enlightenment subject. Nancy Tuana (2004, 2006) continues this critique into our "present," with her use of epistemologies of ignorance. Her analysis of contemporary professional discourses is a mirror held up to our gaze, revealing an uncanny and creepy new view of ourselves. In this mirror, we see that what we know is as much determined by what we actively choose to not know as what we might claim to understand. In this respect, the light that one brings back down into Plato's cave carries a potential for as much ignorance as the shadows on the wall. Even new ways of seeing do not help, because they too create ignorance along with knowledge.

> If we are to fully understand the complex practices of knowledge production and the variety of features that account for why something is known, we must also understand the practices that account for not knowing, that is, for our lack of knowledge about a phenomena or, in some cases, an account of the practices that resulted in a group unlearning what was once a realm of knowledge. In other words, those who would strive to understand how we know must also develop epistemologies of ignorance. (Tuana, 2004, p. 194)

To take two prosaic examples of epistemologies of ignorance in action, consider the role of schools as sites of social reproduction within an ostensibly meritocratic, democratic society, or the pros and cons of tracking. Each of these areas of educational theory and practice demonstrates the ways in which practices maintain ignorance in the light of the mirror of research. Schools as sites of social reproduction have been well represented in the research literature for quite some time (Anyon, 1980; Bowles & Gintis, 1976, 2001; Dolby & Dimitridis, 2004; Farber, Wilson, & Holm, 1989; Kincheloe, 2007), confronting anyone who holds up schools as sites of opportunity. Such research is the wink in the mirror, as are the abundant responses in the form of critical pedagogy (Darder Torres, & Baltodano, 2002; Duncan-Andrade & Morrell, 2008; McLaren & Kincheloe, 2007; Morrow & Torres, 2002; Wink, 2004), border pedagogies (Chávez & O'Donnell, 1998; Fine, Bernadette, Hancock, Jordan, & Sherman; Garza, 2007; Giroux, 1993, 2005; Necochea & Cline, 2005; Romo, 2005), and schooling for social justice (Ayers, Hunt, & Quinn, 1998; Fine, Weis, Powell, & Burns, 2004; Huber-Wang, 2008; Kincheloe, 2005; Kumashiro, 2004). Similar lists for tracking (Loveless, 1999; Oakes, 2005; Sapon-Shevin, 1994) might be compiled; in general, there is little evidence to support separation of students by any category, except for very short term targeted skill training measured by standardized tests (Oakes, 2008; Obiakor & Ford, 2002), while there is overwhelming evidence to support mixing students by as many categories as possible, with positive results for all using any possible criteria (Lee, 2006; Mallery & Mallery, 1999), and many practical ideas for doing so (Cline & Necochea, 2006; Fine et al., 1998; Gustavson 2007; Gutstein & Peterson, 2005; Sapon-Shevin, 1998).

Yet, despite the lengthy bibliographies of resources that one might annotate, theorists are continually plagued with disappointment in large-scale curricular and pedagogical reform. They turn to analyzing the mechanisms of ignorance, those ideological and economic forces and cultural assumptions that maintain professional and institutional knowledge as well as those ignorances of social injustice (see this short sampling from a range of research: Appelbaum, 1995, 2002b; Appelbaum & Clark, 2001; Block, 1997; Giroux, 2007; Hoadley, 2008; Kincheloe et al., 2000). I suppose we cannot presume that current practices are thought of by a large majority of people as "best practices" or the result of scientific research, much to the consternation of supporters of the No Child Left Behind Act and the many educational researchers who actively pursue such a 'best practices' agenda. In Tuana's words,

> Ignorance, far from being a simple lack of knowledge that good science aims to banish, is better understood as a practice with supporting social causes as complex as those involved in knowledge practices. (Tuana, 2004, p. 5)

Working mostly in the context of women's health, she offers three dimensions along which we can analyze ignorance and its active, ongoing creation: (1) knowing we do not know, and do not care to know; (2) not even knowing that we do not know; and, (3) being preventing from knowing by others who do not want us to know (adapted from Tuana, 2006).

In its most positive manifestation, the enlightenment project takes the knower as a connoisseur who has developed over time methods and languages for appreciating and understanding phenomena. Within the field of education, Elliot Eisner (1977, 1991) has made the strongest case for connoisseurship. Here appreciation means an awareness of characteristics and properties of whatever is being critically understood. Where Tuana focuses on epistemologies of ignorance, Eisner celebrates how a connoisseur has learned to see particular things as more important than others, and to intelligently ignore those less important attributes or elements. The connoisseur's conclusions are judgments rather than mere preferences, based on knowing what to look for, and the abilities to recognize skill, form and imagination. Criticism, for Eisner, is the art of disclosure; beyond discerning the characteristics and properties constituting an object or event, the critic renders what he or she has encountered so that others who have not had the same life experience might also develop the same sense of appreciation. Eisner (1977) quotes John Dewey, who wrote that criticism is a reeducation of perception, to describe such work as "lifting the veils that keep the eyes from seeing" (p. 348), providing a bridge for others to traverse the gap between lay person and connoisseur.

It would seem Tuana's ideas might be directly translated from health practices to educational practices, providing a more contemporary discourse for the kind of criticism articulated by Plato, Enlightenment thinkers, and Eisner. Jaime Romo (2005), for example, speaks in schools as an

> education doctor ... I don't wait for the educational disease to grow and manifest in later stages; I already see the crisis ... I go to schools and prescribe developing the strength and forgiveness, not amnesia, to work with those who continue to treat Latinos or others with a need-hate disdain, I also go out to vaccinate: to help people have a sense of warning, a sense of how schools systems in passive and unconscious ways can hurt people, can maim people's identities, can inflict a kind of disease, in a way that the blankets given to native Americans carried diseases, that then decimate those recipients. (p. 200)

Schooling as an *ideological state apparatus* (Althusser, 1971) can easily be the location for this kind of "educational doctoring." Indeed, as I have already noted, there has been much work in, for example, critical pedagogies and border pedagogies that has done precisely this kind of critical critique of schooling as an institution of social reproduction and hegemonic cultural structuration, producing what might be termed "enlightened awareness." Social justice pedagogies also commonly aim to employ such "revealing" analyses through a critical interrogation of and response to this new-found knowledge. But of course, as is circularly evident in a theory that proclaims an epistemology of ignorance, this new-found knowledge will always itself be a process of unlearning and the invention of new forms of ignorance; this is Tuana's point when she notes how a body of knowledge necessarily requires a focus on some things rather than others. In various contexts, such enlightened critical perspectives become knowledge aptly described as "taboo" or "subjugated" (e.g., in the evaluation of school programs, the training of new teachers, etc.). In our haunted house, we are spooked by the ghost of de Certeau (1984) who might have labeled the critical theories assembled here as tactics promoting resistance and innovation, only to be swallowed by the strategic actions of social institutions.

THE UNCANNY VALLEY

As foreshadowed in the prologue, this chapter explores the notion of the uncanny in order to explain both the nature of and resistance to the knowledge/ignorance of critical and border pedagogies, and related educational projects for social justice. I further examine as its value in establishing practices that sublate such knowledge/ignorance. Attempts to dwell in the methods of epistemologies of ignorance and/or in the development of alternative pedagogical practices exhibit many characteristics of the *uncanny valley* (Bryant, 2006; Mori, 1970), a concept from technological design-science, which also proposes a postvalley experience of embrace. My basic argument is that people experience the revulsion of the uncanny when what they see or experience is "too close" to what they know while also being slightly different; for educational practices, border pedagogies and other forms of critical pedagogy are, in other words, too close to what many people have come to "know" as essential to the "real world" and therefore trigger a visceral revulsion.

My own take on the theory of the uncanny valley posits the experience of *carnival*, discussed below, on the other side of the valley, where humans and their designed artifice are so close in similarity that the uncanny resides in the borderland of pleasure. I suggest the embrace can be fostered as carnival. Indeed, educational studies can verify the existence of the uncanny valley where design science has failed. Robotics and video-game technology has not yet bridged the valley, giving rise to a straight forward empirical critique of the concept. Education has demonstrated the achievement of carnival, especially in the theories of border pedagogy, which avoid static entrapment in Tuana's three dimensions of ignorance.

The uncanny valley is haunted. And when we enter it we are electric with anticipation. This is because education is itself in many ways a design science (Simon, 1969). Like the mannequins that prompted Freud to conceive of the uncanny, educational programs are artificial constructs doomed to deny their own efficacy and to foment disquiet in the process. At the center of Freud's seminal essay on the uncanny, a young man falls in love with such a pretend woman; she says little and sings a little too perfectly. Freud pulls from this story the critical role of threats to identity —the claims to reality of our own artificial constructs, and the ways that these constructs toss our own identities into question. *We see things in certain ways, evoking the idea that we come to know via technologies of vision, and when we do, we are subjected to that confusing return of the gaze, forever echoing in the mirror provided by what we see our technologies of vision themselves. This is in essence one way to describe the experiences of the uncanny. All those things we forgot about, or did not want to think about, or simply never knew about, are ghosts who haunt our house of theory. We try to suspend the crisis, in a never-ending anticipation of good fortune interwoven with impending failure: Maybe the kids will increase our yearly test scores ... maybe the scores will go down due to something we did not consider.*

Likewise, our educational programs simultaneously tell us too little and sing a little too perfectly. As we attempt to study the effectiveness of a particular curriculum or institutional organization, the tools we use to do so help us to see, but only in ways that throw our own identity into confusion. We fall in love with these programs, artificial constructs designed by mere mortals that only pretend to exist as authentic. As in the story of the mannequin, their artifice is finally revealed when someone else fights over them; they end up, much to our horror, dismembered. Conflicting constituencies pick them apart until they no longer resemble their earlier, potentially effective forms.

The uncanny as frightening pops up when education is understood as a design science. We must either directly traverse the uncanny valley, or perhaps circumvent it by foregrounding other aspects of educational practice. Enter new theories that carry many promises. We love them for what they promise, as if they are solutions to any and all educational problems, or we take them apart through critique. If these new theories are treated like Freud's mannequin, to be loved or dismembered, they will forever be uncanny in the most difficult sense of the term. They will evoke horror. What would be required for us to see them as singing in just the way they should, rather than, like the mannequin, a little too perfectly, as if they promise to be the perfect solution to all educational hopes and dreams? There are at least two options. Just as some robotics engineers think we should make our puppets look strictly different from humans if we want to avoid the revulsion that can occur when they are too similar, we might make our educational programs clearly distinct from current practice, so as not to confuse them with the "real, natural world" of schooling conjured by the common sense of everyday life. This has been the tactic that most critical and border pedagogues have so far employed with varying success as they attempt to implement social justice practices. The use of very different discourses to theorize, generate and describe critical practices highlights differences rather than similarities. A second option is to make them so like the real programs that we no longer experience the revulsion of the uncanny, and find ourselves in a state of embrace; like robots who look like humans, they would be different yet so like what we are ourselves that we love them for what they are, no longer trapped in an uncanny valley. In robotics this has not been achieved; is it a realistic goal for education?

Japanese robotics engineer Masahiro Mori (1982) was prompted way back in the 1970s to suggest the notion of the uncanny valley. His hypothesis was that robots and other representations of real living things are attractive to people as they become more and more real, but there is a range of closeness to the real that is not real enough, and in this range people are repulsed. He graphed human reactions to robots that he had designed, and in this graph one finds a deep valley of negative response when the representations are lifelike, but not lifelike enough. The hypothesis was used to explain audience negativity in response to the film *Polar Express*, and has been useful in videogame design, film animation, recent robotics work, and theme park design. I am positing that the concept can be extended metaphorically to any design science. In this way, we think of educational programs as designed. They represent a sort of engineered reality to us. When they appear very much like our expected reality, we are attracted to them. But when they are too much like our expected reality, yet not exactly close enough, we find ourselves in that uncanny valley, and are repulsed. The question is what it takes to push us past the range of the valley into the pleasurable, positive reactions that Mori hypothesized for robotics. If we can figure this out, then we can make tons of money as educationists, consulting for videogame companies, theme parks, robotics firms, and any other design scientists. We might also find a new, deep sense of satisfaction in our educational work.

Though originally intended to provide an insight into human psychological reaction to robotic design, Bryant (2006) claims that the concept expressed by the uncanny valley is applicable to interactions with nearly any nonhuman entity. Stated simply, the idea is that if one were to plot emotional response against similarity to human appearance and movement, the curve is not a sure, steady upward trend. Instead, there is a peak shortly before one reaches a completely human "look," but then a deep chasm plunges below neutrality into a strongly negative response before rebounding to a second peak where resemblance to humanity is complete.

This chasm—the uncanny valley of Doctor Mori's thesis—represents the point at which a person observing the creature or object in question sees something that is nearly human, but just enough off-kilter to seem eerie or disquieting. The first peak, moreover, is where that same individual would see something that is human enough to arouse some empathy, yet at the same time is clearly enough not human to avoid the sense of wrongness. The slope leading up to this first peak is a province of relative emotional detachment—affection, perhaps, but rarely more than that.

Figure 11.1 (Bryant, 2006) describe curves of emotional response, plotting it (from top to bottom) first against how closely an entity's motion resembles human movement, then against physical resemblance to human appearance, and last against a synthesis of the two. It is significant to note, judging from the relative depth of the curves, that Dr. Mori apparently considered motion more important than simple appearance, though he stressed that both are affected at least as much by subtle nuances as by more striking factors.

Mori recommended that designers should not try too hard to duplicate human appearance, since some minor flaw would likely drop the unfortunate

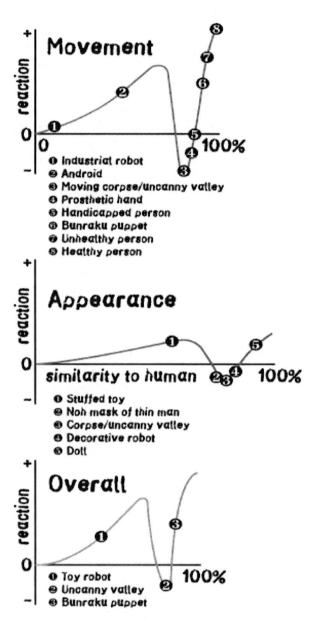

Figure 11.1.   The uncanny valley gets its name from the dip in the graphs and reaction to movement, appearance, or a combination of both.

android or cyborg into the uncanny valley. He favored prosthetics and robots remaining visibly artificial, but smart and stylish in appearance, placing them near the top of the first peak in the graphs. We could translate the recommendation metaphorically to educational programs, where those that look initially a lot like traditional human schooling are appealing until the "flaws" of difference are revealed as uncanny, dropping them into the creepy valley of revulsion. Thus the fate of innovation would be to make programs that employ ideas of critical pedagogy and border pedagogy clearly unlike those that would be understood as "normal." Yet they would seem to need to be stylish, according to Mori, appealing to educational fashion. An alternative would be to make the programs so real that they are no longer repulsive but are instead embraced, being placed to the extreme right on our graphs.

EDUCATIONAL *BUKIMI*

Critical theorists often sound to those less convinced by their arguments as whacky "Peters" "crying" about alarming catastrophic "wolves"—emotional violence predicated by schooling, irrational horrific loss of social justice and reification of economic unbalances, the specter of the creepy corporations, spreading the slimy tentacles of globalization and consumer culture throughout the world. Did the night watchers of Hiroshima get the same response? Surely not. Everyone wondered why their city had not yet been bombed. The people of Hiroshima who experienced *bukimi* had detected the opening up of the conditional space of catastrophe—conditional because, despite the signs that informed its citizens' sense of the uncanny, Hiroshima might finally have been spared rather than razed if conditions had been different on the day of the drop (Saint-Amour, 2000, p. 60). In certain respects, the kind of conditional traumatic space that registered as *bukimi* was unique to human-made devastation, and particularly to early nuclear weapons. The careful sparing of atomic bomb target cities from conventional bombing indicated the American military commanders' confidence in the destructive potential of the bomb and their desire to demonstrate that power in the theater of relatively undamaged cities. Having noticed the passing-over of Hiroshima, its citizens strove to read the intention of the enemy in the signs that constituted that passing-over. Those signs had been returned in a sense from one of two futures: one culminating in the nonevent of preservation, the other in the limit event of catastrophe. When that limit event occurred, its survivors underwent a historically specific, unique trauma. But in the period of eerie suspension before the explosion, those who registered the nuclear uncanny in Hiroshima were also the first to experience a condition that, in a far more explicit incarnation, would become familiar to everyone living in a targeted city during the Cold War: the sense that the present survival and flourishing of the city were simultaneously underwritten and radically threatened by its identity as a nuclear target.

Just as I express discomfort in calling forth this incomparable *bukimi* in our discussion here, Saint-Amour (2000) notes that it is inappropriate to use the tales of nuclear survivors to explain later Cold War fears of potential destruction by residents of targeted cities. Potential devastation does violence to the specificity of the actual historical trauma of nuclear catastrophe. Nevertheless, historians and cultural critics have made connections between the uncanny *frisson* of the Cold War period as a structuring condition of everyday life and the uncanny anticipation recalled by those who managed to live through the horrors, carrying the memories of the anticipation with them (Hartman, 1995; Sontag, 1966). These connections have been used to explain the place of science fiction and horror films in Cold War culture, and more importantly the emergence of *hysteron proteron*, a condition first described by Susan Sontag (1966), in which traumatic symptoms—denial, dissociation, fragmentation, repression, the compulsive repetition of extreme violence—exist not in the wake of a past event, but in the shadow of a future one.

The difference between the use of *hysteron proteron* to understand the allure of disaster films and the calls for change coming from contemporary critical theorists in education is the presence of the actual crimes. School as a tool of social injustice is no hysterical cry of potential calamity. It is very real and present. In this sense, our educational *bukimi* is about the anticipation of recognizing our own ongoing participation in the educational project of injustice. More crudely, every teacher and school administrator lives a perpetual *bukimi*, waiting to be told by a supervisor, or a public evaluation, that they are doing something wrong or that they irresponsibly allowed a bad thing to happen; all educational practices are haunted by this uncanny anticipation.

Leading us further into this haunted house of educational madness are the ghosts of "the learner" and a "liberal education" (Hammond, 1992). School curriculum is repeatedly described in terms of enabling learners to develop their individual potential and to acquire the knowledge, skills, and attitudes needed to contribute to a healthy society and a prosperous and sustainable economy. What one means by "individual potential," "healthy society," or "prosperous and sustainable economy" are up for grabs. I do not mean to create a straw man here; the actual words in this description were analyzed by David Hammond in 1992 and taken from a British Columbia provincial curriculum document. The point made by Hammond so long ago, echoing such giants of educational theory as John Locke, Jean-Jacques Rousseau, John Dewey and Maxine Greene, was that the question of how best to fulfill the private longings of human subjects and still properly satisfy the "needs" of their communities has been long and furiously debated. "[this] remains a basic moral-political dilemma to which there is no correct solution, just congeries of polemical ones" (Hammond, 1992, p. 133).

Julie Webber (2001) notes a commonsense view that one either conforms to the herd mentality cultivated and reproduced at school and in the society, or chooses to allow oneself to be targeted as a scapegoat for the voyeuristic enjoyment and vented frustration of the rest. Scapegoating and projection become the standard means for trying to get out of this condition of impotence:

> The more citizens internalize these projections of traumatic violence as their own, the more impotent (and less active) they become. So, in a sense the problem is not so much a question of forgiving the violence (or even condoning it), as it is one of putting the violence into "perspective." The more these acts are allowed to infect the public's sense of community, the more they begin to dismantle it. (p. 171)

Central to educational *bukimi* are the ways that end-point objectives become in a perverse way starting-points for school programs, lesson plans from external authorities are twisted into the experiences of those inside particular classrooms and school communities, and critics of contemporary fads are used as mirrors for finding the inner beauty of established practices. Enlightenment instruments of reason appear to clarify what we see, but merely distort our gaze. At any given moment, an educational theory is like a triad in classical music, with the latent potential to fragment into a set of component parts that stand in dissonant relation to each other.

> The listener is at any moment at risk of being cast out on a vast sea of tonal indeterminacy, without compass or anchor. Each triad seems to be a port, yet each rests on naught but its own corrodible bottom. The lines between good and evil, life and death, truth and appearance are cast into doubt. Severed heads are so beautiful one cannot but kiss them. The energy of a dying woman is transferred into a fixate gaze. A dissonant harmony bursts into a consonant but bleached-out *Gesang*. Superannuated wraiths sing from their crypts, dead heroes animatedly guard their treasure, and spirits scamper back down their infernal holes. A great composer survives his own death to compose it in tones. (Cohn, 2004, pp. 319–20)

CARNIVAL OF BORDER PEDAGOGIES

So far I have introduced the idea of the uncanny as describing the experience of educational theorizing. As theorists attempt to understand educational phenomena, to act in Eisner's terms as a connoisseur, they are haunted by the ghosts of those things they must ignore in order to accomplish the work that theorizing demands. When theorists are confronted by educational criticism, they are forced to see themselves and their work in the light of these haunting ghosts, and the experience is unsettling to say the least. Thus we might say that educational theorizing is well-described by the Japanese term *bukimi*, which names the feeling of anticipation central to the uncanny haunting and mirrored reflection at the heart of this work. In this next section of my chapter, I turn to border pedagogies as an example of a form of educational theorizing and practice that embraces the uncanny rather than avoids it. In the language of multiculturalism and diversity education, others are the vehicle of the gaze that sets up the uncanny, and, in the process, chasms of difference. That is, "others" are constructed by the assumptions of most forms of multiculturalism in its misleadingly optimistic, liberal perspective; these others become mirrors through which we see ourselves, and thus, through the mirroring process, establish the uncanny. Border pedagogy events,[1] in contrast, enable all participants to celebrate the exchange of identity made possible by the presence of *carnival*, in the sense of Bakhtin, which I explain below. In this way, border pedagogies avoid the uncanny gaze of the mirror of others.

Elizabeth Garza's description of the U.S./Mexican border and its constant cultural indeterminacy, for example, sounds very much like the description of the musical triad quoted at the end of the last section:

> the same barrier dividing the people who live on each side of it also creates a unique set of life experiences that they share in common ... in a counter-intuitive paradox the border itself becomes a unifying factor illuminating surprising similarities among borderlands inhabitants living on both sides. (Garza, 2007, p. 2)

Yet far from describing the uncanny, creepy, haunted house of educational theory, she shares how meetings of teachers from both sides of borders brought hope and ideas to her work as well as their own. Why the difference? Bernardo Estrada (2006) suggests that a paradoxical sense of unity grows out of a focus on the seeming split of a border, as participants in border pedagogy events are challenged to seek changes in unjust barriers to quality education for all students in these border regions.[2]

> The strategies that we discover and develop together create a vibrant energy within each of us, an excitement to go back and try these in our classrooms. Through understanding that there are no recipes or formulas, no checklists or advice that describe the one best way to educate all children, Border Pedagogy participants are discovering new ways of relating and engaging students, *caminos* that allow students to become critical thinkers and creative problems solvers. (p. 36)

Within the context of multicultural education, border pedagogies enable all participants to claim membership in "the borderlands" and in this respect no one is superior or dominant as the authority on borderland experience. Instead of the all too common uncanny, haunting gaze of "the other," a spontaneous regrouping often takes place, based on a sense of a shared identity and experience as borderland inhabitants. Participants are positioned to explore educational topics from that common ground. For example, when discussing the issues of cultural and linguistic diversity in education, Garza's (2007) students, future teachers, drew on their experience as inhabitants of the border region to build deeper understanding. They found many common threads, all of which took on new importance for these students because they saw each thread as woven into preparation for teaching in the border region.

I employ Bakhtin's (1965) idea of *carnival* to describe the rich border pedagogy experiences. For Bakhtin, *carnival* is associated with collectivities. Those attending a carnival do not merely constitute a crowd; participants see themselves as a whole, organized in a way that defies socioeconomic and political organization. According to Bakhtin, "all were considered equal during carnival. Here, in the town square, a special form of free and familiar contact reigned among people who were usually divided by the barriers of caste, property, profession, and age" (p. 10). The carnival atmosphere holds the lower strata of life most important, as opposed to higher functions (thought, speech, soul) usually privileged in the signifying order. At carnival time, a unique sense of time and space causes individuals to feel they are a part of the collectivity, at which point they cease to be themselves. It is at this point that an individual exchanges bodies through costume and mask and is renewed. At the same time there arises a heightened awareness of one's sensual, material, bodily unity and community. Differences are transformed through exchange in *carnival*, rather than analyzed or avoided; that is, rather than juxtaposed.[3]

We commonly look to the juxtaposition of differences as a source of learning and growth. We might claim hope for multicultural encounters because participants are confronted by the experiences of the other. But we can see from the perspective of the uncanny that these mirror experiences that return our gaze are likely to cause revulsion rather than a pleasure of learning about ourselves and others. They create gaps or ruptures instead of bridges or conduits of exchange. Educational theorists like rupture, they themselves are not easily trapped in the uncanny valley of this educational landscape, or at least do not feel so trapped. Yao (2005) has described the appeal to rupture as a potential site of learning—such as between what we know and do not know, or between what we know and cannot know, or between what we know and do not want to know—as the "*unheimlich* maneuver." What we find in such experiences is accusatory "others," an uncanny gaze back at us that shows us—ourselves—to ourselves as different from whom we thought we were. The legacy is the ghostly trace of those encounters that haunt us—uncannily—for the rest of our lives. In many multicultural education contexts, the uncanny experience strengthens resistance to learning rather than encouraging such learning. The gaps between people are crystallized rather than permeated. Thus, the *unheimlich* reinscribes Eurocentric Enlightenment ideology within the post-colonial project, reifying categories and differences rather than reinventing them.

Thus multicultural meetings with difference, while as erotically alluring as the mannequin character that led Freud to write about the uncanny in the first place, tend to be surprisingly disappointing as learning opportunities. This is because they fall into the uncanny valley. The *unheimlich* is a frantic Freudian dependency on estrangement and alienation for a claimed personal or social transformation. Yao urges an alternative to "gaps between," which he paints for us through the notion of a gradient —a conception of difference that operates not through absolute, fixed distinctions, but rather by means of relative, phased dimensions. Instead of a radical discontinuity, this model of difference works with spectra or series of continua of variance. Gradients make it possible not only to undertake comparisons along any number of conceptual or material axes, but also to recognize gradations within and among those dimensions of difference. This shifts the domain of comparison into a multidimensional space of potential relations instead of focusing on discontinuities. The gradient reconfigures the very conditions and possibilities for comparison.

The gradient may be what is happening in those border pedagogy events that Garza and Estrada so glowingly report. For when we think of borders as "borderlands"—either geographically and literally, or figuratively in a conceptual landscape, we place ourselves within a creolized "intercultural" and liminal territory (Clifford, 1988). Borders are concrete lines of differences, whereas borderlands are permeable, ill-defined areas with no specific borders. We are no longer looking in from a critical standpoint outside, as might be the case with epistemologies of ignorance and their three fixed dimensions that situate knowledge along parallel, independent paths. Instead, we are *in* the borderlands, wherever and whatever they might be, with whatever shifting sense of difference and continuity they imply. Jaime Romo (2005) writes, "In contrast to popular negative views, border pedagogy affirms, interrogates, and negotiates sociocultural differences "(p. 194)

Not too long before writing this chapter, the world paid tribute to Aimé Césaire, the Martinican poet, politician and consummate West Indian who passed away in April 2008 at the age of 94. Césaire was known for his anti-colonialist politics, and for the post-colonial interculture in his poetry, for example, in these lines from *Lost Body*:

> when my turn comes into the air
> I will raise up a cry so violent
> that I will spatter the sky utterly
> and by my shredded branches
> and by the insolent jet of my solemn wounded bole
> I shall command the islands to exist (Césaire, 1950)

I am suggesting that this way of being is not trapped in the uncanny valley because it slides along gradients of culture and concepts, rather than jumping into crevasses. The intercultural wrestles with difficult experiences of power and authority while celebrating in this difficult work the joys of the uncanny. Parallel cultures, either geographically or in the realms of knowledge and ignorance, eliminate in some ways the critical issues of power and the interrelationship of subordinate and dominant groups. Border pedagogues seize the very tools of the uncanny—the haunting of what we know, do not know, and cannot know—and make them the tools of practice; the uncanny becomes the point of their work, and power and authority are new materials of theory and practice. In this way, these theorists look for new mirrors because they promise new gazes, rather than anticipating what they might reveal. They enjoy the uncanny expectation as a defining feature of what is special about the intellectual challenges of their work in the borderlands, living the embrace of critical multiculturalism (Appelbaum, 2002a; Chicago Cultural Studies Group, 1992; Kanpol & McLaren, 1995).

Braiddoti (2005) describes a new European version of this carnival in terms of the dominant centers deconstructing their powers and letting them be, while the marginal become the motors of change; her point is to bypass the gaps of a dialectic between center and margin, so that we can celebrate the abilities that accompany not knowing, in order to creatively "be with" the not knowing. Schwart (1995) quotes Audre Lorde in her explication of critical multiculturalism: "It is a waste of time hating a mirror or its reflection instead of stopping the hand that makes glass with distortions" (Lorde, 1992, p. 85). And we need to take this to heart. There is no point in getting mad at educational theory for its uncanniness that haunts our everyday lives and futures. There is no point in being afraid of ignorance. It comes with the territory. It is part of the pleasure. *Bukimi* has a strange and uncomfortable origin in a haunted history we wish we could forget; but it is lived by people who carry that legacy into new borderlands, making use of its pleasures as well as its horrors. It is in the pleasures that we find the carnival.

> What is this something that comes *very close*? That *is disquieting only to the extent that it is close*? As we struggle to break away from hegemonic discourses, the traces of signs, signals and signatures appear in uncanny ways to haunt the work. The ghosts *at work* in the curriculum. (Bruce et al., 2003)

When we theorize as *bukimi*, it is as if we have chosen to live with and love our robots, just because they can teach us about the uncanny valley. But in such a situation, we are no longer *in* that valley. How uncanny! The uncanny has become canny, defining once again how the word is its own opposite. The ghosts at work in the curriculum no longer haunt us simply because we *want them to*. The uncanny valley helped us by postulating a continuous curve with a gradient, rather than disjoint categories. The trick is not to make a new pedagogy informed by new ignorance, but to reconceptualize the already existing pedagogy as uncanny (Appelbaum, 2007). We no longer desire to lift the veil, but instead try on new veils, to see how they change what we can see. This is why we can leap the valley. We are not struggling to love a new curriculum, but embracing what is uncanny in our already existing borderlands, in both political and intellectual landscapes. It is confusing, perhaps, because this type of border pedagogy understands its task as living with not knowing in the face of Others; as *carnival*, this pedagogy dwells in the exchanging character of a double negative: to not want to not know is a violence to others, a violence that obscures and obliterates the categories and norms that simultaneously constrain and enable. Judith Butler (2001) suggested this is living with not knowing in face of the Other; such a notion is *close* to the carnival of border pedagogy, but not quite the same: At carnival time, a unique sense of time and space causes us to feel we are part of a collectivity; we cease to be ourselves. We exchange bodies, not standpoints, and are renewed.

NOTES

1. I use the word "event" for any pedagogical or educational encounter, formal or informal, such as a classroom lesson, teacher group meeting, and so forth.
2. The examples cited here reference the U.S./Mexico border; however, the notion of border region can be extended to many geographic borders, such as South Africa/Zimbabwe, Pakistan/Kashmir/India/China, the Basque regions of Spain/France, and so forth.
3. My use of carnival is in the *longue dureé* sense of Bakhtin (1965), Le Roy La

Durie (1979), and Davis (1975). More recently there has been scholarship on carnival as experienced in unequal ways that seem to suggest class, race, and other categorical differences, so that carnival can be one more social institution of social reproduction; see, e.g., Scheper-Hughes (1992) and Malewski and Sharma (2009). My claim is that border pedagogies more closely resemble the former rather than the latter.

REFERENCES

Althusser, L. (1971). *Lenin and philosophy and other essays*. New York, NY: Monthly Review Press.

Anyon, J. (1980). Social class and the hidden curriculum of work. *Journal of Education, 162*(1), 67–92.

Appelbaum, P. (1995). *Popular culture, educational discourse, and mathematics*. Albany, NY: State University of New York Press.

Appelbaum, P. (2002a). *Multicultural and diversity education*. Santa Barbara, CA: ABC-CLIO.

Appelbaum, P. (2002b). Diss-Conceptualizing curriculum: Is there a next in the generational text? *Journal of Curriculum Theorizing, 18*(1), 7–19.

Appelbaum, P. (2007). *Children's books for grown-up teachers: Reading and writing curriculum theory*. New York, NY: Routledge.

Appelbaum, P. & Clark, S. (2001). Science! fun? A critical analysis of design/content/evaluation.. *Journal of Curriculum Studies, 33*(5), 583–600.

Ayers, B., Hunt, J. A., & Quinn, T. (Eds.). (1998). *Teaching for social justice: A democracy and education reader.* New York, NY: New Press.

Bakhtin, M. (1965). *Rabelais and his world*. Bloomington, IN: Indiana University Press.

Block, A. (1997). *I'm only bleeding: Education as the practice of social violence against children*. New York, NY: Peter Lang.

Bowles, S., & Gintis, H. (1976). *Schooling in capitalist America: Educational reform and the contradictions of economic life*. New York, NY: Basic Books.

Bowles, S., & Gintis, H. (2001). *Schooling in capitalist America* (Rev. ed.). Retrieved April 20, 2008, from http://www.umass.edu/preferen/gintis/soced.pdf

Braiddoti, R. (2005). A critical cartography of feminist post-postmodernism. *Australian Feminist Studies, 20*(47), 169–180.

Bruce, A., Feng, F., Nishizawaumiko, S., Palulis, P., Russel, B. D., & Worthing, C. (2003). Provoking signs: Un/canny moments as curriculum theorizing. *Educational Insights, 8*(2). Retrieved May 31, 2008, from http://www.ccfi.educ.ubc.ca/publication/insights/v08n02/contextualexplorations/theorize/groupofsix.html

Bryant, D. (2006). *The uncanny valley*. Retrieved May 31, 2008, from http://www.arclight.net/~pdb/nonfiction/uncanny-valley.html

Butler, J. (2001). The question of social transformation. In E. Beck-Gernsheim, J. Butler & L. Pulgvert (Eds), *Women and social transformation* (pp. 1-28). New York, NY: Peter Lang.

Césaire, A. (1950). *Lost body [Corps perdu]* (A. Hurly, Trans.). New York, NY: Prospector.

Chávez, R. C., & O'Donnell, J. (Eds.). (1998). *Speaking the unpleasant: The politics of (non)engagement in the multicultural education terrain*. Albany, NY: State University of New York Press.

Chicago Cultural Studies Group. (1992). Critical multiculturalism. *Critical Inquiry, 18*(3), 530–555.

Clifford, J. (1988). *The predicament of culture: Twentieth-century ethnography, literature, and art*. Cambridge, MA: Harvard University Press.

Cline, Z., & Necochea, J. (2006). Teacher dispositions for effective education in the borderlands. *The Education Forum, 70*, 268–281.

Cohn, R. (2004). Uncanny resemblances: tonal signification in the Freudian age. *Journal of the American Musicological Societ, 57*(2), 285–323

Darder, A., Torres, R., & Baltodano, M. (Eds.). (2002). *Critical pedagogy reader*. New York, NY: Routledge.

Davis, N. Z. (1975). *Society and culture in early modern France: eight essays*. Palo Alto, CA: Stanford University Press.

de Certeau, M. (1984). *The practice of everyday Life* (Steven Rendall, Trans.). Berkeley, CA: University of California Press.

Dolar, M. (1991). I shall be with you on your wedding-night: Lacan and the uncanny. *October, 58*, 5–23.

Dolby, N., & Dimitriadis, G. (Eds.). (2004). *Learning to labor in new times*. New York, NY: Routledge.

Duncan-Andrade, J., & Morrell, E. (2008). *The art of critical pedagogy: Possibilities for moving from theory to practice in urban schools*. New York, NY: Peter Lang.

Eisner, E. (1977). On the uses of educational connoisseurship and criticism for evaluating classroom life. *Teachers College Record, 78*(3), 345–358.

Eisner, E. (1991). *The enlightened eye*. New York, NY: Macmillan.

Estrada, B. (2006, January). The border pedagogy initiative: an opportunity for growth and transformation. *Hispanic Outlook*, 34–36.

Farber, P., Wilson, P., & Holm, G. (1989). From innocence to inquiry: A social reproduction framework. *Journal of Teacher Education, 40*(1), 45–50.

Fine, M., A., Bernadette, M., Hancock, M., Jordan, C., & Sherman, D. (1998). *Off track: Classroom privilege for all* [video]. New York, NY: Teachers College Press.

Fine, M., Weis, L., Powell, L., & Burns, A. (2004). *Off white: readings on power, privilege, and resistance*. New York, NY: Routledge.

Freud, S. (1905). *Jokes and their relation to the unconscious*. Retrieved May 27, 2008, from http://www.bibliomania.com/1/7/68/2025/frameset.html

Freud, S. (1911). Das Unheimlieche. (Laurel Amtower, Trans). Retrieved May 27, 2008, from http://www-rohan.sdsu.edu/~amtower/uncanny.html

Garza, E. (2007). Becoming a border pedagogy educator. *Multicultural Education, 15*(1), 2-7.

Giroux, H. (1993). *Between borders: Pedagogy and the politics of cultural studies*. New York, NY: Routledge.

Giroux, H. (2005). *Border crossing: Cultural workers and the politics of education* (2nd ed.). New York, NY: Routledge.

Giroux, H. (2007). *The university in chains: Confronting the military-industrial-academic complex*. Boulder, CO: Paradigm.

Gustavson, L. (2007). *Youth learning on their own terms: Creative practices and classroom teaching*. New York, NY: Routledge.

Gutstein, E. & Peterson, B. (2005). *Rethinking mathematics: Teaching social justice by the numbers*. Milwaukee, WI: Rethinking Schools.

Hammond, D. (1992). Two ghosts in a house of curriculum: Visions of the learner and liberal education in current educational reform. *Canadian Journal of Education, 17*(2), 131-47.

Hartman, G. (1995). On traumatic knowledge and literary studies. *New Literary History, 26*, 537-63.

Hoadley, U. (2008). The reproduction of social inequalities through mathematics pedagogies in South African primary schools. *Journal of Curriculum Studies, 39*(6), 679-706.

Huber-Wang, T. (2008). *Growing a soul for social change: Building the knowledge base for social justice*. Charlotte, NC: Information Age Publishing.

Kanpol, B., & McLaren, P. (Eds.). (1995). *Critical multiculturalism: Uncommon voices in a common struggle*. Westport, CT: Bergin & Garvey.

Kincheloe, J. (2005). *Classroom teaching: an introduction*. New York, NY: Peter Lang.

Kincheloe, J. (2007). *Cutting class: socioeconomic status and education*. Lanham, MD: Rowman & Littlefield.

Kincheloe, J., Steinberg, S., Rodriguez, N., & Chennault, R. (Eds.). (2000). *White reign: Deploying whiteness in America*. New York, NY: Palgrave Macmillan.

Kumashiro, K. (2004). *Against common sense: Teaching and learning toward social justice*. New York, NY: Routledge.

Le Roy La Durie, E. (1979). *Carnival in Romans*. New York, NY: George Braziller.

Lee, J. (2006). *Tracking achievement gaps and assessing the impact of NCLB on the gaps: An in-depth look into national and state reading and math outcome trends*. Cambridge, MA: The Civil Rights Project at Harvard University.

Lifton, R. (1967). *Death in life: survivors of Hiroshima*. New York, NY: Random House.

Lorde, A. (1992). Good mirrors are not cheap. In Audre. Lorde, *Undersong: chosen poems old and new*: 85. New York, NY: Norton.

Loveless, T. (1999). *The tracking wars:sState reform meets school policy*. Washington, DC: Brookings Institution Press.

Malewski, E., & Sharma, S. (2009). The unstudied and understudied in curriculum studies: Toward historical readings of the "conditions of possibility" and the production of concepts in the field. In E. Malewski (Ed.), *Curriculum studies handbook: The next moment* (pp. 365–373). New York, NY: Routledge.

Mallery, J., & Mallery, J. (1999). The American legacy of ability grouping: Tracking reconsidered. *Multicultural Education, 7*(1), 13–15.

McLaren, P., & Kincheloe, J. (2007). *Critical pedagogy: Where are we now?* New York, NY: Peter Lang.

Middleton, N. (1997). Philosophy & the uncanny. Retrieved May 27, 2008, from http://www.geocities.com/SoHo/Lofts/1430/thesis/thesis4.html

Mori, M. (1970). The uncanny valley. *Energy, 7*(4), 33-35.

Mori, M. (1982). *The Buddha in the robot*. North Clarendon, VT: Charles Tuttle.

Morrow, R., & Torres, C. A. (2002). *Reading Freire and Habermas: Critical pedagogy and transformative social change*. New York: Teachers College Press.

Necochea, J. & Cline, Z. (2005). Borderland education and teacher education reform in California: Unfulfilled promises. *Journal of Borderlands Studies, 20*(1), 129-141.

Oakes, J. (2005). *Keeping track: How schools structure inequality (2nd ed.)*. New Haven, CT: Yale University Press.

Oakes, J. (2008). *Beyond tracking: Multiple pathways to college, career, and civic participation*. Cambridge, MA: Harvard Education Press.

Obiakor, F. & Ford, B. (2002). *Creating successful learning environments for African American learners with exceptionalities*. Thousand Oaks, CA: Corwin Press.

Outram, D. (1999). The Enlightenment our contemporary. In William Clark, et al. (Eds), *The sciences in enlightened Europe* (pp. 32-42). Chicago: University of Chicago Press.

Park, J. (2003). Unheimlich maneuvers: Enlightenment dolls and repetitions in Freud. *The Eighteenth Century, 44*(1), 45-94.

Romo, J. (2005). Border pedagogy from the inside out: An auto ethnographic study. *Journal of Latinos and Education, 4*(3), 193-210.

Saint-Amour, P. (2000). Bombing and the symptom; traumatic earliness and the nuclear uncanny. *Diacritics, 30*(4), 59-82.

Sapon-Shevin, M. (1994). *Playing favorites: Gifted education and the disruption of community*. Albany, NY: State University of New York Press.

Sapon-Shevin, M. (1998). *Because we can change the world: A practical guide to building cooperative, inclusive classroom communities*. New York: Allyn & Bacon.

Scheper-Hughes, N. (1992). *Death without weeping: The violence of everyday life in Brazil*. Berkeley, CA: University of California Press.

Schwart, E. (1995). Crossing borders/shifting paradigms: Multiculturalism and children's literature. *Harvard Educational Review*. Retrieved May 27, 2008, from http://www.hepg.org/her/abstract/299

Simon, H. (1969). *The sciences of the artificial*. Cambridge, MA: MIT Press.

Sontag, S. (1966). The imagination of disaster. In S. Sontag (Ed.), *Against interpretation* (pp. 209–225). New York, NY: Dell.

Tuana, N. (2004). Coming to understand: orgasm and the epistemology of ignorance. *Hypatia,19*(1), 184–232.

Tuana, N. (2006). The speculum of ignorance: The women's health movement and epistemologies of ignorance. *Hypatia, 21*(3), 1-19.

Vidler, A. (1987). The architecture of the uncanny: The unhomely houses of the romantic sublime. *Assemblage, 3*, 6–29.

Webber, J. (2001). Why can't we be Deweyan citizens? *Educational Theory, 51*(2), 171–190.

Wink, J. (2004). *Critical pedagogy; notes from the real world*. New York, NY: Allyn & Bacon.

Yao, S. (2005). The unheimlich maneuver; or the gap, the gradient, and the spaces of comparison. *Comparative Literature, 57*(3), 246–255.

CHAPTER 12

READING
HAVE WE KNOWN RIVERS?

Indigeneity, Language, and the Significance of Epistemologies of Ignorance for Curriculum Studies

Erik Malewski

We need to imagine home as the places where we live, walk, write, work, and go to school; the physical, emotional and spiritual places where we learn to be at home with others, as well as, ourselves; the place where others means not only neighbors but ancestors, spiritual and familial, theirs and ours, as well as our descendants. We need to offer a home that recognizes we inhabit these places with all animate beings (the land, the stars, the animals, the plants), those with no power to purchase comfort or survival. And perhaps most importantly, as curriculum theorists, we must proffer the reality of a home where we learn the hard lessons of living with our enemies.

—Cynthia Chambers

This mode of conversing with all the inhabitants of the world, be they rock, tree, animal, or human, is one which we should be careful not to assimilate to current prevalent notions. To assume when a peasant tells you that she is conversing with the soil or the wind that she is speaking metaphorically is to assume that Andean peasants are the intellectual heirs to the Reformation and the Scientific Revolution, in

Epistemologies of Ignorance in Education, pp. 243–266

243

which nature does not speak directly, but can be interrogated in the laboratory through experiments, in which to "hear nature speak" one has to be specially trained and taught to construct mechanical devices for proper interrogation.

—Frederique Apffel-Marglin

As the archeology of our thought easily shows, man is an invention of recent date. And one perhaps nearing its end.

—Michel Foucault (1978/1990, p. 139)

READING ONE: INTRODUCTION

The title of this essay is taken from two poems composed by two different U.S. American poets. The first piece titled, *The Negro Speaks of Rivers*, was written by Langston Hughes in 1920. He reported in an interview that the idea for the poem came to him as he crossed the Mississippi River by train on the way to see his father in Mexico. Seized by its greatness, he began to think about the significance of this commanding muddy tract, flowing toward the heart of the South, for African Americans and the ways in which slavery and emancipation were intricately tied to its channels. Decades later, poet Sonya Sanchez (2004) would pay tribute to Langston Hughes and this particular work under the title, *I've Known Rivers*. Most revealing, she describes Hughes as a visionary poet who had the ability to see where before there was nothing ("to fill vacancies"). That is, a capacity to displace ignorance with the revelation of stories less untold than unacknowledged. Accordingly, her poem reads as a testament to the key role Hughes played in moving the Black experience onto the stage of history.

Both of these poems with their references to organic memories and a present that is always already a culmination of the past and future conjure up images of being subdued into rest ("it lulled me to sleep") and moved to celebrate ("I heard the singing"); a sense of time and space that is beyond human understanding and yet always an intimate part of becoming human; and an earthly discourse where the experience of watching muddy rivers turn golden in the sunset, in the case of Hughes (1995), or dancing on the tongues of poets in celebration, in the case of Sanchez (2004), is encouraged to surface.

I imagine that to many of us the title of these two poems and the thoughts spurred by their words are intriguing precisely because they seem distant from and incongruent with the contemporary terms used to give meaning to curriculum in particular and education in general: higher standards, stronger accountability, increased competition, to name but a few. In fact the lure of such poems might be the ways the authors highlight an earthly epistemology and the ways more expansive understandings are contingent upon making connections between seemingly disparate realities, ones that extend beyond bodily knowledge to what the land, air, and water that compose our bodies know. Certainly these poems are attractive for their recognition of how one becomes insinuated with forces that rush us at "break-neck" speeds through the hours and minutes of each day, ones where the image of being caught among the crisscrossing currents of the mighty Mississippi, but remaining ignorant toward the knowledge the river holds, function as an appropriate metaphor for our lives as educators.

What is more, in addition to living in an era of fundamentalist analytics that fail to account for the tacit forces that shape perceptions within the world, we are also faced with proliferating speech acts that leave few spaces for coming to terms with language or pondering the mysteries of the universe. Wonder has little wriggle room. And, just as troubling, we educators, so caught up in the rushing currents of simplistic reasoning and endless self-reporting what we know, find it difficult to see how we contribute to the roaring nature of our lives. Speaking quickly, linearly, and with authority is equated with developing competencies or mastery over the requisite skill sets within a certain field. With the possibility our voices might be heard, education scholars promise the capacity at a moments notice to put knowledge in the service of modern advancement, to declare this new insight or that notable thought within the mania of mass produced ideas and among thousands of groups peddling this or that notion of a fulfilling life, will tell us which curriculum to deliver.

Most disturbing, we educators have been pushed and pulled by these modern forces for so long that we risk mistaking learning how to survive among the currents for all the earthly knowing and wonder that surrounds us. In our ignorance, it has become increasingly difficult to see, hear, feel, or in any other way know (and therefore appreciate, protect, and shepherd) the natural worlds upon which we are unavoidably dependent. In a Foucauldin-esque age of confession (see Foucault, 1976, p. 58), where the secrets of consciousness are revealed through continuous self-reporting, and self-declarations disclose the character of our personalities, the claustrophobia induced by the chorus of cries to be heard conceal the profound gift of human silence. That is, they mask the gift of the animate worlds and living languages that surrounds us. Speaking slowly, cyclically, and with pause, to lose ones place, to punctuate thought with silence, has come to signify ineptitude or, worse yet, an inability to prove mastery and press ourselves onto the world that surrounds us; speaking has become synonymous with awareness. Sitting in silence, diverting one's eyes to seek out ontological breathing space, to search for that "inner space wherein we can create "wriggle room" as Pinar (2009, p. 319) describes it, has come to signify susceptibility or an incapacity to be heard among the cacophony of self-reports that mark the fields of education and curriculum studies. Silence. Animate worlds, living languages, those that "our nerves and skin remember" (Miller, 2000, p. 264), those sights, sounds, touches, smells, and the spaces necessary to hear them, wait for us to heed their calls. This is something other to arrogant consumerist, modernist discourses that promise salvation by way of synthesis and closure on the way toward intellectual advancement and purer forms of knowledge. A sort of Hegelian philosophy of knowledge "which believes it knows all there is to know" (Ellsworth, 1997, p. 67), what indigenous knowledge confronts is discourses of deliverance with the possibility that redemptive agendas provide ever deeper folds in which anthropomorphism might hide.

In 1988, Madeleine Grumet offered a profound and compelling question, why the contradiction between the structure of our teaching and what we know of dwelling in the world as it was experienced in our youth? What makes this question as profound as it is troubling is that regardless of our hopes and dreams for intellectual progress and a better future for our children, we likely embody what the next generation will become. That is, the contradictions between the theorizing we do and the way we live our lives everyday speaks to the relationality between me, my actions, and those who absorb my inconsistencies and will live on long after me.

Within the last year I have followed stories on three districts that have re-configured their annual evaluations and merit increases based on the ability of teachers to contribute to the Annual Yearly Progress (AYP) requirements of the No Child Left Behind Act of 2001. I shake my head in disapproval (each time I read these stories Pinar's (2004) "nightmare that is the present" (p. 5) comes to mind) as I rush off to a meeting where I instruct teaching assistants on how to coax the required-short-yet-meaningful online reading responses from preservice teachers, attempt to forecast when my edited book will come out in relation to the promotion and tenure guidelines for the college, and work frantically to meet the proposal deadline for a grant that most importantly will allow me to hire research assistants who will bear some of the responsibility for a study already underway. In the spaces between us, my students, graduate and undergraduate alike, ingest my becoming as they become on their own. This energy I help create between us, between our bodies "embodied, intercorporeal, and folded with, in, and through each other" (Springgay, Irwin, & Kind, 2007, p. 86), this is the real curriculum I offer regardless of what I profess in lectures and scholarship.

For me, the realization that the Tylerian (see Tyler, 1949) approach to curriculum, the assumption that human thought, feeling, and word are formed apart from the surrounding world, is still dominant within public education is more than a little troubling. What the continued privileging of reason that positions humans at the center of the universe forces us to confront is this: rather than a more expansive curriculum that seeks out relationships among the seemingly disparate elements of the natural world (such as the ways we create and are created by an ecology that knows only infinite centers), we are offering the next generation bodies of knowledge and knowledge of bodies out of which individualized, self-present modes of living are not only attainable but most sought after. Here one is inhibited from knowing anything beyond the ever-changing, dynamic forces of the river's currents because one can never approach an earthly onto-epistemology, what Riley-Taylor (2009) terms an eco-spirituality, to develop a sophisticated understanding of the mutual integrative relationships of the water, land, and air. Too embroiled in urgent negotiation with its continuous and indeterminable effects upon our being, struggling to keep our heads above water so to speak, educators are forced to expend exorbitant amounts of energy on developing mechanisms for survival, as evidenced in the rhetoric of fights, battles, and competition that dominate contemporary discussions of public education (see Race to the Top Description in the White House, 2010).

Wang (2009) attributes this crisis in education "to an inadequate understanding of the impacts a network can have on the singular" which she views as a symptom of a more general failure "to translate well across difference" (p. 383). Almost as if predicting Wang's meditations, nearly a decade earlier Esteva and Prakash (1998) taught us that the inability to translate and make meaning across difference is in part due to the "dis-membering" of societies that made possible the emergence of the "modern individual self" (p. 51). This phenomenon of "individual identity as 'life project' " (Gee, 2000, p. 112) they attribute in part to education systems that emphasize Enlightenment rationality, ones that assume there is an independent original source of order that when discovered and analyzed will provide a coherent explanation for human experiences.

We have been educated (indoctrinated?) into aspirations that "divide," "split," and "separate" and, most importantly, they wash over the lesson taught to us by the Greeks: that the process of abstraction separates ideas from reality (Feyerabend, 1999). These aspirations are often the ones that cut us off from more fully coming to terms with and exploring the implications of our experiences with the natural world for the public, the self, and the production of knowledge. Instead, we are schooled in aspirations that draw our attention upward toward far off visions of utopia, development, and mobility that free us from communities (which means having no community), inward toward a Cartesian subject that becomes the starting point for all certain and essential knowledge or, possibly most disturbing, outward into the "observing gaze" of the knowledge regimes of the state, ones where "the task of administering life" has produced atomized and alienated beings devoid of relations to the humus from which we have come (Foucault, 1978/1990, p. 139).

In *The History of Sexuality: An Introduction, Vol. 1,* where the quote above is taken, Foucault teaches us that since the classical age the West has experienced significant reconfiguration of the mechanisms of power. In this shift, deduction (those social relations that impede or destroy) is no longer the privileged form of power but merely one among many "working to incite, reinforce, control, monitor, optimize, and organize the forces under it" (p. 136). Once the sovereign power of life and death was supplanted by the mundanely compelling and deeply penetrating "administration of bodies" (p. 140), academic knowledge became an indispensable element for adjusting the phenomena of populations to the productive, life-giving and economy-enhancing capacities of the state.

Thus, according to Foucault (1976/1995), public schooling was associated less with the need to educate for freedom and democratic participation than it was for "distributing the living in the domain of value and utility" (p. 144). Framing resistance as the very incitement toward a bodily intervention and the emergence of new discursive practices, disciplinary knowledge, and therefore subject knowledge, became yet another mechanism for aligning bodies and ordering subjectivities. As Foucault explains in regards to formations of disciplinary knowledge:

> The disciplines function increasingly as techniques for making useful individuals. Hence their emergence from a marginal position on the confines of society, and detachment from the forms of exclusion or expiation, confinement or retreat. Hence the slow loosening of their kinship with religious regularities and enclosures. Hence also their rooting in the most important, most central and most productive sectors of society. They become attached to some of the great essential functions: factory production, the transmission of knowledge, the diffusion of aptitudes and skills, the war-machine. Hence, too, the double tendency one sees developing throughout the eighteenth century to increase the number of disciplinary institutions and to discipline the existing apparatuses. (p. 211)

Somewhere in the horror of the outward draw of our schooled aspirations toward state and industry is an invitation that is beyond the limitations of the Enlightenment subject, Age of Reason, and roar and rush of modern forces. It is an invitation to engender a keen sense of place and rootedness in the land while selectively taking advantage of contemporary opportunities to improve quality of life and efficacy of lifestyles (Vitek & Jackson, 1996). Eschewing fixity and essentialism, what is made available in accepting this invitation involves sense making marked by the conjunction of the lived past with select aspects of contemporary economic, political, and social relations. Articulation. Such an invitation might be best actualized through the restoration of "place and place-making for culture, nature, and economy" (Escobar, 2001, p. 141). Place. To which I would add a curriculum that illuminates the significance of both articulation and place. This recognition of the need to know the humus, this land of which we are an extension (culminating) and to which we will return (integrating), has its origins in remembering that includes local culture and national heritage as well as historical investigations that include literature, oral histories, site specific social relationships, and art, ones with the ability to reconnect education to a sense of rootedness in the earth that makes us and which we make.

Attunement to place acts as a challenge to the ahistorical presentism, economic determinism, and intellectual fundamentalism that uproot a sense of place and dissolve a feeling of belonging and realistic scope of influence, offering in exchange for what Berry (1990) describes as "a man with a machine and inadequate culture"(p. 8) an earthly recognition that events take place outside of our wanting and doing. These occurances outside our control speak to our limits; they act as a measure of and re-gard for what is within the realm of human influence. On one register, a Foucauldian analytic sheds light on this concern: the power/knowledge affair attends to the mechanisms that allow for the "state intervention in and regulation of the everyday lives of citizens" (Lather, 2004, p. 24). Yet, even as many dimensions of the knowledge/power project invite further exploration, it remains a concern born out of a European intellectual tra-dition, one unable to account for a subject that is displaced not just by discourse but also by the natural world and its unfathomable mysteries (natural events that happen without or without our self-presence, self-awareness, and academic knowledge). For example, the likely path of a fish, currents, and movement of debris and sediment within a river are at the nexus of inseparable relationships of the cosmos and as interconnect-ed events they take place whether or not they are witnessed by human be-ings. And each of these events, because they occur outside of our wanting and doing, require that we look upon them as gifts inextricably bound to life forces to which we are always already beholden, ones that know no way to speak to us through human language, whether it is Spanish, French, English, or Latin. Out of each of the daily experiences of place there ex-ists the silent collectivity of the Earth, an integrative system with natural cycles that sustain all life and human thoughts, feelings, and words where each aspect is indebted to all other aspects of the universe. Attunement to this life force raises to the surface a primordial obligation all life has to the spherical, cyclical time of the earth: human boundedness to the air that fills our lungs; minerals, organisms, and all the other elements of the land that constitute our flesh, blood, and bone; and sun, clouds, and sky that give sustenance to the body and sustain our existence.

The worldview that humans have a responsibility for maintaining harmonious relationships with the natural world, ones successively repressed in the exercise of domination for economic and political gain, promises to uncontrollably belittle our theories of subject-hood with unfathomable ecological disasters. That is, they threaten to end in ecological disasters far beyond any rationale human effort at their management (The British Petroleum oil disaster in the Gulf of Mexico, for example). Through ceremonies and rituals we honor the concepts that provide the foundation to our field and speak and write with excitement at the intellectual advancements taking place at the crossroads of cultural studies, autobiography, critical geography, teacher education, internationalization, post-structuralism, and so on. We endlessly speculate what the future might hold in terms of the next new story that so installed will make a contribution to curriculum thought. We bemoan the lasting influence of curriculum development on schools. Yet, in doing so, we regularly neglect the fleshy, material, dynamic, and undecipherable world that makes our theorizing possible, one where we are but one of infinite centers positioned among the ever-changing natural forces that make up the universe. This is the very real foundation that provides the nutrients that constitute our bodies; an act of nurturing that is always already more fundamental to thinking our thoughts and speaking our words than any successor narrative offering the promise of increased understanding. Gifts. These are gifts that must be honored through the cultivation of harmonious relationships with the earthly world, an ancient planet that Hughes so aptly points out has known rivers "older than the flow of human blood through human veins" (Hughes, 1994, p. 23).

READING TWO: LA COMIDA: SINGULARITY AND INTERCONNECTEDNESS

Not only are humans endowed with consciousness, but so are all things of the environment.

—Angayuqaq Oscar Kawagley

The Negro Speaks of Rivers and *I've Known Rivers*. The rhythms, words, and titles of these two poems proclaim a feeling of both the vibrant spiritual connectedness among all the elements of the cosmos and the dramatic seclusiveness of the natural world. In excess of binary formations or attempts to reduce objects of the natural world to successively smaller parts, both poems fulfill both of these feelings, not merely an either-or but an also-and, both the interrelationship of the dynamic and ever-changing elements of the earthly world and the invaluable, solitary, and complete uniqueness of each element of the universe. For what the Mississippi River reveals in its singularity, exceptionality, and incomparability it also reveals in its flowing down toward the South and its ongoing transformation into an-other form, such as the continuous cycle of vapor rising from its waters and collecting again among nearby plants as the morning dew.

That is, the Mississippi River is unique and incomparable as a force of nature and it is undeniably interrelated with every other force of nature within the universe. It culminates as a river and it is undergoing continuous transformation and regeneration as it integrates with every other element of planet: forming the moisture that fills the air and making the land that is right under our feet inhabitable. It invites a notion of interrelationships and connections that emanate from uniqueness and invaluability toward what is yet to come; they are not in contradiction with each other but complimentary cosmic forces that form a holistic spherical scheme. It is an invitation that works against a conventional notion within the curriculum field, drawn from Descartes and reaffirmed all too clearly by Bobbitt (1921): "The first step in curriculum-making is, of course, to decide upon the developmental results that are to be the outcomes of the training" (p. 607). This regime of thinking central to our formations of curriculum (whether or not it is central to the field) sheds some light on the artificial isolation that characterizes much of our lives and that we quietly pass on to the next generation under the pretenses of high-quality, newly reformed public education and the individualized, frenetic consumption of knowledge for self-advancement, and along with this mania all the standards to achieve and competencies to meet in an effort to move ahead, develop, and feed "our obsession with 'getting to the top'" (Berry, 2000, p. 57).

Hughe's description of rivers "ancient as the world" and "older than the flow of blood in human veins" teaches us two things: every force within the natural world and every human becoming are always already dependent upon and inadequate to the unfathomable mysteries of nature. "Each thing stands before us on behalf of all things, as the absolute center of all things, and at the periphery of all things" (Jardine, 1999, p. 265). Each element is solitary and invaluable because its existence relies upon its relationship to the existence of all other elements of the universe. The next meal from which you will garner nourishment cannot simply reveal the truth of its existence, provide an authentic representation of what it is. It is not incomparably this meal, your meal, simply because it can exist without anything else. In reasoning counter to that produced out of the scientific revolution, it is not its own constitution. Rather, it exists as it is before you because of what in its singularity it cannot otherwise be. Sitting before you, waiting to be consumed, it speaks to the land from which it took its nutrients, the water that provided its sustenance, and the sun that enabled the process that transformed the nutrients into sustenance. It speaks to the migrant workers who harvested the grains for it, the peasant workers who were displaced from their land to allow for the price of it, and the change in the lives of their children and their children's children because of it. It speaks to the coal that was burned to run the factories that provided the processing, the pesticides that guaranteed a bountiful harvest and ran off into a nearby stream, and the soon to be mother downstream who ingested those pesticides and gave birth to a "deformed" child and that families sorrow and joy and cries and laughter. This meal before you speaks as one solitary element of a holistic, integrative system with both infinite vectors and a unifying life force. This one meal in all its exceptionality depends upon its relationship with every other element in the cosmos so that it might exist just as it is, just as it will be, right before you in all its singularity. Dispose of this meal and there is a reconfiguration of every element in the network of natural forces that make up the universe.

Thus, when indigenous woman Jeanette Armstrong (2005) tells others that she is Okanagan, that she originates from the Okanagan Valley between the Selkirks and Cascades rocky mountain ranges of British Columbia, and that to understand what it means to be Okanagan one must understand the profundity of the act of taking numerous strands of hair and rubbing them between one's fingers until finally they form one strand, she is speaking to this exceptionality and interrelationality. This sense that one is both solitary and a part of everything else is why it is reasonable to assert that if this meal before you, your next meal, was to no longer exist, everything else would no longer exist, for what now exists with this meal, just as it is, has this meal as a constitutive force of its existence. Dispense with this meal and everything has literally undergone reconfiguration, it is no longer the same. The lesson that the categories of our language are inadequate to such experience invokes a wondrous sense of vertigo: to be seized by the reality that any object of the universe, from the most substantial to the most minute, is at the same time vital to this integrative matrix and also just one of an infinite number of points of convergence involves an unequivocal reconfiguration of modern thought.

The meal before you might be unremarkable and yet it is at the center of all elements in the cosmos. And, to extend this reconfiguration further, circular temporality is at issue as well. Cultural, material, and spiritual time and space are revealed as functioning, not in a linear fashion, but in continuous repeating cycles. Each and every moment is not only at the core of all elements but moments that exist in spherical schema of the universe or uninterrupted sets of systems. Dwiggins (1999) captures these natural cycles in a description of indigenous Andean peasants' non-chronological temporality. In particular, Dwiggins refers to a non-Western cosmosvision that is,

> circumambient, producing a sort of "surround sound" effect. Events that are from a historicist perspective in the 'past' are in the 'future' in the Andean point of view because the referenced event is affecting actions that will eventually take place ahead of the point in time where we are situated at the present. Subterranean spirits, from a modern locus of "below," are, in the Andean point of view, *approaching* Earth's surface to arrive at a future date, even though the ancestor may have passed away centuries ago. In this case then the 'future' is approaching from 'behind', a 'below' in the historicist terminology. Predictions, projections, and prognostications thus become a function of past events because these events will re-manifest as part of the cyclicity of the Andean cosmos. (emphasis in original, p. 33)

In summary, as something other than the humanist's subjects, biologist's organisms, and the chemist's molecules, what we have are two ecological revelations: the existence of every element is embedded in every other element of the cosmos and at any given moment our past and futures overlap and are shared collectively across time and space.

Recognizing this as an invitation both equal to and more than heightened awareness, it opens the possibility of moving through our philosophies of self-presence, self-definition, and self-volition, drawing our hands, heads, eyes, and feet down to the real foundation of curriculum studies, the real humus that gives us life, the real becoming in our exquisite incomparability and unfathomable interrelationships. This is not just an "intellectual breakthrough" (Pinar, 1999), or a "next moment" (Malewski, 2009) in understanding made possible via the work of Benjamin, Foucault, or Derrida, or others. Undeniably, deriving wisdom and ethics from direct experience with the natural world offers a different set of constraints, yet ones where the suspicions of modern rationality, philosophies of presence, and universalizing projects put in check the rampant desire to position human subjectivity at the center of all elements of the universe. As a field we might pay tribute to Foucault's assertion that humans are a recent invention that emerged within sixteenth century Europe, that it was not around the figure of man that "knowledge prowled for so long in the darkness" (Foucault, 1970/1994, p. 386), not by looking upward, inward, or outward, but downward, toward the generative, rich, and fundamental humus right beneath our feet.

READING THREE: PLACE-MAKING AND HOME-MAKING/
PRODUCTION AND CONSUMPTION

Flowing rivers are not insinuated with land, air, and surrounding water by way of causal relationships, ones so isolated that they cannot imagine the innumerable interaction effects of what is at play in everyday life. They do not attempt to order the world, to bring the objects of the world into a controlled space, removed from situation or context, labeled and placed on a shelf in a Western museum or university laboratory. And what suitable images the museum and laboratory are for the logic of empiricism and the structures created to sort the concepts born out of the staged organization of progress. And too what important images are they for our unquestioned investments in curriculum studies. So enamored are educators with the idea of progress that even with the "recent impulse to deconstruct developmentalism" in order to "rescue the child from developmentalism's clutches" what we end up with becomes yet "another chapter in a long-standing narrative of progress" (Baker, 1999, p. 829). In our ignorance of our own epistemological investments we have a difficult time thinking otherwise. A museum, a laboratory that separates the relational self from what the real breath of life and what the land, air, and water that compose our bodies know, what becomes available involves isolating variables, replicating studies, and numerical conversions of reality based on the protocols of scientism and education's own developmental commitments. By way of evidence-based practices and data driven decision-making that are the next step in the narrative of progress and advancement, what becomes more difficult to see involves the complex web of interactions and the interrelatedness of seemingly disparate realities.

Increasingly segmented, experimental designs associated with knowledge of most worth, life becomes depressingly episodic, where understanding implicit orders and tacit assumptions is eclipsed by a focus on already unfolded orders, simple patterns, and invariants in time. Here life is reduced to a series of snapshots, what has already occurred, what has already been ordered, and diminished to what is divisible into increasingly smaller, insular parts. When conjoined with a "salvation narrative of superiority" that "relies on exaggerated and essentialized notions of difference between the colonizing and colonized" (Bergeron, 2007, p. 88), our research practices become unwittingly insinuated with the reproduction of hierarchical relationships worldwide. Producing feverously to contribute to a "robust" body of knowledge, hoping to make a difference but uncertain of our larger effects, we fail to see how we contribute to the worst aspects of Western knowledge production.

Unsettled by what is occurring beyond our academic disciplines, we write and think about a future time when all will be right in the world, when all the knowledge fragments will form a whole, when our knowledge will provide us with salvation. Faced with the traumatic practices occurring within schools, where our curriculum work has yet to make a lasting intervention, our home-making becomes decontextualized. That is, our sense of time and place become out of place and distorts our understanding of our own capacities, our relationships with all that surrounds us, and our effectualness. As space and time become more fragmented, captured in episodic time rather than lived in mutual interrelationships, the most insignificant ideas take on resounding force. That is, as pointless information proliferates with manifold intensity, finding wriggle room at all demands retreat from the public sphere. Here the river of information on all that is wrong with the world and seemingly beyond our control is confronted with a sense of place based only on our most immediate surroundings, what professional societies we belong to, what journals we write in, what we live in, what we commute in, and what gives us comfort in our retreat into daily routines; how we think and feel about what immediately surrounds us are the measures of satisfaction.

So what has become of actual homes where each of us live? No longer viewed for the most part as a place for producing, a location from which to prepare for public engagement, the home has undergone a transformation over the past 4 to 5 decades. Less often are homeowners planting gardens, mending their own clothes, canning their own meats, or engaging in other activities whereby the household plays an integral role in economic and public life. Instead the home has become a retreat from the brutality of the world: a place where we sleep at night, prepare for the activities of the next day, and take leisure time in evenings and on weekends. Historically homes were the sites of useful production and engagement with the public economy but in more recent times they have become centers for consuming resources and producing what sickens the earth. As Wendell Berry (1986) teaches us on no uncertain terms, the contemporary home has shifted away from being a productive unit:

> With its array of gadgets and machines, all powered by energies that are destructive of land, air and water, and connected to work, market, school, recreation, etc., by gasoline engines, the modern home is a veritable factory of waste and destruction. It is the mainstay of the economy of money. But within the economies of energy and nature, it is a catastrophe. It takes the world's goods and converts them into garbage, sewage, and noxious fumes– for none of which we have found a use. (p. 52)

What would it mean to see our academic home as well as the homes in which we live not in isolation but in relation? How would our living need to change so that our thinking and being were more harmonious with our doing? If we write prolifically on social injustice and yet our students breath in our frenetic and wasteful lives, ones where we act as if the world is ours to consume and disciplinary knowledge will save us from destruction, then regardless of what we say in writing, our practices mask deeper and more profound earthly knowing.

READING FOUR: HUMAN-EARTHLY/EARTHLY-HUMAN CONNECTEDNESS AND SINGULARITY

The flowing river is insinuated with the land, air, and surrounding water; it harmonizes with all those elements that make up the earth and moves in relation to them, when it is not dammed or enclosed. The waters of the flowing river are not devoid of character; they are not components of hydrogen and oxygen and energy longing to be put to use, to be managed by humans, and therefore yearning to come into existence in the Western imagination, to move onto the stage of history once labeled and categorized. In this sense it is no mere liquid at all. It is no mere symbol. To exist as it does it moves into and out of all the earth and therefore it is everything and nothing all at once; named or unnamed it speaks to deep-seated relationships that so unenclosed, so moving out into the existence of all other things reveals human interconnectedness with the infinite elements of the earth, humans also simultaneously everything and nothing, all at once.

Just as the flowing river is both part of us and apart from us, existing in indeterminable relationships with each of us in ways beyond language, so too are we both a part of and apart from the children and youth we teach. That is, they exist in relation to us, their teachers, and yet they have minds, bodies, and spirits of their own, both in relation to and distinct from those holding the role of educator. Working within psychoanalysis, Jennifer Gilbert (2009) traces this indeterminable relationship through the formation of generations and the paradox of being a part of and apart from the students we teach. She asks two questions that highlight the enabling and constraining capacities of generational change: What does it mean for the older generation to challenge the younger generation's ideas without merely capitulating or attempting to contain them? What does mean for a younger generation to actualize a future without destroying the previous generation's ideals or becoming mere clones lurking in their shadows? The questions she asks are akin to the idea that the river can only continue to flow because it remains its own entity and at the same time transforms into an-other. That is, a river can only flow down toward the South, as Hughes describes, because it remains itself and because it also takes on a new form. In an irresolvable paradox of Western reason, at its limits, only by way of the ability to flow, to move from one place to another, does it remain itself. So too, for human life to continue, there remains the irresolvable tensions whereby for humanity to remain itself it must continually change with each new generation. In the birth of anew there is both continuity and change.

Entirely via our ambivalence toward newcomers who are both a promise, a hope that the future might be different from today, and a threat, a reflection of our mortality and failures, what comes about is neither a sameness subsumed within our own image or a difference which is beyond our comprehension, but all the possibilities associated with affiliations with an-other. Here what is required to engender this affiliation is recognition that the future might be different from the past, that the flowing river must change to remain itself, and that our practices and thoughts in the past could have been different than they were, that our reasoning and living might be insufficient to the needs of the present moment. The children and youth of today are who they are because they are not the children of yesterday; they bring promise of a future different from our now and confrontation with the reality that in educating new life, an-other life, our own life will come to an end. Pinar (2008), exploring our own finiteness, suggests "[o]ur predecessors render our very presence possible; they provide the medium through which we articulate our educational experience and midwife experience yet to come" (pp. 5–6). To this I add, the existence of an-other, of a younger generation, speaks to all the land, air, and water that stands apart from them *and* composes their bone, blood, hair, and skin, them, us, me, apart from and a part of the earth. This is the ongoing transformation that allows us to be ourselves; this is genuine education.

An-other. Conflict. Difference. Affiliation. Hospitality. Gift. The gift of life the earth gives and its hospitality when it welcomes us in and provides us shade, food, and drink. This is a gift that to us is given but cannot be understood as a gift. That is, following the work of Derrida (1992/1994), the gift of life the earth gives, as a genuine gift, cannot be conceptualized as a gift, as it must exceed the demands of both giving and taking, as well as any calculated reasoning or self-interest (p. 30). His point is that a genuine gift demands of the giver a certain anonymity, that by giving the giver is not caught up in self-aggrandizement or any form of self-promotion. In this sense, the giver cannot seek recognition or even be aware they are giving, for such awareness by the self or other risks a sort of reabsorption of the gift, a statement about the benevolent capacities of the self: "see what I have done, how good I am; with my privileges I give back." Genuine gift giving raises the question of nature's limits, of how long before the earth stops giving and demands reparations. This impossible possibility demands educators in particular and humans in general think differently about their relationship with the earth.

Indeed, this impossible possibility might be experienced as an appeal to see anew the very grounds upon which we understand curriculum. What Derrida wants to problematize is the very idea of a gift that can be disarticulated from notions of giving and taking. There is no solution to this type of problem and no Western dialectic that might synthesize the incommensurable, the impossible possibility of the problem that confronts us with what the earth gives us as a gift. Yet, Derrida teaches us, what we are left with is not a sort of paralysis, a sort of endless vacillation within Western logic between this and that side of the binary, infinite deferral. Rather, the idea is to actually seek genuine giving and at the same time recognize the actual limits of these concepts, to acknowledge that these notions are elusive and their absolute forms cannot actually be achieved. Here what becomes possible involves the search for reasoning that is the other to the other of Western thought. What this other to the other might mean for us is that we are not at the center of an earthly epistemology nor other to it, but that the earth might live on with or without us, that we have been living as the recipients of the genuine gift.

Not a purpose that can be set in motion by way of scope and sequence on the way toward some sort of evaluation that speaks to what has been accomplished, children and youth learn neither to seek out the elusive nature of genuine giving nor their interrelatedness with all the earth. We need to call attention to both this absence and this ignorance: the question of the genuine gift is the gift that grounds curriculum understanding and all the aporias the question of the genuine gift reveals to us. For it is the impossibility of absolute altruism and our simultaneous search that compels us toward children and youth. In our affiliations they are us and we are them and yet we are not the same, and this ensures that the very conditions of possibility regarding genuine giving between educators and children, and youth are intricately linked to their very impossibility. This paradox seems to invoke a certain anxiety in modern curriculum thought and practice, that in contemporary times great faith is invested in the articulation of "things unto themselves" as if there is no relationality, as if isolation and fragmentation will somehow alleviate our lives of paradoxes, tensions, and impossible possibilities. And it is here that education, including teachers and students, is caught up in atomization and acts of neglect, that purpose, meaning, and irresolvable questions are displaced by facts without context, and appeals to reasoning devoid of questions of significance and ethics. Equally disturbing, we are left without any way of asking the question, what makes this life meaningful? Or even possible?

Wendell Berry also is concerned about this atomization of our modern lives. In his 2005 essay "Contempt of Small Places," he highlights the interconnection between realities that have become disparate under instrumentalism. In the case he presents, it is the linkage between the "dead zone" in the Gulf of Mexico and the practice of strip mining coal in Kentucky that is of key interest, but unfortunately, masked within contemporary thought:

> The health of the ocean depends on the health of the rivers; the health of the rivers depends on the health of the small streams; the health of the small streams depends on the health of their watersheds. The health of the water is exactly the same as the health of the land; the health of small places is exactly the same as the health of large places. As we know, disease is hard to confine. Because natural law is in force everywhere, infections move. (p. 7)

This incapacity to see relationships and interconnections makes possible an image of curriculum as knowledge to be transmitted, self-actualization to be completed, and language to be studied, but not life as one of infinite centers and deeply dependent upon the earth. That is, it can speak to formula and causality but little to the humus that cools the flesh, water that wets the lips, and air that fills the lungs. Here the difference between the teacher who focuses on the facts of nature in order to prepare students for a test and the teacher who invites students to be seized by the wonders of nature and explore the forest, pick up a leaf, and see its veins, to study it as one of a multitude of vectors of existence and ponder its connection to the universe, speaks to the magnitude of pedagogical and curricular implications. Thus, without the latter, the study of curriculum,

> [r]emoves teachers and students from an understanding of the compelling intellectual and political issues of the day. This is a fatal pedagogical mistake as it sets up a dichotomy between school and the "real world." Such a division will always undermine motivation, as teachers and students come to see the mandated activities of school as trivial and irrelevant. (Tobin & Kincheloe, 2006, p. 11)

In this quagmire of regressive curriculum studies, teaching and learning become less immediate, less connected to the concerns of nature and community and to student interests and desires, and less concerned with eco-ethical issues regarding life in and out of schools and the knowledge we produce. Equally compelling, the rationalization of a facts and figures approach to curriculum further removes public education from the environmental, economic, and cultural changes that surround schools and the very real problem that the earth might not need us as much as we need the earth. It is only with these disconnections that hyper-individuality and a false pretense of independence from the earth can flourish.

READING FIVE: THEORIZING ECO-POLITICAL EPISTEMOLOGIES OF IGNORANCE IN CURRICULUM STUDIES

Far from a lack of knowledge that the social sciences aim to eliminate, ignorance is more accurately understood as the parallel product of knowledge production. This is what Paul de Man (1983) termed blindness and insight, where what is excluded is the very organizer through which intelligibility is made possible and "knowledge loses itself in the necessary blind spots of understanding" (Lather, 2007, p. vii). Accordingly, it is important to study who benefits and loses in regards to knowledge production and the production of ignorance. What might be termed the politics of ignorance, academic debates over knowledge of most worth are less a Kuhnian process of dialectical synthesis leading to an eventual agreement upon a settled form. Instead, they are viewed as the eco-political results of structural inequalities, intentional and unintentional concealments, and conflicting interests and agendas. My sense is that too often ignorance is conceptualized as innocence not yet lost, as in "I did not know," and not the very exclusions necessary to the insights, discoveries, or truth claims that are made.

Therefore, epistemologies of ignorance cannot be theorized merely as a gap, oversight, or omission, as something outside of complicity, but must be understood as an active construction. In this sense, ignorance involves a series of operative nondiscursive and discursive productions embedded within the act of knowing itself. Insinuated with concerns over differential authority, the press of narrative formulas, methodological proceduralism, and discourses of credibility, knowledge production is never free from its own contamination. Frances Rains (1999), for example, argues that it is the refusal to consider knowledge not derived from within an impervious system of Western knowledge formation that has led to the active production and preservation of ignorance:

> It is an interesting system, this "Western" knowledge production, it is self-contained, self-sustaining, handy, convenient, and even tinged with a sense of self-righteousness. It has certainly worked. Hermetically sealed, the closed system of "Western" knowledge production has been institutionalized, in a matter of several hundred years, to such a degree as to dismiss indigenous knowledges based on thousands of years of experience, analysis, and reflec-

tion as primitive. It is this system, this intellectual apartheid, that merits examination in how it operates in conjunction with historical amnesia to deny indigenous knowledge. (p. 317)

Although such intellectual productions cannot be mapped seamlessly onto oppressive practices as a sort of unfallible explanation, they are interrelated in complex and often not easily distinguishable ways. As Eve Kosofsky Sedgwick (1990) so aptly notes,

> If ignorance is not, as it evidently is not, a single Manichaean, aboriginal maw of darkness from which the heroics of human cognition can occasionally wrestle facts, insights, freedoms, progress, perhaps there exists instead a plethora of *ignorances,* and we may begin to ask questions about the labor, erotics, and economics of their human production and distribution. (p. 8)

Clearly, viewing the unknown as ways of knowing and the ecological, cultural, and economic politics of such nonknowledge must be a central element of our educational analyses. Epistemologies of ignorance have the capacity to expose the force of power relations within the construction of the knower and the known and to provide a lens for exploring the anthropomorphic values at work in our knowledge producing practices.

Similarly, epistemologies that uphold a colonial perspective that ignorance is a frontier to be settled and ordered risk underwriting modernist frameworks that are dangerous to both the earth and humans. Traditional accounting practices in the United States and elsewhere, for example, mask the actual or true costs of bringing a product to society by failing to account for all dimensions, from production and shipping to environmental degradation and proper disposal. In this way, we have knowledge of accounting practices that are more accurate and present a fuller picture of reality. Yet, there is resistance toward using them for what they might expose in terms of harm to environments, particularly those of the poor and "third world," and costs to the public in terms environmental clean up and sickness, destruction, and death. Many socially just organizations in the United States and abroad practice this "true" or "actual" cost accounting. Epistemologies of ignorance must not only focus on the unknown as ways of knowing, the understudied and unstudied histories of knowledge production, but also those situations where particular forms of knowledge are ignored or subjugated for political-economic purposes. We must join indigenous peoples and scholars in asking who benefits and who loses in these forms of centering and marginalizing.

Given my post-structural suspicion of grand narratives and "one best way" approaches to theory and practice, it seems while the concept of ignorance as a gap or omission awaiting a discovery that will fill it is risky business, so is the pursuit of a model by which to make judgments over truth claims. Instead, it might be beneficial to study the specificity of ignorance: What has led to our contemporary not knowings? How might we conceive of the unknown as ways of knowing? Who is in the know and who is ignorant and why? How has knowledge and ignorance shifted historically and contemporarily and why? What are the conditions that have led to our ignorance and knowledge and what historical thresholds had to be passed through in order to arrive at our current state of knowing and not knowing? In addition, in thinking through particularities and specificities, what are the parallels between ignorance and knowledge and how do they diverge and reveal disjunctive logics? The analytic tools for examining knowledge production might or might not function for examining how ignorance is crafted, sustained, and made more robust. In regards to curriculum and indigenous knowledge, in order to account for what we know it is imperative that we also account for what we do not know and who benefits and who suffers under current regimes of knowing and not knowing.

Colonialism/postcolonialism, Western/non-Western theories and practices are particularly fruitful sites for studying the relationships between knowledge and ignorance. The intersection of earthly knowledge and knowledge produced by humans has a fertile history for understanding the significance of epistemologies of ignorance in relation to our theories and practices of teaching and learning. It is with this study that we might honor grassroots cosmovisions within curriculum studies.

READING SIX: CONCLUSION

What do I think of Western civilization? I think it would be a very good idea.
—Mahatma Gandhi

What would it mean to turn our eyes away from a relentless quest for development, this effort to produce purer and purer knowledge, which hovers further and further above the real complications of life on the ground, and toward the very humus that sustains us and gives us life, and makes living on, and therefore the next generation, possible? It seems the answer is not a battle against epistemologies of ignorance, for such a move merely establishes another binary, an-other for which affirms an-other against, and therefore plays into an already crowded reactionary terrain of modern epistemological frameworks. And, as the Gandhi quote above reminds us, it is not productive to think of terms such as "civilized" and "primitive" separate from the systems of thought that sustain their hierarchical relations. Nor is it productive to think of discourse and ideas as other to this place, this life, to where it is we plant our feet, and who it is we live with.

In the moment of our now, real education is an economic, political, and social matter *and* a matter that draws us toward the land, air, and water to which we are inextricably bound, that which is apart from and a part of us. Real education does not issue forth from a textbook as this or that idea, to be "banked" as Freire termed it, and regurgitated on a test; *the "real test" is how we find ourselves practicing and thinking, and that means living, in our everyday lives, the ways we relate in and to the world and how this speaks to the children and youth we teach.*

The teacher seeing the specificity of each child, realizing that children deeply experience being seen, understanding that children will compare what we say with our eyes with what we say with our words, these are recursive moments in teaching, ones that resonate with our complete responsibility toward an-other, a newcomer, and the demands this makes on the character of our affiliations. If Langston Hughes' poem becomes just another commodity, just another form of cultural capital put on display in the next new regime of knowledge assessment to justify a place at the top, then the real test has been failed and real education lost. For what we are left with in the vacuum of unmet expectations is the pornographic, what Audre Lorde (1984) refers to as the false separation of the spiritual from the political, a certain "plasticized sensation" (p. 54) where the good is defined "in terms of profit rather than in terms of human need" (p. 55). The issue that arises is not merely that as educators we "embody possible ways of being for the child" (van Manen, 2002, p. 16); rather, the issue is how in the present day context of education teachers and students are enabled *and* constrained to ask questions regarding how they want to be in the world and how they want to practice as a sort of answer. At the crossroads of our teaching, the questions made available, and the possibility of acting differently is the real work of schooling.

So as to make this point clear, to not let it cloud my claims, it is a White male academic who shares these thoughts, who is located in the safety of an academic position in the midst of a global "great recession." And it is this White male academic who recognizes that while he too is attempting to survive among the river's currents, he is privileged in many ways in relation to the global majority. That is, there are spaces for me to write and think through these ideas while the worst aspects of internationalization, developmentalism, and cultural imperialism silences many (and also provokes many toward decolonization and indigenous ways of knowing, just to be clear). Yet, I work from the realization that what is rarely discussed in "developed" societies

> are the ways in which the knowledges of people being developed are ignored or treated as mere obstacles to rational progress. In order for them to progress, these people have first to be constituted as "underdeveloped"

and ignorant. Conversely, without such underdevelopment and ignorance, the West could not represent itself as developed and possessing knowledge. (Hobart, 1993, p. 2)

As I spend time with my nephews, and the girls and boys at the schools where I do research, I see how distant the curriculum is from their real lives and issues (they worry about war, ecological devastation, and the state of the world the previous generation is leaving them; yet, when they talk of school, the focus inevitably turns to grades, test scores, and the categorization of winners and losers). I fear two things from all of this: that to survive schooling these children and youth will crowd their lives with objects and outlooks that will do little more than perpetuate self-indulgent onto-epistemological outlooks of mastery, individualism, imperialism, and development. And, because of this, they will not have room for relationality and the humility and understanding that issue forth from genuine affiliations with an-other. I am determined that schooling become something different for them, an experience where they understand that they are both a part of and apart from each other and the earth, and infinitely indebted to both. I wonder if, as the generation that follows mine, they will have to pay for the consumerist self-indulgent lifestyles that have been a problem for grass root communities for far too long. I also wonder what they will think of me in years to come if they are the ones who must deal with the mess my lifestyle has caused. If they discover that what I said was different from how I lived, then how will they experience my life as an educator? How do we meet the call to educate our own to the best of our ability when our students, just as us teachers, carry on our lives under the very economic, political, and cultural conditions that have created devastation for the global majority? The issue beckons us to respond, just as Sanchez did, to the question raised by Hughes: *Have we known rivers?*

REFERENCES

Armstrong, J. (2005, November 8). I stand with you against the disorder. *Yes Magazine*. Retrieved November 5, 2009, from http://www.yesmagazine.org/issues/spiritual-uprising/i-stand-with-you-against-the-disorder

Baker, B. (1999). The dangerous and the good? Developmentalism, progress, and public schooling. *American Educational Research Journal, 36*(4), 797–834.

Bergeron, S. (2007). Colonialism and imperialism. In A. Lind & S. Brzuzy (Eds.), *Battleground: Women, gender, and sexuality* (pp. 87–97). Santa Barbara, CA: Greenwood Publishing.

Berry, W. (1986). *The unsettling of America*. San Francisco, CA: Sierra Club Books.

Berry, W. (1990). *What are people for?* New York, NY: North Point Press.

Berry, W. (2000). *Life is a miracle: An essay against modern superstition.* Washington, DC: Counterpoint Press.

Berry, W. (2005). Contempt of small places. In *The ways of ignorance: And other essays* (pp. 7–8). Berkeley, CA: Counterpoint.

Bobbitt, F. (1921). A significant tendency in curriculum-making. *The Elementary School Journal, 21,* 607–615.

de Man, P. (1983). *The blindness of insight: Essays in the rhetoric of contemporary criticism.* Minneapolis, MN: University of Minneapolis.

Derrida, J. (1994). *Given time: Counterfeit money* (P. Kamuf, Trans.). Chicago, IL: University of Chicago Press. (Original work published in 1992)

Dwiggins, D. (1999). Ancient symbols/contemporary tools: Forging counterhegemonic coalitions in Ecuador. *Wicazo Sa Review, 14*(1), 29-43.

Ellsworth, E. (1997). *Teaching positions: Difference, pedagogy, and the power of address.* New York: Teachers College Press.

Escobar, A. (2001). Culture sits in places: reflections on globalism and subaltern strategies of localization. *Political Geography, 20*(20), 139-174.

Esteva, G. & Prakash, M. S. (1998). *Grassroots post-modernism: Remaking the soil of cultures.* London: Zed Books.

Foucault, M. (1990). *The history of sexuality: An introduction* (Vol. 1) (R. Hurley, Trans.). New York, NY: Vintage Books. (Original work published 1978)

Foucault, M. (1995). *Discipline and punish: The birth of the prison.* New York, NY: Random House. (Original work published in 1975)

Foucault, M. (1995). *The will to knowledge: History of sexuality* (Vol 1). London: Penguin Books (Original published 1976)

Feyerabend, P. (1999). *Knowledge, science, and relativism: 1960-1980.* Cambridge, MA: Cambridge University Press.

Foucault, M. (1994). *The order of things: An archaeology of the human sciences.* New York: Vintage Books. (Original work published 1970)

Gee, J. P. (2000). Identity as an analytic lens for research in education. *Review of Research in Education, 25,* 99–125.

Gilbert, J. (2009). Reading histories: Curriculum theory, psychoanalysis, and generational violence. In E. Malewski (Eds.), *Curriculum studies handbook: The next moment* (pp. 63–72). New York, NY: Routledge.

Grumet, M. (1988). *Bitter milk: Women and teaching.* Amherst, MA: University of Massachusetts Press.

Hobart, M. (1993). *An anthropological critique of development: The growth of ignorance.* New York, NY: Routledge.

Hughes, L. (1994). *The collected poems of Langston Hughes.* New York, NY: Vintage Books.

Hughes, L. (speaker). (1995). *The voice of Langston Hughes* [CD]. Washington, DC: Folkways Records.

Jardine, D. W. (1999). A bell ringing in the empty sky. In W. F. Pinar (Ed.), *Contemporary curriculum discourses: Twenty years of JCT* (pp. 262–277). New York, NY: Peter Lang.

Lather, P. (2004). This is your father's paradigm: Government intrusion and the case of qualitative research in education. *Qualitative Inquiry, 10*(1), 15–34.

Lather, P. (2007). *Getting lost: Feminist efforts toward a double(d) science*. Albany, NY: SUNY Press.

Lorde, A. (1984). *Sister outsider: Essays and speeches*. Berkley, CA: The Crossing Press.

Malewski, E. (Ed.). (2009) *Curriculum studies handbook: The next moment*. New York, NY: Routledge.

Miller, J. L. (2000). What's left in the field ... a curriculum memoir. *Journal of Curriculum Studies, 32*(2), 253–266.

Pinar, W. F. (1999). Not burdens, breakthroughs. *Curriculum Inquiry, 29*(3), 365–367.

Pinar, W. F. (2004). *What is curriculum theory?* Mahwah, NJ: Lawrence Erlbaum.

Pinar, W. F. (2008). Understanding curriculum as gender text: Notes on reproduction, resistance, Male-male relations. In S. Appel (Ed.), *Psychoanalysis and pedagogy* (pp. 103–124). Charlotte, NC: Information Age.

Pinar, W. F. (2009). Response essay: The agency of theory. In E. Malewski (Ed.), *Curriculum studies handbook: The next moment* (pp. 318–321). New York, NY: Routledge.

Rains, F. V. (1999). Indigenous knowledge, historical amnesia and intellectual authority: Deconstructing hegemony and the social and political implications of the curricular "other." In L. M. Semali & J. L. Kincheloe (Eds.), *What is indigenous knowledge?: Voices from the academy* (pp. 317–332). New York, NY: Falmer Press.

Riley-Taylor, E. (2009). Reconceiving ecology: Diversity, language, and horizons of the possible. In E. Malewski (Ed.), *Curriculum studies handbook: The next moment* (pp. 286–298). New York, NY: Routledge.

Sanchez, S. (2004). *I've known rivers*. On *Full moon of Sonia* [CD]. New York, NY: Via International Artists.

Sedgwick, E. K. (1990). *Epistemology of the closet*. Berkeley, CA: University of California Press.

Springgay, S., Irwin, R. L., & Kind, S. (2007). A/r/tographers and living inquiry. In J. G. Knowles & A. L. Cole (Eds.), *Handbook of the arts in qualitative research in qualitative research: Perspectives, methodologies, examples, and issues* (pp. 83–92). Thousand Oaks, CA: SAGE.

The White House. (2010, January 19). *Background on the President's events today in Falls Church, Virginia*. Washington, DC: Office of the Press Secretary. Retrieved on July 5, 2010 from http://www.whitehouse.gov/the-press-office/background-presidents-events-today-falls-church-virginia

Tobin, K., & Kincheloe, J. (2006). Doing educational research in a complex world. In K. Tobin & J. Kincheloe (Eds.), *Doing educational research: A handbook* (pp. 3–13). Boston, MA: Sense.

Tyler, R. (1949). *Basic principles of curriculum and instructuon*. Chicago, IL: University of Chicago Press.

van Manen, M. (2002). *The tone of teaching: The language of pedagogy*. Ontario, Canada: The Althouse Press.

Vitek, W., & Jackson, W. (1996). *Rooted in the land: Essays on community and place*. New Haven, CT: Yale University Press.

CHAPTER 13

THE RIOT IN MY SOUL—PART I

A Critical Rant on Race, Rage, Ignorance, and the Limits of Formal Education on These Matters

Denise Taliaferro-Baszile

A PREFACE (NO THIS IS A WARNING. I AM ABOUT TO BREAK THE RULES)

Most of us in our writing substitute it *for* I. *This practice is generally deceitful (unless one is writing fiction). The* it *style excuses the absence of feeling. Feeling is not accepted as a critical component of any truth worth seeking.*

—Robinson (2000, p. 37)

Would you bear with me for a few pages please? I need to rant for a moment. Yes, I realize that ranting is quite un-academic, but it is necessary to make the point I need to make. I know that as academics we are expected to take messy and complicated realities and study them, analyze them, organize them, present them and explain them objectively, as if they were never messy or complicated at all. We are quite driven to and sometimes

Epistemologies of Ignorance in Education, pp. 267–282

obsessed with rational argumentation, so much so that we miss important dynamics *(or we struggle to keep them private, to repress them)*, ones that are unspeakable or even unknowable from the perspective of Western rationality as we have come to know and practice it. In Western culture, the discourse of rationality insists that we deny (as an attempt to control) the extent to which deep feelings—whether passion, frustration, resentment, fear or elation—impact our understandings, our politics, and our claims to truth. In so doing, we often overlook in Megan Boler's (1999) words "the power of feelings" or more aptly the extent to which emotion is a site of social control. I have a few things to say about race, rage, ignorance, and the limits of formal education for addressing these matters. And in order not to get too caught up in reproducing the problems I want to tackle, I need to speak to and through the emotions that make teaching about race and racism both possible and impossible. In short, I need to un-objectively and unapologetically shoot straight from the hip.

First, let me just say a few words about why I think it is important to walk out on a limb and forego the traditional academic analysis on matters of race. To offer a traditionally rational—that is objective and unemotional—perspective on race is to seek a *legitimate* understanding of the ways in which race has shaped society, historically and in the present moment. A legitimate understanding is typically generated through the episteme of rationality, where "emotion is verboten" and "objectivity is the object" (Robinson, 2000, p. 36). To this end, rationality—as we have come to know it—seeks an understanding that is objectively knowable and therefore controllable, not to mention Eurocentric in its separation of emotion and reason, body and mind. Consequently, that which is not knowable or well understood from the perspective of rationality is often considered illegitimate and unreliable knowledge. Our efforts to know rationally, then, are sustained by a seemingly necessary epistemological ignorance—that which we ignore, which we refuse to know, which we repress, and which we ultimately and dysconsciously[1] act out and/or project on to others. Patricia Williams (1991) reiterates this point when she argues that "much of what is spoken *(and written)* in so-called objective, unmediated voices is in fact mired in hidden subjectivities and unexamined claims that make property of others beyond the self, all the while denying such connections" (p. 11).

Inarguably, rationality makes it all too easy to deny our deep feelings about race and/or simply ignore those of others and to dismiss the ways in which such feelings impact attitudes, practices and policies around race. The consequence of such denial and ignorance is that they bolster and are bolstered by ideological perspectives and practices that ultimately work to maintain racial injustice. Colorblind ideology—the insistence that racial difference is inconsequential—is one such example which works to normalize and rationalize the power and privilege associated with whiteness, and in so doing also absolves White people of not only their feelings of guilt and self-doubt, but also their individual and collective responsibility to a just democracy (Bonilla-Silva, 2001; Giroux, 2006; Goldberg, 2006; Mills, 2006).

In contrast, I want to work toward a fuller understanding of race that can only come from a multiepistemological stance: one that recognizes the importance of moving in and out of the rational; that embraces and seeks to understand the complicated and sometimes volatile feelings that are race; and that accepts contradiction as a real and sometimes irresolvable part of knowing and living in a society that has staked its democratic dreams on the tragic contradiction between freedom and chattel slavery. A multiepistemological stance means that I will not, as every good academic should do, wed myself to a theoretical framework or specific paradigm. Instead, I will call on Patricia Hill Collins (1990) sense of "going a piece of the way" which speaks to the importance and power of calling on the experiences, discussions, organizations, and theories necessary for doing what one needs to do when one needs to do it, in spite of the labels or contradictions they may represent. In this vein, I intend to engage what Collins calls a "critical rationality" which means "negotiating, articulating, and interrogating simultaneously a variety of resistant discourses relationally and depending on context, historical, and political circumstances" (p. 47). And as should be obvious by now, I intend to be both thoughtful and quite explicit about the feelings that are tangled up in the processes of coming to know and coming to testify.

Specifically what I would like to think about (*Are ranting and thinking compatible?*) is the place and importance of rage—Black rage in particular—in a pedagogy of race. In 1968 Black psychologists William Henry Grier and Price Cobbs released a book titled *Black Rage*, which purported that Black people living in a society dominated by White supremacy are psychologically damaged by persistent racial oppression. Grier and Cobb's work goes a long way in demonstrating how persistent racism can lead to feelings of inadequacy and rage, and how such feelings are far more likely to be turned in on one's self and as such become far more harmful to the one who embodies feelings of rage than it does to those who are the source and/or object of that rage. The weak point, however, in Grier and Cobb's discussion is that Black rage is framed as pathological, rather than as a "logical" response to the pathological conditions of White supremacy. On this point, bell hooks (1995) insists that,

> Many African Americans feel uncontrollable rage when they encounter White supremacist aggression. That rage is not pathological. It is an appropriate

response to injustice. However, if not processed constructively it can lead to pathological behavior—but so can any rage, irrespective of the cause that serves as a catalyst. (p. 26)

hooks (1995) goes on to underscore the importance of acknowledging the pathology of White supremacy. Until we do this, she argues, "we will never create a cultural context wherein the madness of White racist hatred of Blacks or the uncontrollable rage that surfaces as a response to that madness can be investigated, critically studied and understood" (p. 26).

When I speak of Black rage I am not by and large referring to violent outbursts directed at White people by Black people. Although Black rage unchecked can lead to such action, I am talking about the *feelings* of intense frustration—the killing rage, as bell hooks (1995) termed it, that creeps from the depths of one's soul as a response to the profound and persistent White ignorance (Mills, 2006) that shapes much of what we do in academia. I want to focus, not so much on the way in which that rage explodes or may explode but rather on the ways in which it gets repressed, and thus becomes far more harmful to one's self than to anyone else, and subsequently helps to maintain rather than challenge White ignorance (*Don't get too frazzled. I'll explain in a minute*). I am talking about the kind of rage that reflexively clenches your teeth, furrows your brow, and bites your lip until it bleeds, as it waits for your split second decision to speak or not to speak for the hundredth-millionth time; that is the hundredth-millionth time that you have had the almost undeniable urge to tell some White person exactly what you think about their attempt to make you invisible, unimportant, incompetent, and so on. It may linger as a headache or sleepless night but after a while it dissipates, goes away, or does it? Where does such rage come from? Where does it go? And what impact does it have on the enraged? And what impact does it have on the work—in this case the teaching—of the enraged? In an effort to tackle some of these questions creatively, realistically, and I hope effectively, allow me to share the riot in my soul—that is the ongoing struggle between my rational professor self and my angry Black woman within (*the parentheses*).

CLAIMING RAGE

Rage cannot be hidden. It can only be dissembled. This dissembling deludes thoughtfulness and strengthens rage and adds to rage contempt. There are, no doubt, as many ways of coping with the resulting complex of tensions as there are Black men in the world, but no Black man can hope to ever be entirely liberated from this internal warfare—rage, dissembling, and contempt having inevitably accompanied his first realization of the power of White men.

—James Baldwin (1985, p. 85)

I will never forget this during April of 2008 and for several weeks before I was home on maternity leave, feeding, changing and rocking the baby and flipping obsessively between MSNBC and CNN to catch the latest on the race for the White House. I had been consumed with all of the hoopla around the comments of the good Reverend Wright. I have heard the Reverend Jeremiah Wright speak on several occasions, although not in his church or any church for that matter, and I raised my hand in agreement and shouted "Amen!" quite a few times. And I imagine that over the 20 or so years that Barak has attended Trinity Baptist Church, he has responded in kind to many of Reverend Wright's high-spirited truth-telling sermons. But, of course, admitting that would surely mean political suicide. Arguably Black Americans in general know that Wright's words capture and reflect a righteous rage about the historical tragedy and the continued struggle that shapes our lives as Black folks in America. And in fighting against slavery, Jim Crow, and the much more subtle contemporary racisms that prevent America from living up to its own image as free, equal, and just, Black Americans have lived and died among the most patriotic. There is nothing really irrational or crazy or even hateful about it. It is all quite "logical" if you will.

I spent the many days frustrated about how the media pundits portrayed the one who is pointing out the racism as the racist, fascinated to witness that Wright has been called everything but a liar, unsurprised that most people do not consider the contradictions between the media image of a crazed Black man and the narratives of his military and community service, and incensed that few have questioned Wright about why he feels that America is hypocritical *(I am just fit to be tied right now)*. Without taking any of these issues into account, Reverend Wright has been written off as the crazed Black man, whose rage is an expression of hate rather than injustice. And although Barak Obama, in his now famous race speech, attempted to not only put the good reverend in context, but to also point out the ways in which our tragic history continues to haunt our present feelings about race in America, it was not enough to address the insatiable public need to mythologize Wright and to dance around or flat out ignore the racial history against which and because of which he speaks.

The whole drama is a glaring display of White ignorance (Mills, 2006), an ignorance generated from an inability and unwillingness to place Reverend Wright, Black liberation theology, Black church practices, and Black people in a historical context. Honestly and typically, White folks have no pressing obligation to reposition themselves (hooks, 1992) to understand or to empathize with the plight of a people who logically have complicated and contradictory feelings about a country that has enslaved them both physically and psychologically for centuries; a country that has, nevertheless, become home, a home that would not exist if it were not for Black people's labor and determination that the United States live up to its image as a free, equal, and just democracy. Unfortunately, many people have chosen to forget *(Hmmm … is it a choice? Or is there something else that explains the profundity and persistence of such ignorance?)*, or to ignore the importance and the presence of our tragic, complicated, and shared history. While "forgetting" seems too trite a description for the problem at hand, "ignoring" seems unimaginably cruel. But given the context and profundity of what Goldberg (2006) calls a raced racelessness and Charles Mills (2006) calls White ignorance both are accurate. Racelessness, an ideological perspective that racial difference is and should be inconsequential, as Goldberg argues (2006),

> the neoliberal attempt to go beyond—without (fully) coming to terms with —racial histories and their accompanying racist inequities and iniquities; to mediate the racially classed and gendered distinctions to which those histories have given rise without reference to the racial terms of those distinctions; to transform, via the negating dialectic of denial and ignoring, racially marked social orders into racially erased ones. (p. 59)

In a similar line of argument, Mills (2006)—elaborating on his concept of White ignorance first mentioned in *The Racial Contract* (1997)—argues that

> White normativity manifests itself in a White refusal to recognize the long history of structural discrimination that has left Whites with the differential resources they have today, and all of its consequent advantages in negotiating opportunity structures. If originally whiteness was race, then now it is racelessness, an equal status and a common history in which all have shared with White privilege being conceptually erased. (p. 28)

Racelessness is raced, then, in many respects, not the least of which is that the denial and ignorance it substantiates is not simply about the racial histories but also then necessarily about denying and ignoring the very existence of the racial subjects—the identities—formed by such histories, as they happened and as they are told and not told. Hence, it is much easier to simply write off Reverend Wright as the crazed Black man, or for that matter to lambast Michelle Obama,[2] whose attempt to express pride in her country, was used to cast her as unpatriotic, radical Black woman. It is so much easier to ignore the history, the context and instead feed moral panics that play on White folk's deepest unacknowledged fears, fears that Black rage will inevitably lead to revenge. I know this scenario well.

One of the unfortunate realities of being a Black woman teaching about race and racism in academia is that I am often mythologized as the angry Black woman, one whose pedagogy mounts to little more than an opportunity to discuss the weighty chip on my shoulder. At first, I must admit, I was certainly caught off guard when students referred to me as "angry" and/or "racist." Trying to teach about race in predominately White spaces and in honest and rigorous ways has often rendered me suspect mostly by White students but not always and only by them. The first time, I pointed out to my mostly White class how problematic it was that there was no representation of Black people's educational dilemma in the video we were watching about the common school movement. It was almost a week later before I learned that this comment initiated a big discussion outside of class, in which I was being framed as the angry Black professor. Another time I made a comment about understanding where the Black students were coming from in a discussion about some of the challenges they face when they chose to attend predominately White schools. Not an hour after class, the word was out that I was a "racist" because I, as one student put it, liked Black students better than White students. The incidents go on and on, so much so that eventually I began to accept the fact that these kinds of mythologizations would always be a consequence of my pedagogy.

From my perspective, I entered my work with the desire to promote a sense of cross-racial understanding. My mistake, however, was in assuming that if people were simply exposed to the data, to the history/ies, they would be far more likely to understand the position of the other. I did not count on people's resistance to knowing and/or acknowledging the impact of America's racist past on its racist present. I underestimated the depth of their racial priming in the context of U.S. racelessness:

> Too often, academics who teach race-based classes, as well as ethnic studies professors, treat White students as if they are racial *tabulae rasae*. They underestimate the degree to which White students enter their classrooms with sophisticated racial scripts, which they have inherited, and how well they have been groomed to oppose critiques on Whiteness, merit, and other topics that are taught as unfair racial inequities while endorsing individualism and employing racist stereotypes. (Smith, 2004, p. 179)

Even though I always referred students to theories and sources for consideration, that was hardly ever enough to confront their collective amnesia (Mills, 2006). Never mind the many years of study in the history, politics and philosophy of race that inform my pedagogy; I quickly learned two things. First, I learned that a rational presentation of the knowledge at hand was not ever going to be enough to eradicate racism. I also learned that my raced and gendered body would bear the burden of everything students did not want to hear, did not want to believe, and did not dare to ask. Thus, regardless of my seemingly rational approach —my attempt to stick to theory and empirical studies—my perspective, pedagogy, and presence would often conjure in the imaginations of my privileged students' notions of Black rage, which project me as unreasonable about race and them as the innocent victims of my unreasonableness.

In the beginning I resisted any insinuation that I was angry or actually enraged about racism or at White folks, for that is what the rules of racial etiquette dictate. As Eduardo Bonilla-Silva (2001) explains, one of the ways racial ideology structures racial orders is by providing the basic rules of engagement for actors along with the racial episteme to make decisions about "Other" and "Same" based on racialized readings of bodies. But over the years as I have come to better understand the complexities of Black rage. I know that I embody it, manage it, and as such bring it to bear on my pedagogy of race in complicated ways. For a long time, I was not conscious of the rage *(not really)*. At least, I did not act it out in irrational outbursts of any kind *(at least not publicly—I have been known to grumble at the four walls in my office)*. I did not kill any students or myself for that matter *(For what is a good rant without sarcasm?)*. But perhaps the Black rage seeped out anyway. Could such rage have been manifested in my insistence on presenting a history of the United States that often goes unacknowledged; or in my willingness to make students uncomfortable enough to think, to learn; or in my unwillingness to be a neutral text? Certainly at times students have thought so. As the semesters and years have gone on, I have had moments of striking clarity, moments where I can physically feel the killing rage creeping through my body forcing clenched teeth, a furrowed brow and a split second decision to speak or not to speak. I recognize this as Black rage—not so much because of the visceral—but because of where it happens, when it happens, and how I choose to deal with it.

In fact, it was just last summer that I found my professor self negotiating with the Angry Black Woman within. I was teaching two summer courses back to back. One was a course on critical race theory, which consisted of nine Black and 1 White doctoral student. It was an exciting class, the most rewarding that I have taught in a long time. The conversations were meaningful, agonistic, and complex. The readings inspired deep insight as well as explicit rage about the depth and breadth of White supremacy. Quite a few times I jumped to my feet, drew on the board, and talked loudly to emphasize a point in this class. Oftentimes, I walked into the class with little energy but left energized and ready to talk more, to think more, to write more.

The other course was on critical media literacy and consisted of 19 White students, most of who were teachers seeking their master's, and 1 Black student from Nigeria. I had an unusually difficult time getting excited about this class. From my perspective, it was depressing, boring, and full of liberal minded White folks with good intentions but with no critical sense of how whiteness framed their perspectives. Even though I know that there was little reason to expect that somewhere along the way they would have been made aware of their whiteness or would be open to exploring it in a class that was supposedly not about race, their not knowing, their not wanting to consider their whiteness annoyed me. So much so that I did get a little angry one day, and raised my voice an octave as I tried to support bell hooks' assessment of racism in mainstream media. I could tell in that very moment that the class was a bust. Whatever I did from that point on would not have mattered, for they had caught a glimmer of my rage, and they would use it to discount whatever knowledge I had to offer thereafter. I received the worst evaluations that I have ever received in my 10 years of teaching at the university level. Interestingly, while I usually obsess over that one critical and accusatory evaluation, this time I was not surprised or even disappointed. I expected, accepted, and understood the evaluations given the context. The thing is, though, I have had plenty of classes with the same racial make-up and the same issues, which were not so depressing and anxiety ridden as this one was for me. It was this quandary that consumed me over the next several months. I wanted to understand how and why my own attitude had changed.

It was, I believe, the juxtaposition of these two courses. You see, the relationship between the two courses compelled me to unearth something that had been muddling around in my head and heart, but which I had yet to deal with. The question that the Angry Black Woman within was screaming at the top of her lungs was, *why the hell are you spending your time and energy teaching White folks who really don't want to know, who resist any understanding of race, racism, or White supremacy—unless it is the KKK or the Nazis—when you could be teaching Black folks who want to know but aren't often given the opportunity or the resources?* The beauty of the critical race course was that the insight, the inspiration, the teaching/learning were fueled by rage, and not just my own but the rage of the students as well. It was a safe place for the angry woman to be passionate, to exhale, and still be taken seriously. In contrast, the critical media literacy course was rageless and the little glimmer that shone was taken to disrupt rather than energize the teaching/learning in the course. This realization hit me hard and propelled me onto another difficult train of thought. Where does such rage come from? And what have I been doing with it over the years?

UNDERSTANDING RAGE

Our racial crisis has made us realize that White racism in America is no aberration, but an ingredient of our culture which cannot be fully understood apart from the rest of our total situation.... I shall consider our racial dilemma as the product of the historical unfolding of Western culture. The irrational power racism holds over us may then be seen as part of the larger unreason in which we live.

—Joel Kovel (1984, p. 3)

It's a funny thing, a messy thing. When I had no obvious feelings of rage, the students kept saying that I was angry (*which of course was sometimes enough to piss me off*), and they often thought I was angry about the fact that slavery happened, as evidenced in the endlessly annoying "the past is the past" storyline (Bonilla-Silva, 2001). Although I am still not sure if they saw my anger or a reflection of how angry they themselves would be if they were Black, and had to deal with racism. The real irony, for me anyway, is that I could acknowledge the history of slavery—for instance—teach about it, talk about it, watch films about the horrible things that happened and not feel anywhere near the anger or rage I feel when people dismiss, or deny the relevance of that history on the present moment. It is the denial —blatant and persistent—that most causes flares of Black rage.

This denial that so many students hold is unbelievably complex, as it often cannot be addressed with data or logical argument for that matter. The rational, as I have learned, is not going to alleviate the largely ir-rational (*that is emotional and only sometimes nonsensical*) reactions that race engenders, precisely because it is the production of the rational that ne-cessitates the denial. That is, in the production of rational discourse, the other is to be distanced, objectified and dominated, and any connection, similarity, or empathy is to be denied. As Toni Morrison (1992) argues so brilliantly in *Playing in the Dark*, America has a deep and complicated psychohistory around matters of race that significantly impacts what and how we come to know or refuse to know our "selves" and our "others." In the discourse of the rational, there can only be one right perspective and that must come from those who deem themselves the most rational, all others must be denied.

DuBois (1935/1962) makes this argument in his sharp critique of American historians and the history they choose to present. In *Black Reconstruction*, he points to the profound denial that shapes the histories of the Reconstruction era and iterates the idea that history—as we have come to tell it—functions more as propaganda than as a representation of what happened. In the discourse of the rational, feelings are denied and yet simultaneously drive the whole agenda—feelings of fear, feelings of superiority, feelings of greed, and feelings of guilt. Mills (2006) offers a prolific read of White denial as well, arguing that to the extent White people see Black people as a threat to their interests, they will have—where race is concerned—cognitive distortions of various kinds, including colorblindness, refusal to perceive systemic discrimination, the convenient amnesia about the past and its legacy in the present, and hostility to Black testimony on the continuing White privilege and the need to eliminate it to achieve racial justice. Mills goes on to note that all of these distortions are interlocking and reciprocal, basically creating a White epistemology of ignorance. He surmises that,

> White ignorance has been able to flourish all of these years because a White epistemology of ignorance has safeguarded it against the dangers of an illuminating blackness or redness, protecting those who for "racial" reasons have needed not to know. Only by starting to break these rules and meta-rules can we begin the long process that will lead to the eventual overcoming of this White darkness and the achievement of an enlightenment that is genuinely multiracial. (Mills, 2006, p. 35)

They need not to know. These are the words that reverberate, that resonate. They remind me of just how daunting the task before me is and will always be, because as surely as White folks need not to know, I need them to know. It is not, as I have been pretending it to be, a simple presentation of knowledge, a potential exchange of ideas that inspires me to teach about race and racism. It is my rage that compels me to take up such a challenge, but at the same time it is the repression of that rage that ultimately makes that challenge an impossible success.

RAGE MANAGEMENT

Oppressed people cannot remain oppressed forever. The yearning for freedom eventually manifests itself.

—Martin Luther King, Jr., (1963/2003, p. 41)

(This goes for repressed people too!)

From the lashes of the slave whip, constant rape, lynching, cross burnings, loss of livelihood, and other measures of physical and psychological control, White folks have worked hard to make sure Black folks contain their rage. As hooks (1995) so poignantly notes in *Killing Rage* (*you can probably tell by now that this book is one of my favorites. It has been quite theory-peutic*), "to perpetuate White supremacy, White folks have colonized Black Americans, and part of that colonizing process has been teaching us to repress our rage, to never make them targets of any anger we feel about racism" (p. 14). Joy Degruy Leary (2005) also speaks to our propensity for such repression in her theorization of posttraumatic slave syndrome, when she comments on just how much time and energy we spend worrying about what White folks will think and consequently make every effort to protect their feelings (*Ain't that the truth Ruth!*).

My way of repressing the Angry Black Woman within has been to develop a style, a way about my teaching that is like giving medicine to a baby. I have become the Cool as Hell Professor, highly engaging, student centered, and creatively gentle with the way I expose them to the unrelenting image of a racist America and give them an opportunity to ponder—quietly even silently—their positionality in it. In other words, I coo, smile, and *chuga chuga choo choo* as I try to convince them that I am exposing them to critical perspectives on race for their own good. This "cool as hell" image I have managed has no doubt allowed me to accomplish a lot—raising some awareness of the issues and decent student evaluations, to name a few. But the Angry Black Woman within is dying to interject amongst all the coddling, vociferously insisting that we will never get anywhere unless her testimony is heard, acknowledged, and used as a basis for healing. So my rage management looks something like this: the Angry Black Woman within (denoted by parentheses) the Cool as Hell Professor. The Cool as Hell Professor stays calm, cool, but not collected because she is already herself and not herself, an oxymoron like "cool as hell."

And it goes a little something like this: It is the White kid who continues to complain about how it's not fair that Black kids can use the N-word, but he cannnot? (*Fair? Fair? Things ain't been fair at least since 1619. Why is it suddenly central now and in relationship to this issue?*). I attempt a rational response, directing him to a historical consideration of the word as well as the dynamics of language as a form of resistance among oppressed groups. No matter, though, he tries several more times to interject an ahistorical notion of fairness with regards to several issues.

It is the White student who stands up and announces that she would have more Black friends, if it were not for the fact that they all lived in the Black dorm (*What audacity! Does she really believe that the primary reason Black students come to this campus is to diversify her experience? What about the fact that they see this multicultural—not all Black—living space as a safe haven from the overwhelming whiteness they must negotiate daily?*). I attempt, yet again, to set the facts straight. I remind her and the rest of the class that in fact the dorm in question is the most multicultural on campus, housing Black

(African American, Afro-Caribbean, and African), Latino (Puerto Rican and Dominican), and White (tough few) students. There are no restrictions on who can live there. The majority of Black students live in other dorms on campus, and the great majority of students who do live in this dorm, do so only for 1–2 years at which point they live in one of the typically all White dorms on campus. This argument was an endless one. It comes up every semester without fail and inconspicuously enough the controversy seems to convince students of color not to choose to live in the dorm (*Hmm ... the art of domination. So they get what they want in the end, because the Black students finally decided—so the story goes—that it was the right thing to do. Is it possible that they were perhaps indirectly harassed into such a decision?*).

Another student insists that the only way to improve diversity on campus is to get rid of the dorm. He lived there for a year and nobody talked to him. (*Who the hell are you? Never mind the fact, you made no attempt to talk to anyone either. What you are really saying is that you do not give a damn about what this place means to the students of color. It makes you uncomfortable, so it must go. That's real nerve!*). I explain the historical circumstances—the White terror that drove Black students on campus to demand a safe space. This too is an endless debate. It is a repeat performance from year to year as if the data do not matter at all. It is that student of color who sits in silence and offers no rebuttal, no support (*until after class...where were you when we needed backup?*) for the one who has the guts to challenge her White classmates on their perceptions of affirmative action. It is also the Black student who will not speak up in class at all because they do not want to be seen as speaking for all Black people (*That's just a stupid excuse given to you by liberal minded White folks, an excuse that results in silence. If they think you speak for the whole race, whose inadequacy is that? Yours or theirs?*). I assure the student that their point of view is crucial to the dialogue.

It is that White student who makes his way to the front of the room after class to ask me if I support historically Black colleges and then proclaims that I am a racist when I say yes (*Well isn't that the pot calling the kettle black?*). It is the student who wants to convince me, who refuses to acknowledge the context of my position, who will not agree to disagree, that racial profiling is necessary for the security of our country (*Why does he insist on being in my face when the White professor next to me has taken the same position?*). It is the White students who use "extreme" to characterize the views of a Black cultural critic, who because she is angry cannot be making a valid point (*What really burns me up is that that burns me up. They literally make me what they imagine me to be, and then the only response is to pretend not to be what I now am. Have mercy!*). Or it is the colorblind White students who deny the relevance of the other's experience by constantly noting that this or that has happened to them too, so it could not possibly be an indicator of racism (*Never mind the fact that they continue to see themselves as the standard against which all other realities must be validated).* I could go on really, but I will stop here with just one more thing that enrages me. It is giving A's and B's to students who master the language to pass the test or write the paper, but who in our conversations continue to deny the history of White supremacy and its impact on the present, especially those students who might one day be teaching my children (*I'll be damned!*).

Although I often imagine the Cool as Hell Professor as passionate and real, she is problematic, because she is ultimately an oxymoron. The cool exterior disguises the hot as hell rage that bubbles to a point and then cools to a point and then heats up again, giving life to the ebb and flow of the ongoing riot in my soul. I have spent years trying to convince people —White students especially—that I am not enraged, I am not angry, I am only trying to raise their awareness about matters of race. Yet, as I think about it now, that is frankly not true. Perhaps it has been truer in the past than it is today, because the more I teach and the more I learn, the more important I think it is to wrestle with rather than repress the rage. I have been and I continue to be enraged on a daily basis about the way racial dynamics burden my life and the lives of people everywhere. In fact, if I were not enraged, could I teach about race with any passion, with any sense that it is for the greater good that it would make for a stronger more socially just democracy? I have learned to suppress, to redirect, and to do anything with rage other than lay it bare. To lay rage bare would be to risk my good reputation as cool, rational, and intelligent. In not speaking my rage, I pretend not to know what I in fact do know—that White supremacy is alive and well, reproduced in the context of everyday practices. Speaking my rage honestly and regularly would certainly not allow me to preserve a sense of myself as a rational and thoughtful woman, but would cast me as threatening, which would then of course make it okay for people to treat me as if I were crazy (*Damned if I do. Damned if I don't. It's a complex catch 22*). Personally, I pay a high price to maintain such repression, as I am plagued with bouts of racial battle fatigue (Smith, 2004). But to go a step further, the repression works against any possibility of an emancipatory dialogue around racial injustice and racial healing.

RELEASING RAGE AND
THE LIMITS OF FORMAL EDUCATION

As long as Black rage continues to be represented as always and only evil and destructive, we lack a vision of militancy that is necessary for transformative revolutionary action.

—bell hooks (1995, p. 19)

So here is where things get quite tricky. I am not so sure I am ready to expose the Angry Black Woman in full dress as part and parcel of my pedagogical strategy. It will no doubt take me sometime to figure out how to engage her honestly, strategically and effectively *(I will not go back in the bottle!)*. For now, it is still too dangerous, even with tenure, because students —especially well to do ones—can make life miserable for an uncooperative professor. But this first step of acknowledging her existence is critical because it throws into flux many of the assumptions we make—as socially just educators—about the possibility and potential of the work that we do or try to do in the classroom.

I end with some questions. Are we engaged in honest and open dialogue? Is everyone having the opportunity to speak his or her truth? Is that even possible when there are multiple relations of oppressed and oppressor at work in the classroom and potential cycles of self and other silencing? What are we really trying to do anyway? Unearth a lifetime of racial priming in a semester or just trying to raise their awareness? Do we have any real opportunities, outside of the fabricated test or paper, to discern the effect of our work? Is presenting the history, the factual data enough to do the job? What about the psychological and emotional drama that is racism or sexism or heterosexism? What about the impact on real lives, particularly the trauma White supremacy imparts on everyday lives? How can we acknowledge the trauma if those who have been traumatized cannot speak their rage for fear that it will upset those who need not to know? And what about those of us who do this social justice work in the classroom day in and day out? How does this kind of work affect our own mental, emotional and spiritual well-being? How might our answers to such questions stay in stride with or begin to dismantle this white epistemology of ignorance? And what does dismantling this epistemology of ignorance mean for our obsession with rationality as the best, most appropriate approach to (racial) knowledge?

NOTES

1. Joyece E. King (1991) defines dysconscious racism as an uncritical habit of mind in regards to race.
2. Speaking about the tremendous support for her husband's campaign, Michelle Obama commented that for the first time in her adult life she was proud of her country. In some of the media coverage the comment was used to suggest that she was unpatriotic.

REFERENCES

Baldwin, J. (1985). *The price of the ticket*. New York, NY: St. Martin's/Marek.

Boler, M. (1999). *Feeling power: Emotions and education*. New York, NY: Routledge

Bonilla-Silva, E. (2001). *White supremacy and racism in the post-civil rights era*. Boulder, CO: Lynne Rienner.

Collins, P. H. (1990). *Black feminist thought: Knowledge, consciousness, and the politics of empowerment*. Boston, MA: Unwin Hyman.

DuBois, W. E. B. (1962). *Black reconstruction*. Millwood, NY: Kraus-Thompson Organization. (Original work published 1935)

Giroux, H. (2006). Spectacles of race and pedagogies of denial: Antiblack racist pedagogy. In D. Macedo & P. Gounari (Eds.), *The globalization of racism* (pp. 68–93). Boulder, CO: Paradigm.

Goldberg, D. T. (2006). The global reach of raceless states. In D. Macedo & P. Gounari(Eds.), *The globalization of racism* (pp. 45–67). Boulder, CO: Paradigm.

Grier, W. H., & Cobbs, P. (1968). *Black rage*. New York, NY: Basic Books.

hooks, b. (1992). *Black looks: Race and representation*. Boston, MA: South End Press.

hooks, b. (1995). *Killing rage, ending racism*. New York, NY: Henry Holt.

King, M. L. (2003). Letter from Birmingham jail. In J. James (Ed.), *Imprisonedintellectuals: America's political prisoners write on life, liberation and rebellion* (pp. 31–48). New York, NY: Rowman and Littlefield. (Original work published 1963)

Kovel, J. (1984). *White racism: A psychohistory*. New York, NY: Columbia University Press.

Leary, J. D. (2005). *Post traumatic slave syndrome: America's legacy of enduring injuryand healing*. Portland, OR: Uptone Press.

Mills, C. (2006). White ignorance. In S. Sullivan & N. Tuana (Eds.), *Race and epistemologies of ignorance* (pp. 11–38). Albany, NY: SUNY Press.

Morrison, T. (1992). *Playing in the dark: Whiteness and the literary imagination.*Cambridge, MA: Harvard University Press.

Robinson, R. (2000). *The debt: What America owes Blacks*. New York, NY: Plume.

Smith, W. (2004). Black faculty coping with racial battle fatigue: The campus racial climate in the post civil rights era. In D. Cleveland (Ed.), *A long way to go: conversations about race by African American faculty and graduate students* (pp. 171–193). New York: Peter Lang.

Williams, P. (1991). *The alchemy of race and rights: The diary of a law professor*. Cambridge, MA: Harvard University Press.

CHAPTER 14

EPISTEMOLOGIES OF IGNORANCE

Erik Malewski and Nathalia Jaramillo

EPILOGUE

Twelve chapters on epistemologies of ignorance in education. Now you are back with us. You heard from a wide range of scholars who brought together a myriad of theoretical and practical examples, ones that might help you gain a better appreciation for the unknown, what epistemologies are about, and why knowledge and its counterpart (nonknowledge) should matter to educators. Maybe you no longer hold the belief that knowledge production is innocent or that the domains of nonknowledge are merely voids or omissions. Maybe we have helped render suspect notions that neutral or objective curriculum content and instructional practice is possible or even desirable. We know that it is impossible to produce knowledge that is outside of politics; institutional agendas; power relations; and capital, cultural, and personal investments. Therefore, epistemologies of ignorance manifest when not-knowing is connected to contemporary interests and the very terms and processes by which a topic of study is judged (un)worthy of our attention.

Epistemologies of Ignorance in Education, pp. 283–288

Epistemologies of ignorance have always been shaped by the broader logic of capitalism and coloniality. This is clear. Any understanding of our becoming and knowing in the world needs to take into consideration the underlying relations that frame our social organization. This frame does not define our existence, or predict our actions, but it does provide form to how we respond to and participate in the field of knowledge production. It has become more prescient to consider what Slaughter and Rhoades (2009) termed "academic capitalism," or the further alignment of research agendas and processes with the needs, desires, and interests of business and private enterprise. Lucrative contracts, government research interests, and the decimation of public spaces and funding are intricately linked with epistemologies of ignorance. Yet, we are only just beginning to make in-roads to the symbolic and material spaces of contestation over nonknowledge, capitalism, colonialism, and education. Epistemologies of ignorance envelopes a multitude of such efforts.

In addition to what is considered worth knowing, or what we do not care to know, are epistemologies of ignorance in education that emerge from the ways knowledge blocks other forms of knowledge. To return to one of the quintessential statements that frame the curriculum field—curriculum is what the older generation chooses to tell the younger generation. Epistemologies of ignorance expand beyond this statement to ask how what is told masks or obscures other forms of knowledge. Take, for example, a key finding taken from my (Erik Malewski) recent research with gay men. Two research participants spoke of their recent visit to a gay male doctor who urged them both to get anal Pap smear tests as a precaution against anal cancer. Most telling, both men talked about their belief, until they met with this doctor, that only women received Pap smear tests and that they were conducted vaginally, not anally. Participants reported that even other general practitioners who frequently work with gay male clients admitted that they were unaware of the need to test gay males for rectal abnormalities by way of a Pap smear tests. A matter not just of ignorance and knowledge, but life and death, these tests detect cell abnormalities that if left untreated might lead to cancer.

I would argue that ignorance of the health needs of gay males was due in large part to heterosexual biases embedded within medical knowledge and concordant educational programs. In this example, we see both in practice and theory gay men were employing epistemologies of ignorance as a key component of their epistemologies of resistance, challenging the complex interests that had produced ignorance. Accordingly, they spoke out to other gay men about the need to become embodied knowers and advocates for their own health.

Beyond the ways in which knowledge blocks other knowledge is concern over the ways that ignorance is systematically cultivated. This type of ignorance in education abounds. The controversy over the recent move by the Texas Board of Education to, among other things, make changes to the social studies curricula that include replacing "capitalism" with "free enterprise system," "democracy" with "federal republic," and the figure of Thomas Jefferson with those of St. Thomas Aquinas, John Calvin, and William Blackstone, largely because the former coined the term "separation of church and state" is one example. Epistemologies of ignorance demands that educators study the ideas, concepts, and people marked dangerous or troublesome, how they came to be deemed so by way of historical and contemporary events and documents, and the political practices through which ignorance has been institutionalized and normalized. What are the implications when one of the largest states in the U.S. rewrites the social studies curriculum in ways that will misrepresent ideas, people, and concepts in history and economic textbooks for not just Texas but possibly the nation? More specific, what are the implications when students will study in great detail the conservative resurgence of the 1980s and 1990s including Phyllis Schafly, the Contract with America, the Heritage Foundation, the Moral Majority, and the National Rifle Association but not Che Guevara? Our claim is that it was not that the Texas Board of Education does not know the dangers of a narrow curriculum so closely aligned with dominant perspectives and power blocs, but that they do know and were consciously constructing and maintaining public ignorance in order to protect their privileges and interests.

We hope epistemologies of ignorance invite dialogical debate within a range of educational fields. The notion that ignorance is a void—an empty space of nonknowledge without character and conditions of existence—to be displaced by teaching and learning belies issues of complicity and the very real fact that blindness is created in insight. That teaching and learning have become so sanitized and distant from more complex issues of complicities, omissions, and refusals, and their implications for not knowing as a way of knowing, speaks to the profound bureaucratization and "disembodiment" of learning in and out of school contexts. Instead of asking difficult, troubling questions regarding the conditions under which claims to truth are made, investigating subjugation as implicated and necessary to teaching and learning, and studying the interrelationship between shifting systems of thought and the terms under which knowledge is deemed (un) worthy, students are faced with simple truths and false promises. Therefore, epistemologies of ignorance engender complicated discourses that enrich our own capacity for relating through difference—that of being affected by the other. The work contained in this collection "talks back" to curriculum content and instructional practice where schooling erases curriculum and pedagogy predicated on conversations had by others in government or business, or framed and managed by textbook publishers erases student and community voices.

Epistemologies of ignorance demand that students become not merely problem solvers—that is, that they employ mimetic devices to solve problems for which there are already solutions—but problem detectors who investigate and name problems that are unknown or yet-to-exist, and find as-of-yet solutions toward ethically responsible ends investigating, finding, and naming problems that are unknown or have yet-to-exist—and finding as-of-yet unknown solutions toward ethically responsible ends. Indeed, subjugation is itself a product of epistemology as educational disciplines have been "shot through with the positivity of knowledge" (Foucault, 1972, pp. 193–144) for centuries. Epistemologies of ignorance are an attempt to disarticulate that very certainty of knowing that comes with established truths. That is, they attempt to "take back" curriculum and pedagogy from those government officials and business leaders who forgo the study of one's educational experiences toward ends that constrain the promise associated with a participatory democracy. Toward such ends, epistemologies of ignorance offer tactics for reading and intervening within curriculum and pedagogy, as contested sites, multiple locations where meaning making over teaching and learning are made and remade. We invite readers to participate in such a reconceptualization.

In relocating epistemologies of ignorance to the scene of education, our intent is to employ the construct of ignorance to think critically about our work as educators, our symbolic and material contexts, and the shared universe in which we generate meaning about the social world. Let us be clear. The aim of epistemologies of ignorance is not to produce educational practices more conducive to the culture of test taking predicated (in rhetoric) on the logic of competition and accountability. The aim of epistemologies of ignorance is not to create another academic discipline unrelated to issues of equity or the relationship between theory and practice. The aim of epistemologies of ignorance is, however, to encourage us to think critically on what has been left out, on how intelligibility inhibits other forms of intelligibility, and on how historical and contemporary interests shape what we do not know. In this sense, epistemologies of ignorance asserts without reservation that to theorize and practice with intelligence, courage, and sensitivity in both public and private spheres— and with ethical responsibility toward others—we must also theorize and practice in ways that account for the unknown as a way of knowing and tendencies toward cowardice and insensitivity in spite of our best efforts.

As scholars of gender, race, class and sexuality in education have shown, private and public spheres are interrelated (Fraser & Honneth, 2003; Mouffe, 1995; Munro, 1998) and while we often make distinctions between these spheres for analytical purposes, they are not lived separately. To enter the contested sites of curriculum and pedagogy, where larger meaning is made over what constitutes education, is to refuse to let politicians and business leaders frame teaching and learning for us. To "take back" curriculum and pedagogy demands we study not only what we know, what the older generation deems worthy enough to pass along to the younger generation, but also what we do not know, and what older and younger generations consider unworthy knowledge, if it is considered at all. That is, as soon as we engage curriculum and pedagogy critically, for what it hides as well as what it reveals, we have an opportunity to reconceptualize teaching and learning, as well as schooling and education, in ways never before imagined. We have the opportunity to enter the contested sites of curriculum and pedagogy and make efforts to change them. We can rearticulate teaching and learning by the ways we talk about them, think about them, study them, and move between action and reflection, from what is intelligible to what is unknown and back again, toward the actualization of a participatory democracy that is yet to come. Curriculum and pedagogy ceases to be merely processes known beforehand (the Tyler Rationale), an object of study, and becomes not just things we react to (passive) but things we produce, shape, influence, and direct (active). Here teaching and learning—engaged study whereby the aim is to read and intervene within the symbolic and material world—requires that we treat nonknowledge and nonrules as verbs, as continuously changing and demanding and that we produce new theories and ideas, practices and actions about them.

This edited collection, then, looks back to look forward to fuse both horizons in the here and now. That was our aim. We wanted to think ignorance of the past in parallel to what is not-yet-known regarding the future, to think blindness alongside insight in the contemporary moment. Education has been in crisis for some time. We wanted to think through the implications of ignorance for working the ruins of the field after post-structuralism brought its fund of doubt to bear upon curriculum and pedagogy. We hope we have, in whatever small ways, as authors of this collection, succeeded in complicating our understandings of knowledge and ignorance. We hope that students and colleagues alike have been spurred to think in more complicated ways about the thresholds that had to be passed through for curriculum objects to come into view. And, concurrently, we hope readers were inspired to think about the objects that dropped out of sight. All fields exist within systems of thought and historical contexts that shape what is thought of as worthy knowledge and its concordant nonknowledge. We hope readers recognize that fields of knowledge are not givens; they are produced by people with agendas, goals, and ideas, often ones they (as well as us) might not even recognize. For this reason, we see the proliferation of perspectives and practices in education as a sign of its health and vibrancy, even if schooling has been under siege by those who wish to deal only in the illusion of certainty that comes with simple truths (we contend that the constant crisis in education is due, in part, to the failure to account for emergence, uncertainty, and the unknown).

Epistemologies of ignorance, relocated in the scene of curriculum and pedagogy, we hope, invites more complicated conversations about contaminated knowledge, complicity with knowledge production that oppresses in spite of our efforts toward empowerment, and reading with and against our own research. We also hope that epistemologies of ignorance can be translated into practice, in the everyday and mundane activities that take place between us and our designated roles: teacher-to-student, student-to-student, professor-to-colleague, and administrator-to-professor. As we write this concluding essay, we are aware that colleges and schools of education are becoming increasingly vulnerable to debt-ridden state budgets, programs of study in the foundational fields of education are being slashed by state legislatures, and our colleagues—both tenured and nontenured faculty—are being released as "free agents" in the university system. All of these acts demonstrate a willful ignorance to the ideas, realities, and complexities that the authors of this collection speak about. For these reasons and many more, we feel that this edited collection is so timely.

Educators of the world, unite!
Erik Malewski & Nathalia Jaramillo
"Agents" @ Purdue University, 2011

REFERENCES

Foucault, M. (1972) *The archaeology of knowledge and the discourse of language.* New York, NY: Pantheon.

Fraser, N., & Honneth, A. (2003). *Redistribution or recognition? A political-philosophical exchange* (J. Golb, J. Ingram, & C. Wilke, Trans.). London: Verso.

Mouffe, C. (1995). Feminism, citizen, and radical democratic politics. In L. Nicholson & S. Seidman (Eds.), *Social postmodernism: Beyond identity politics* (pp. 315–331). Cambridge, MA: Cambridge University Press.

Munro, P. (1998). Engendering curriculum history. In W. Pinar (Ed.), *Curriculum: Toward new identities* (pp. 263–294). New York, NY: Garland.

Slaughter, S., & Rhoades, G. (2009). The academic capitalist knowledge/learning regime. In A. S. Chan & D. Fisher (Eds.), *The exchange university: Corporatization of academic culture* (pp. 19–48). Vancouver, Canada: UBC Press.

ABOUT THE AUTHORS

Pete Appelbaum is professor of education at Arcadia University, Philadelphia, United States, where he coordinates the Curriculum Studies and Mathematics Education Programs, and is the director-at-large of the University Curriculum. He is the author of *Children's Books for Grown-Up Teachers: Reading and Writing Curriculum Theory, and Multicultural and Diversity Education: A Reference Handbook,* and directs the Strangely Familiar Music Group.

Sandro R. Barros is assistant professor of modern languages at DePauw U. He earned his BA in music and Spanish and his PhD in romance languages and literatures with a dissertation on current representations of Latin American marginality in foreign literary markets. Sandro has published several articles on authors Reinaldo Arenas, Cervantes, Paulo Lins, and Fernando Vallejo. His current interests include critical/resistance pedagogies and the political implications of Latino literature in the U.S. curriculum. His first book titled *Competing Truths in Latin American Literature: Narrating Otherness and Marginality* is forthcoming through Floricanto Press.

Dolores Calderón is an assistant professor at the University of Utah in the department of education, culture, and society and the ethnic studies program. She is also the associate director of the critical race studies center. She earned her PhD at UCLA'S graduate school of education with an emphasis in race and ethnic studies and cognate in american indian studies. Professor Calderón also has a JD from Texas Tech School of Law. Her research interests center on the following areas: indigenous epistemologies;

critical race/tribalcrit theories in education; and jurisprudence and education. Specifically, her work examines how these components challenge traditional curriculum and instruction development and implementation.

Alexandra Fidyk, Jungian psychotherapist, holds the positions of assistant professor in the Department of Secondary Education, Universtiy of Alberta, Canada, and adjunct faculty in depth psychology at Pacifica Graduate Institute in California. She has written and coauthored numerous articles, poems, dialogues, and chapters on silence, eros, intersubjectivity, the liminal and ethics. Current interest continues in these areas and those of transgenerational and transspecies questions.

Twyla Gibson is assistant professor of culture and technology at the Faculty of Information at the University of Toronto. She received the PhD and MA in philosophy of education and a BA in philosophy and religious studies from the University of Toronto, and pursued postdoctoral research in the history of ideas in the Departments of History and Classics at the University of Michigan at Ann Arbor. Her research and publications concentrate on the ancient Greek philosophical foundations of knowledge in education. Her work in the digital humanities focuses on the implications of computer-mediated communication for our understanding of the ancient world through to contemporary cultures. She has a forthcoming book, *Comparative Orality and Literacy,* and a textbook on writing and composition in development for Oxford University Press.

Nathalia Jaramillo is an assistant professor of cultural foundations in the College of Education and affiliate faculty in the Department of American studies in the College of Liberal Arts, Purdue University. She is coauthor (with Peter McLaren) of *Pedagogy and Praxis in the Age of Empire* (Sense Publishers, 2007).

Richard Kahn (Antioch University Los Angeles) is the author of *Critical Pedagogy, Ecoliteracy, and Planetary Crisis: The Ecopedagogy Movement* (Peter Lang, 2010); as well as of the forthcoming titles, *Education Out of Bounds: Reimagining Cultural Studies for a Posthuman Age* (w/ Tyson Lewis; Palgrave Macmillan, 2010), and *Ecopedagogy: Educating for Sustainability in Schools and Society* (Routledge, 2011). His work has been collected in a wide variety of books and journals, including *The Critical Pedagogy Reader* (2nd ed.); *The Blackwell Companion to Globalization;* and *Cultural Studies: Keyworks.* Additional information about him can be obtained at: http://richardkahn.org

Deborah Biss Keller teaches cultural foundations courses at Indiana University School of Education at Indianapolis. Her research interests include service-learning locally and abroad, semiotics in education, and multicultural education.

J. Gregory Keller is senior lecturer in the Department of Philosophy at Indiana University-Purdue University Indianapolis. His research interests include the relationship of dialogue to cosmopolitanism, ethics, reasoning, and teaching. His other interests include critical theory, hermeneutics, and philosophy of literature.

Erik Malewski is an associate professor of curriculum studies at Purdue University. His research interests include curriculum theory, state of the field studies, internationalization by way of study abroad, and difficult knowledge and ignorance within education. He has had articles appear in various peer-reviewed journals, such as *Teaching and Teacher Education,* and published book chapter in numerous edited collections, including The *Praeger Handbook of Latino Education in the U.S.* He is editor of the *Curriculum Studies Handbook: The Next Moment.*

Stuart J. Murray is assistant professor of rhetoric and writing at Ryerson University in Toronto, Canada. He received his PhD (2004) in Rhetoric from the University of California at Berkeley, after which he held a 2-year SSHRC postdoctoral fellowship in philosophy at the University of Toronto. His work is concerned with the ways that "life" is produced as a rhetorical and political production, including the relation between biopolitics and bioethics. He has a collected volume edited with Dave Holmes, titled, *Critical Interventions in the Ethics of Healthcare: Challenging the Principle of Autonomy in Bioethics* (Ashgate Publishing, 2009). Current research includes a three year SSHRC-funded study titled, "Ethics and Mental Health Care: An Analysis of Professional Practices in Correctional Institutions," and a book-length project on the rhetorical dimensions of biopolitics and thanatopolitics, tentatively titled, *The Living From the Dead.*

Molly Quinn is associate professor of education at Teachers College, Columbia University, in New York. The author of *Going Out, Not Knowing Whither: Education, the Upward Journey and the Faith of Reason* (2001), much of her work as a curriculum theorist engages "spiritual" and philosophical criticism toward embracing a vision of education that cultivates wholeness, beauty, compassion, and social action.

Teresa Rishel is an associate professor in the Department of Teaching, Leadership, and Curriculum Studies at Kent State University where she teaches Middle Childhood Education and Multicultural Education. Teresa researches adolescent suicide in terms of sociocultural relationships, student alienation, power issues, policymaking, and leadership roles in schools, as well as the effects of the hidden curriculum. Teresa's research explores and focuses on critical theory/pedagogy, reflective thinking, curriculum theory, multicultural issues of education and social justice.

Celeste Snowber is a dancer, poet, and educator who is an associate professor in the Faculty of Education in the area of arts education at Simon Fraser University. She has written numerous essays and is sole author of *Embodied Prayer* and coauthor of (2009) *Landscapes of Aesthetic Education with Stuart Richmond*. A lover of improvisation, she continues to perform and is mother of three sons, together a tribe of artists.

Denise Taliaferro Baszile is an associate professor in the Department of Educational Leadership at Miami University, where she teaches courses on curriculum theory, critical race theory, critical media literacy, and African American education. Her research interests are in the historical, political and philosophical foundations of race and its relationship to curriculum and pedagogy.